The *Comedy* tells the story of Dante's experiences, feelings and thoughts as he journeys through the three realms of the afterlife. In the core of this book, Patrick Boyde argues that the way in which Dante represents what he (or his fictional self) saw and felt was profoundly influenced by the thirteenth-century science of psychology. The author offers a clear and authoritative account of the way in which vision and the emotions were understood in Dante's lifetime and he re-reads many of the most dramatic and moving episodes in the poem, throwing fresh light on Dante's narrative technique.

Seeing and feeling were known to be inextricably bound up with thinking and voluntary action, and they were treated as special cases of motion and motive force. Professor Boyde therefore sets Dante's treatment of perception and passion in its intellectual context by presenting some of the leading ideas in Aristotelian epistemology, ethics and physics. Here too it is shown that a knowledge of Dante's philosophical ideas can help us to understand his poetic representation of mental processes and value judgements, and even the meaning of his journey towards the source of goodness and truth.

D1103633

Perception and passion
in Dante's *Comedy*

Perception and passion in Dante's *Comedy*

PATRICK BOYDE

*Serena Professor of Italian in the University of Cambridge
and Fellow of St John's College*

CAMBRIDGE
UNIVERSITY PRESS

CAMBRIDGE UNIVERSITY PRESS
Cambridge, New York, Melbourne, Madrid, Cape Town, Singapore, São Paulo

Cambridge University Press
The Edinburgh Building, Cambridge CB2 2RU, UK

Published in the United States of America by Cambridge University Press, New York

www.cambridge.org
Information on this title: www.cambridge.org/9780521370097

First published 1993
Reprinted 1995
This digitally printed first paperback version 2006

A catalogue record for this publication is available from the British Library

Library of Congress Cataloguing in Publication data
Boyde, Patrick.
Perception and passion in Dante's Comedy / Patrick Boyde.
p.   cm.
Includes index.
ISBN 0 521 37009 4
1. Dante Alighieri, 1265–1321. Divina commedia.   2. Psychology in literature.
3. Philosophy in literature.   I. Title.
PQ4412.B63   1993
851'.1–dc20   92-40938   CIP

ISBN-13 978-0-521-37009-7 hardback
ISBN-10 0-521-37009-4 hardback

ISBN-13 978-0-521-02855-4 paperback
ISBN-10 0-521-02855-8 paperback

E se la stella si cambiò e rise,
qual mi fec' io che pur da mia natura
trasmutabile son per tutte guise!

Dante, Paradiso v, 99–101

The passions are feelings associated with pain or pleasure which so change a man as to affect his judgements.   Aristotle, *Rhetoric* II, i, 8, 1378a

The Philosophers, as well natural as moral, the one for Speculation, the other for Practice, wade most profoundly in the matter of our Passions.

The natural Philosopher contemplating the natures of men and beasts' sensitive souls (for Passions are common to both) consequently enters into discourse about the actions and operations thereof; for, without the knowledge of them, it were impossible to attain unto the perfect understanding of either of them.

The moral Philosopher, describing manners, inviting to virtue, dissuading from vice, showeth how our inordinate appetites must be bridled with fortitude and temperance. He declareth their natures, their craft and deceit, in what sort of persons they are most vehement, and in whom more moderate; and to be brief, he spendeth well nigh in this disputation all his moral Philosophy in teaching how they may be used or abused.

Thomas Wright, The Passions of the Mind in General (1604), I, 1

And here again I find strange (...) that Aristotle should have written divers volumes of Ethics and never handled the affections, which is the principal subject thereof. (...) Better travails, I suppose, had the Stoics taken in this argument. (...) But yet it is like it was after their manner, rather in subtilty of definitions (...) than in active and ample descriptions and observations.

But the poets and writers of histories are the best doctors of this knowledge; where we may find painted forth with great life, how affections are kindled and incited; and how pacified and refrained; (...) how they disclose themselves; how they work; how they vary; how they gather and fortify; how they are enwrapped one within another; and how they do fight and encounter one with another; and other the like particularities.

Francis Bacon, The Advancement of Learning (1605), II, xxii, 6

'I think I'll go and meet her,' said Alice, for, though the flowers were very interesting, she felt that it would be far grander to have a talk with a real Queen.

'You can't possibly do that,' said the Rose: '*I* should advise you to walk the other way.'

This sounded nonsense to Alice so she said nothing, but set off at once towards the Red Queen. To her surprise, she lost sight of her in a moment, and found herself walking in at the front door again.

A little provoked, she drew back and, after looking everywhere for the Queen (whom she spied out at last, a long way off), she thought she would try the plan, this time of walking in the opposite direction.

It succeeded beautifully.

Lewis Carroll, Alice through the Looking-Glass, chapter 2

Contents

Preface

For a number of years I have been teaching early Italian literature in a Faculty of Modern Languages, working with students who have a relatively limited knowledge either of the language or of medieval culture, and giving regular public lectures for people who are not studying Italian at all but who want to know more about Dante. In this time I have become ever more conscious of the exceptionally close link between Dante's fiction and his ideas, and have increasingly felt the need to read the *Comedy* in the light of the poet's own beliefs about the nature of language, art, morality, history and God. For better or worse, this work has grown out of my teaching and the consequences will be obvious at every turn.

If the book has a motto over and above its five epigraphs, it is the much-quoted injunction of E. M. Forster: 'Only connect'. It presents many individual philosophical concepts which become clearer as they are reintegrated into their system. The exposition of Dante's ideas is always related to a reading of one or more episodes in the *Comedy*. Each episode is interpreted in the light of its place in the whole poem which is itself set in the context of Dante's other works. And all the time I am trying to make connections between an early fourteenth-century poem and a reader in the late twentieth century.

There are, of course, other important relationships of a different kind between the book as a whole and its predecessors – the giants of Dantean and medieval scholarship, for example, or an earlier work of my own written in the same spirit. These relationships too deserve to be spelt out, but they will be of interest only to a minority, and at this stage there are just two things that need to be made clear. First, the book's main claim to originality lies precisely in the connections that it seeks to re-establish between a medieval poem and medieval ideas. Second, the only close link with my earlier study of Dante's thought and poetry is that I occasionally use the adjective 'philomythical', as a correlative to 'philosophical', in order to signify the kind of creative writing that is open to and nourished by philosophy. Anyone who is curious to know how I conceive the relationship between *mythos* and *sophia* in Dante, or who would like to read my own sketch of his development and his other works, is referred to the first forty pages of *Dante Philomythes and Philosopher; Man in the Cosmos.* But this book stands entirely on its own feet.

The editions of Dante's works and the abbreviations used are given on p. 302 below at the beginning of the notes section. All unattributed translations and all italicisations for emphasis are mine.

My thanks are due to many people. First and foremost, to the friends who read and commented on drafts of one or more chapters, particularly Peter Brand, Fergus Campbell, Robbie Carroll, Ruth Daniel, Robert Gordon, Michael Horton, Martin Kemp, Robin Kirkpatrick, Laura Lepschy, Alison Morgan, Roger Morgan, Elizabeth Mozzillo, Christopher Ryan, Malcolm Schofield and Chris Stevens. They helped to make the 'crooked straight and the rough places plain' as well as pointing out a good many slips and inconsistencies. (It should go without saying that all the remaining anfractuosities and errors are my own responsibility.) And this is the place to record my debt to the staff of the Cambridge University Press for their patience and their admirably professional service, particularly to the editor, Kevin Taylor, and to the copy-editor, Rachel Neaman, who went through the final draft with something more than the proverbial toothcomb and made suggestions for scores of vital improvements.

During the long years of gestation, however, there have been other less tangible kinds of support which it is a pleasure as well as a duty to acknowledge. My thanks go therefore to the Fellows of St John's College for their intellectual stimulation, good humour and affection. It is a unique privilege to spend one's working life in the middle of such a community. At another level I must express my gratitude to the general audiences in England, Germany and North America whose warm responses have encouraged me to persevere in the attempt to present Dante, even to non-specialists, in his own language and as a medieval intellectual. I am still more deeply indebted to our Cambridge students whose moments of bewilderment or boredom have done as much to improve the book as their questions in tutorials or seminars. Last, but not least, I must thank all my immediate colleagues in the Department of Italian at Cambridge for their advice, friendship and cheerful support throughout the making of this book. It is perhaps invidious to single out one name, but I want to end by expressing special gratitude to my fellow Dantist and keenest interlocutor, Robin Kirkpatrick, whose generous offer to shoulder the ever-more intrusive duties of Head of Department in 1990 had the effect of liberating and focusing my energies and thus bringing the work to its conclusion.

PART ONE

Coming to terms with Aristotle

CHAPTER ONE

The prestige and unity of the Aristotelian corpus

'The Master of those who know'

The first line of the *Comedy* tells us that the events to be narrated took place when the narrator was 'in the middle of the journey of our life'. The words are usually interpreted (with a certain amount of circularity in the reasoning) to yield the very precise sense that it was 1300, when Dante was in his thirty-fifth year. But it is equally possible, and highly desirable, to understand the phrase less narrowly as meaning 'in our middle age', that is, in the second of the three ages of man, which, in Dante's view, extends from the twenty-fifth to the forty-fifth year of a normal human life span.[1]

There are several linked advantages in this more flexible formulation. It helps us to see that the protagonist is portrayed with critical detachment by the author of the poem, who writes from the superior vantage point of full maturity gained in the *third* age. It prepares us to recognise that Dante-the-author depicts his earlier, wayward self as a typical representative of that time of life, as someone who manifests both the weaknesses and the 'signs' of innate goodness which theory would lead one to expect in a well-endowed man during his middle years. Taken together, these considerations remind us that Dante-the-pilgrim is a character in a work of fiction: he is partly drawn from life, partly a free creation and partly modelled on a type.

If we want to discover what the *historical* Dante was really like in the crucial years of his second age, at a time when his work gives clear indications that he was approaching some kind of crisis, we must turn to the *Convivio*, and especially to the fourth and last book,

3

probably written in 1307 or 1308, when Dante was not much over forty.

Few sections of that book could be more revealing than chapters xi–xiii, which develop and amplify an argument which he had formulated in just five lines of verse in the poem to which the book is a commentary. The central chapter (xii) is very well known, because it is there for the first time that Dante explicitly uses the image of the 'journey' of human life. And it will be instructive to quote the opening of his extended simile, since it can reasonably be interpreted as evidence of the creative or 'philomythical' Dante growing impatient with his self-imposed role as commentator and teacher:

> Imagine a traveller who is taking a road along which he has never been before. Every time he sees a house in the distance, he believes it to be the inn; and each time he finds he was wrong, he extends the same belief to the next house. And so he goes on from house to house until he does come to the inn. The soul is like this traveller. It has never been on the strange journey of this life before ['nel nuovo e mai non fatto *cammino* di questa *vita*']. As soon as it sets out, it turns its eyes towards the supreme good, which constitutes its goal; and every time it sees something that seems to embody some good, it believes it has found that goal.
>
> At first, its judgement is defective because it lacks experience and instruction. So it believes that small objects of little value are large and valuable, and it begins by desiring them. This is why we see small boys long for an apple above all things, and then, when they are a little more advanced, set their hearts on a pet bird. From this they go on to desire a fine suit of clothes, then a horse, then a woman. Next they aspire to a modest fortune, then to a larger one, then to a still bigger one. And this happens because the soul never finds what it is looking for in any of these objects, but believes that it will find its heart's desire further on.
>
> (*Con.* IV, xii, 15–16)

The chief interest of these three chapters, however, with their sustained attack on the pursuit of riches, and their celebration of the quest for knowledge, lies in what they reveal about Dante the thinker and philosopher in his second age. And we could sum this up by saying that he is still under the spell of Aristotle.

Aristotle was the inventor of the syllogism, which is used in the strictly logical passages. Aristotle figures prominently among the authorities (indeed, if we include the previous chapter in our count, he is quoted more frequently than any other source in this section, since there are six references to his works, as against five to the Bible and five to Boethius). Lastly, it was from Aristotle that Dante derived his most important new argument, namely, that human beings *can* achieve a perfect human happiness in *this* life, because the 'natural' desire for certain knowledge (in which this happiness consists) *can* be satisfied, notwithstanding the limitations of our intellect. Nor is this composite debt in any way surprising, since Aristotle had been described in the first eight chapters of the same fourth book of the *Convivio* as 'the master of human reason', the 'guide of human life' and the 'master of the philosophers'. In fact, Dante is nowhere more representative of his time than in the reverence he felt for the man whom everyone called '*the* Philosopher'.

The rediscovery of Aristotle

Aristotle's reputation had not always stood so high. Before the middle of the twelfth century his fame in the Latin West rested on two short introductions to the science of logic (although it has to be said that these had been of crucial importance for the new breed of dialecticians who laid the foundations of the scholastic method in the monastic and then in the cathedral 'schools' of northern France). But in the hundred or so years between the death of Peter Lombard in the early 1160s and the death of Aquinas in 1274 – the years in which the University of Paris became the most important intellectual centre in Western Europe – he had climbed slowly but inexorably to a position of absolute supremacy. By the latter year, virtually all his works had been translated and re-translated, 'commentated' and 're-commentated', attacked and defended, re-attacked and re-defended. A Parisian Master of Arts in the 1280s or 1290s was in a position to know what Aristotle had actually said and what he really meant in some of his more cryptic utterances. He could hold an informed opinion (although not an uncontroversial one) concerning the truth of certain propositions which seemed to run counter to Christian belief. And he could and did deploy Aristotelian concepts, terminology and methods in his own questions and disputations. Back in the 1150s his course would have been limited to works relevant to the seven Liberal Arts; in the 1250s the curriculum of the Arts Faculty in Paris is known to have consisted almost exclusively of 'bookes (...) of Aristotle and his philosophie'.[2]

Obviously, one cannot do justice to a hundred years of complex

5

development in a single paragraph, nor condense that paragraph into a single phrase. There is, nevertheless, more than a grain of truth in the textbook cliché that forms the title of part one. The history of philosophy and theology in the first part of the thirteenth century had been one of 'coming to terms with Aristotle' in the most pregnant sense of that expression. And this is why any serious reader of Dante must sooner or later 'come to terms' with Aristotle in the more limited sense of acquiring at least a nodding acquaintance with the essential concepts and terminology of his philosophy.

Aristotelian moral science: one among three, or three in one?

The known writings of Aristotle may be divided into three main groups: (a) an inquiry into the meaning of knowledge itself, that is, 'true' or 'demonstrable' knowledge (*scientia*); (b) knowledge about the universe (*scientia naturalis*); (c) knowledge about man considered as a being distinguished from the rest of the universe by his capacity for knowledge and by his capacity to initiate or control action in accordance with his knowledge (*scientia moralis*). At the risk of oversimplification, one might say that his writings were devoted to truth, nature and human nature. And Dante clearly had these distinct groups in mind when he described Aristotle, in different places and contexts, as (a) 'the master of those who *know*', (b) 'the glorious philosopher to whom *Nature* had revealed her secrets more than to any other man', and (c) 'the master of our life', who 'showed the purpose and goal of *human* living'.[3]

My last book drew extensively on the texts dealing with the science of nature. The present volume, by contrast, is affected more strongly by the gravitational pull of works in the third group, especially by the *Nicomachean Ethics* (hereinafter known simply as the *Ethics*).

Now, it is important to acknowledge that the *Ethics* may be studied without constant reference to Aristotle's other writings. It is not a difficult or pronouncedly theoretical work. The approach is for the most part commonsensical and down to earth, and there are many real life examples to illustrate the general points. Aristotle addresses himself to mature men who are assumed to have wide experience of the world and 'sound judgement'; and he often concludes that the adages and rules of thumb enshrining the practical wisdom of this class of reader are at least tolerably well founded from the point of view of the professional philosopher. He is generally cautious and undogmatic; and he does not lose sight of the principle, enunciated near the beginning of the work, that one cannot demand the same degree of exactitude in the study of human affairs that one may reasonably expect from the theorems of geometry. Many of the issues he defined are still at the centre of ethical debate, even though the terminology has changed; and however much individual members of the legal profession or members of the general public might disagree in theory about the definition of such matters as 'personal responsibility', the 'age of consent' or the 'admissibility of circumstantial evidence', it is clear from the decisions reached in the law courts of the free world that, in practice, judges and jurors find themselves very much in agreement with the content and spirit of Aristotle's work.[4]

It is also arguable that the Aristotle whom we feel we get to know in the *Ethics* is a less forbidding, less monolithic figure than the author of the *Metaphysics* or *Concerning the Heavens*. Reading the work, one comes to understand why some twentieth-century scholars have been at pains to bring out the inquisitive character of his mind, why they are inclined to view internal inconsistencies between one work and another as signs of a desirable evolution in his thought, and why they admire him as the man who kept asking questions and checking his hypotheses against the evidence, rather than as the oracle who delivered all the answers.[5]

Nevertheless, the reader of Dante must always bear in mind that the 'false' image of Aristotle, which modern scholarship has consigned to the lumber room, was precisely that of 'the Philosopher' with a capital P – the image which had been so lovingly pieced together and set on a pedestal in the course of the thirteenth century. Like so many of his near contemporaries, Dante was strongly attracted to Aristotle, not simply because he had investigated every branch of knowledge in turn, but because he seemed to offer a *unitary* vision of knowledge, nature and man.

The three groups of works were expressions of a single endeavour and formed a unified system of thought. It was not possible, so it then seemed, to acquire knowledge about 'nature' without knowing what 'knowledge' was, or without mastering the linguistic tools and the 'primary' concepts provided in the writings on logic and in what Aristotle himself called 'First Philosophy' (only later were these books so seductively named *Metaphysics*). Similarly, one could not understand 'human nature' unless one understood the structures, properties, powers and functions of *animal* existence, because man was seen to be – to paraphrase Dante – 'up to his neck' in the natural order.[6]

Again, one could not grasp what was distinctive about the power that differentiates man from all other existing species unless one knew enough about animals to be able to perceive how human 'reason' differs from the 'cunning' of a fox, the 'docility' of a horse or the 'imitative' ability of a monkey or parrot (in Aristotle's model of rational knowledge, concepts like these are reached and successively refined by a process of comparison and contrast). The more one studied what was distinctively human, and what was therefore good for man considered as a human being, the more inescapable seemed the conclusion that the purpose of our life, and the nature of our happiness, lay in the 'actualisation of a potential for knowing' (this is a paraphrase of a definition accepted by Dante).[7] And so the path of investigation seemed to lead full circle through 'natural science' and 'human science' back to the original question: 'What is knowledge'?

Aristotle's commentators and disciples

The medieval commentators – from Averroes (d. 1198) in Moorish Spain to Aquinas (d. 1274) in Paris – excelled above all in interpreting Aristotle '*with* Aristotle'. They would use their understanding of the whole body of his thought to justify one translation of a difficult phrase against another, or to reject an apocryphal work as being un-Aristotelian. They filled out the lacunae in Aristotle's frequently elliptical utterances and reconstructed the 'missing stages' in what they took to be a syllogistical train of thought. Hence, when a student of Dante's generation read the *Ethics*, he found the text embedded in an extensive commentary which presented the 'moral science' in the framework of 'science' and 'natural science'.

As often as not, Dante would have encountered Aristotle's ethical thought at second hand in the lapidary fragments that were quoted by his teachers or contemporaries in the course of their own independent enquiries (typically, the quotations were used as points of departure or as proofs of an intermediate stage in the argument). As a result, Aristotle came to seem more authoritarian and technical than he really was. And while medieval philosophers and theologians no doubt prided themselves on conducting their investigations in a thoroughly professional – that is, Aristotelian way – they frequently turned a deaf ear to their master's warning concerning the degree of certitude which is possible in the study of human *mores*.

They also forgot that Aristotle liked to consider ethics as a branch of practical knowledge, and therefore as no different in principle from medicine. A doctor studies the workings of the human body in order to keep his patients 'well' or to restore them to good health. Similarly, the student of ethics should investigate the operations of the whole man – body and mind – in order to take the right decisions in everyday life. Even today, an ordinary non-philosopher could still read the *Ethics* for guidance on how to bring up his children so that they would achieve happiness and well-being. But he would be deterred or frustrated by the scholastics. They continued to define, distinguish and syllogise in the discussion of ethical problems exactly as they would do in solving a puzzle in formal logic. They treated feelings, obsessions and conflicts of interest and duty as if they were dealing with the interaction of impersonal physical forces. And it was precisely this approach to moral issues that was to form the principle target of attack for later opponents of scholasticism such as Petrarch and Francis Bacon.

'Natural', 'human' and 'combined' operations

It would therefore be seriously misleading to remove the *Ethics* from the elaborate contemporary 'frame' in which it was perceived by Dante, or to clear away the areas of 'over-painting' that are to be attributed to the good intentions of thirteenth-century experts; and this is why the present book is structured in such a way that discussion of the simpler ethical issues is located – and seen to be located – within an appropriate context of non-ethical assumptions and ideas.

Actions that can be performed only by human beings – intellection and voluntary acts – will not be treated in any detail until parts three and four, which may be thought of as establishing a beachhead and exploring the coastal plain of the vast territory which Dante called 'operazioni umane'.

In the four chapters forming the second part, man will be treated as a member of the natural order, and as the object of a purely 'natural science'. We shall examine some of the more important processes or activities that Dante described as 'operazioni naturali', by which he meant involuntary actions, such as seeing or running, which are indeed carried out by man, but which are no different in principle from those performed instinctively by the higher species of animals. (To put it in Dante's own perspective, we shall study the powers of sensation and movement, which belong to us by virtue of our common, *generated* nature, before we study the rational and volitional powers, which are directly *created* by God in each individual human being and therefore stand outside the order of nature.)[8]

The process of 'coming to terms with Aristotle', however, begins immediately in the remainder of part one, because these three brief chapters will offer a highly selective introduction to Aristotle's 'primary philosophy' and physics – an introduction which will be confined to those concepts and terms which are necessary for the understanding of Dante's psychology and ethics.

Hence, the four parts of the book may be compared to the concentric circles of a target on an army rifle-range. Working from the circumference towards the centre, the 'outer' ring of physics provides the necessary frame for the poetically named 'magpie' (devoted to natural operations) and the 'inner' (devoted to specifically human operations). Together, the 'magpie' and the 'inner' circumscribe and define the 'bullseye', which will study Dante's poetic representation of what might be called 'combined' operations, that is, actions performed by human beings which involve the exercise of both our natural and our God-given powers.

A brief course in Aristotelian physics may seem an odd way of preparing for a journey to the heart of Dante's poetry; but, as my last epigraph suggests, there is a looking-glass logic at work. We are going to 'try the plan' of walking purposefully 'in the opposite direction' from the text. Who knows? It may 'succeed beautifully'.

CHAPTER TWO

Movement and change in lifeless bodies

Nature, mobility and mutability

In ordinary English usage, 'physics' is taken to be just one branch of the 'natural sciences', but in the university Latin of Dante's time the corresponding words *physica* and *scientia naturalis* were exactly synonymous, the Latin noun *natura* being the counterpart of the Greek *physis*.

The definition of *physis* that Aristotle gives in his *Physics* was common coin by the end of the thirteenth century, but has become so unfamiliar nowadays that it may seem quite bewildering on first encounter. 'Nature', he said, 'is the origin of movement and change': *natura est principium motus et mutationis.* From this it follows – logically but still challengingly – that 'the subject matter of natural science is that which exists but does not remain in the same place or state': *subiectum Physicorum est ens mobile.*

Part of the difficulty in the second definition lies in the noun *ens* ('that which exists'); and this stumbling block may be removed by substituting the familiar word 'body' (*corpus*, plural *corpora*), which suggests something reassuringly solid and accessible to the senses. The object of study in physics can then be redefined as 'bodies in motion', or 'bodies subject to change' (*corpora mobilia*). This certainly sounds more natural in modern English, and, despite an element of tautology, there are distinct advantages in going back to this locution, provided it is borne in mind that the word 'body' may refer to something as vast and fluid as the ocean or atmosphere, or as minute and irritating as the speck of dust in the eye that we still describe as a 'foreign body'.

However, the main causes of difficulty for the modern student are that Aristotle focusses attention on movement rather than on the bodies which do the moving, and that he leaves his reader in doubt as to the semantic relationship between 'movement' and 'change'. Is change simply a kind of motion, as the adjective *mobilis* seems to imply? Or vice versa? Or are they both species of the same genus?

There is little one can do about the first difficulty except exercise patience and trust. But the precise connection between 'change' and 'movement' will become clearer once it is realised that all three of the suggested relationships are possible in different contexts. There is no doubt, for example, that Aristotle frequently uses *motus* in a very broad sense, in which it is synonymous to all intents and purposes with *mutatio*.[1] It is this usage which makes it possible for the adjective *mobilis* (derived from the same verb, *movere*, as *motus*) to do duty for either noun and thus to signify 'inconstant' or 'mutable', as well as 'capable of movement' or 'swift to move'. On the other hand, it is equally beyond doubt that *motus* occurs in contexts where it implies the adjective *localis* or where it could be replaced by the compound noun *locomotio*. And in this narrower sense Aristotle treats *motus* as if it were simply a species of 'change'.[2]

'John Brown's body': the four species of change

Aristotle distinguished four main classes of natural change which can be illustrated through the medium of an imaginary biographical sketch.

> John Brown was born on Clydeside and lived in Glasgow until the age of ten. He was a sickly child, and small for his age, until his parents took him to live in Palermo, where he shot up in height, excelled in sport and acquired a tan that made him almost indistinguishable from the local population. He was the pride of his parents' heart, but, alas, as he was returning home after his twenty-first birthday celebration, he was killed in a traffic accident. He is buried in the Protestant Cemetery there.

How would an Aristotelian have analysed these events? The journey from Glasgow to Palermo would obviously have been classified as a change of place – *locomotio* or *motus localis*. The biological developments by which John reached maturity and full adult height would have been described as 'growth'; but they would have been perceived as a change in size or quantity, and hence the preferred term would probably have been 'increase' – *incrementum* or *augmentum*. His acquisition of a tan is a clear example of a 'qualitative' change, or *alteratio*; and, finally, the fatal accident was the cause of a change in 'formal identity', or a 'substantial change'.

This last concept is the most difficult and requires some further elucidation. At the moment of his death, John Brown ceased to exist and another formally distinct body came into being – an *inanimate* body, that resembled the deceased for a time, until it began to decompose or be absorbed by other less complex animate bodies. In the Aristotelian analysis, the matter that 'lies a-mouldering in the grave' is not 'John Brown's body', and has no greater claim to that title than the matter that had slowly accumulated and assumed human form in his mother's womb. That earlier, unnamed 'body' was transformed into John in the instant that his heart and lungs began to function independently. He continued to exist through all the changes of place, quality and quantity over the next twenty-one years, but he ceased to be John Brown when his heart stopped beating and he 'breathed his last' (Aristotle would not have accepted that 'his soul goes marching on'). No matter was created during his gestation or birth, and no matter was destroyed at his death and decomposition; but at each decisive stage a 'new body' came into being. In the first case, the new body (John Brown himself) was more complex than its embryonic predecessor, and this kind of substantial change was called *generatio*. In the second case, the resultant body (the corpse) was less complex simply because it was *in*animate; and this complementary change of identity was known as *corruptio* (the root being the verb *rumpere*, 'to break', 'to break down').[3]

Body, esse, subsistere, *substance, accident*

The brief life of John Brown can take us straight to the core of the topic of 'change' or 'mutability'. But we cannot make any further progress until we have paused to consider more closely what it is that is presupposed in every instance of change, and what persists through all the different varieties. In short, we have reached the point where we must refine the indistinct and confused notion of 'body' that has been adequate for our purposes until now.

A body (*corpus*) is a unified whole (*totum*), which Aristotle analyses as a composite (*coniunctum*) of matter and structure (*materia et forma*), or, rather, as a composite of this particular matter under this particular structure. It extends in three dimensions and is thus said to possess magnitude. It is limited and bounded by a continuous surface, and therefore occupies a finite volume in space (*locus*). It is 'located', and no two bodies can be in the same place (*locus*) at the same time.

Matter and form can be distinguished analytically, but they cannot 'subsist' and cannot 'be' in the strong sense (to be explained in a moment) that these two verbs had in scholastic Latin. A *corpus*, on the other hand, not only can, but *must* 'subsist' or 'be'. And whatever 'is' or 'subsists' in nature is by definition a body, whether it is as simple and homogeneous as one of the four elements, or as complex and heterogeneous as man; whether it is as minute as the motes that dance in a sunbeam ('le minuzie de' corpi'), or as vast as the outermost of the heavenly spheres ('il maggior corpo').[4] Our next task, therefore, is to look more closely at the meaning of the two verbs 'to be' and 'to subsist' (*esse* and *subsistere*).

The verb *esse* is often no more than a link between subject and predicate in simple sentences of the type 'John Brown is tanned', or – to use Aristotle's recurrent example – 'Socrates is pale skinned'. But as we have just seen, it can also be used absolutely, with the meaning 'to exist independently in one's own right'. Hence, to say *Socrates est*, without further qualification, is tantamount to saying that he 'exists in the real world' (*Socrates est in rerum natura*). When used as a noun, in the context of natural science, *esse* means 'existence' or 'being *there*' ('Dasein', as the German equivalent suggests).

In medieval Latin, *subsistere* did not have the modern pejorative connotation of 'to eke out a bare living' (as in 'subsistence-economy'), but meant 'to enjoy full, autonomous and separate existence'. Dante clearly found it a radiantly positive word, since he claims that God created the angels so that each might say 'I subsist' (*subsisto*); and he uses the noun *subsistentia* (in Italian 'sussistenza') to refer to the angels, the blessed and to God Himself.[5]

The noun most commonly associated with *subsistere*, however, is not *subsistentia* but *substantia*, and we must now look at the meaning and usage of this important term – within the framework of Aristotelian natural science – in order to establish how far and in which contexts it might serve as a possible synonym for *corpus*.

The best way to grasp and remember the technical meaning of

substantia is to see it as the product of three factors: the verb *subsistere*; its component roots *sub-* and *-stantia*; and, most important, its opposition to the equally common term *accidens*, to which it stands in the same relationship as 'day' does to 'night', in the sense that each is perceived as being what the other is not.

A *substantia*, then, is that which is *per se subsistens*, enjoying autonomous existence in its own right and not simply as a part or attribute of something else. By contrast, an *accidens* is a quality, state or disposition, such as colour, warmth or health, that cannot exist *per se*, but must always be attributed to a *substantia*.[6] The etymology of *substantia* (*sub* = 'under', and *stantia* = 'staying') implies that it 'underlies' and 'sustains' its attributes or qualities. A student of natural philosophy will normally indicate a *substantia* by means of a proper noun (e.g., Socrates), or by a common noun used with a demonstrative adjective (*hic homo*, 'this man'); and he will regard the adjective (e.g., 'tanned', 'warm', 'healthy') as the primary linguistic sign for an *accidens*.

In nature, then – at least, in all contexts relevant to this book – every *substantia* is a *corpus*, every *corpus* is a *substantia*, and either noun presupposes the fundamental predicate *est* or *subsistit*. But *substantia* would not be substituted for *corpus* unless the context required or implied a contrast with 'accidental qualities'. Conversely, *corpus* would not seem appropriate as a possible variant for *substantia* except in a passage where a distinction was to be drawn between *forma* and *materia* – and it is to this pair of correlated terms that we must now turn.

Body: subject-matter, form, properties, powers and differentiae

In the analysis of a body – still considered in itself, as a *coniunctum*, without reference to change in the past or future – matter was thought to be necessary, but entirely passive. It was the *ex quo*, the 'stuff out of which', mere receptivity. It was often compared to a piece of wax receiving and retaining the imprint of the signet, or, more tendentiously, to the female fertilised by the male. And because of this passivity, it was regularly designated by another word beginning with the prefix *sub*. Matter is the *subiectum*, literally, 'that which is placed underneath'; and the modern English compound noun 'subject-matter' is a tautological dead metaphor, derived from what was once held to be a physical fact – *all* 'matter' was 'subject'.

The 'dominant' partner is therefore *forma*, a noun which in this context was often qualified by the adjective *substantialis* to remove any possible ambiguity. The *forma substantialis* was said to be 'that by which a body exists' (*id quo est*). It is also that which makes the body '*what* it is' (*id quod est*); and Dante was merely repeating a textbook cliché when he wrote that 'man is what he is by virtue of his substantial form': *homo est id quod est per formam substantialem.*[7] Whenever the scholastics speak of the essence or nature or quiddity (i.e., 'what-ness') of a thing (*essentia, natura, quidditas, quod quid est*), they are in fact referring to what we would be most inclined to call its 'structure' and what they called 'substantial form'.

The *forma substantialis* endows the body which it 'informs' and causes to exist with a set of properties (*proprietates*, from *proprium*, 'belonging to'), which in different contexts are known as *potentiae* and *virtutes* ('powers' or 'capacities', and 'virtues'). Some of these properties will be common to all bodies at or above a given level of being (e.g., to all plants and to all animals, but not to minerals); some will be shared by all bodies of a given kind or *genus* (e.g., crustaceans or fish); but at least one such property will be limited to, and therefore distinctive of, bodies in a particular *species* (e.g., tench or bream), and this is said to constitute its *differentia, vis ultima* or *ultimum.*[8]

Any two bodies that exhibit the same set of properties – or even, simply, the same *differentia* – are assumed to have the same *forma substantialis*, and to belong to the same species. Conversely, any two bodies which are claimed to belong to the same species must be identical with respect to their substantial form, and possess the properties inseparable from that form. This is not to say, of course, that any two bodies of the same species must be identical in *every* respect. But the differences between them will be 'accidental', and not 'substantial'. In other words, they will differ in qualities, states and dispositions – such as size, age, colour, warmth, health – and not in the connatural properties, powers and virtues. The *accidentia* that produce unlikenesses in two bodies of like form are not different from the *accidentia* that befall any given body during its existence, and make it unlike what it was before. And with that conclusion we are ready to return to the theme of change, and to shift the emphasis from the noun *corpus* to the verb *mutare* or the adjective *mobilis*.

Corporeity, mutability (mobility): swords, shares and sharpening

We can both summarise and synthesise the most important concepts and terms that have been introduced so far by stating explicitly what it is that remains *un*changed in the four kinds of 'mutation'.

In the first and simplest kind, 'locomotion', that which is carried from location A to location B is obviously the body itself considered as a *totum*. The sword that Arthur drew from the stone is the same that others had failed to move. The ploughshare that Dickon guides along the furrow will be the same at the far end of the field as at the near.[9]

In the most drastic kind of change, however, when body A is transmuted into body B, all that persists is the matter which had been 'subject' to the form of body A. When a sword is beaten into a ploughshare, it is only the matter which is common to the 'corrupted' body A and the 'generated' body B. Matter is therefore the *subiectum* of the process of 'substantial change', as well as the *subiectum* of 'form' within the body.

If the sword were simply sharpened and shortened, it would still be a sword and the *same* sword, just as the shoes we fetch from the cobbler's are the same as we took in for repair. An Aristotelian would say that a number of 'qualities' had been modified, but that the 'quiddity' had been left intact, or that the changes were not 'of the essence', but merely 'accidental'. Technically speaking, therefore, what persists in the case of 'alteration' is the *forma substantialis* (the 'what it is that makes it what it is'), or the body considered as a *substantia* underlying the supervening *accidentia*.

It is not possible to be quite so clear-cut about the final category, 'growth', which must be understood to include '*de*crease', as well as 'increase'.[10] Insofar as these entail no more than a change in quantity or magnitude – as, for example, when an adult animal puts on weight or loses it again – they would seem to be 'accidental' in character, and therefore most akin to 'alteration'. But insofar as growth and diminution are regarded as aspects of the young animal's development and the mature animal's decline in old age, they would seem to be related more closely to 'generation' and 'corruption'. On balance, however, it is safer to consider the *forma substantialis* as the constant element, and therefore to link *augmentum* more closely with *alteratio*.[11]

Rectilinear locomotion as the paradigm of all change

We admire a new-born baby, smile at the meanderings of a drunk, and infuriate the children of our visitors by exclaiming 'How you've grown!' And our reactions show that it is not in the least difficult to recognise the *results* of change, even though the *processes* called generation, alteration and growth cannot be observed by the naked eye. On the other hand, if we watch a boy on a beach throwing a pebble up into the air, we can witness the whole event, following every instant of the pebble's progress from the moment it was picked up until the moment it returned to the ground.

Galileo and Newton – or the mythical figures who masquerade under these names in the popular consciousness – were able to overturn a major part of Aristotle's *Physics* through the universal laws of motion which they deduced from their observation of falling bodies that were scarcely more significant than a pebble. But in a sense they were not so bold in their speculations as Aristotle himself had been. For what he did was to take the visible *progress* of bodies moving through space (*motus localis*) as his paradigm for the analysis of the three invisible *processes* of change (*mutatio*) that occur within the confines of a body. He himself did not refer directly to boys or beaches, but we know exactly how he would have analysed the trajectory of the pebble, and we can use this humble example to illustrate the next group of concepts and axioms with which we have to 'come to terms'.[12]

Time and immobility: the concomitant and the correlative of motion

Not without a pleasing hint of paradox, we must approach the analysis of movement by recalling that the pebble lay *motionless* on the beach before the boy's arrival and after his departure. This will enable us to dispose of two important preliminaries, one concerning time, which is the concomitant of motion, the other concerning stillness or rest, which is its correlative or antonym.

The first point, then, is that Aristotle regarded the concepts of time and motion as inseparable. By definition, a body cannot be in two different places simultaneously, and so its transition from location A to location B, however close these may be, must involve the passage of time, however brief. Our very perception of movement, moreover, entails an awareness of successive moments – of a 'then' and a 'now', or a 'before' and an 'after', a *prius* and *posterius*. Conversely, we should not be conscious of the dimension we call time if we were unable to perceive some kind of movement or change.[13]

The second point is that, for Aristotle, no explanation of movement could be satisfactory unless it could also account for the absence of motion or its cessation – the state of stillness or rest, which in medieval Latin was called 'quiet' (*quies/quietis*). The dictum with which we began – 'Nature is the origin of movement and change' – has thus to be modified to read: 'Nature is the origin of movement and repose', *natura est principium motus et quietis*.[14]

Mercifully, there is no need to go into the details of how Aristotle would have explained the pebble's immobility.[15] But it must be borne in mind that, for him, a movement begins and ends in a state of *quies* or rest, during which the *corpus mobile* in question is 'located' at some specific point in space. Or, to express the same insight with a different emphasis: in every instance of local movement here on earth there is a *prius* and a *posterius*, a before and an after, in which the body is motionless even if the duration of this stillness is so brief as to be imperceptible to the senses.

The 'terms' of rectilinear motion

The next stage in the exposition will be easier to follow if we deal first with the elementary terminology associated with rectilinear motion. Let us imagine, then, for the time being, that the boy simply *pushed* the pebble from its initial resting place at A to its second resting place at B, as though he were advancing a pawn on a chess-board.

Position A would be called the *terminus a quo*, literally the 'boundary from which', while position B would be the *terminus ad quem*, the 'boundary towards which'. The qualifying phrases *a quo* and *ad quem* were necessary, because the word *terminus* still retained something of its original meaning of a 'boundary' or 'limit', and did not necessarily refer to the 'termination' of movement. Hence, one of the most important implications of this pair of terms is that the rectilinear movement of any body must be finite and limited in space.[16]

Less formally, positions A and B would be known as the *principium* and *finis*, while the stretch of beach that separates them would be the *medium*. It is worth stressing once more that these three words could and did refer to space, and might well be translated, in the appropriate context, as 'starting point', 'finishing post' and 'course'. More commonly, however, they are to be translated as 'beginning', 'end' and 'middle', with reference either to time or to space or to both (then, as now, it was often difficult to determine which idea was prevalent).

By Dante's time the three nouns had long been used in the extended senses which require us to translate *principium* as 'source', 'origin' or 'cause', *finis* as 'objective', 'target' or 'goal', and *medium* as 'method', 'instrument' – or 'medium'. But whereas nobody today associates 'principles', 'ends' and 'means' with the idea of locomotion, in the thirteenth century it would have been impossible to ignore the link or the continuity between ethical discourse and the language of natural science.

The pebble ascending: propulsion; agency, patience; vis motiva, violentia

Our hypothetical pebble did not, however, proceed from A to B by means of a flat push, as when a pawn is advanced on a chessboard. It was *thrown* there. And since its flight will serve to introduce and exemplify a number of important concepts and distinctions, let us attempt to visualise the events on the beach in greater detail.

The boy bent down, took hold of the pebble in his outstretched hand and stood up again so that the pebble came to rest temporarily near his body. Next he took a short run, as throwers often do. Then he leant backwards, lowering his right arm, before straightening up and simultaneously extending his arm with all his power. At the crucial moment he relaxed his grip, so that the pebble began its flight into the air.

In each of the three main phases – drawing to himself, carrying, throwing (*tractio, vectio, propulsio*) – all the energy required to displace the stone came from the boy. He would therefore be known as the 'mover', or 'moving cause' (*motor, movens, causa movens*).[17]

More generically, however, he may be described as the 'agent' of the 'action' (*agens* and *actio* being derived from *agere/actum*, 'to do', 'drive', 'perform'). The pebble, by contrast, would be described as 'passive', or, most commonly, as the 'patient body' (*patiens*, from *pati/passum*, 'to suffer', 'undergo', 'endure'). The relationship between the boy and the stone is that of 'agency' and 'patience', and this is one of the most important correlative pairs in the whole system of Aristotle's thought. We shall see that there must be an 'agent' and a 'patient' in every instance of movement or change, even if these have to be distinguished purely analytically within the same *substantia* (as we would have to do, for example, if we were trying to understand the boy's own movements).

In every instance of movement or change, also, the energy or power applied by the agent was known as the 'motive force', *vis motiva*, or simply as the 'motive', *motivum*. But whenever the agent and the patient are quite distinct, such that the patient contributes nothing to the change it undergoes and all the motive force comes 'from without' (*extra*), the *vis* could be called *violentia*, and the change would be described as 'violent'. The projection of the pebble is in fact a perfect example of what Aristotelians called a *motus violentus*.[18]

A great many movements in the universe were thought to be 'violent' in this sense – including the daily revolution of the sun and stars around the earth! Moreover, it was regarded as entirely 'natural' that some bodies should cause violent change to others. We must therefore remember that *violentus* and *violentia* were neither emotive nor pejorative in thirteenth-century physics. Nevertheless, in this context, 'violent' is the contrary of 'natural'; and so it may be inferred that a truly 'natural motion' is one in which the source (*principium*) of the movement or change is in some sense 'within' the body (*intus*, *intrinsecus*). Or, to put it another way, a movement is 'natural' when the same body is both agent and patient, and is therefore '*self*-moved'.

The pebble descending: natural movement

The time has come to explore the subject of *natural* motion in more detail. It is generally agreed that the weakest part of Aristotle's account of locomotion lies in his explanation of what later came to be called 'momentum', that is, in his explanation of how and why a projectile continues to travel through the air after it has lost contact with the body that had first 'impelled' and then 'expelled' it (this was to be the area where Galileo and Newton made their most important contributions). His errors – or those of his followers, because

Aristotle says tantalisingly little on the subject – probably arose because he relied too easily on the analogy of the transmission of sound, and also because his primary concern was to show that there is no such thing as a vacuum.[19] In other words, he assumed that a medium such as the atmosphere or water was necessary if the projectile were to be able to move at all, and that the particles of air and water did not so much *resist* the body in its passage as *help* it on its way by acting as links in a 'knock-on' series of instrumental causes. But these misconceptions did not have important consequences for the rest of his natural science considered as the context of his *Ethics*; and, in any case, he would have insisted that the boy was the 'first mover' in the series (*primum movens*), and that every inch of the pebble's ascent and lateral movement was attributable to the *motus violentus*, for which the boy was clearly responsible.[20]

For the sake of simplicity, let us assume that the boy managed to launch the pebble almost vertically into the air, so that we may discount the lateral displacement (which in reality would have combined with the up-and-down movement to make the whole flight a smooth and uninterrupted parabola). We shall then be able to accept that the 'violent motion' reached a *terminus ad quem* at the altitude where the pebble ceased to climb, and that there was an instant at which the pebble was not moving and at rest (*quies*).

Why did the pebble not remain at a standstill? What was the force that caused it to return to the beach below? Both the medieval Aristotelian and the post-Newtonian physicist would reply with the same word – 'gravity' – but they would give the word two quite different meanings.

For Aristotle, 'weight' or 'heaviness' (*gravitas*) was a property inherent in the form of two of the four elements (Earth and, to a lesser extent, Water), just as 'lightness' (*levitas*) was a connatural property of the other two elements (Fire and, to a lesser degree, Air). Compound bodies in which the elements of Earth and Water predominate (e.g., minerals and metals, respectively) are therefore heavy by their very form or nature.

'Heaviness' was defined as an inclination to move downwards (*deorsum*), and 'downwards' meant 'towards the centre of the universe', which, in Aristotle's cosmology, coincides with the centre of our globe. This centre was thought to be the 'natural place' for a naturally heavy body.[21]

It is one and the same connatural property that causes a stone to feel heavy when we pick it up, to fall to the ground when we let it go, and to remain in its proper place. Heaviness is the cause both of movement and of stillness; or, to put it in the technical terms of Aristotle's definition of Nature, *gravitas* is a *principium motus et quietis*. Hence the motive force that caused the pebble to descend to its *terminus ad quem* on the beach lay inside the pebble itself, *intus* or *intrinsecus*, in the property of weight that it possessed simply by virtue of its form. Its fall was therefore (although admittedly in a special sense) an instance of '*natural* motion'.[22]

The last shall be first: 'whither' and 'whence'

There is one last lesson to be extracted from the parabola of the pebble, and, fittingly, it is not the least.

The reason why the change from one kind of motive force to the other can so easily pass unremarked is that the 'end' of the violent motion is less significant than the 'beginning', whereas the 'beginning' of natural motion is less significant than the 'end'. In order to explain the pebble's ascent, Aristotle would direct his attention to the *principium*, the 'whence', that is, the boy from whom (*a quo*) the motive force derived. But in order to explain its descent, he would look to the 'whither', or the *terminus ad quem*. *Finis* acquires the extended connotations of 'objective' or 'goal', and it is assumed that the pebble falls *in order to* return to its natural place.

There are of course many exceptions to this polarising tendency, and Aristotle did not limit himself exclusively to the 'whither' in order to explain natural motion, nor to the 'whence' in order to explain violent motion. It is enough to imagine that the boy on the beach threw his stone at a passing seagull to be reminded that violent motion can have a purpose when it is considered from the standpoint of the agent; and the standard Aristotelian example of movement directed to a definite goal was in fact that of a projectile – the flight of an arrow to its 'proveduto fine'. In this perspective, the *violent* motion of a patient body must have its immediate or ultimate source in the *natural* motion of some agent or other. Hence, in the last analysis, all movement is natural; and all movement is therefore 'directed to a specific goal' or 'for the sake of something': *in determinatum finem*, or *propter aliquid*.[23]

It was Aristotle who taught posterity to distinguish between these two kinds of explanation, which came to be called the 'efficient cause' (*causa efficiens*, from *efficere/effectum*, 'to bring about', 'to produce an effect') and 'final cause' (*finalis*, from *finis* in the sense of 'purpose' or 'intention'). It was he, too, who showed that the two causes are complementary: for example, if a colleague were to ask me 'What brings you to the British Library?', it would be equally correct (although equally facetious) to reply either 'my research', or 'my car'; and a full answer to this kind of question should include both the 'motive' and the 'motor'.[24]

Lastly, it was Aristotle who convinced the scholastics at least that, insofar as the two kinds of explanation are commensurable, the final cause takes priority. The end comes first. It is 'that for the sake of which' any movement has its origin (*cuius gratia, propter quid*). Metaphorically, the end is already 'pulling' before the efficient cause begins, literally, to 'push'. All Aristotle's investigations into the 'origin of change' (*principium motus et mutationis*) were inspired by the conviction that 'the beginning lay in the end', and that nature always acts for a purpose (*propter aliquid*).[25] He specifically rejected a theory of natural selection, attributed to Empedocles, involving random mutations and the survival of the fittest.[26] For him there could be no true knowledge of nature, and therefore no *scientia naturalis*, unless one could discover what purposes are served by bodies and by the changes they undergo. And this is what historians of thought mean when they stress that his philosophy is profoundly and distinctively teleological (the Greek word for *finis* was *telos*; and *teleologia* used to mean the 'study of final causes'). So much for the paradigm of change afforded by the pebble.

From mobility to corporeity: the four 'causes'

Aristotle was perfectly aware that there is something paradoxical in saying that a stone is capable of 'moving itself'. He accepted the commonsensical view that the power of self-movement is not to be found in minerals, nor even in plants. And we shall see in chapter 4 that the 'properties' which enable a wolf, a lamb or a shepherd to change their location are more numerous and complex than a mere 'inclination to the centre'. But before we can examine self-locomotion as found in animals and man, we must consider the operations of plant life in relation to the other three species of change – that is, in relation to quality, quantity and substance. And before we can do that, we must return to the notion of *corpus* as such, and see how Aristotle's account of 'corporeity' was influenced by his analysis of 'mobility'.

The relationship between 'matter' and 'structure' *within* a body (provisionally described above) is clearly analogous to that between the pebble and the boy in the simplest possible case of a *motus violentus*: the *materia* is 'patient', contributing nothing; the *forma substantialis* makes the body exist and determines its characteristics. These two correlated principles help to explain the nature and being of the body, and hence they too could be called 'causes' in the old sense of the word. And it will be found that, in the appropriate context, the simple nouns *materia* and *forma* can be replaced by the phrases *causa materialis* and *causa formalis*.

A body comes into being as the end-product of the process of 'substantial' change known as 'generation'; and since no body can be self-generated, it must owe its existence to some other pre-existent body outside itself – a *principium extrinsecum*. And just as there was an 'efficient' cause of the flight that took an arrow to its target, so a body must have had an 'efficient' cause of its very being, which needs to be identified if the body is to be fully understood.

The target is the *finis*, or *terminus ad quem*, or *causa finalis* of the arrow's flight; and the newly generated *substantia* is the *finis* of the process of generation. Aristotle continues to press the analogy between *motus* or *mutatio*, on the one hand, and *corpus* or *substantia*, on the other, by asserting that any existing body must itself have a *finis*, in the sense that it has a purpose to fulfil, a function to discharge, an active or a passive role to play in the workings of the cosmos. It has a *propter quid* within itself. It too has a 'final cause'.

There are, therefore, four different kinds of explanation for the existence and nature of a *corpus naturale*, which were known to the scholastics as the 'material cause', the 'formal cause', the 'efficient cause' and the 'final cause'. And in a well-known passage of the *Physics*, where he summarises this part of his teaching, Aristotle insisted that the 'natural scientist' (*physicus*) should seek to acquaint himself with all of them:

> Plainly, then, these are the causes, and this is how many they are. They are four, and the student of nature should know about them all, and it will be his method when stating on account of what [*ipsum propter quid*] to get back to them all: the matter, the form, the thing which effects the change,

and what the thing is for [*materiam, formam, moventem, et quod est cuius causa*].   (II, vii, 198a 22; translated by W. Charlton)

The cooking pot: the pre-eminence of the 'final cause'

But just as the *finis* of natural movement proved to be more significant than its *principium*, so the 'final cause' of a natural body is pre-eminent with respect to the other three. An example will serve to illuminate this point and to make the terminology more familiar; and nothing could be more suitable than the kind of humble artefact from which students of the human past can deduce so much about a culture that has ceased to exist.[27]

An earthenware cooking pot or casserole is made out of a special substance, familiarly called 'potter's clay', which is found in nature, but has been transformed by the action of prolonged and intense heat in a kiln. This clay is its 'material cause'. Its 'efficient cause' was clearly a potter, who used a wheel, kiln and fire as his tools or 'instrumental causes'. And it is enough to imagine a pot made out of ordinary garden clay, or thrown and fired by an amateur, to realise how important the material and efficient causes are to the pot's nature and its continued being.

Nevertheless, it is the shape or design – the 'formal cause' – that makes this piece of baked clay a casserole rather than some other item of domestic pottery or some fragment of a broken pot. And every significant feature of the form is determined by the fact that the casserole was made in order to stew enough meat and vegetables for a family meal: this is its purpose or 'final cause'.

The pot must be able to retain fluids (unlike a flowerpot of comparable dimensions) so it has to be glazed; it must be big enough to hold a meal for the entire family (unlike a soup bowl); and the nature of the stewing process demands that it shall have high sides and a lid (unlike a frying pan). It should have a thick bottom to prevent the food from sticking and burning, and it must be sufficiently robust to withstand repeated scouring and the knocks of daily use. The cook must be able to lift it from the stove when it is full and hot, so it needs two small handles placed rather high (unlike a cup). If it is intended to appear on the dinner table, it will probably have some suitable decorative pattern on the outside. But the ornamentation will not be so elaborate or so finely executed as it would have been if it were a show-piece for display in a cabinet. If it is not meant to come out of the kitchen, it will be left perfectly plain. Unlike a jug or a teapot, it will not need a lip or a spout suitable for pouring ... and so on. If the potter knows his craft, he will ensure that the casserole has no feature which is not functional, and that it lacks nothing which is essential to its purpose. And since Aristotle believed that 'craft imitates nature' (*ars imitatur naturam*), he generalised these insights in two often-quoted axioms that distil the essence of his teleology: 'Nature does nothing in vain', and 'Nature is not deficient in necessaries': *Natura nil facit otiose*; *natura non deficit in necessariis.*

A further brief example will serve to underline Aristotle's distinctively teleological approach – and this time the artefact is of his own choosing. A saw (*serra*) requires a hard metal such as iron for its 'material cause'; it must have teeth (*dentes*) as a distinctive feature of its 'formal cause'; and it would never come into being without a tool-maker as its 'efficient cause'. But it is the '*final* cause' – the accurate cutting of a thick resistant material such as a log of wood or a block of stone – that determines both matter and form. And if the tool-maker had not intended to fashion an instrument that would cut that kind of material in that kind of way he would not have made a saw, but a knife, an axe, a sword or a pair of shears.[28]

Mud, mud pies and casseroles: potentiality in substantial change

Let us now imagine that the boy has left the beach and gone to play beside a stream near a deposit of potter's clay. He scoops up a handful of the clay and squares it off until it has the shape of a brick. Next, he rolls it between his hands to make it into a ball. Still experimenting, he breaks off a small piece and puts it on one side, while he hollows out the remainder with his thumb until it looks like a bowl. Then he flattens the smaller piece so that it resembles a coin or lid and places it over the bowl to make a mud pie. If he were to dip his hand into the stream from time to time in order to keep the clay moist, he could continue his game almost indefinitely; but we have followed him far enough to conduct an Aristotelian analysis of the material and its transformation, and in so doing to introduce another crucial pair of correlated terms – *actus* and *potentia*.[29]

The first and most obvious point to notice is that it was the same piece of clay that underwent the successive metamorphoses; the brick did not preclude the ball or the bowl, nor has the mud pie even begun to exhaust the possibilities for further remodellings. Aristotle would hold that, so long as the clay remains clay, and so long as it stays moist, it will be in a state of permanent availability, waiting 'patiently' for the next demand on its resources. His word for this state is *potentia*, which originally meant no more than 'power', but which came to acquire – largely through the influence of his thought – the shades of meaning that are variously rendered as 'potency', 'potential' or 'potentiality'. He would refer to the brick, ball, bowl and pie as being 'in potency', or as having 'potential being' within the clay (Michelangelo would hold the same opinion about statues in marble). And he would find it natural to say that the clay is *in potentia* with respect to the bowl, and that the bowl is *in potentia* to the pie.

The next point is that the clay is not 'pure' matter, nor just 'any old material'. Significantly, it is *not* hard, sticky or friable, otherwise it would be useless for making mud pies. It *is* incombustible, but that is irrelevant as far as the boy is concerned. All that counts for his immediate purposes is the peculiar consistency of the clay, the distinctive property that enables him to mould it into one shape after another without any preparation or any tool other than his hands.

Should the boy grow up to be a potter, he would discover that this particular species of clay has a further, more significant potential. When it is heated to a very high temperature and then allowed to cool in the right conditions, it will emerge from the kiln in exactly the same shape as it went in, but under another substantial form – that of the 'substance' called terracotta. (By contrast, a wax image would have lost its shape, but retained the form which made it wax.) Hence, what went into the kiln as a glorified mud pie may come out as the earthenware casserole of our earlier example. Considered in its 'material cause' – that is, terracotta – the casserole is as hard, dry and brittle as the potter's clay had been soft, moist and mouldable; and as a result the casserole no longer has a *potentia* to assume the shape of a brick, ball or bowl. But considered as a *substantia* in its own right – as an independently existing earthenware cooking pot – it has acquired a new potential, a potential for use by human beings. And, as we saw earlier, this potential use as an instrument for stewing the dinner is precisely the 'final cause' of its existence, which determines all the features of its 'formal cause'.

The concept of 'potency' is necessarily somewhat elusive and far from limited to those properties of inanimate substances which give them a potential for use by other *substantiae*. But this humble example should nevertheless bring out the close link between *potentia* and *forma substantialis* and help to explain why the concept is so fundamental to the Aristotelian analysis of change.

Actuality and form

The technical term that correlates with *potentia* in Aristotle's system is *actus*. Historians of thought are still inclined to transliterate the word rather than translate it, and they continue to speak of 'potency' and 'act'; but if the concept is to be conveyed in ordinary modern English, one is compelled to use the derivatives 'actuality' or 'actualisation', or to fall back on roundabout phrases involving 'real' or 'reality'.

The meaning of the term is not usually in doubt, because it is determined by its opposition to whatever sense of the word *potentia* is relevant in the given context. Nevertheless, there are a number of usages that require illustration and comment. The casserole of our example existed only *in potentia* through all the phases of shaping, firing and cooking, but it will remain *in actu* – 'actualised in its existence as a cooking pot' – from the moment when it is safely extracted from the kiln until it is broken beyond repair. Similarly, John Brown was *in actu* – an 'actual human being' – from the time he drew his first breath until he breathed his last, whereas his existence in his mother's womb, or as a glint in his father's eye, was only *in potentia*. In other words, the phrase *in actu* is to be understood every time that the verb *esse* is predicated absolutely, meaning 'to exist' or 'to subsist' (it was often supplied by the writer to confirm that this was indeed the desired sense). And since a *corpus* – whether natural or artificial – exists by virtue of its substantial form, the form of a body may be described as its 'actuality', or as 'the principle by which its existence is actualised': *forma est actus corporis*.

Potentia *and* actus *in relation to* motus

In the last few sections we have been dealing either with bodies considered in themselves, that is, in their four 'causes', or with bodies viewed as the result of the process of change called 'generation'. The time has now come to shift the emphasis back to the *corpus* as *mobile*, and to see how the concepts of *actus* and *potentia* entered into the analysis of the other three kinds of change (alteration, growth and generation).

We saw earlier that Aristotle conceived all change as a *motus* from a *principium* or *terminus a quo* to a *finis* or *terminus ad quem*; so it will come as no surprise to learn that he would always locate the point of departure in a *potentia* of some kind, and the point of arrival in an *actus*. John Brown possessed *potentiae* for locomotion, alteration and growth that are not present in Ben Nevis, an Ethiopian or a baby elephant. He was potentially in Sicily while he was still in Scotland, potentially suntanned while still pallid, and potentially a man while still a boy. Residence in Palermo, the possession of a tan, and the state of manhood can be understood as the actualisations of these potentialities. And it is possible to describe every conceivable change in every conceivable body as a passage from a state of potentiality to a state of actuality, or as a transition from *potentia* to *actus*.

A description of this informal kind is all that is required for most practical purposes.[30] But when Aristotle came to offer a general definition of change that would be acceptable to a 'natural scientist', he felt it necessary to insist that change itself is 'real' or 'actual' while it lasts, and that it could lay claim to the status of 'actuality' just as much as any other attribute that may be predicated of a body. If it is legitimate to say that Thomas Green is 'actually' on the platform at Brighton at 0745 and 'actually' at London Victoria at 0850, then it is no less legitimate to say that he is 'actually changing places' between those times. And so Aristotle incorporated the word *actus* into his definition of *motus* (in its widest possible meaning) to assert that change is neither an actuality nor a potentiality in the normal sense, but 'the actuality of something existing potentially, considered precisely in its potentiality': *motus est actus existentis in potentia inquantum huiusmodi*.[31]

Terminal terms: perfectio *and* perfectus

It is most unlikely that Mr Green will remain at Victoria Station, and it is safe to assume that he will immediately seek some other form of transport to take him to his office in the City. But the journey from Brighton to London will nevertheless be 'completed' when his train comes to a halt at the terminus. And a medieval physicist would have said that his *motus* was *perfectus*, or that his arrival constituted the *perfectio* of his *motus localis*.[32]

Perfectio and *perfectus* could denote the completion of any and every process of change, and thus they are the last terms to be introduced in this chapter devoted to *motus et mutatio*. They do not present any particular difficulties, provided one bears in mind that both adjective and noun derive from the verb *perficere/perfectum*, meaning something like 'to carry on doing or making until the end', 'to round off', 'to complete'. In its primary sense, then, *perfectio* referred to the fulfilment or the fullest actualisation of a potential; and it could be used as a synonym for *actus* in any context where a given natural body, or any of its current attributes, was viewed as the result of change. The beatitude enjoyed by Dante-the-pilgrim as he experienced the direct vision of God was 'perfect' in the modern sense ('lacking nothing', 'fully actualised') precisely because he had 'perfected' (i.e., 'completed') the journey which brought him to the Empyrean.[33]

In the final stage of that journey, the pilgrim passed beyond space and time, beyond the greatest and swiftest body, beyond *motus* and *mutatio*, and therefore beyond Nature and the scope of Aristotelian physics. And there is clearly a profound meaning in that transcendence. But the key terms of Aristotle's natural science can nevertheless help us to interpret the first two-thirds of his journey. The protagonist's 'locomotion' through Hell and Purgatory to the Garden of Eden was not just a paradigm but a symbol of other kinds of change. He underwent 'alteration' and 'growth' to such an extent that he not only 'actualised' his 'potential', but was enabled to re-'generate' his 'corrupted' nature, 'perfecting' it through the recovery of the 'powers' and 'virtues' which had been lost by Adam at the Fall. That, or something like that, was the preliminary result of his 'nuovo e mai non fatto cammino'.[34]

CHAPTER THREE

Self-change: growth and reproduction in plant life

Life and soul

From the study of change as such, in all bodies whatsoever, we pass now to the study of *self*-change in those bodies – plants, animals and human beings – which have an internal *principium mutationis* known as the *anima*.

Like the Greek 'psyche', to which it corresponds, *anima* has been conventionally translated into English as 'soul'; and the modern reader's first task is to clear his or her mind of the connotations that this word has acquired in popular Christianity, and to re-establish the etymological link with the adjective 'animate', which still conveys both the meaning and the neutral tone of the medieval original. In other words, the 'souls' that concern us in the present chapter are not necessarily 'immortal', and are to be found in dogs and in trees as well as in human beings. Everything that has life is by definition 'en-souled' (a *corpus habens vitam* must be *animatum*). Everything that is 'animate' must be 'animated' by an *anima* of some kind.[1]

The term *anima* may be correctly paraphrased as the 'vital principle' or the 'first principle of life' (*primum principium vivendi*), or as 'that by which the body first lives' (*id quo primum vivit*). But the simplest possible definition is 'the substantial form of a living body' (*forma substantialis corporis viventis*).[2]

A *forma substantialis*, it will be remembered, is that by virtue of which a body exists or subsists in its own right (*id quo est*), and also that by virtue of which it possesses a certain number of characteristic properties or powers. 'Soul' is simply the name given to those species of substantial form that confer the power called 'life'. And it is important to grasp that it is one and the same form that makes a living body exist and makes it live. 'Life' is the special mode of being found in living things: 'vivere è l'essere de li viventi', as Dante put it in a close translation from Aristotle.[3]

We have seen that the substantial form of a body may be described as its 'actualisation' (*actus*), and that in this context *actus* may be replaced by *perfectio* ('fulfilment'). It follows therefore that the same pair of words may be applied to 'life-conferring forms' – *animae*. And Aristotle's preliminary working definition of 'soul' may be translated: 'soul is the first actuality of a natural body having life potentially within it'.[4]

This preliminary definition of 'soul' is relatively easy to understand if one is familiar with Aristotle's concept of *corpus*, and with the terms *esse, forma, proprietas, potentia* and *actus* as applied to *in*animate bodies. Similarly, there is no difficulty in grasping what Aristotle understood by 'life' – the other key word in the definition of soul, and the rhyme word in the first line of the *Comedy* – provided that one is familiar with his account of the four kinds of change (*motus*), and his distinction between 'enforced' and 'natural' change.

How, then, do we know that a given body is in fact 'alive' (*habens vitam*)? The answer is: through our observation of changes in that body, for which we cannot assign any external cause.

If, for example, we want to know whether an exotic shrub has survived the frosts, or whether a favourite elm has succumbed to the Dutch disease during the winter, we wait to see if they put out new leaves in the spring. If they do, they are still alive. We recognise, of course, that the light and warmth of the sun are necessary conditions for the changes we observe (otherwise we should not have waited for the spring). But we also know that the sun by itself could never 'draw forth' elm-leaves from the shrub or shrub-leaves from the elm; and that it can shine down on a patch of mud all through the summer without calling into being a leaf of any kind. We therefore conclude that there is some *internal* cause of this evident growth.[5]

Each of the two bodies, then, in some sense 'changes itself' – *movet seipsum*. And in Aristotle's view, 'the essence of life consists in the power to initiate self-change', so that 'we call a being lifeless when it can be changed only by some force acting from without'.[6]

Virtus, operatio: principium motus

A plant, then, is not simply 'passive' or 'patient'. It does not simply endure 'violent' changes originating from without. Like all living things, it is to some extent an 'agent'. And it is convenient to have two distinct terms to denote the two sets of properties (all of them inherent in the life-conferring form) which enable a living body to be acted upon and to act.

Aristotle used the single word *dynamis*, but the medieval Latin translator or the independent scholastic philosopher could describe these properties either as *potentiae* or *virtutes*. Admittedly, the two terms were not always contrasted, nor was the contrast anything like consistent; but there was at least enough consistency to justify Dante in saying that the element Earth is given 'powers' to suffer (*terra* [*est*] *potentiata ad patiendum*) while the heavenly bodies are given 'virtues' to act (*virtuatum est caelum ad agendum*). We shall therefore be slightly more rigorous than our authorities and reserve the term *virtutes* for those properties that enable a body to *initiate* change.[7]

The example of the shrub and the elm shows that a 'virtue', such as the capacity to put forth leaves, can remain dormant or 'in potency' over a long period. But when it is woken or 'actualised', it becomes active in its own right. It 'does' something (*agit*, from *agere/actum*). It carries out a 'job of work' (*opus*). And the most common and the most precise term in medieval Latin to denote the activity of a *virtus* is *operatio*, which is derived from the noun *opus* (plural *opera*) through the verb *operari/operatum*.

An *operatio* may be defined, then, as 'an activity which actualises a *virtus*', where *virtus* is understood as a capacity for a certain kind of action inherent in the *anima*, which is understood in its turn as the life-conferring, substantial form of a living body. Every *operatio* is an instance of change that is 'self-caused', or 'natural', or 'caused from within', because the 'origin of the change' (*principium motus*) lies in the *anima* of the body that performs the operation. The *anima* is therefore the ultimate object of study for the student of nature. But since it can only be known through the perceptible effects which it is assumed to cause, the study of the psyche must always begin with its *operationes*.

Operationes animae vegetativae

In Aristotle's analysis, even the simplest of animate bodies – plants – have 'virtues' in their 'souls' that enable them to initiate three of the four kinds of change. These are known collectively as the 'operations of the plant-soul' (*operationes animae vegetativae*), and some familiarity with them is necessary, because they are present in all living things including man. The first is the capacity to absorb and assimilate moisture and the mineral nutrients which are carried by the rising sap to nourish all parts of the plant. The operation itself is called *nutrimentum*, and the virtue is the *vis nutritiva*. It is probably to be classified as a kind of 'alteration', and its immediate purpose is to keep the plant alive and thus to preserve its being. Technically speaking, its *finis* is the *conservatio vitae, conservatio esse,* or *conservatio sui.*[8]

The operation of the second virtue, which presupposes that of the first, is called 'increase' or 'growth' (*augmentum, incrementum*), and it gives its name to the general category of 'quantitative' change. It is not, however, limited to mere enlargement, since it presides over the successive development of all the different parts that are found only in the mature plant. In some sense, therefore, it is related to the antecedent process of 'generation', through which the growing plant came into existence as a seedling. And its function can be described as the 'actualisation', 'completion' or 'perfection' of the capacities that had previously been present only 'in potency' (*augmentum est quo aliquid proficit in maiorem perfectionem*).

The third virtue comes into operation only when the plant is *perfecta*, that is, fully grown. It is known by the same name as the general category of 'substantial change' (*generatio*), and its function is to produce, from the patient matter of the soil, other living bodies with the same structure and properties as its own. Hence it can also be called 'self-reproduction'. Like nutrition, its goal may be defined as the preservation of being; but what it labours to preserve is the existence of the *species*. It strives to ensure that its specific form will survive not only its own death, but also the necessary corruption of all individual members of the species. Expressed in technical language, its *finis* is *conservatio speciei* rather than *conservatio sui.*[9]

Plurality of ends and unity of substance: distinction and subordination

This analysis of the processes involved in plant life is characteristic-ally Aristotelian in that it is thoroughly teleological. As always, a *motus naturalis* is assumed to have a *finis* and to occur for the sake of that *finis*. But here for the first time we are faced with a body that seems to be moving towards more than one goal, whereas the paradigm of rectilinear motion suggests that it is not possible to travel towards two different destinations at the same time.

The difficulty is a recurrent one in Aristotle's system of thought since every living thing proves on inspection to be 'impelled' to a plurality of ends, and the most complex of living beings – humans – have the greatest number of *operationes* and the greatest number of goals.[10] We must therefore pause to take note of how Aristotle combines the weapons of distinction and subordination to defend his doctrine of final causes.

Let us begin with the necessity of making distinctions. One simply has to accept that the definition of a *finis* will vary according to the point of view from which one chooses to consider the *motus*. Is one looking objectively, from the detached viewpoint of a supreme being? Or subjectively, with the eyes of a participant? Is one talking in broad terms (*large*), as is appropriate in an introductory chapter, or narrowly (*stricte*), as is necessary in a scholarly debate? Is the body being studied as an individual *substantia*, as a member of a certain species, or as a representative of a level of being such as plant life? Again, is one seeking a formula that will fit all possible cases universally and without qualification (*absolute, simpliciter*), or is one relating the *motus* and its *finis* to the particular circumstances and the operation of other contributory factors (*secundum quid*)? Or, more simply still, has distinction been made between the four different modes of change?

In some cases of conflict between the rival claims of two or more 'final causes' the apparent contradictions can be reconciled by distinction alone. Thomas Green – to revert to an earlier example – is fully capable of breathing, digesting his breakfast, twiddling his thumbs and reading a newspaper, while taking the train to the City. He can perform all these *motus* simultaneously, because their *fines* belong to different categories of change, and the underlying *virtutes* are genuinely distinct. What he cannot do is to breathe and hold his breath at the same time, or to travel – on this line – simultaneously to London and to Brighton.

Other conflicts can be resolved simply by invoking the principle of subordination, that is, by demonstrating that one end is in reality subservient to the other. It is perfectly possible for Mr Green to be travelling simultaneously to Haywards Heath and to London, because Haywards Heath is an intermediate station through which he must pass on his journey to the terminus. The first objective proves to be no more than a *medium* with respect to the ultimate *finis* – a means to an end.

In other cases, pure distinction has to be supplemented by the process of subordination, as will become clear if we go back to the 'operations' of plant-bodies, and consider a particular species, such as grass. In addition to its three *virtutes*, grass has a number of *potentiae* which render it suitable for use by other beings. For example, insects may find shelter underneath it, cows may graze on the tips, a dog may swallow a mouthful to act as an emetic, or a boy may stretch a blade between his thumbs and blow on the improvised reed to make a singularly raucous and penetrating wind instrument.

Higher beings – that is, those which possess a wider range of 'virtues' and 'operations' – will always define the purpose of a lower being in relation to its utility for themselves, exactly as in the earlier case of the cooking pot, whose *finis* was its *usus* by man. And in this perspective, the *virtutes* of the inferior body are always judged to be 'for the sake of' and therefore 'subordinate to' its *potentiae*. (We tend to think that grass takes nourishment and grows in order that cows may eat it, and that cows take nourishment and grow in order that we may eat them.) But this does not invalidate or exclude the subjective or 'self-centred' definition, according to which the grass exists simply in order to absorb nourishment, grow to maturity and reproduce.

Operatio propria *as the keystone in the arch*

The three *operationes* of the plant soul – which are of course present as the foundation of life in all higher bodies – are both distinct in kind and subordinate one to another.

From one point of view, *nutrimentum*, *augmentum* and *generatio* are as unrelated as qualitative, quantitative and substantial change; and this independence is already a sufficient explanation of how one and the same body can move towards several destinations at the same time. But from another point of view, self-preservation, which is the goal of nutrition, is merely the pre-condition of growth to maturity, which, in its turn, is merely the pre-condition for generation: plants and animals reproduce only when they are fully grown. The first is therefore subordinate to the second, and the second to the third.

In this latter perspective, self-reproduction is seen as the highest of a plant's active properties – its *virtus suprema* – and its 'actualisation in activity' (both senses of *actus* are pertinent) can be described as a plant's 'proper operation', its *operatio propria*. This is the 'job of work' – other synonyms might be 'task' or 'function' – which cannot be performed except by a plant with the given specific form: only elms can produce more elms; only grass is generated by grass.[11]

It will be found that the additional activities of an animal or a man can be analysed along exactly the same lines, and that *every* living body is assumed to have a 'proper operation' which is the actualisation of its 'supreme virtue'. And if any one concept can claim to be the keystone of Aristotle's natural philosophy, it must surely be that of *operatio propria*.

The concept cannot be adequately explained until all the other building-blocks have been, so to speak, cut to size and temporarily held in position on the right and the left of the arch by the kind of commentary that has been provided in this chapter and its predecessor. But once the keystone has been dropped into place, the temporary scaffolding can be dismantled, and the stone serves to bind the hitherto separate units into a single self-supporting span of thought. Anyone who has fully understood the meaning and implications of *operatio propria* should be able to rediscover and reassemble the ideas and axioms which it presupposes, whether these lie on the side of 'corporeity', or on the side of 'mobility' and 'change'. He or she will have 'come to terms' with Aristotle's science of nature, at least insofar as it constitutes the framework and foundation of his moral science.

Operatio propria *in relation to* differentia, causa finalis *and* corpus organicum

There are, of course, many other connections or correspondences within the unified system of ideas; and our next task will be to trace some of these pathways, and especially the one that links the adjective 'animate' to the adjectives 'organic' and 'organised'.

We saw earlier that the 'final cause' or *raison d'être* of an *artefact*, such as a saw or casserole, is the use to which it is put by human beings, and that every relevant property of its form or 'formal cause' is determined by the purpose it is designed to serve. It should therefore be clear, by analogy, that the final cause of a *living* body can be described as the use which that body makes of *itself*, and that every significant feature of the 'life-conferring' form – every *virtus* of the *anima* – is determined by the activity which the whole body is primarily intended to perform. 'Self-movement' is a kind of 'self-use'.

It should also be evident on reflection that the *differentia* of a living body – that is, the unique characteristic that marks off its specific form from those of related species – will coincide with its 'supreme virtue'.[12] And it also seems to follow that the *activity* of this 'differen-tiating virtue' – that is, the *operatio propria*, conceived now as the body's 'self-use' – can be identified with the *causa finalis*. In other words, the body exists in order to perform its characteristic activity, or 'for the sake of' its characteristic activity, and not the other way round. Ordinary Latin usage requires the noun *corpus* to precede the adjective *mobile*, but in Aristotle's conceptual syntax, we might say, *mobilitas* takes priority over *corporeitas* or *esse*.

Now, a living body will always possess a number of dissimilar or 'heterogeneous' parts (even a plant exhibits roots, stem, leaves, flowers and fruits); and if one finds such a body in nature, one can assume that it is, or has been, alive.

These unlike parts are held to be just so many 'tools' or 'instru-ments' (*instrumenta* or *organa*) by means of which the whole body performs its various operations. And it may be taken as axiomatic – since Nature does nothing in vain, and does not fail to provide what is necessary – that each distinct part corresponds to a distinct operation, and vice versa. So it is a matter of definition that a *corpus animatum* is always *organicum* or *organizatum*. The words which we transliterate as 'organic' and 'organised' used to mean no more than 'equipped with the appropriate tools'.[13]

Operatio propria *in relation to* perfectio

We must now revert to Aristotle's definition of 'soul' in order to introduce a simplification and to refine the crucial concept of 'fulfil-ment' – *actus* or *perfectio* – in the light of what has been said about the 'organisation' and the 'operations' of a living body.

It will be remembered that the provisional definition of *anima* ran like this: 'soul is the first actuality of a natural body potentially having life within it'. A few lines later in the same chapter, however, Aristotle uses a briefer formulation, in which the clumsy phrase 'potentially having life within it' is replaced by the single word 'organic' in the acceptation which has just been explained. The simpler version is therefore: 'soul is the first actuality of a natural organised body': *anima est perfectio prima* (or *actus primus*) *corporis physici organici.*[14]

Even in this shorter version, the noun *perfectio* is still qualified by the adjective *prima*, and the inference to be drawn is that there is some second, higher level of actuality beyond that of merely being alive. It will help us to see what this higher level may be if we begin by looking at the example of an *in*animate body.

A cartwheel is what it is by virtue of its form; and it will remain a wheel as long as the rim stays roughly circular and remains firmly attached to the axle by its spokes. But while the cart is stationary, the wheel might just as well be a support like the leg of a table. It only fulfils its potential while it is actually revolving and helping the cart to move from one location to another.

Similarly, a plant is a living body which subsists in its own right even when it is still a seedling. Even then, it already has a soul which has 'actualised its potential for life', and it will continue to exist by virtue of this same actualising principle as long as it remains alive. But clearly a plant does not fulfil the whole potential of its specific form until it has grown to maturity and begun to perform the task of self-reproduction, which is its *operatio propria*.

It becomes clear, then, that it is the 'proper operation' of a living body that constitutes its second and higher level of actuality. And while the noun *perfectio* is sometimes used as a synonym for 'maturity' (i.e., the *terminus ad quem* of the *motus* called *augmentum*), the phrase *perfectio secunda* refers to the current exercise of the supreme virtue of the soul. That which brings the whole potential to fulfilment is the *operatio propria*.

'Good', 'better', 'best' on the Aristotelian scale

We may round off this brief introduction to the basics of Aristotelian 'psychology' by looking well ahead to see how the natural scientist's category of 'perfection' will overlap with the moral scientist's category of 'goodness' or the 'good'.

Until recently, there has been relatively little professional contact between scientists and students of ethics, because it was widely felt that their respective aims and procedures are quite distinct. Science is objective, or so the story goes, and will never seek to pronounce as to what is good or bad, right or wrong, within its field of study. Ethics, by contrast, is properly concerned with value judgements, but it is inescapably subjective since it has not proved possible to reach agreement on a scale that would act as the unit of measurement.

Aristotle would have agreed that there is an important difference between the two disciplines. In his view, *scientia naturalis* offers generalisations and pursues truth for its own sake, whereas *scientia moralis* is a branch of practical knowledge, codifying the fruits of experience with a view to guiding individuals as to the correct action to be taken in particular situations. But he certainly did not accept that the concept of 'goodness' was merely a matter of personal opinion or local tradition and therefore impossible to define. And he could use the adjective 'good', and its comparative and superlative forms 'better' and 'best', in exactly the same way, whether he was referring to human affairs or to the realm of nature. The only premise to which we are asked to assent without demanding a proof is that 'Being is good'.

Of course, there is much more to this dense proposition than first meets the eye. *Esse* here means corporeal existence; and it entails the concepts of *corpus*, *materia* and *forma* as defined earlier. And since everything that exists in nature must exist as a body, analysable as *this* matter, under *this* substantial form, invested with *these* properties, it follows that the only mode of being that is good for bodies in a given species is that which is actualised by their own specific form: vegetable life is good only for plants; oak-life is good only for oaks; reed-life is good only for reeds.

Nevertheless, the proposition 'Being is good' can be predicated of each and every body in its particularity, and of the universe in its entirety. And the link between *esse* and *bonum* is not unlike that between zero on the Celsius scale and the freezing point of water. The link may be arbitrary, but it establishes an uncontroversial, verifiable root meaning for the adjective 'good'; and simultaneously it makes possible a system of measurement, with plus and minus values. Every affirmation of the goodness of particular qualities, quantities and actions, every statement about value which is couched in negative form ('not good', 'bad') and every assessment of relative value ('better', 'best'; 'worse', 'worst'; 'superior', 'supreme'; 'nobler', 'noblest') can be derived from the positive sense of 'good' by a series of necessary deductions, using the categories and concepts of natural science with which we have now become familiar.

Negative statements are easy to exemplify. If being is good, *ceasing to be* is not good (and there is no 'question' as to whether it is 'nobler' 'to be or not to be'). Death is bad for animate bodies. Plant-life, as such, is bad for both minerals and animals. Oak-life is bad for reeds, and vice versa.

The *comparative* degree of adjectives like *bonum* or *malum* is founded on the principle of physics that anything which exists in its own right and for its own sake is prior to something which exists for the sake of something else or merely as an attribute of some existing body. Hence, substance is 'better' than accident; potentiality is 'less good' than actuality; the end is always 'superior' to the means. Alternatively, the claim that species A is 'better' or 'of greater value' than species B rests on the observable fact that A possesses all the essential characteristics of B together with other additional properties.

The *superlative* degree – and there is an *absolute* superlative on the Aristotelian scale – is a consequence of the fact that the universe is finite, and that the substantial form of every body in the universe confers a limited number of virtues and powers. Whenever a body has fully actualised the whole potential of its form, it can be described as 'best' – best in its *kind*, obviously – even though there may be other bodies in existence which are in the same optimum condition at the same time.

As we have seen in the analysis of numerous examples, animate as well as inanimate, the 'final cause' of a body is conceptually prior to its 'formal cause'. Moreover, the final cause of an *animate* body is always a kind of 'self-use' involving a number of self-caused movements or changes, which are all for the sake of, and therefore subordinate to, a supreme activity known as the 'proper operation', the current exercise of which constitutes the 'second perfection' of the whole organism. It follows therefore that if the first perfection (*esse*) is good, the second perfection (*operatio propria*) is better or best.

42

'When I perceive that men as plants increase'[15]

Even from this very cursory presentation of the Aristotelian scale of value, it will be clear that it is not at all difficult – in principle, at least – to determine what is good or bad for a plant, and to what degree. Just three more examples will be enough to illustrate how teleological criteria are brought to bear.

First, external bodies or conditions can be described as 'good for' the plant if they are indispensable for its continued being (e.g., air, moisture, sunlight and nutrients in the soil). Conversely, such bodies or conditions are 'bad for' the plant if they threaten to destroy or to maim it, to deprive it of its necessaries, or to overload its capacities (e.g., grazing animals, falling boulders, overhanging trees and prolonged heat-waves).

Second, the plant's own body may be described as 'good' if its soul has articulated all the heterogeneous parts that are necessary as organs (*instrumenta*) for the plant to carry out its three operations. It can be called 'bad', 'defective' or 'monstrous' if it has too many or too few 'tools' for its purposes, or if these are in any way 'non-operational'.

Third, although the 'being' of a plant is a means to the end of its 'activity', the activity of reproduction is itself a means to the end of the continued being of the species (*conservatio esse speciei*). Hence the 'goodness' of 'being' can be both assumed as a *principium* and deduced as a *finis*.

Human beings are much more complex than plants (Dante once remarked that human beings are so diversified that almost everyone seems to constitute a separate species).[16] But they are *corpora mobilia*, they have within them a *principium motus et mutationis*, and they may therefore be both studied and judged in accordance with criteria based on the same universal categories and concepts with which we have 'come to terms' in this chapter. In other words, one may give a reasoned verdict – not just an opinion – on the merit of human operations by ascertaining to what extent they are conducive to the end or purpose of our being – our *causa finalis*.

Before we make that leap from psychology to ethics, however, we must consider the powers, organs and operations found in the animal world, and make a much closer study of how Dante conceived and represented the perceptions, passions, motive forces and bodily movements that human beings share with the higher animals.

CHAPTER FOUR

Self-movement: sensation and locomotion in animal life

Anima sensitiva

Let the scene be set in springtime on a hill in medieval Tuscany. A lamb enters and makes its tentative way to a clump of particularly succulent grass. It has scarcely begun to nibble the tips, however, when it is surprised by a young wolf and scampers away with its attacker in hot but inexpert pursuit. The shepherd boy drops his piece of bread and cheese, springs to his feet shouting 'Wolf, wolf', and hurls a stone from his sling in the direction of the wolf, who abandons the chase and lopes away.

There are four 'bodies' in this Aristotelian pastoral – boy, wolf, lamb and grass – and all of them are 'animate'. In their different ways, moreover, they are all actively engaged in taking or procuring the food that is necessary to preserve their 'being' and to enable them to 'grow' to maturity so that they may begin the task of 'self-reproduction' (food being 'good' as a 'means' to the 'end' of continued existence, which is assumed to be good both 'in itself', 'for its own sake', and also as a means to the end of the higher good of reproduction, which ensures the continued existence of the 'species').

The clump of grass, however, does not need to do anything further to 'save its soul' and 'fulfil its potential'; and, since capacities are always determined by needs, it cannot perform any 'task' beyond these 'operations of the vegetative soul', *nutrimentum*, *augmentum* and *generatio*. It is rooted to the spot (this being the only way it can absorb nourishment), whereas the other three 'agents' are all capable of moving from one location to another (this being the only way they can find sufficient nourishment). And it is of course the additional power of changing location that 'differentiates' animals from plants.

To the onlooker, or to the protagonists in the drama, nothing could seem easier or more spontaneous than movements of the kind described in the opening paragraph. But to the scientist, whether modern or medieval, it is clear that the internal causes are numerous and highly complex. The limbs are activated by the flexion of muscles in response to messages or commands transmitted along the nerves from a localised area of the brain. The commands are energised by feelings of pleasure and pain, and the feelings are aroused by the perception of some external body which the percipient judges to be either 'good' or 'bad'. In other words, it was recognised, then as now, that 'self-movement' is the consequence of a complex process of sensation, and could not occur without that preliminary phase: no sensation, no movement. This is why the kind of 'substantial form' that conferred the power of locomotion was named after the concomitant power of sensation, and was always known as the *anima sensitiva*.[1]

The boy's use of language and of a weapon points to his possession of still further, higher powers – faculties of the mind – which derive from what is distinctively human in his nature and which set him apart from the animal world as a member of another 'kind' – the *genus humanum*. But the anatomical parts and the physiological processes involved in his act of locomotion are almost identical to those of the wolf and the lamb. It is therefore perfectly possible to consider him, in the first instance, simply as a member of an animal 'species'.[2] And everything that will be said about the *anima sensitiva* of the wolf and the lamb in the following sketch of the 'powers', 'organs' and 'operations' which culminated in their self-caused movements in space must be understood as applicable to the boy as well. The higher, human powers of reason and will – significantly not yet fully developed in the immature specimen – will never replace the lower, animal powers, but will extend, complement and regulate them.[3]

Apprehension (a) principium, medium, terminus *in the external phase*

Let us now return to the Tuscan hillside in order to reconstruct the first phase – *apprehensio* – in the Aristotelian analysis of the events that led up to the various acts of locomotion, particularly those of the wolf.

As in every process of change (*motus*) there must be a 'beginning', a 'middle' and an 'end'. In this case, the *principium* is to be identified in the lamb. It is the efficient cause of no less than three changes to the surrounding body of the atmosphere, in that it communicates colour, gives off a characteristic odour and – intermittently – utters a high-pitched, wavering, ostinato call, conventionally transcribed as 'baa-aa-aa'.

The *medium* is constituted by the atmosphere. When it is suitably 'disposed', the body of the air is 'in potency to' or 'patient of' all three kinds of change which originate in the lamb and spread in every possible direction to create what we might call a 'hemisphere of influence'.

Generally speaking, any solid, opaque body will act as a *terminus* for all the atmospheric changes emanating from the lamb, simply because solid, opaque bodies do not have the 'potential' to 'undergo' any of the three kinds of change to which air is susceptible. But the wolf is a *terminus* of a very remarkable kind. His head has three pairs of orifices (nostrils, eye-sockets and ear-holes), which house three sets of specialised organs, each of which is in potency to just one of the three kinds of change, the eyes being patient of colour, the ears of sound and the nose of odour.[4]

Each of the external organs is said to receive an 'impression' (*impressio*) of the lamb; and the original metaphor of an 'imprint' left by a seal in a piece of molten wax is significant, because it reminds us that eyes, ears and nose do not take the initiative, but are acted upon from outside. In this case the wolf's seeing, hearing and smelling are caused by the lamb.

In Aristotle's analysis, however, the lamb does not emit particles of any kind, and the so-called *impressiones* are not the result of bombardment by a stream of minute projectiles passing through the atmosphere, as the earlier Greek atomists had believed.[5] To prevent any misconception on this point, one must stress the indispensable role of the medium. The eye is 'altered' by the atmosphere in precisely the same way that each particle of air in the hemisphere of influence is either 'altered' or 'moved' by its neighbour, except that the eye is susceptible to colour, and not to sound or odour.[6] *Mutatis mutandis*, the same is true of the changes that result in hearing and smelling. If the lamb were to be pressed hard against the wolf's eyes, ears or nose, thus eliminating the medium, the wolf would perceive something woolly and warm, and nothing else.[7] In other words, he would experience two of the qualities which are received by the less specialised sense of touch.

Apprehension (b) sensus communis *and* imago

We must now consider a typical medieval account of the *internal* organs of sense, bearing in mind that these inevitably posed far greater problems for the early psychologists and physiologists. Aristotle himself was teasingly vague about this part of the subject. His commentators and followers diverged even as to the number of such organs – three, four or five – and as to the precise nature or distribution of their functions. Nor can we be sure of Dante's own allegiances. There was, however, general agreement on the joint principles that there must be one distinct organ for each distinct task, and that there must be one 'master sense' – 'the fount and origin of the power of sensation', as Dante will call it – which alternates between periods of wakeful activity and periods of suspension (for example, during dreamless sleep or other kinds of total unconsciousness). And there was no serious disagreement about the features and functions that will prove important for the study of the *Comedy* in part two.

The organ of the central, controlling power was thought to be located in the frontal lobe of the brain ('la parte del cerebro dinanzi'), and it was universally known among the scholastics as the 'common sense' (*sensus communis*).[8] It was to this organ that the separate impressions received by the wolf's eyes, ears and nose were conveyed, instantaneously and without interruption, through the hollow conduits of the nerves (*nervi*), which were thought to be filled with a highly refined, volatile substance called 'spirit' (*spiritus*).[9] It was in this organ, too, that the incoming impressions were 'grasped', 'seized' or, as they said, 'apprehended' by the conscious wolf. 'Apprehension' (*apprehensio*) takes place in the common sense – in the brain, not on the surface of the body.

There are two further aspects to the process of 'apprehension' which also help explain why the organ was called the *common* sense. When impressions of different kinds are received simultaneously from the same external object, they are recombined or synthesised to make a composite impression, which, in the case of our *lupus in fabula*, would have been odoriferous, bleating and white. It is from the composite impression (which in other circumstances might include information relayed from the senses of taste and touch), that the *sensus communis* can extract and apprehend features such as shape, size, number and movement, which were always referred to as the 'common sensibles' (*sensibilia communia*) to distinguish them from the 'proper sensibles' (*sensibilia propria*), namely colour, sound, odour, taste and the tactile sensations, which are 'proper to' (i.e., belong exclusively to) the five external receptors.[10]

The composite impression, reconstituted and apprehended in the *sensus communis*, was usually referred to as an 'image' (*imago/imaginis*), rendering the Greek word *phantasma*, which was also used in medieval Latin.[11] Primarily, of course, 'image' denoted an impression received by the sense of sight, which is very often the only external sense to be activated, and was in any case regarded as pre-eminent. There is therefore a possibility of ambiguity as to which meaning of 'image' is the one required in a given context. To avoid this, the composite impression could be described as a 'sensible form' or 'sensible species' (*species sensibilis*). And this would be the preferred term, if it were necessary to insist that what the wolf perceives, for example, is the 'form' or 'figure' of the lamb, that is, its 'outward appearance', disjoined from the physical matter of its body.[12]

Apprehension (c) aestimativa *and* intentio

From the common sense, the apprehended image passes into the centre of the brain, which was widely held to be the seat of a distinct faculty called 'estimation' (*aestimativa, aestimatio,* 'la stimativa'). As the name suggests, this is the faculty that 'assesses' or 'estimates' whether the object currently being perceived represents something 'good' or something 'bad' for the percipient.[13]

There are two points to make about the operation of this very important organ of the sensitive soul. First, the assessment is instinctive and immediate without any process of reasoning or deliberation. It was thought that a young wolf will 'estimate' that a lamb is 'good' for him, even if he has never seen one in his life before. The power to distinguish friend from foe *at a distance* was assumed to be inherent in the soul of higher animals, just as the powers of nutrition, growth and generation are inherent in the vegetative soul.

Second, estimation clearly involves some assessment of the given *circumstances* in addition to a simple judgement as to whether the object perceived is good or bad. The wolf might well estimate that the lamb is attractive in itself, but *un*attractive in the present situation, because it is on the other side of a ravine or protected by a shepherd. And the assessment will also be affected by the urgency of his personal needs, for example, by such factors as when he last had a meal.

An image that has been 'estimated' as good or bad could be described as an *intentio*, and just as it is convenient on occasions to distinguish the mere 'impression' from the consciously perceived 'image', so it is sometimes helpful to make a distinction between the mere 'image' and the 'intention', which has received, so to speak, a positive or negative charge, in that it has been identified as deriving from an external object which is either friendly or hostile.[14]

Apprehension (d) imaginatio *and* memoria

The brain is the seat of two further organs which enable an animal to retain and 're-view' what it has apprehended in the past. 'Images' or 'phantasms' are kept, rather precariously, in a storehouse (*thesaurus*) in the front of the brain called the *imaginatio* or *phantasia*, while 'intentions' are more carefully preserved at the rear in the *memoria sensitiva*.[15]

At first sight, neither organ would seem to play any part in the very simple act of self-movement exemplified in our fable. But each does in fact make an important contribution, even when the object remains within range of the external senses.

It is thanks to the memory, obviously, that higher animals can learn from past experience. If a young wolf were to perceive the heat, tang, crackling and colour of a fire for the first time, he might fail to 'estimate' it as a *malum* and burn his paw or nose because he failed to avoid physical contact. But the burnt wolf will fear the fire just as much as the proverbial burnt child, and will keep at a safe distance on future occasions. His acquired wariness implies that he is able to 're-cognise' fire – to 'know it again' – by successfully matching an incoming 'image' with the stored 'intention'. It also implies that his *aestimativa* has been modified and improved. Conversely, a lower animal (such as the no-less proverbial moth) will perish in the flame, because it has no memory of an earlier occasion when it singed its wings.[16]

The role of the imagination is a little more difficult to understand, since it was credited with two activities. It was thought to serve as what we would now call a 'short-term memory', able to retain all images long enough for the animal to perceive movement by comparing the present image with the '*re*-presented' image from the immediate past (we saw earlier that the perception of change presupposes some kind of comparison between a 'then' and a 'now'). In this way the imagination would help the wolf to pursue the escaping lamb. But the imagination also has the power to retain certain images over a long period, to decompose them and to rearrange the original series, in such a way that the images which it 're-presents' to the consciousness no longer correspond in shape or sequence to the objects and events from which they originally derived.

This apparently arbitrary and capricious power (registered in the later semantic development of the adjectives 'fantastic' and 'fanciful') is extremely important for human beings, since it is to this that we owe our art, our fiction, our inventions, even our power to translate other people's words into images.[17] But it does not seem to be of much practical use to the wolf (Aquinas, indeed, doubted whether animals possess this faculty).[18] The consensus of opinion, however, was that a wolf must possess some power to *form* images, although this power was limited to images relating to the immediate future of the objects immediately present to his senses. In other words, the wolf is assumed to be able to 'foresee' the moment when he will literally seize the lamb, and to 'foretaste' the pleasure he will experience when he sinks his teeth into its flesh. Foreseeing and foretasting take place in the present (*praesentialiter*); and it is in effect the foretasted pleasure which stimulates the wolf's muscles and causes him to move in the direction of the lamb.[19]

Appetition (a) passio, delectatio *and* tristitia

We shall look more closely at the processes of seeing and imagining in part two, but for the time being we must leave the subject of perception in order to begin to 'come to terms' with the Aristotelian and scholastic analysis of the feelings that follow the successful act of *apprehensio* and lead on to *locomotio.* Here, too, we shall confine ourselves to a preliminary survey, limited to the general principles.

All the feelings in question were known as *passiones* and were classified under just two main heads, since they were all considered to be species of, or conducive to, the fundamental sensations of pleasure or pain (*delectatio* and *dolor*).[20] For our immediate purposes, all we need to keep in mind are the following three points.

First, pleasure and pain were themselves regarded as 'passions'. Second, they are the result of present union or contact with an outside cause. And third, they are indissolubly linked with the concepts of 'good' and 'bad', as defined in connection with plant-life at the end of chapter 3.[21]

It was assumed that present union or contact with what is good for a specific animal causes pleasure; and it was further assumed that whatever causes pleasure must *ipso facto* be good. By seeking pleasure, the animal will instinctively conserve its being, perpetuate the species and perform its distinctive activity, because it will be seeking the particular bodies, qualities or states that constitute the necessary means to those three interlocking ends (*conservatio sui, conservatio speciei, operatio propria* or *perfectio secunda*).

Conversely, the 'bad' (*malum*) is synonymous with the 'harmful'. The harmful always causes pain; and pain is the consequence and indicator of harm ('harms' being subdivided into *mala corruptiva,* which directly threaten the animal's survival, *mala contristativa,* which impede its operations, and *mala privativa,* which deprive it of some necessary *bonum*).

Appetition (b) consecutio, fuga, quies; passio, appetitus, vis appetitiva

In the very simple model offered by the predator and his prey, the polar opposites of pleasure and pain are also correlated with the two fundamental species of rectilinear motion (i.e., movement towards or away from a point). The passion of hunger experienced by the wolf is a species of desire for the good and it causes 'pursuit'; while, in the lamb, the passion of fear is a species of aversion from the bad and it causes 'flight'. Hence a passion can be defined, provisionally, as a feeling aroused by 'apprehension' leading to either 'pursuit' or 'flight' (*consecutio* or *fuga*).[22]

Dante and his teachers never tired of repeating that every self-caused movement can be analysed in terms of this single opposition ('questo appetito mai altro non fa che *cacciare* e *fuggire*').[23] They also insisted that, since flight from 'harm' is *for the sake of* the 'good' of existence, all movement can, in the last analysis, be ascribed to desire for the good.

There are, nevertheless, two distinctions to be drawn. First, the passion of anger will often lead an animal to attack and therefore to move towards a *malum*. Second, the 'passion' of pleasure may well be the cause of stillness, rather than motion, when it is excited by the senses of taste and touch: the 'passion' is still the result of apprehension in the brain, but it presupposes physical union or contact with the object that caused the sensation, and it may therefore induce the animal to prolong that union. (There is, however, no contradiction, since Aristotelian physics sets out to explain the causes of stillness or coming to rest as well as the causes of motion itself.)[24]

The noun *passio* derives from the verb *pati/passum* meaning 'to suffer' or 'to undergo', and the scholastics sometimes dwelt on the etymology in order to stress that this alleged cause of self-movement is simply a necessary effect of an *external* cause – no more, as we should now say, than an automatic response to a stimulus.[25] But they were also faithful to Aristotle in insisting that a passion, such as the lamb's fear or the wolf's desire, was the actualisation of a capacity for that kind of feeling, a capacity which was an inherent property or power of the sensitive soul, considered as the substantial form of a living body. In scholastic terminology, a *passio* is the *actus* of a *potentia animae sensitivae*.[26]

Each distinct species of passion is the *actus* of a distinct *potentia*, and each such *potentia* was called an *appetitus*. The collective noun for all these related powers was the *vis appetitiva*. And in this case the etymology suggests the active role played by the 'actualised power', because both adjective and noun are derived from the verb *adpetere/ adpetitum* meaning 'to reach out for', 'to seek' or 'to strive after'.[27]

Ordinary modern English usage has separated 'passion' from 'appetite'. 'Passion' normally refers to anger or to sexual infatuation, while 'appetite' is limited to the desire for solid food (when we speak of 'sexual appetite', it is generally perceived as a metaphor). Medieval scholastic Latin, by contrast, never separates *passio* from *appeti-*

tus, and it treats all feelings of aversion, as well as all species of desire, as the actualisation of an *appetitus*. It is the same appetite that finds wormwood bitter and honey sweet, the one 'repulsive', the other 'attractive' (these terms too derive from the Aristotelian analysis of the causes of rectilinear motion).[28]

Appetition (c) transmutatio corporalis, cor

We are now ready to pass from the soul to the body, that is, from the powers inherent in the living structure to the material instruments or organs through which the powers come into operation.

A passion reveals itself by causing some perceptible change in the body. Indeed, a passion cannot be described as such unless it produces a *transmutatio corporalis* in one or more of the categories distinguished in chapter 2.[29] It may, for example, cause dilation or contraction (*augmentum*), loss or gain of heat in the affected part (*alteratio*), or the flow of one of the bodily fluids (*motus*). Often, the passion will provoke all these changes simultaneously or in quick succession, as when we shiver with fear and a cold sweat breaks out on our brow. And since all these transformations seem to affect the pulse in some way, it was generally assumed in the thirteenth century that the *vis appetitiva* had its principal seat in the heart, just as the *vis apprehensiva* had its 'master power' in the *sensus communis* in the front of the brain.[30]

We may therefore reconstruct the psycho-physiological consequences of the wolf's perceptions somewhat as follows. When the impressions emanating from the lamb had been transformed into an 'image' (possessing size and shape), and when this image had been converted into a storable 'intention' (identified, and indeed 'fore-tasted', as good), the intention was communicated to the heart by the agency of the animal spirits running along the nerves and arteries. In the heart, this 'message' aroused the passion of hunger, which became the immediate, efficient cause of a constrictive pang in the stomach, a quickening of the heartbeat and a surge of warm blood. This provided the *impetus* or *vis motiva* that energised the muscles in the legs, causing them to flex and extend alternately in a complex sequence of movements and arrests that carried the wolf, 'body and soul', over the ground towards the lamb.

Contemporaneously, a similar sequence of *transformationes*

corporales was taking place within the lamb. The main differences were that it suffered a *loss* of heat; the blood fled *towards* the heart; and contractions probably occurred in the bladder and intestines, causing them to void their contents. The lamb may also have experienced a moment of terrorised immobility before the leg muscles were convulsively agitated by the passion of fear to carry the lamb away from the source of the hostile *intentio*.[31]

Appetition (d) vis irascibilis *and* vis concupiscibilis

The foregoing account is complete as far as it goes; and a scholastic natural philosopher would have analysed all self-caused acts of locomotion by all animal species (including human beings) as being directed either towards some particular *bonum* or away from some particular *malum*, and as involving all the stages of apprehension and appetition that have just been described.

It does not follow, however, that an animal will always move towards a good or away from a bad. A great deal will depend on the 'circumstances' that surround the primary object of attraction and repulsion.[32] Clouds may have a silver lining; roses usually have thorns; the roots of learning are bitter. And so – to return to the animal world – a bear may retreat from a honeycomb if it is defended by bees, or it may attack a hunter and his hounds in order to defend its cubs.

To account for these apparently contradictory but undeniable phenomena, Aristotle and his followers posited the existence of a further, distinct group of appetites within the *vis appetitiva*. Those in the first group – illustrated in the wolf and the lamb – were known collectively as the 'concupiscible power' (*vis concupiscibilis*), while those in the second group constituted the *vis irascibilis* or 'irascible power'.[33]

The irascible passions are aroused whenever a perceived good is seen to be attended by some danger or difficulty, and the purpose of their existence is to complement and protect the concupiscible passions. We shall examine them in more detail in chapter 12 when we explore Dante's representation of *ira*, 'anger', the passion which gives the group its name.[34] At this stage, however it would be counterproductive to complicate the simple binary model of pursuit and flight. It will be enough to keep the existence of anger in mind, secure in the knowledge that nothing will be said to shake the fundamental principle that all passions are aroused by perception and that their function is to provide the 'motive force' for some kind of 'operation'.

Conclusion to part one: Aristotle, Dante and the ens mobile

The subject of part one has been Nature, understood as the *principium motus et mutationis* – as the source of the changes in quality, quantity, location and identity to which all bodies are necessarily subject.

Having noted Aristotle's definition of 'enforced' change (that in which 'the source lies outside and the patient body contributes nothing'), we have in effect been hunting for examples of *natural* change in which the *principium* lies unequivocally within the patient body, such that it can be described, without any further qualification, as 'self-moving', a *corpus seipsum movens*. At first sight, it would seem that the quest has not been successful. To adapt the simile from Dante's *Convivio*, quoted at the beginning of chapter 1, we have gone from inn to inn – or from one-star hotel to four-star hotel – without ever finding a completely autonomous body.

Even though we identified *internal* 'principles' of increasing number and complexity, we learnt to attribute them to powers or properties inherent in, and limited by, the *forma substantialis* to which the given body owes its existence. We noted that no body is the efficient cause of its own existence or the designer of its own structure or 'formal cause'. In every case, moreover, the internal *principium mutationis* proved to be activated from without. The stone will not fall unless it has been thrown into the air. Plants will not grow without light and warmth. Animals, too, are 'more acted upon than acting' (*magis aguntur quam agunt*), because they cannot help responding in predetermined ways to the impressions they receive from external objects.[35]

On the other hand, we have seen that the *internal* principle becomes progressively more important as we climb the 'ladder of being' from minerals to animals. At each successive 'rung', the role of the external agent becomes correspondingly less significant, dwindling from the sole efficient cause to a contributory factor (*concausa*), and then to a mere necessary condition or 'dispositive' cause (*conditio sine qua non*; *causa dispositiva*). And if we re-examine the concept of enforced change in the light of the perceived analogy between natural bodies and human artefacts, it will become clear that there are relatively few instances of change in which the activity of the external principle is totally unrelated to the needs or purposes of the patient body. The cart needs a horse as much as it needs wheels. The potential of a casserole can be actualised only by the cook. It would be absurd to suggest that an arrow is 'violated' or 'abused' when it is shot through the air, since this is precisely the final cause of its existence. A dandelion will not reproduce successfully unless the wind disperses its seed. Throughout the animal kingdom the patient female needs the male, as much as the agent male needs the female. Hence, in many cases, it is natural and not 'violent' for lower bodies to be acted upon and actualised – fulfilled or perfected – by higher bodies.[36]

Perhaps the most important lesson to be learnt, then, from this highly simplified introduction to the concepts and terminology of Aristotle's natural science is that all the bodies in the universe form a single system of interlocking, interacting parts. Change is either reciprocal or cyclical, and it is continuous. Every change involves the actualisation of a potential, and yet the whole potential of 'primary matter' (which underlies even the four elements) is always fully actualised, despite, or rather because of, the continuous processes of change.[37]

The subject-matter of natural science (defined, it will be remembered, as the *ens mobile*, i.e., 'that which exists but does not remain in the same place or state') proves to be co-terminous with the universe. And the universe may be compared to a single *corpus organicum*, a single living body with many distinct and unequal organs, each performing an essential operation and each helping to conserve the being of the 'universal frame' or *machina mundi*.

For Aristotle, this could be no more than a comparison (an unhelpful comparison); and he would have rejected any Platonist notion that there is an *anima mundi*, a 'world soul', that literally animates the cosmic *corpus*. He nowhere speculates as to the *telos* or final cause of the universe; he does not have a concept of divine providence; he rejects the possibility that the universe could have been created from nothing 'in the beginning'. But thanks to his characteristically teleological approach to the study of change (every *mutatio naturalis* is for the sake of an 'end' that is 'good'), it was possible for thirteenth-century Christian thinkers to absorb his ideas into their existing mental picture of the cosmos – a universe created by an omnipotent, loving God who presides over all its operations.

Dante's first great philosophical 'hymn', in the opening canto of *Paradiso*, is permeated with concepts and images deriving from the Bible, the Stoics and the Neoplatonists, as it celebrates the 'bow-string' of 'providence' that carries all 'creatures' over the 'sea of being' to their different 'havens' in an 'order' of unequal parts, an order which constitutes the 'imprint' of the divine 'Source' and confers a 'likeness' to God. But it may also be interpreted as a meta-phorical synthesis of Aristotle's teaching on the *principium motus et mutationis*; and it makes free use of the words with which we have been 'coming to terms' – words like 'natura', 'essere', 'forma', 'fine', 'muoversi', 'istinto', 'permotore' (to be followed by 'virtù', 'volgersi', 'quiete', 'pingere', 'piegare', 'impeto', 'impedimento'). It is too long to quote in full, but there could be no better text with which to bring this first part to a conclusion than the lines which present 'instinct' as the universal 'motive force' carrying animate and inani-mate beings to their distinct and appointed goals (the paradigm of locomotion being valid, as so often, for all species of change).

> 'Le cose tutte quante
> hanno ordine tra loro, e questo è forma
> che l'universo a Dio fa simigliante.
>   Qui veggion l'alte creature l'orma
> de l'etterno valore, il qual è fine
> al quale è fatta la toccata norma.'   (*Par.* I, 103–8)

'All things have order among themselves, and this is the formal cause through which the universe resembles God. Here the highest of God's creatures see the impress of his eternal goodness, which is the final cause of the whole system.'

> 'Ne l'ordine ch'io dico sono accline
> tutte nature, per diverse sorti,
> più al principio loro e men vicine;
>   onde si muovono a diversi porti
> per lo gran mar de l'essere, e ciascuna
> con istinto a lei dato che la porti.
>   Questi ne porta il foco inver' la luna;
> questi ne' cor mortali è permotore;
> questi la terra in sé stringe e aduna.'   (109–17)

'Within this order all natures have their bent according to their different destinies, nearer to their source and further from it. And hence they move to different ports over the great sea of being – each endowed with an instinct to bear it on its way. Instinct it is that carries Fire towards the moon; this is what provides the motive force in mortal hearts; this is what binds Earth and makes it one.'

PART TWO

The operations of the sensitive powers in man

CHAPTER FIVE

Perception of light and colour

The pre-eminence of vision and the 'proper visibles'

All the external senses exist in order to detect bodies in the world outside the percipient, to register their movements and to discriminate between them. They are, however, unequal in their performance. The three senses illustrated in the fable of the wolf and the lamb are superior to those of touch and taste because they enable animals to distinguish between *bona* and *mala* while they are still at a distance, and then to 'move themselves' in accordance with their 'estimation'. And sight has always been regarded as the highest and most perfect of the senses, if only because it affords the finest discriminations at the greatest distance.[1]

Aquinas noted that, in ordinary speech, 'to see' had become the verb of sensation *par excellence* ('see how hot it is'), and that it was also commonly extended to the act of understanding ('do you see what I mean?'). And anyone who studied philosophy in the late thirteenth century would have known the opening paragraph of Aristotle's *Metaphysics*, where the Philosopher observes that 'we take pleasure in the senses for their own sake, and above all in the sense of sight, preferring it to all the other senses because it is the principal source of knowledge'.[2]

Dante clearly endorsed this view of the matter whole-heartedly. For him, as poet, no operation of the sensitive component of the human soul was anything like as important as seeing. He took the keenest interest in the contemporary science of optics, using his knowledge on almost every page of the *Comedy* with amazing variety and virtuosity, so that the most severe restraint has been required to condense the following introductory survey into two longish chapters.

The distribution of the material between this chapter and the next is based as far as possible on the distinction we have already encountered between the role of the eye – the proper organ of vision – and the role of the *sensus communis* – the seat of the sensitive power located in the front of the brain, which is where vision actually takes place.

We can certainly perceive shape and size with our eyes, but these properties can also be registered by the sense of touch. Size and shape are therefore known – together with number, movement and rest – as 'objects of common perception' (*sensibilia communia*). Each of the five senses can, however, apprehend at least one property that is inaccessible to the others – its *sensibile proprium*. And the qualities that are specific to the sense of sight are colour and light. It is these and these alone that are to be called 'objects of vision' in the strict sense (*visibilia propria*). As so often, it is difficult to improve on Dante's own brief account:

> Dove è da sapere che, propriamente, è visibile lo colore e la luce, sì come Aristotile vuole nel secondo de l'Anima, e nel libro del Senso e Sensato. Ben è altra cosa visibile, (...) sì come è la figura, la grandezza, lo numero, lo movimento e lo stare fermo, che sensibili comuni si chiamano: le quali cose con più sensi comprendiamo. Ma lo *colore e la luce sono propriamente*, perché solo col viso comprendiamo ciò, e non con altro senso.
>
> (*Con.* III, ix, 6–7)

> It must be borne in mind that, strictly speaking, the visible properties are colour and light, as Aristotle insists in the second book of *De anima* and in *De sensu et sensato*. Other things are indeed visible, as, for example, shape, size, number, movement and stillness, which are known as the 'common sensibles'. But colour and light are visible in the proper sense of the term, because we perceive them with sight alone and not with the other senses.

Light in the different contexts of scientia naturalis *and* perspectiva

It was by no means uncontroversial to consider *light* as a proper object of vision (*obiectum visus*), as we can confirm by glancing at a sentence from the first book of the *Convivio*, where Dante says that 'the sensitive part of the soul has eyes with which it discovers the differences between things, inasmuch as they are coloured on the surface' ('la parte sensitiva de l'anima ha suoi occhi, con li quali apprende la differenza de le cose in quanto elle sono di fuori colorate'). Aristotle, indeed, had made it clear that in his view the only quality that could be called *visibilis per se* was colour.[3]

On the other hand, it is obvious that we are able to register the presence of light thanks to the sense of sight alone. And we are aware of sunlight through our eyes even when our eyelids are closed.[4] There are, moreover, two sentences in *De anima* where Aristotle comes very close to saying that 'colour is light' or that 'light is colour'.[5] Nor can we understand what Aristotle meant by colour, and how he thought it acted upon the atmosphere to modify the eye and cause vision, until we are familiar with the concept of light as it presents itself within the framework of his natural philosophy.

It is also vital to remember that Dante and his contemporaries were trying to reconcile the philosophical concept of light, which they took from Aristotle, with their close knowledge of its behaviour, which they owed to Aristotle's successors, particularly among the Arabs, who had elaborated the science of *perspectiva* or optics by means of a startlingly modern combination of strict geometry and ingenious experimentation.

Dante frequently speaks of 'rays' of light 'issuing' from a 'source' and 'passing' or 'falling' in a straight line until they are 'halted' when they 'strike' a surface, from which they are 'struck back', 'bent' or 'broken' (the last three verbs will be more familiar through the English nouns 'repercussion', 'reflection' and 'refraction'). From this surface the light is said to 'spring up' and 'return' in such a way that the 'climbing' ray makes exactly the same angle to the perpendicular as the 'falling' ray had done (again this observation may be more recognisable in the familiar proposition that 'the angle of reflexion is equal to the angle of incidence').[6]

In all these usages Dante is implicitly treating light as though it were a body capable of motion – a *corpus mobile secundum motum localem*. But if there is one point on which Aristotle is absolutely clear, it is that light is not a body, nor the substantial form or matter of a body. For him it is an active quality inherent in the substantial form of a luminous object – such as the sun – or a passive property inherent in the form of other things, which is actualised by an external source – again, such as the sun.[7] Aquinas was therefore perfectly correct when he added the following note to his commentary on *De anima* II, vii:

We have got into the habit of saying that a ray 'passes through' the air, or is 'reflected', or that rays 'intersect each other' – all of which seem to refer to a body. But everything that is said about the 'movement' of light or its 'reflexion' is said metaphorically.[8]

It is equally metaphorical, Aquinas continues, to speak of *heat* as 'advancing' or being 'turned back' by an obstacle. But there are some important and revealing differences between heat and light in Aristotelian physics. Heat is one of the four 'primary qualities', the so-called 'four contraries'. As such, it is directly opposed by another equally active quality – that of Cold – and, as such, it is by definition found at the level of the four elements.[9]

Light, on the other hand, 'has no contrary'. What we call darkness (*tenebrae*) is simply an unrealised potentiality for illumination, the 'absence' of light, or its 'privation'. There is therefore nothing to resist the communication of light (to the extent that a body has the *potentia* to receive it), whereas a cold body offers active resistance to the diffusion of heat. This is why illumination takes place instantaneously (*in instanti, statim*), whereas warming requires the passage of time.[10]

Light, moreover, is found everywhere in the universe. It was said to be the property of a 'sort of common nature' (*quaedam natura communis*) in which all things share.[11]

Luminis susceptivum: lucens, diaphanum, coloratum

This common nature was conceived as something capable of 'taking up' or 'receiving' light: *id quod est luminis susceptivum*. Not all bodies share in this 'susceptibility' in the same way, however, and we must learn to distinguish three main levels – the 'shining', the 'transparent' and the 'coloured' – each of which admits a scale of greater or lesser intensity.

In the first and highest group, the potential for the reception of light has been totally filled and actualised. As a result, such bodies are said to be *lucentia* (from *lucere*, 'to shine'), or *illuminativa*, in that they communicate *lumen* to other bodies. Each one acts as a *principium* or *terminus a quo* in a process of illumination, and each can be described metaphorically as a 'fountainhead' or 'source' ('fontale principio').

The most brilliant of these *corpora lucentia* circle above us in the heavens – chief among them being the sun. But they are also found here on earth, for example, in a bonfire (where the element Fire is made manifest as flame), or in the tiny phosphorescent creatures and plants that shine so faintly that they can be seen only at night.[12]

The second group comprises all *transparent* bodies. Those at the top of the scale are so completely 'susceptible' to light deriving from an active source that they are able to receive it in their every part. In medieval Latin they were known by any one of three synonyms: *diaphanum, transparens* and *perspicuum.* And as the etymology of each name suggests, a body of this kind allows light to pass *through* itself to illuminate other bodies. Hence a *corpus diaphanum,* such as the atmosphere, is perfectly fitted to be the *medium* in the process of illumination or in the process of vision, because it both receives and relays light (it is both *recipiens* and *reddens*).[13]

Included among these *corpora perspicua* are three of the four sublunary elements (Water, Air and Fire), and also the fifth element, Aether, which constitutes the matter of the invisible celestial spheres and of the 'lucent' planets and stars which they carry. Transparency is also present, almost in the pure state, in a small number of minerals and in clear glass. It is found to a lesser extent in amber or coloured glass, and, minimally, in substances like alabaster and mica, which we should describe as 'translucent' rather than 'transparent' (these last are unable to act as the medium for vision).[14]

The third and lowest group includes the remaining element, Earth, nearly all mineral compounds, and all plants and animals. These bodies are 'opaque' (*opaca*). They are the least able to 'take up' light, and indeed they 'receive only on their surfaces'. They therefore act as a *terminus ad quem* or *finis* in the process of illumination.[15]

Opaque bodies are, by definition, 'coloured' (*colorata*); and the different colours were believed to form a descending scale of brightness, from white at one extreme to black at the other. It is, however, very important to grasp that all opaque bodies participate in the quality of colour because they all partake of the common nature that consists in a 'susceptibility' to light. Even the blackest object has some minimal trace of the *natura communis* by virtue of which it is coloured and therefore an object of vision.[16]

Corpora colorata differ in the texture of their surfaces as well as in their particular hues. All of them – even the blackest and mattest – do reflect light. But in proportion as their surfaces are more or less smooth or polished (*politum, tersum*) they become more or less 'refulgent' (*fulgidum, nitidum*), gleaming like gold, sparkling like precious stones, or, in the case of a mirror, becoming so bright that they can dazzle the eye almost as effectively as the true source of the light which they reflect. And in all these *corpora fulgida*, the *terminus ad quem* of the process of direct illumination becomes the *terminus a quo* of a significant process of indirect illumination or reflection (*reverberatio, reflexio*).[17]

Dante on the reception of sunlight

Somewhat confusingly, the 'common nature' in which all bodies share was known by the same name as the intermediate group. In other words, the genus took its name from the species called 'transparent' (*diaphanum* or *perspicuum*); and it is in this generic sense that the term 'diafano' appears in a striking passage from the third book of the *Convivio* where Dante displays his knowledge of these ideas.

It will be seen that the examples are not presented in the most logical sequence (Dante passes from gold to amber, and thence to mirrors and earth). This is partly because he is drawing closely on an independent work by St Albert, rather than on *De sensu et sensato*, and partly because the choice of examples and their sequence are dictated by the needs of the extended comparison in which they occur.[18] But the passage is worth quoting in full because it demonstrates Dante's keen delight in these distinctions and gradations:

The sun's light is one in nature and derives from a single source, but it is received in different ways by bodies here on earth (...).

There are some, like gold and certain stones, which contain a high proportion of brightness ['molta chiaritade di diafano']. As soon as the sun strikes them, there is a kind of multiplication of their own incorporated brightness and the light on their surface, and they relay a great brilliance from themselves to other bodies.

There are others again that are transparent in every part ['del tutto diafani'], and these not only receive light from the sun, but allow it to pass through unimpeded; or, rather, they colour the sun's light with their own colour as they communicate it to other objects. There are some, like mirrors, in which the incorporated brightness is so pure and predominant that they irradiate light and overwhelm the mean temperament of the eye and cannot be looked at without distress.

And there are still other bodies, such as Earth, which contain so little of

this brightness ['sono tanto sanza diafano'] that they scarcely receive light
at all.   (*Con.* III, vii, 3–4)

Dante and the terminology of light: lux, lumen, splendor

Before passing on to the subject of colour and vision itself, we must
take note of the precise definitions – 'secondo l'usanza de' filosofi' –
of three of the most important words relating to light in medieval
Latin and in Dante's Italian.

The most general word for light in all its manifestations was
lumen/luminis, 'lume', from which are derived the verb *illuminare* and
the noun *illuminatio*. It was often necessary, however, to distinguish
three main phases in the process of illumination and to use a
different word to describe light in each phase. Thus, light is called
lux/lucis, 'luce', when it is considered in a *corpus lucens* such as the
sun. It is called *lumen* again, but in a narrower, specific sense, when it
is received in a *corpus diaphanum* (for example, when it is present as
daylight in the atmosphere), and finally, it is called *splendor*, 'splendore', when it refers to illumination caused indirectly by reflection
from a *corpus opacum*, especially from a *corpus album* such as a white
wall, or a *corpus politum* such as a mirror. Or, to put the same
distinction in terms of the paradigm of rectilinear motion, light is
called *lux* in the *principium*, *lumen* in the *medium*, and *splendor* after it
has reached the first *terminus ad quem*.

From the standpoint of the philosopher, as opposed to that of the
behaviourist, *lumen* is that which actualises or fulfils or 'perfects' the
potential transparency of bodies like air and water, which remain 'in
potency to transparency' – that is, in darkness – until they are
illuminated by a *corpus lucens*. *Lumen* – in the narrow sense – can
therefore be economically defined as 'the actuality of the transparent'
(*actus diaphani*).

Dante often exploits the technical distinction between *lux*, *lumen*
and *splendor* in his poetry; and we ought therefore to glance at his
own explanation of these terms in the same third book of the
Convivio. It will be seen that he avoids the possible ambiguity arising
from the two meanings of *lumen* by opting for the 'behaviourist' term
'raggio' (*radius*, 'light-ray') to describe light in a medium. And it
should also be borne in mind that his explanation is tailored to meet
the needs of an extended comparison in which the two kinds of

illumination – direct and indirect – are taken as analogies of the two modes in which God acts on the universe (either directly, 'sanza mezzo', 'per modo di diritto raggio'; or indirectly, 'con mezzo', 'per modo di raggio reverberato').

> Ma però che qui è fatta menzione di luce e di splendore, a perfetto intendimento mostrerò la differenza di questi vocabuli, secondo che Avicenna sente. Dico che l'usanza de' filosofi è di chiamare 'luce' lo lume, in quanto esso è nel suo fontale principio; di chiamare 'raggio', in quanto esso è per lo mezzo, dal principio al primo corpo dove si termina; di chiamare 'splendore', in quanto esso è in altra parte alluminata ripercosso.
>
> (*Con.* III, xiv, 5)

> Since mention has been made of 'luce' and 'splendore', I shall explain the difference between them, as Avicenna understands it, in order to make my meaning absolutely clear. Philosophers are accustomed to call light 'luce', when it is considered in its source, 'raggio', when it is considered in the medium, that is, from the source to the first body where it terminates, and 'splendore', when it is considered as reflected into another illuminated area.

Colour and 'colouration' as the prerequisites of vision

With these distinctions in mind, we are ready to grapple with Aristotle's concept of colour and of the process called 'colouration' (*coloratio*).

Colour is what prevents an opaque body from 'taking up' *lumen* (or, in the alternative description, it is what causes the direct or incident ray of light to 'come to a halt' at the surface of such a body and to 'bounce off' in another direction). It is a property of that body, inherent in its substantial form, and always *in actu*. If we scratch the surface of a coloured body, or peel it off layer by layer, the newly exposed surface will always be coloured.[19] Colour is therefore quite different from the images that appear and disappear on the surface of a mirror; and it is quite different from *lumen* in the atmosphere, which is only present *in actu* while it is being 'activated' by a *corpus lucens*.

Despite its resistance to illumination, however, colour is the quality through which an opaque body participates in the 'common nature' which Dante called 'il diafano' and which we may refer to as the 'diaphanous principle', to distinguish it from mere transparency.

It is a 'cousin' to *lux* – even if it is something of a 'poor relation'. It is an active quality; and its activity is analogous to that of light itself.

In the Aristotelian account (as we saw), *lux* is the active quality in a *corpus lucens*, which becomes the 'agent' in the kind of change called illumination. It actualises the potential transparency of a *corpus diaphanum* so that it becomes transparent 'in act' (*diaphanum actu*), which is to say, filled with *lumen*. It achieves this by communicating its own form or nature to the 'patient body', or, rather, by communicating that degree of likeness to itself (*similitudo sui*) which the patient is able to receive.

Similarly, *color* is the active quality in a *corpus coloratum*, which becomes the agent of a process of change called 'colouration' (this being, among other things, the external cause of vision). It too acts by communicating a likeness of its form to a *corpus diaphanum*. But it is weaker than its 'cousin'; and it reveals its relative impotence in two ways. First, it can modify the patient body (e.g., the atmosphere) only when this has already become *diaphanum actu* (that is, only when the 'patient' has been suitably 'disposed' by illumination). Colour cannot act on an unilluminated medium, which is why we cannot see it in the dark. Second, the likeness it communicates is not visible while it is in the atmospheric or other transparent medium, whereas we can be aware that the air has been illuminated even when our eyes are closed. Colour is not present in the air as a natural quality in a material subject in the way that heat can be. It is said to be there 'incompletely', in a half-actualised form, 'spiritually', or 'after the manner of an *intentio*': *secundum quoddam esse incompletum, spirituale, intentionale.*

The effects of 'colouration' remain latent unless the illuminated and 'spiritually transformed' medium touches the surface of another body. And even then the effects appear only if this body is specially receptive, either because it is opaque but lightly coloured and highly polished, as in a piece of burnished silver, or because the receiving body is opaque but covered with a film of clear, still water, as in a pool – or in the pupil of the eye. And even here the colours do not cause any change to the matter of the receiving body, as heat would do. They are mere 'likenesses' of colour – *intentiones* – not *impressiones* in the strict sense of the word.[20]

Colour also 'behaves' like *lux* in the sense that it appears to emit 'rays' in all directions – like spokes (*radii*) from the hub of wheel – each of which 'travels' in a straight line until it is 'arrested' by the surface of an opaque body. Hence colour can and does convey the shape (*figura, forma*) of the body to which it belongs, together with the other 'common sensibles', like size and number, described above. It is also convenient to speak of 'visible forms' 'passing through' the illuminated medium to 'enter' the eye.

Aquinas and Aristotle, however, would say that all these locutions are merely metaphorical. 'Philosophically' speaking, colour acts by causing a 'spiritual alteration' (*immutatio spiritualis*) to the transparent medium, which then causes a similar change to the transparent, aqueous substance in the pupil. And to avoid confusion with modern theories, it is worth pointing out here that Aristotle specifically rejects the view that colour is transmitted by reflected light, or that light activates the colour on the surface of the *corpus coloratum*, rather than preparing the medium to receive colour.[21]

As was hinted earlier, Aristotle does permit himself some paradoxical expressions that seem to run counter to these formulations. For example, he suggests that light (*lux*) is 'more visible' than colour; that colour is a 'sort of light obscured by an admixture of something opaque'; or that light might be called the 'colour of the transparent': *lumen est quasi quidam color perspicui.*[22] But all these suggestions are duly qualified by an 'as it were' or an 'in some sense'; and, at bottom, they are all consequences of the fact that *color* and *lux* are species of the same genus, the 'common nature' which we called the 'diaphanous principle'. From our point of view, it is enough to keep in mind that *color* is distinct from *lux, lumen* or *splendor*, and that the process of 'intentional colouration', on which vision depends, is not to be identified with the process of illumination (which is, however, presupposed as a necessary condition), nor again with the reflection of light (with which it happens to coincide).

Stages in the 'journey' of an image from the the object to the brain

Now that we have explored the nature of 'lo colore e la luce', we can return to the subject of vision and to the chapter in the *Convivio* where Dante distinguishes these 'proper visibles' from the 'common sensibles' – shape, size, number, movement and rest – which can be perceived by the sense of sight 'and by other senses'.

In the continuation of the passage quoted above, Dante begins by describing the visually significant events that take place outside the eye, or within the eye itself considered as a passive receptor or 'patient body'. It will be seen that he makes liberal use of the 'metaphorical' locutions employed by students of the behaviour of light. The visible form is said to 'pass through' the transparent medium of the air and to 'enter' the equally transparent liquid contained in the pupil, before it is 'brought to a halt' by the opaque coating at the rear of the eye, where it appears as though in a mirror. But it will be remembered that Aristotle himself frequently described all species of change in terms derived from the paradigm of rectilinear motion; and the passage also demonstrates Dante's clear grasp of the more 'philosophical' components, evident in his use of terms like 'trasparente', 'diafano' and 'lucido', and evident above all in his distinction between 'realmente' and 'intenzionalmente'.

> The objects of vision, whether they are accessible to sight alone, or whether they can be perceived by other senses as well, pass through a transparent medium into the eye, as though into a piece of clear glass: it is, of course, not the objects themselves that travel, but their forms, and their presence is not 'real' but incomplete or 'intentional'.
>
> The passage of the visible form through the medium comes to an end in the water contained in the pupil of the eye. It cannot pass any further because the water has a boundary, such that it resembles a mirror, which consists of glass bounded by lead; and so the form stops short there, like a ball when it strikes an obstacle. The form cannot be seen while it is in the transparent medium, but it does become visible on the polished surface that forms a boundary to the eye. And this is why an image appears in glass that has been coated with lead, but not in ordinary glass.
>
> (Con. III, ix, 7–8)

Next, Dante reveals what happens to the image after it has made its first appearance in the eye (and in this case, it is crucial that we read the original Italian):

> Di questa pupilla lo spirito visivo, che si continua da essa, a la parte del cerebro dinanzi – dov'è la sensibile virtude sì come in principio fontale – subitamente sanza tempo la ripresenta, e così vedemo.　　(ibid., 9)

> The spirit in the optic nerve, which is in unbroken contact with the pupil, immediately and instantaneously carries the visible form away from the pupil and presents it for a second time in the front part of the brain, which is the seat of the power of sensation; and this is how we see.

There are at least three significant points to notice about this one brief sentence. First, Dante gives due weight to the Aristotelian component in the theory by stressing the 'continuity' of contact between the pupil and the spirits, which is necessary if one body is to cause change in another. Second, he shifts the emphasis away from the role of the external agent to that of the percipient. Syntactically, the 'forma visibile' ceases to be the subject and becomes the object acted upon by the 'spirito visivo'. And perception is shown to take place in the brain, that is, in the 'organ' so signally lacked by the 'inorganic' mirror, which can register images but not perceive them.

Third, and most important, the verb chosen to denote the activity of the spirit is 'ripresentare', which might be somewhat lengthily paraphrased as 'to set down a likeness in some suitable medium, so that the recorded object may be contemplated even when it is absent or has ceased to exist'. As is well known, 're-presentation', 'mimesis' or 'imitation' was a central concept in Aristotle's *Poetics*. And Dante here implies that the representative or mimetic skills of the painter – or of the poet as painter in words – are instances of the truth that 'art imitates nature' not only in the objects depicted, but in the very process of 're-presentation' itself.[23]

This close and characteristic attention to the internal phase of perception – to what the brain does with the patches of colour received in the eye – can be further illustrated in a passage earlier in the *Convivio*. There Dante was trying to explain how it is that, although several visible forms can enter the eye simultaneously ('avvegna che più cose ne l'occhio a un'ora possano venire'), only one of them is perceived in the full sense of the word. The explanation that he took from his sources is concerned with the geometry of the external phase: the privileged form is the one that travels without refraction from the centre of the pyramidal base of the current field of vision into the apex of that pyramid in the pupil ('quella che viene per retta linea ne la punta de la pupilla'). For his own part, however, Dante dwelt more on the role of the 'spirits of sight' and on the orientation of the optic nerve ('il nervo per lo quale corre lo spirito visivo'). And, as in the later passage, he insisted that vision consists in the formation of an image in the brain. The object or visible form that is truly seen ('veramente si vede') is that which alone imprints itself in the imagination ('ne la imaginativa si suggella solamente').[24]

The journey of images in the Comedy

The sequence of events described in these paragraphs from the *Convivio* is condensed into a single phrase in the opening canto of

Paradiso, where Dante tells us how he imitated the example of Beatrice and looked directly into the sun. Her action is said to have been 'poured through his eyes into his imagination'.[25] But Dante's continuing interest in the two distinct phases of perception is seen more clearly in two extended similes that appear later in the cantica and demonstrate to perfection some of the highly personal ways in which his technical expertise is pressed into the service of his narrative.

Dante's first encounter with the souls of the blessed takes place *inside* the body of the moon, the 'eternal pearl', into which he and Beatrice had miraculously entered without compromising its unity, just as a ray of light can enter water. We are told – in language that is strongly reminiscent of the texts quoted earlier, and, in particular, of Dante's paraphrase of St Albert – that the moon has covered them like a cloud, with the double difference, however, that the cloud is 'solid and dense', and yet 'burnished and brilliant like a diamond sparkling in the sun'.

> Parev' a me che nube ne coprisse
> lucida, spessa, solida e pulita,
> quasi adamante che lo sol ferisse.
> Per entro sé l'etterna margarita
> ne ricevette, com' acqua recepe
> raggio di luce permanendo unita.   (*Par.* II, 31–6)

After a long discourse by Beatrice (in which the behaviour of reflected light is subjected to close investigation), the story resumes with the first of the two similes in question. This is inspired by certain problems connected with perception in the external phase; and even the most cursory glance at the nouns, adjectives and verbs ('vetri', 'acque', 'pupille'; 'trasparenti', 'tersi', 'nitide'; 'tornare', 'venire') will confirm that they are drawn from texts of the kind that have been quoted extensively above.

> Quali per vetri trasparenti e tersi,
> o ver per acque nitide e tranquille,
> non sì profonde che i fondi sien persi,
> tornan d'i nostri visi le postille
> debili sì, che perla in bianca fronte
> non vien men forte a le nostre pupille;
> tali vid' io più facce a parlar pronte.   (*Par.* III, 10–16)

If we look into glass that is transparent and smooth, or into water that is limpid and still, but not so deep that the bottom is lost to view, our features return to us – yet so faintly that a pearl on a pale forehead would scarcely be more reluctant to enter our pupils. That was how I saw a group of faces, showing their eagerness to converse.

The scientific vocabulary of the opening lines is, however, by no means incompatible with the most mellifluous verbal music; and the qualification introduced in the third line is just as striking for its internal assonance ('profonde', 'fondi') as it is for Dante's meticulous attention to the sense data. Similarly, the climactic word 'pupille' is at once the most conspicuously technical term and the most arresting element in the complex pattern of sounds, thanks to its position as the third of the rhymes on '-ille'. And yet the simile is perhaps less remarkable for its effortless fusion of verbal beauty and scientific observation than for the contribution it makes to the story and to the characterisation of the protagonist.

Dante here corrects his earlier, over-confident assertion that reflected images do not appear in ordinary uncoated glass ('nel vetro piombato la imagine appare, e non in altro').[26] Of course they do, even if only weakly. Indeed, the phenomenon is so familiar that his own spontaneous reaction on noticing the eager faces of the blessed was to 'estimate' that they were *reflected* likenesses ('specchiati sembianti') and to look behind him in order to see from whom the reflections might derive – only to see nothing!

> Sùbito sì com' io di lor m'accorsi,
> quelle stimando specchiati sembianti,
> per veder di cui fosser, li occhi torsi;
> e nulla vidi ...   (*Par.* III, 19–22)

It is a delightful and quite unexpected moment, but not without its deeper significance and thematic relationships. The protagonist is mistaken; and his error consists in trying to interpret a supernatural event in the light of purely natural criteria. He will fall into the same trap again and again in order that the reader may learn with him that 'where God rules without intermediary, the laws of nature have no standing'.[27]

The second of the two similes begins by describing the impact of light rather than colour. Light, it will be remembered, is the more powerful of the two 'proper visibles', and can force its way through closed eyelids and past the successive 'tunics' (that is, the 'coatings' which separate the internal parts of the eye) to proceed up the optic nerve and into the common sense. Moreover, it is capable of rousing a sleeping subject, thus enabling him to perceive the impression it has made on his senses (Dante will not let us forget that we do not truly see the re-presented image unless the power of sensation is in a state of wakefulness, *vigilia*).[28]

> E come a lume acuto si disonna
> per lo spirto visivo che ricorre
> a lo splendor che va di gonna in gonna. (*Par.* XXVI, 70–2)

As we are roused by the presence of a piercing light, because the visive spirits rush towards the radiance that is advancing from one 'tunic' to the next.

Even in this internal phase, and even with regard to the events that take place between the eye and the brain, Dante gives due prominence to the external cause. But the simile is so worded that the action of waking is attributed to the 'spirito visivo' rather than to the light; and the following terzina serves to underline the importance of the percipient himself and of the internal organs. The sudden and violent awakening results in shock, confusion and a temporary failure to understand ('nescience'). But the faculty called *aestimativa* comes quickly to the rescue. And we are reminded that the process of perception or 'apprehension' culminates not in imagining, nor even in paying attention to the re-presented image, but in the act of 'assessment'.

> E lo svegliato ciò che vede aborre,
> sì nescïa è la sùbita vigilia
> fin che la stimativa non soccorre. (*ibid.*, 73–5)

The rudely awakened sleeper recoils from what he sees, because in his sudden state of wakefulness he is quite unable to understand, until the power of estimation comes to his aid.[29]

Appearances, reality and the causes of 'mis-apprehension'

Dante, then, was keenly interested in what we see (*lux* and *color*), and in how we see it (*illuminatio*, *coloratio* and the *vis apprehensiva*). But he was even more keenly interested in why we sometimes fail to see, or why the apprehended image does not correspond in colour, shape or size to the *corpus coloratum* from which it derives.

As a lover of wisdom, he accepted Aristotle's view that all

knowledge has its origin in sense experience. And since knowledge could not claim to be 'certain' unless it could be shown to rest on secure foundations, he had to be able to account for the occasional fallibility of the senses in order to uphold their reliability in normal operation.

As story-teller and lover of fiction, Dante came to appreciate that if the first-person narrator begins by describing his '*mis*apprehensions', he can stimulate the reader's curiosity to discover the true cause of those erroneous initial impressions. The narrator will also make himself seem more human in his proneness to error, and yet more worthy of trust in his evident concern to set the record straight: he becomes more 'authentic' in both the modern and the original meanings of the word. And we shall find that Dante frequently and deliberately exploits his understanding of the faults and deficiencies associated with sense-perception in order to heighten suspense and to make his alleged experiences seem more credible.

The obvious place to begin a survey of the causes of 'misapprehension' is the chapter in the *Convivio* quoted earlier, in which Dante explained the difference between 'proper visibles' and 'common sensibles', and in which he described the passage of a visible form from the object to the brain. The very next sentence raises the problem of possible discrepancies between appearances and reality, or, as he will later say, between the 'intenzione' and the 'essere verace'.

> If vision is to be truthful ['acciò che la visione sia verace'], that is, faithful to the visible object in itself, the medium through which the form comes to the eye must be entirely without colour, and the fluid in the pupil must be similarly colourless. Otherwise, the visible form would be stained by the colour of the medium or the pupil.　　　　　(*Con.* III, ix, 9)

After a brief digression, Dante illustrates the two sources of error by considering our perception of a star. From his point of view, the star is a perfect example. It participates in the nature of both 'luce' and 'colore', in that it shines ('è lucente'), and yet has a clear colour ('è chiara'), such that one can distinguish a star from the planet Mars by means of colour alone. On the authority of Aristotle, moreover, it was known that a star is eternally free from alteration, growth or corruption, and admits change only in respect of place ('non riceve mutazione alcuna se non di movimento locale').[30]

The light and colour of the star are therefore invariable within the lucent body itself. It is *'d'un modo* chiara e lucente'. To the human observer, however, the star may appear to be neither shining nor clear in colour; and Dante goes on to list some of the causes of such illusions.

> The star may appear to be *'non* chiara' and *'non* lucente' because the atmospheric medium is continually changing. It changes from strong light to dim light, depending on whether the sun is absent or present. And in the presence of the sun the transparent medium is so full of light, that it overpowers the star, which no longer appears to shine.
>
> The medium is also subject to change with respect to density and moisture because of the exhalations that are continually rising from the earth. And these changes to the medium bring about changes in the visible form passing through it, such that the star seems more or less dark, in proportion to the density of the vapours, and coloured according to whether they are wet or dry. (*ibid.*, 12)

Dante next discusses some of the causes of 'mis-apprehension' that are attributable to the perceiving subject, distinguishing with his usual care between the results of illness, which affect the pupil and lead to discolouration, and the results of strain, which affect the 'visive spirits' and lead to blurring.

> The star may also appear other than it is in reality because of the organ of sight – that is, the eye – which may be coloured by illness or weakened by strain. It often happens that the 'tunic' enclosing the pupil becomes bloodshot because of damage resulting from illness, and in this case everything seems to take on a reddish hue. (...)
>
> Or again, there may be a scattering of the visive spirits, if the sight has been weakened, so that things no longer seem united, but scattered, rather like the writing on a piece of damp paper. And this is why people who want to read something often push the writing away from their eyes, so that the image may become sharper and penetrate more easily: in this way the letters seem more distinct to the eye. (*ibid.*, 13–14)

This admirable clinical sketch of the presbyopia that comes with age makes one think of the famous simile, used in connection with Brunetto Latini and his companions, of the old tailor 'sharpening' his eye to thread his needle, or of Farinata's reference to the metaphorical 'long-sight' of the damned with regard to their knowledge of events on earth. But these foreshadowings of the *Comedy* are immediately forgotten as one reads the next sentence with its rare snatch of autobiography. For a moment we are shown the physical cost to

Dante of his period of intense study, when he became an 'amatore di sapienza' and composed the canzone beginning 'Amor che ne la mente mi ragiona', to which the prose is a commentary. And one also understands why he should later have a particular veneration for the saint who protects eyesight, the aptly named 'Lucia'.[31]

> E io fui esperto di questo l'anno medesimo che nacque questa canzone, che per affaticare lo viso molto, a studio di leggere, in tanto debilitai li spiriti visivi che le stelle mi pareano tutte d'alcuno albore ombrate. E per lunga riposanza in luoghi oscuri e freddi, e con affreddare lo corpo de l'occhio con l'acqua chiara, riuni' sì la vertù disgregata che tornai nel primo buono stato de la vista. (*ibid.*, 15–16)

> I myself had personal experience of this in the very year that saw the birth of this canzone. By straining my sight through persistent study, I weakened the visive spirits to such an extent that all the stars seemed veiled by a kind of white halo. But thanks to a long rest in cool, dark places, and by cooling the body of the eye with clear water, I reunited the scattered power and regained my former good sight.

'Poca luce' and lux in tenebris

Stars remain something of a test-case for the nature of vision in the *Comedy*. The last astronomical simile in the poem describes how the stars fade from view one by one as the dawn advances, and two earlier similes tell how they re-emerge at dusk, when the sun, 'which illumines the whole universe, descends from our hemisphere, and the day is consumed on every side'. As one reads these passages with the *Convivio* chapter in mind, one is struck by the way in which Dante suppresses the word 'star' altogether, while insisting on words for 'sight', 'seeming', 'appearing' and 'appearances' ('vista', 'parere', 'parvente', 'parvenze'). And so perhaps the most revealing of the three similes is the first, in which he dwells on the uncertain moment, at the onset of twilight, when the stars 'appear to appear', and one cannot really be sure whether one is seeing them or merely imagining what one wants to see:[32]

> E sì come al salir di prima sera
> comincian per lo ciel nove parvenze,
> sì che la vista pare e non par vera,
> parvemi lì novelle sussistenze
> cominciare a vedere ... (*Par.* XIV, 70–4)

At the first ascent of evening, new *appearances* begin in the sky, so that the *sight seems* true, and yet not true. That was how I *seemed* to begin *seeing* new beings ...

The stars also remind us that lucent bodies other than the sun require a transparent medium whose transparency is still in a state of potentiality. The total or relative 'privation of light' that we call darkness (*tenebrae*) is 'good' for these lesser sources of light, whether they are the minute and indistinguishable stars that make up the Milky Way (as Dante well knew), the candles on a chandelier, or the fireflies – aptly named 'lùcciole' in Italian – which the peasant sees on a midsummer evening in the valley below him. It is because the air in the Underworld is prevailingly murky that two flames ('fiammette') can act as a signal to summon the ferryman from the other bank of the Styx (the signal is acknowledged by another flame).[33]

The darkness of Hell is so important as a narrative resource and as a symbol of the state of damnation that it deserves a whole chapter to itself, but we shall have to content ourselves with an examination of two outlying or 'flanking' passages, where we are made aware of that darkness by contrast – first, when it is temporarily overcome, and second, when it is definitively left behind.[34]

Having been ferried across the river Acheron in a deep swoon, Dante comes to his senses to find himself in a 'blind world' on the rim of the valley of Hell, which is so 'dark and cloudy' that he cannot distinguish anything at all below him ('per ficcar lo viso a fondo, / io non vi discernea alcuna cosa'). He and Virgil make their way along the cliff edge through a 'forest' of spirits, who are 'suspended in this Limbo' – neither in Hell, nor out of it. Before long Dante sees, at some distance, 'a fire which was driving back a hemisphere of darkness' ('io vidi un foco / ch'emisperio di tenebre vincia').[35]

The source of this light ('lumera') proves to be a noble castle, surrounded by seven walls, through which the two poets pass into a 'meadow of fresh greenness' – the colour being visible because the 'place is open, high and illuminated', thus allowing Dante to pick out all the spirits who are assembled there.[36] So well can the protagonist see that he is able to give a roll-call of great names from the cultures of Greece, Rome and Islam. The 'spiriti magni' include heroes and heroines of the active life, poets and, on the highest ground, a group of scientists and philosophers who are all paying honour to Aristotle, 'the master of those who have true knowledge':

Vidi 'l maestro di color che sanno
seder tra filosofica famiglia.
  Tutti lo miran, tutti onor li fanno.   (*Inf.* IV, 131–3)

The vocabulary relating to light, colour and vision is very precise
('oscuro', 'non discernere'; 'luminoso', 'vedere'; 'verdura', 'verde'),
and nowhere more so than in the observation that the fire was
'overcoming a *hemisphere* of darkness'. But the precision of that
phrase does not preclude a multiple allusion to the Gospel of St
John, which provides the best possible commentary to the symbolic
meaning of the whole scene. Aristotle and his 'retinue of philosophers' did indeed 'lighten the darkness of ignorance' – but only to a
limited degree and to a limited extent. They are in Limbo, cut off
from God, still surrounded by *tenebrae.* Aristotle's teaching is not the
'most true teaching of Christ', which, as Dante reminds us in the
Convivio, is 'the way, the truth and the light', and which is properly
called the 'light' because 'it illuminates us in the darkness of worldly
ignorance' ('perché *allumina* noi ne la *tenebra* de la ignoranza
mondana'). Christ alone – in the words of St John, which Dante
clearly had in mind – is the 'true light', the 'light of the world', the
'light shining in the darkness' (*lux in tenebris*), who 'illuminates every
man who comes into this world'.[37]

Colour and the rebirth of delight

That episode came at the start of Dante's journey through the 'valle
dolorosa'. The next begins in the very last line of *Inferno,* where
Dante and Virgil emerge into the southern hemisphere 'to see the
stars again'. The opening lines of *Purgatorio* look back to the 'dead
poetry', describing the 'dead air' which had 'oppressed Dante's eyes
and breast'.[38] And the moment of 'resurrection' from that 'death'
(after three days of 'harrowing' in Hell) is marked by the return of
colour and light.

The light has several distinct sources. We hear first of the familiar
constellation of Pisces, which is being outshone and 'veiled' by the
equally familiar but praeternaturally radiant planet Venus, appearing
as a morning star and 'causing the whole East to smile'. Above these,
near the southern celestial pole, there are four unnamed stars – never
seen in the northern hemisphere – which are shining with such
supernatural brilliance that 'their rays seem to adorn with light' the

face of a mysterious old man, and the protagonist sees him 'as though the sun were on him':[39]

> Li *raggi* de le quattro *luci* sante
> fregiavan sì la sua faccia di *lume*,
> ch' i' 'l *vedea* come 'l *sol* fosse davante.   (*Purg.* 1, 37–9)

Meanwhile, the still invisible sun, which is not far below the horizon, is beginning to illuminate the atmospheric medium ('mezzo'), which is 'pure and cloudless as far as the first of the celestial spheres', with the result that the whole sky is becoming slowly blue. And it is *colour* – the '*sweet* colour of an oriental sapphire', which has the privilege of 'renewing delight' for Dante's eyes, which are still smarting from the 'dead air' of the Underworld:

> *Dolce* color d'orïental zaffiro,
> che s'accoglieva nel sereno aspetto
> del mezzo, puro infino al primo giro,
>   a li occhi miei ricominciò *diletto*,
> tosto ch'io usci' fuor de l'aura morta
> che m'avea contristati li occhi e 'l petto.   (1, 13–18)

The precision of all these details does not make the episode any less moving or any less symbolic. As so often, Dante will remind us of the normal laws of physics in order that a supernatural phenomenon may be perceived and felt by the reader for what it is – an infraction or transcendence of the 'legge naturale'. And, as so often, there is a rich and satisfying symbolic meaning, which is to be deduced from the literal meaning of the passage by studying it in the context of the whole poem and of Dante's other works.

In this case, the significance of sunlight in Purgatory and of darkness in Hell can be further clarified by reference to the opening stanza of one of Dante's long poems, 'Amor, che movi tua vertù da cielo'. The sun's power to drive out 'darkness and cold' was taken there as an analogue of the power of love – cosmic love – to banish 'baseness and aggression' from our hearts. Without love, all our potential for doing good remains unfulfilled. A human being unilluminated by love is 'like a picture kept in a dark place, where it cannot reveal itself or give delight in its art or colour' (once again, we must note the close association of *delectatio* and *color*):

> sanza te è distrutto
> quanto avemo *in potenzia* di ben fare,
> come *pintura* in *tenebrosa* parte,
> che non si può mostrare
> né dar *diletto* di *color* né d'arte. (*Rime* XC, 11–15)

Throughout *Purgatorio*, the sun will symbolise not just divine goodness and love in general, but divine grace. There can be no ascent on the mountain of Purgatory during the night, because human beings are not able to 'move themselves' on the journey to their predestined 'end' without the assistance of grace. And with all these considerations in mind, we can establish three important points about the symbolism of darkness, or 'poca luce', in Dante's Underworld. First, it denotes a 'privation of the good', a waste of potential, rather than evil hypostatised as an independent force in the universe. Second, it represents not just ignorance as such – an unrealised potential for knowing the truth – but the limitations set on human reason (we have seen that darkness can be 'pushed back' by the efforts of philosophers, but that it will be 'dispelled' only by Christ, considered as the Word of God, the *lux vera*). And third, the darkness of Hell symbolises more than anything else the consequences of sin, a weakening of the appetitive rather than the cognitive faculties.[40] Darkness is an inability to love God. Human beings no longer 'move' towards their *bonum* of their own accord, because they do not desire it as they should. Fallen man needs a *principium extrinsecum* to realise a *potentia* that he should have been able to actualise for himself. Left in the dark without a lamp, he must wait for the dawn.

'In oscuritade e in colore'

One of the naturalistic reasons why the planet and stars shone with such unnatural brilliance in the dawn sky was that the atmosphere – the 'aspect of the medium' – was 'puro' and 'sereno'. The two adjectives seem vaguer and more emotive than the nouns ('aspetto', 'mezzo'), but they are in fact used with equal precision. 'Sereno' means 'cloudless' (as it still does in Italian weather reports), while 'puro' means 'without any suspended particles of dust', because Dante is clearly referring to the absence of 'moist and dry exhalations', which, as we were told in *Convivio* III, ix, are 'continually rising from the earth'. The two kinds of exhalation – the difference between them is, roughly, that between steam and smoke – reduce the transparency of the atmosphere and render it less suitable as a medium for vision by making it darker ('in oscuritade'), or by making it coloured ('in colore'); and Dante alludes to both effects in the *Comedy*.[41]

Let us begin with obscuration. When the moist exhalations (or 'vapori' as they were also called) condense to form haze, mist and finally cloud, the air is progressively starved of illumination.[42] In the extreme case, the 'aere' may become so 'stipato' – 'choked' or 'clogged' – that one can see nothing at all; and this is the situation that Dante asks us to imagine in the opening lines of the sixteenth and seventeenth cantos of *Purgatorio*, which act as the frame for his encounter with the souls of those penitents who are purifying themselves of an excessive inclination to anger. Dante and Virgil see a cloud-like substance rolling towards them which engulfs them in total darkness, 'robbing them of their eyes and the pure air' ('questo ne tolse li occhi e l'acre puro'), the unpleasant state being described with a flourish of rhetorical exaggeration:

> Buio d'inferno e di notte privata
> d'ogne pianeto, sotto pover cielo
> quant' esser può di nuvol tenebrata,
>   non fece al viso mio sì grosso velo
> come quel fummo ch'ivi ci coperse,
> né a sentir di così aspro pelo.   (*Purg.* XVI, 1–6)

The blackness of Hell or a night deprived of every luminary, under a glowering sky and obscured by cloud to the limits of the possible, never made so thick a veil to my eyes as did the smoke that enveloped us, nor such a rasping surface to the sense of touch.

Dante's eyes are stinging so much that he is unable to keep them open and he lays his hand on Virgil's shoulder as though he were a blind man following his guide. His conversation with the 'voice' of Marco Lombardo, which occupies the rest of canto XVI, takes place in this artificial 'oscuritade'; and the opening of the next canto compares the 'fummo' to the kind of hill mist which makes the traveller as blind as the proverbial mole. These lines are, however, chiefly remarkable for the marvellously *un*rhetorical description of the moment when the mist begins to thin out and disperse, allowing the pallid disc of the sun to become visible in its midst:

> Ricorditi, lettor, se mai ne l'alpe
> ti colse nebbia per la qual vedessi
> non altrimenti che per pelle talpe,
>   come, quando i vapori umidi e spessi
> a diradar cominciansi, la spera
> del sol debilemente entra per essi;
>   e fia la tua imagine leggera
> in giugnere a veder ...   (*Purg.* XVII, 1–8)

Reader, if you have ever been overtaken in the mountains by a mist, through which you could see as well as a mole does through its skin, think back to how the sun's sphere feebly penetrates the dense, moist vapours as they begin to thin out, and your imagination will easily make the leap to see.

Alternatively, exhalations may deceive the eye by colouring the atmospheric medium, which in turn communicates that colour to the visible form as it 'passes through'. The planet Mars is red because of its intrinsic heat, but it will glow redder than usual, 'because of the dense exhalations', if it is 'caught by the morning, as it sets low in the West over the surface of the sea':

> Ed ecco, qual, sorpreso dal mattino,
> per li *grossi vapor* Marte *rosseggia*
> giù nel ponente sovra 'l suol marino.   (*Purg.* II, 13–15)

And 'vapori' are the cause of the redness of the sky at sunset or sunrise, as Dante reminds us in an evocative simile drawn from personal experience, where he contrasts the 'rest of the sky', which is cloudless and therefore blue, with the rose-colour of the 'eastern part' at daybreak:

> Io vidi già nel cominciar del giorno
> la parte orïental tutta *rosata*,
> e l'altro ciel di bel sereno addorno.   (*Purg.* XXX, 22–4)

'Troppa luce'

The real point of this simile, however, emerges only in the following terzina, where we read that, in those conditions, 'the face of the sun was shaded by the tempering of the exhalations, so that the eye could endure it for a long time':

e la faccia del sol nascere *ombrata*
sì che per *temperanza di vapori,*
l'*occhio* la sostenea lunga fïata.   (*ibid.,* 25–7)

And these lines embody two linked paradoxes which lead to the last
and perhaps the most important facts about the two *visibilia propria.*
First, the exhalations, which are normally an impediment to 'truthful
vision', are the only means by which we are enabled to see *lux* in its
most intense manifestation (that is, as an active quality inherent in
the sun). Second, we can only look steadily at this *corpus lucens par
excellence* when it is made to appear as a *corpus coloratum* – a 'pallid
disc' or a 'rosy face'.

Like the other external organs of sensation, the eye is fitted by its
nature to receive impressions in the middle of a range. It may
become accustomed to tolerate levels that are higher or lower than
the norm, and this acquired power may become 'second nature', but
it will never be able to cope with the possible extremes. There will
always be a 'too little' and a 'too much'. Like the other organs, also,
the eye can be damaged or destroyed if it is exposed to impressions
that exceed its natural or its acquired capacity. The ear may be first
overwhelmed, and then rendered permanently deaf. The eye may be
dazzled, then blinded.[43]

It is not entirely misguided to ascribe these limitations to our
'*material* cause' – that is, to an impotence inherent in the four
elements of which we are compounded. But it is more correct to
attribute them to our '*formal* cause', our *forma substantialis.* And it is
important to recognise that these limitations are paralleled in the
distinctively human powers of our moral and intellectual nature. It
was clear to Dante, as a philosopher, that we can learn to 'see' truths
which had been too 'dazzling' on first encounter, and that we can be
trained to acquire good habits which will 'perfect' our natural
inclinations. But it was also clear to him that certain truths will
always surpass the capacity of even the highest and best-trained
intellects, and that the moral virtues recognised by Aristotle consist
largely in a habitual inclination to choose the 'mean', avoiding the
'too much' as well as the 'too little' of what is good for us as bodily
creatures.

On the other hand, it was no less obvious to Dante, as a Christian,
that the human heart can never be satisfied by anything except an
infinite Good, 'a Good beyond which there is nothing to which one
might aspire', and that the human mind will never be stilled in its

quest for understanding until it has grasped the Truth which embraces all truths. He also believed that God – who is, supremely, both Goodness and Truth – would give his grace to certain human beings in order to raise them above the limitations of their human nature, 'transhumanising' them to such an extent that they would be able to know him and love him directly, and thereby to assuage the desire of their intellect and their will. And Dante, the lover-of-myth, conceived his *Paradiso* to express this transhumanisation ('trasumanare') in images that would be comprehensible and attractive to his fellow humans here in this life.[44]

In the language of Aristotelian natural science, the change required in 'going beyond humanity' would be tantamount to *generatio* (that is, to a change in formal identity resulting in a new *substantia*, which would be 'nobler' because it had 'higher powers'). But in the narrative of the *Comedy*, the process is enacted in terms of the other categories of change. The protagonist is represented as though he were on a pilgrimage to a shrine beyond the bounds of space – as though he were literally travelling towards God (*motus localis*) in order to come to rest in him. And at each stage on the journey (as it were, at each 'albergo' in the heavens), he is subjected to massive doses of light-radiation which 'temper' or 'condition' his eyes until they are strong enough to take delight in the highest possible intensity of light (technically, this kind of change would be *alteratio* or *augmentum*).

The consummation of the process comes at the very end of the poem, when the pilgrim looks directly into the Godhead, who is figured as *lux* in its *principium fontale*. Light becomes not just the instrumental cause of colour vision, not just the efficient cause of an increased capacity for enduring light, but the object of vision itself.[45] And Dante-the-poet rises to his greatest heights when he transforms this nexus of ideas and images into fiction, as we can confirm by examining three of the crucial moments in the 'tempering' of his capacities.

Sungazing and transhumanisation

The protagonist's experiences in the Garden of Eden, on the summit of the mountain of Purgatory, restore him to the fullness of human nature, which Adam had forfeited through his refusal to accept the limits set on that nature.[46] And his new condition is symbolised in the enhancement of his power of vision, which forms the subject of the very first episode in *Paradiso*. He looks at Beatrice as she turns her gaze up to the sun in the noonday sky, and then does likewise, imitating her with such fidelity that *her* glance could be compared to a beam of direct light falling on a horizontal surface, and *his* to the beam of reflected light which necessarily 'climbs' from it. And the upshot is that Dante fixes his gaze on the sun itself 'beyond our human custom':

> quando Beatrice in sul sinistro fianco
> vidi rivolta e riguardar nel sole:
> aguglia sì non li s'affisse unquanco.
>   E sì come secondo raggio suole
> uscir del primo e risalire in suso,
> pur come pelegrin che tornar vuole,
>   così de l'atto suo, per li occhi infuso
> ne l'imagine mia, il mio si fece,
> e fissi li occhi al sole oltre nostr' uso.   (*Par.* 1, 46–54)

[It was noon] when I saw Beatrice turn to her left and look into the sun. No eagle ever held his gaze there as steadily as she did. And just as a second ray will climb from the first, rising like a pilgrim longing to return, so her action, passing through the eyes into my imagination, became the model for mine, and I fixed my eyes on the sun beyond our custom.

While conceding that, even in Eden, he could not endure the sun for long, the narrator underlines the extraordinary nature of his feat. Then he supplies a superb simile to convey the effect on him of the sun's *lux*, followed by a hypothetical miracle to suggest the re-doubling of its *lumen* (or of his power to 'receive it'):

> Molto è licito là, che qui non lece
> a le nostre virtù, mercé del loco
> fatto per proprio de l'umana spece.
>   Io nol soffersi molto, né sì poco,
> ch'io nol vedessi sfavillar dintorno,
> com' ferro che bogliente esce del foco;
>   e di sùbito parve giorno a giorno
> essere aggiunto, come quei che puote
> avesse il ciel d'un altro sole addorno.   (*ibid.*, 55–63)

Many things that would be unlawful for our faculties here on earth are lawful there, thanks to the place expressly created for mankind. I could not endure the sun for long; but it was long enough for me to see it showering sparks all around, like molten iron being poured from the furnace. And suddenly day seemed to have been added to day, as though the Omnipotent had adorned the heavens with a second sun.

Significantly, Beatrice continues to look upward; and significantly, too, it is only when Dante looks at her outward appearance ('suo aspetto') that he feels within him ('dentro') the decisive change which he calls 'trasumanare' and which he compares elliptically to Ovid's story of the fisherman Glaucus, who was metamorphosed into a god. The immediate consequences of this 'divinisation' of his faculties is an extension of his power of hearing, which enables him to perceive for the first time the celestial harmony of the spheres.[47] But this is followed by yet another 'flooding' of light, described in one of Dante's finest evocations of *lumen*.

> Parvemi tanto allor del cielo acceso
> de la fiamma del sol, che pioggia o fiume
> lago non fece alcun tanto disteso.   (*ibid.*, 79–81)

It was as though the sun's flame had set the vault of heaven on fire over so vast an area, that no rainstorm or river ever made a lake of comparable size.

'Cielo di fiamma o vero luminoso'

The immediate cause of this apparent conflagration is Dante's 'free flight', which has begun to carry him up towards God through the sphere of Fire. In the nine aetherial spheres above, he will experience ever-higher levels of radiation as he penetrates the very body of the planets. Within the sun, for example, he sees the souls of the blessed as *corpora lucentia* brighter than the sun itself. And such is the radiance of the souls that even after he has experienced an 'ecstasy', induced by the epiphany of Jesus in the Heaven of the Stars, the protagonist will be temporarily blinded for his presumption when he tries to look into the 'fire' that envelops St John the Evangelist.[48]

> Qual è colui ch'adocchia e s'argomenta
> di vedere eclissar lo sole un poco,
> che, per veder, non vedente diventa;
> tal mi fec' ïo a quell' ultimo foco.   (*Par.* xxv, 118–21)

Looking into that 'fire' I became like someone who screws up his eyes in an effort to catch a glimpse of a solar eclipse, and unsights himself in his effort to see.

However, we must pass over all these intermediate 'illuminations' and pick up the story at the close of the last great pyrotechnical display, which was enacted for the pilgrim's benefit in the outermost of the physical heavens. As the fiery circles and the point of light fade from his view, Dante turns to Beatrice to find that her beauty has reached a new intensity, a fullness of perfection such that it could be enjoyed only by her Creator, and therefore such that it lies beyond the resources of his poetry.[49] They are now beyond the universe, in the Empyrean.

In the *Convivio* Dante had explained that this heaven has no location except in the Divine Mind; that it is the abode of the blessed; and that its name means, literally, 'the heaven of flame or the luminous heaven' ('cielo di fiamma o vero luminoso'). Here, in the *Comedy*, he makes Beatrice insist that the 'flame' or 'light' in question is not the light which is accessible to the senses, but that which illuminates the mind and the will, giving a sweetness incommensurably greater than the delight which colour gives to the eyes:

> 'Noi siamo usciti fore
> del maggior corpo al ciel ch'è pura luce:
>   luce intellettüal, piena d'amore;
>   amor di vero ben, pien di letizia;
> letizia che trascende ogne dolzore.'   (*Par.* xxx, 38–42)

'We have issued from the greatest body into the heaven that is pure light – an intellectual light filled with love of the true good, the love being filled with joy, and the joy transcending all sweetness.'

Beatrice continues with a promise that Dante shall see 'both armies of Paradise'. Then the reader is confronted with an anticipatory simile, which should strike with the same totally unexpected force as the phenomenon it describes.

> Come sùbito lampo che discetti
> li spiriti visivi, sì che priva
> da l'atto l'occhio di più forti obietti,
>   così mi circunfulse luce viva,
>   e lasciommi fasciato di tal velo
> del suo fulgor, che nulla m'appariva.   (*ibid.*, 46–51)

Just as a sudden flash of lightning scatters the visive spirits and deprives the eye of its power to see even the most visible objects, so a living light shone round about me and left me wrapped in such a veil of brightness that nothing whatsoever appeared.

It is difficult to know which of the disparate elements in this superb compound to single out for comment. But whereas another Christian writer might have borrowed the Latinism 'circunfulse' from the account of St Paul's blinding on the road to Damascus, or used the paradoxical metaphor of a 'veil of brightness', the characteristically Dantean features are those which will have now become familiar: the physiologist's attention to the role of the 'spiriti visivi' in the optic nerve; the unobtrusive reference to the philosophical concepts of *privatio* and *actus* (seeing is both the 'activity' and the 'actualisation' of the eye); the scientist's 'obietti', qualified by the layman's 'più forti'; and the final 'nulla m'appariva', which is at once colloquial and marvellously exact, since all perception is limited to 'appearances'.

Just as the 'subito lampo' was flashed without warning before the reader's eyes, so Beatrice's reassuring words, which entered Dante's consciousness while he was unsighted, are 'poured' directly into the reader's awareness without any preparatory formula.

> 'Sempre l'amor che queta questo cielo
> accoglie in sé con sì fatta salute,
> per far disposto a sua fiamma il candelo.'   (*ibid.*, 52–4)

'The love that keeps this heaven in perfect stillness always bids welcome with a life-giving greeting of this kind, in order to prepare the candle for its flame.'

After this dramatic use of dialogue and rapid cross-cutting, the narrator chooses an extended sequence of images projected, as it were, from the distant viewpoint of memory. And thanks to this perspective he can represent the effects of the 'subito lampo' on his faculties in a way that reminds the reader of the 'day added to day' and 'the lake of fire' in canto I, while at the same time preparing him for the culminating sequence in canto XXXIII.

> Non fur più tosto dentro a me venute
> queste parole brievi, ch'io compresi
> me sormontar di sopr' a mia virtute;
>   e di novella vista mi raccesi
> tale, che nulla luce è tanto mera,
> che li occhi miei non si fosser difesi;
>   e vidi lume in forma di rivera.   (*ibid.*, 55–61)

No sooner had these brief words entered my mind than I knew that I was rising above my powers. And I was kindled with a new power of sight, such that no light [*lux*] is so pure that my eyes could not have withstood its onslaught. And I saw light [*lumen*] in the form of a river.

The final fulguration

Most of the visual experiences recorded in the remaining five hundred lines of the poem are *sensibilia communia* and therefore belong with the material of chapter 6; but there are two moments in the final canto that demand our attention, since they bring to completion the process of transhumanisation by exposure to light.

When Bernard has finished his prayer to the Virgin, asking her to intercede on Dante's behalf so that he may receive the power to 'lift himself with his eyes to the supreme beatitude', the saint turns his own eyes upwards into the 'etterno lume', while urging Dante, with a smiling gesture, to imitate his example. No such encouragement, however, is needed.[50]

> Ché la mia vista, venendo sincera,
> e più e più intrava per lo raggio
> de l'alta luce che da sé è vera.
>   Da quinci innanzi il mio veder fu maggio
> che 'l parlar mostra, ch'a tal vista cede,
> e cede la memoria a tanto oltraggio.   (XXXIII, 52–7)

My sight was becoming purer and purer as it entered more and more into the living ray of the supreme light, which is 'true' without qualification. From that moment on, my seeing exceeded what language can show, which acknowledges defeat with respect to such a sight, just as memory yields to so great an overmastering.

Far from being overpowered by the 'alta luce', Dante declares that the intensity of the ray was such that 'I would have been dazed if I had turned away from it'. Thanks to the 'abundance of God's grace', he continues, 'I could now dare to presume to fix my eyes on the *lux aeterna* and to consummate my power of seeing there'.

> Io credo, per l'acume ch'io soffersi
> del vivo raggio, ch'i' sarei smarrito,
> se li occhi miei da lui fossero aversi.
> (…)
>   Oh abbondante grazia ond' io presunsi
> ficcar lo viso per la luce etterna,
> tanto che la veduta vi consunsi!   (*ibid.*, 76–8, 82–4)

His power of sight continues to gather strength, owing to changes within himself ('la vista ... s'avvalorava ... *mutandom' io'*). He becomes able to see three circles or spheres, of like colour and equal circumference (symbolising the three Persons of the Trinity), and even the presence of our 'human likeness', 'painted in its own colour' within the second of these circles.[51] Try as he may, however, his own powers will not enable him to see how the divine and the human are united in the Person of the Son – 'how the image fits the circle'. But at this point his mind is struck by a flash of lightning through which its wish is granted:

> Veder voleva come si convenne
> l'imago al cerchio e come vi s'indova;
>   ma non eran da ciò le proprie penne:
> se non che la mia mente fu percossa
> da un fulgore in che sua voglia venne.   (*ibid.*, 137–41)

Even *his* soaring power to form images failed him – he had no perception. But his desire and will were brought by God's love into a perfect circular orbit, the 'orbit' which glorified human beings will share with 'the sun and the stars':[52]

> A l'alta fantasia qui mancò possa;
> ma già volgeva il mio disio e 'l *velle*,
> sì come rota ch'igualmente è mossa,
>   l'amor che move il sole e l'altre stelle.   (*ibid.*, 142–5)

CHAPTER SIX

Perception of shape, size, number, movement and stillness

'Ben è altra cosa visibile'[1]

Light and colour are prominent in the scene of arrival described in the second canto of *Purgatorio*. Pisces, Venus and the four stars near the southern celestial pole fade from our memory as we follow the two poets down to the shore to witness the ceremony in which Virgil 'uncovers the *colour*' in Dante's cheeks by washing away the 'fog' deposited by Hell. When the sun reaches the horizon, the dawn sky changes from 'white and vermilion' to 'orange'; and against this background a 'reddish light' appears over the sea, growing ever 'more radiant' as it approaches. An indeterminate 'whiteness' ('un non sapea che bianco') appears on either side of the red light. Then 'another whiteness' gradually issues from below the first. The closer the light approaches, the 'clearer' it becomes, until it overpowers Dante's eyes and he is forced to look down.[2]

But other things than light and colour are visible; and the impact of the *visibilia propria* is completely transformed in this description – as in so many others in the *Comedy* – by the skilful way in which Dante blends them with his perception of the five *sensibilia communia*. These were listed in the *Convivio*, it will be remembered, as 'la figura, la grandezza, lo numero, lo movimento e lo stare fermo'; and all five are present in this passage.[3]

The final 'stillness' is registered in the past definite of the phrase 'it came to the shore' ('sen venne a riva'); and this contrasts, obviously, with the rectilinear 'movement' of the red light towards the two spectators, which was detected not only by the growing intensity of the light, but by a rapid increase in its 'size'.[4] The perception of 'number' is implicit in the distinction made between the 'whiteness' lying to either side of the light, and the '*other* whiteness' that issued underneath the first. Lastly, 'shape' is recorded when the 'first whitenesses' are identified as wings ('i primi bianchi apparser ali').

Until that moment Dante-the-author confined himself to recording the way things *appeared*. And the verb 'apparire' is repeated four times in this passage to remind us that we perceive *corpora colorata* as they seem to be, and not necessarily as they are in themselves (the eye apprehends 'parvenze' or 'apparenze'; it cannot see 'essenze').[5]

It is the correct identification of the wings that enables a hitherto silent Virgil to know or to recognise ('conoscere' denotes an act of the human reason) that the approaching figure is an 'angel of God'. And in the following nine lines of direct speech, which the 'all-knowing' narrator puts into the mouth of a '*relatively* knowing' Virgil, the still-ignorant protagonist and the reader are given further items of information to fill out the visual impressions of light, colour, shape, size, number, movement and rest.[6]

More precisely, we are given a number of clues which enable us to draw certain inferences and to ask further questions (these being the characteristic processes of human reason in its quest for understanding). When Virgil invites his charge 'to see' that the angel is using not 'oars and sails', but 'eternal pinions' between 'such distant shores', we are not in fact helped to see anything new. But we are moved to wonder: '*which* shores?' And we can already deduce that the angel is a 'helmsman' of some kind, and that the 'other whiteness' below the wings must be some sort of 'vessel'. A few lines later, our deductions are duly confirmed (they are identified as a 'nocchiero', and a 'vasello' respectively), while our curiosity about the shores will be satisfied towards the end of the canto, where we learn that the angel is ferrying the souls of the penitent dead from the mouth of the Tiber to Mount Purgatory.[7]

Sensation and suspense: the 'worm's-eye view'

The approach of the angelic ferryboat is offered as a representative example of the narrative technique that Dante evolved and perfected in the *Comedy*. The author does not immediately tell us what happened. He shows us what his earlier self perceived at the time without the benefit of hindsight or foresight (and he usually succeeds in making us forget that he is not 'remembering' anything but 'inventing' everything).

A typical sequence will begin, as in the present case, with the appearance of something new. Typically, too, generic impressions of colour, light, mass and movement will precede the perception of a recognisable shape. Very often, as we shall find in later passages, Dante will dwell on his initial 'mis-apprehensions' and on the concomitant emotions of puzzlement, fear, curiosity and wonder. Only then – but unfailingly then – will the author clarify the link between appearance and reality by intervening in his own person (or by attributing words to another character in the poem) in order to explain the causes of the phenomenon.

Stated thus baldly, the technique may not seem particularly original. Any born story-teller will instinctively use similar devices to keep his reader in a state of pleasurable suspense. But although Dante certainly was a born story-teller – it is one of the qualities that make him a 'philomythes' – he was also a 'philosopher'. And his handling of the technique is distinctively Dantean for two main reasons.

First, he was trying to educate the reader's mind and emotions by simulating what he knew to be the natural process of learning. Angels, he believed, can intuit universal truths immediately and simultaneously. Human beings, however, must seek them out one at a time by a complicated and laborious process of abstraction from sense-experience.[8] It was an axiom that 'there is nothing in the intellect that was not first in the senses' (*nihil in intellectu quod non fuerit prius in sensu*). And Dante consciously tried 'to address the human mind through concrete images, because it is only from objects presented to the senses that the mind apprehends what it subsequently makes fit for the intellect':

> Così parlar conviensi al vostro ingegno,
> però che solo da sensato apprende
> ciò che fa poscia d'intelletto degno.   (*Par.* IV, 40–2)

We are meant to identify with the protagonist; to perceive and to feel with him; to err with him; and to be corrected and learn with him.

Second, the method is personal and distinctive in that it is founded on a close familiarity with the contemporary account of the mechanics of sense-perception. It is because Dante had been made analytically aware of the causes of delay, deception and self-deception that he could weave so many variations on the one theme. And the main purpose of this chapter will be to establish the known causes of error one by one and then to investigate how they are dramatised and woven together in some of the most memorable and moving episodes in the poem.

At the risk of labouring the obvious, it will be as well to stress that Dante does not confine himself exclusively to what one might call the 'worm's-eye view' of the protagonist. On the contrary, he is always varying his viewing point, alternating flashbacks and close-ups with moments of reflection and commentary, and splicing in long-distance shots which presuppose the 'bird's-eye view' of the traveller who has lived to tell the tale, or which were taken, so to speak, from the partially obscured vantage-points of his guides or of the souls whom he meets and questions during his journey. But in the final section of this chapter we shall see that these 'retrospective' or 'lateral' views of the dramatic action do not necessarily dissipate suspense, because they usually offer clues rather than solutions, and because their very intrusion delays the moment when the 'parvenze' will be reconciled with the 'esseri veraci' from which they derived.

'Il senso s'inganna di lontano'

The healthy eye can be rendered unseeing by too much or too little light, but it is not deceived about colour, which is the *obiectum visus per se*. The *sensus communis*, by contrast, is easily misled with regard to the *sensibilia communia*.

As Aquinas pointed out, all five common sensibles depend on an assessment of quantity, understood as linear magnitude.[9] When the common sense has to rely on the sense of sight to assess the length of a line – the height of a tree, for example – it can do so only on the basis of the angle subtended at the eye by that line. But the size of the subtended angle varies not only in proportion to the length of the line, but also in proportion to its distance from the eye. There is no perceptible difference between the angle subtended by a twenty-foot tree at a distance of sixty feet and that subtended by a forty-foot tree at a hundred and twenty feet. Our judgement of distance, however, is notoriously subject to error, and so we are very frequently mistaken in our estimate of height. (The only way to be sure about distance is, in effect, to call upon our sense of touch, and to measure it by means of a yardstick, pole or chain.)

The young, healthy eye can discriminate between angles that are very narrow indeed – not just a degree, but a minute of arc. Nevertheless, there is a lower limit to this crucial angle of vision. Some angles are so fine that they cannot be registered. And any object, or any feature of an object, that fails to subtend that minimum angle will be invisible, inasmuch as it will be indistinguishable from its surroundings at the given distance. Moreover, if we were looking at two objects of different height, standing side by side, we should not be able to perceive them as being either distinct or unequal, unless the gap or the difference in height between them was sufficient to produce that minimum angle at the distance in question.

These purely trigonometrical factors are obviously compounded in ordinary experience by inadequate illumination or impurities in the atmosphere (outlines seen through a haze are like angles drawn with a soft, blunt pencil, and fine discriminations are not possible). Dante presumably had both aerial and geometrical considerations in mind when he wrote the following passage in the *Convivio*:

> When a person looks straight ahead of him, he sees the nearest objects clearly. Then, as his gaze extends further, he sees less clearly; a little further still, and he begins to doubt; and at the extreme limit of his vision, he sees nothing at all. (*Con.* III, iii, 13)

Even if the medium were perfectly transparent, however, and even if the surface of the earth were not curved, there is a distance at which we would not be able to see something as big as an elephant – not even as a black speck. And distance alone would certainly make it impossible to see an ant in the sky (this example was proposed by Democritus and discussed by Aristotle and Aquinas).[10]

Given that all five common sensibles are assessed on the basis of subtended angles, it follows that all five are increasingly likely to deceive the common sense the further they are removed from the eye. And Dante makes a number of specific references to deceptions or optical illusions caused by distance. In the *Convivio*, for example, he reports that outward appearance can be 'totally misleading, especially in the case of the common sensibles, where the apprehensive power is often deceived'. Again, the sun appears to be no more than a foot in diameter, but Dante's astronomical authority had calculated that its diameter is really five-and-a-half times that of the earth.[11]

In the *Comedy*, he makes similarly explicit comments in connection with two very different episodes, contrastingly set in the murky depths of Hell and in the perfect atmospheric conditions on the summit of Mount Purgatory. What looked like distant towers turn out to be giants when Dante draws closer. What seemed to be seven gold trees prove to be the seven arms of an elaborate candelabrum. But the cause is the same. In the first case, Virgil warns his pupil in advance that he will soon discover 'how much the senses are deceived from afar' ('quanto 'l senso s'inganna di lontano'). In the second, the narrator tells us from the outset that 'the vast extent of the medium was falsifying appearance' ('falsava nel parere il lungo tratto / del mezzo'). And he goes on to specify – with a brief flurry of technical terms which require a little paraphrase – 'that the faculty which provides reason with its special nourishment perceived that they were candlesticks' only after he had 'come so close to them that the common sensible of shape, which can deceive the senses, was losing nothing of its actuality [i.e., none of its distinctive features] because of distance':[12]

> Ma quand' i' fui sì presso di lor fatto,
> che l'obietto comun, che 'l senso inganna,
> non perdea per distanza alcun suo atto,
>   la virtù ch'a ragion discorso ammanna,
> sì com' elli eran candelabri apprese.　　　(*Purg.* XXIX, 46–50)

Distance and disappearance

In the first two canticas Dante usually exploits these simple facts in episodes like those we have just considered, in which an unfamiliar or unexpected *obiectum* is progressively revealed in its true shape or nature, either as he advances, or as it approaches. But it is also characteristic of his working methods that he should devise a number of scenes in which a person or group becomes invisible by vanishing into the distance; and these passages too are marked by explicit references to the optical facts.[13]

In *Inferno* XXVI there is a well-known simile which recalls the biblical story of how the prophet Elijah was carried up to heaven in a fiery chariot drawn by fiery horses, and how his younger companion Elisha 'saw him ascend, called out, and saw him no more'. Dante as author empathises with Elisha and significantly departs from the biblical text by insisting that the prophet 'could follow the chariot with his eyes only to the extent that he could see the flame alone, rising aloft like a little cloud':

> che nol potea sì con li occhi seguire,
> ch'el vedesse altro che la fiamma sola,
> sì come nuvoletta, in sù salire.   (*Inf.* XXVI, 37–9)

In *Paradiso*, Dante clearly took Elijah's ascent and disappearance as a model, using it as the theme for a number of variations in order to describe how the souls of the blessed, who had come down to greet him in each of the celestial spheres, withdrew from his sight as they returned to their true abode in the Empyrean.

The first encounter is the exception that prepares for the rule. As we saw in chapter 5, it takes place in the body of the moon itself; and it will be remembered that the moon was compared to a 'cloud', 'shining and burnished', but also 'solid and dense'.[14] The protagonist is greeted by Piccarda Donati; and when she withdraws at the end of their conversation, Dante dwells lovingly on the length of time that he was able to follow her departing figure with his eyes. But by comparing her to a heavy object sinking into dark water, he implicitly attributes her disappearance not so much to distance, as to the medium:

> e cantando vanio
> come per acqua cupa cosa grave.
> La vista mia, che tanto lei seguio
> quanto possibil fu ...   (*Par.* III, 122–5)

The 'variations' begin in earnest in the Heaven of Mercury, where the souls of the ambitious depart with such rapidity that they disappear in the instant, 'veiling themselves in sudden distance':

> e quasi velocissime faville
> mi si velar di sùbita distanza.   (VII, 8–9)

No less rapid is the ascent of the whole company of contemplatives from the seventh heaven. They are said to sweep up their golden ladder 'like a whirlwind'.[15] In this case, however, a single gesture from Beatrice drives Dante up the ladder behind them at equally supernatural speed, and hence there is no explicit mention of the souls' disappearance. By contrast, when Jesus and Mary return to the Empyrean from the Heaven of the Stars, leaving Dante to undergo his public examination in the theological virtues, fully nine lines are devoted to the evocation of the vastness of the space they have to traverse. We are told that even the nearer, inner surface of the outermost heaven was 'so distant that its appearance did not appear'. And it was because of distance alone that Dante's eyes 'had no power to follow the crowned flame', concealing Mary, 'as it rose to follow her Son'.[16]

> Lo real manto di tutti i volumi
> del mondo
> (...)
> avea sopra di noi l'interna riva
> tanto distante, che la sua parvenza,
> là dov' io era, ancor non appariva:
> però non ebber li occhi miei potenza
> di seguitar la coronata fiamma
> che si levò appresso sua semenza. (XXIII, 112–13, 115–20)

The last of the variations is played in the Empyrean itself, beyond the limits of space and matter. Dante turns to Beatrice at his side – and finds St Bernard! The saint directs his anxious gaze up to Beatrice's throne in the third highest tier of the Celestial Rose. She is now 'more distant from the sight of his mortal eye than is the bottom of the ocean from the uppermost region of the atmosphere where the thunder rolls'. But it makes no difference, 'because her likeness is not "mixed" by the medium' as it travels down towards him.

> Da quella regïon che più sù tona
> occhio mortale alcun tanto non dista,
> qualunque in mare più giù s'abbandona,
> quanto lì da Beatrice la mia vista;
> ma nulla mi facea, ché süa effige
> non discendëa a me per mezzo mista. (XXXI, 73–8)

There is no atmosphere in Paradise to be darkened or coloured by exhalations. And in any case we have already been informed that the very rules of geometry have no validity in the Empyrean. No subtended angle is too large or too small.[17]

> La vista mia ne l'ampio e ne l'altezza
> non si smarriva, ma tutto prendeva
> il quanto e 'l quale di quella allegrezza.
> Presso e lontano, lì, né pon né leva:
> ché dove Dio sanza mezzo governa,
> la legge natural nulla rileva. (XXX, 118–23)

My sight was untroubled by the height and breadth of Paradise, and I could encompass all its joyfulness in every dimension and quality. In that place, near or far can neither add nor take away. Where God rules without any intermediary, the laws of nature have no sway.

'La vigilia dei nostri sensi'[18]

We pass on now to the kinds of error and delay that arise because seeing takes place not in the eye, but in the *sensus communis* in the front of the brain. The visual impressions are pre-eminent, as we noted earlier, but they have to compete for attention with impressions arriving from the other external senses, and also with images and 'intentions' proceeding from the *imaginativa* or the *memoria sensitiva* under the influence of the passions or the mind.

We saw earlier that an animal must have just one 'master' sense, if only because the whole organism is a unit and must move in one direction in response to the feelings aroused by the perception of other bodies. However favourable the lighting conditions, and however close a *corpus coloratum* may be, it will not be apprehended in the *sensus communis* unless this is fully attentive to the incoming 'visible form'. And there are many occasions where Dante shows his awareness of the possible impediments. The seat of the *vis apprehensiva* may be clouded with wine or weighed down by drowsiness or fatigue. A swoon will 'close the mind'. Sleep acts as a 'fetter' to bind the senses (*ligamentum sensus*); and 'the eye does not see when the body lies bereft of all feeling'.[19]

Pleasures and pains, or emotions like fear and anger, may effectively block the reception of subsequent impressions, until such time as the heart – the seat of the *vis appetitiva* – restores what Dante calls the 'power of outside', 'la virtù di fuori'. A lover will carry the image of his lady permanently 'painted' or 'sculpted' in his heart, contemplating that image to the exclusion of all external objects. The rational faculties may be absorbed in the processes of pure speculation, or they may be wholly taken up by the pursuit of a train of practical reasoning unconnected with the immediate circumstances, so that the contemporaneous input from the corporeal senses is simply ignored. In ecstasy or rapture, as described in *Paradiso* XXIII, the whole mind is 'enlarged' and seems 'to go outside itself', returning with no recollection of its experiences.[20]

Intentiones stored in the memory may supplant the incoming images rather than collaborate with them in the process of identification. The *imaginativa* may flood the consciousness with images, either in response to its own capricious promptings, or under the 'dictation', so to speak, of some outside spiritual agent, such as a demon or an angel; and the resultant fantasies or visions may occupy the mind and 'so confine it within itself that nothing coming from outside will be received'. Another, more common possibility is that one of the external senses may 'turn the mind to itself so strongly' that all the others will be 'extinguished'. Seeing can 'make hearing vain', and listening can make one oblivious of the passing of time. Even more strikingly, concentration on one object within the potential field of vision can erect a 'wall of indifference' on either side, rendering everything else invisible.[21]

Dante was also acutely aware of the importance of expectation and association in sense perception and of the synaesthetic illusions to which they can give rise. The wolf of our fable in chapter 4 assembled a composite image of the lamb as something odoriferous, bleating and white; and if he were simply to catch sight of the lamb subsequently, he might be deceived into thinking he could smell it and hear it, even if it were well upwind. Similarly, when Dante is gazing enraptured at the miraculously expressive relief carving of King David dancing in front of the Ark of the Lord, his eyes tell him that he can hear singing and smell incense, but his ears and nose disagree:[22]

> Dinanzi parea gente; e tutta quanta,
> partita in sette cori, a' due mie' sensi
> faceva dir l'un 'No', l'altro 'Sì, canta.'
> Similemente al fummo de li 'ncensi
> che v'era imaginato, li occhi e 'l naso
> e al sì e al no discordi fensi.   (*Purg.* x, 58–63)

In the foreground there were people, divided into seven choirs, and all of them made my two senses exclaim: 'No, they're not singing', and 'Yes, they are.' Likewise, my eyes and nose were at odds with respect to the smoke of the incense that was imaged there.

Co-operation

Anachronistically, the external and internal senses might be compared to the many reporters and sub-editors who work to produce a newspaper, recording and interpreting the events of the day under the direction of a single editor – the reason. It is only when the editor is weak, or the pressure of news unusually great in some time of crisis, that the necessity of sharing a single office – the common sense – may produce the kind of confusion or paralysis that Dante noted with such evident fascination.

In normal circumstances, the different members of the team – be they journalists or senses – complement each other through their various specialisations in order to produce a fuller and more accurate account of the outside world than could be assembled by any one of them working alone. And Dante also took delight in representing the many ways in which the senses co-operate with each other, by giving assistance when required, or by deputising for a colleague who has been prevented from filing his report.[23]

In the *Comedy*, it is the protagonist's recollection of an Aesop fable that sets him thinking about the likely reaction of a group of devils after they have been baulked of their prey. His thought process redoubles his fear; his fear produces a vivid mental image of pursuit in his *imaginativa* ('io li *'magino* sì, che già li *sento*'); and this in turn disposes him to run away or hide, even before he does in fact catch sight of the devils 'with their wings outspread, not far away, trying to catch us'.[24]

As Dante prepares to leave the cornice of the Proud in Purgatory he feels the guardian angel's wing brush his forehead. Shortly afterwards, he is given cause to wonder at the effect of that fleeting contact. He therefore lifts his hand to his brow to 'ascertain' whether one of the seven Ps (inscribed there by the Keeper of the Gate) has indeed been wiped away. And in this way 'his hand helps to make sure, and searches and finds, and carries out the task which cannot be accomplished by the sense of sight':[25]

> per che la mano ad accertar s'aiuta,
> e cerca e truova e quello officio adempie
> che non si può fornir per la veduta. (*Purg.* XII, 130–2)

A little later Dante is unable to see his guide because of the dark smoke on the third circle of Purgatory. He can still 'keep in touch', however, by placing his hand on Virgil's shoulder. But the first spirit whom they encounter as a disembodied voice in the smoke has to be content with 'audition', consoling himself with the reflection that 'if smoke prevents us from seeing, hearing will keep us joined in its place' ('l'udir ci terrà giunti in quella vece').[26]

The sense of hearing acts as a kind of permanent watchdog, whose task it is to rouse the mind and direct the eyes towards any new object of concern in the vicinity.[27] The stimulus may be a clap of thunder, such as the 'greve tuono' that wakens Dante from his swoon in the first circle of Hell. It may be the quiet words spoken by his companion at his side. It may be a 'cry', a 'lament', a 'confused sound' or the 'fearful roaring' of a wind.[28] Or it may even be a thunderous horn call – a summons which had the effect, we are told, of directing *all* Dante's eyes to one place:

> Quiv' era men che notte e men che giorno,
> sì che 'l viso m'andava innanzi poco;
> ma io senti' sonare un alto corno,
>   tanto ch'avrebbe ogne tuon fatto fioco,
> che, contra sé la sua via seguitando,
> dirizzò li occhi miei tutti ad un loco.   (*Inf.* XXXI, 10–15)

There it was less than night and less than day, so that my sight went only a little way ahead of me; but I heard a horn ring out so loudly that it would have made any peal of thunder seem faint; and by following the path of the sound backwards, my eyes were directed all to one spot.

This teamwork of the senses is even more splendidly illustrated and exploited for the purposes of narrative suspense in Dante's description of his flight down to the eighth circle of Hell on the back of the monster, Geryon. The body of the monster blocks his vision below, but his sense of touch enables him to feel the passage of air across his face and from underneath, and thus to become aware that he is both wheeling and descending (the verb 'accorgersi' denotes apprehension of the common sensible of movement).

> Vidi ch'i' era
> ne l'aere d'ogne parte, e vidi spenta
> ogne veduta fuor che de la fera.
>   Ella sen va notando lenta lenta;
> rota e discende, ma non me n'accorgo
> se non che al viso e di sotto mi venta.   (*Inf.* XVII, 112–17)

I saw I was airborne on all sides, and saw my sight of everything except the beast snuffed out. It was 'swimming' very slowly, wheeling and descending, although I was only made aware of this by the wind blowing across my face from below.

A generic natural noise – the roar of a waterfall at the foot of the precipice – prompts him to lean out and look down. In this way he is able to register the torments of the damned, seeing them as flames and hearing them as lamentations (a noise specific to human beings). Fear of falling makes him huddle back ('raccosciarsi' could also refer to gripping his mount more tightly with his thighs); but by now he is so close to the ground that he can actually 'see' the spirals of his descent, because the torments keep changing sides as they draw nearer.

> Io sentia già da la man destra il gorgo
> far sotto noi un orribile scroscio,
> per che con li occhi 'n giù la testa sporgo.
> Allor fu' io più timido a lo stoscio,
> però ch'i' vidi fuochi e senti' pianti;
> ond' io tremando tutto mi raccoscio.
> E vidi poi, ché nol vedea davanti,
> lo scendere e 'l girar per li gran mali
> che s'appressavan da diversi canti.　　　(*ibid.*, 118–26)

To the right, I could already hear the dreadful roar of the waters beneath us, so that I leaned out with my head to look down. Then I became even more afraid of falling, because I could see fires and hear lamentations; and so I shrank back again, trembling all over. And then I saw – not having seen it before – the circling and the descent, through the great torments that were drawing closer, now on one side, now on the other.

Looking and seeing

These two passages from the *Inferno* serve not only to exemplify collaboration between the senses, but also to reaffirm the primacy of the sense of sight. A sound may restore or heighten consciousness; the mind becomes attentive and forms conjectures; but it is the eyes that will be directed to search for confirmation or more precise information. Seeing is believing.[29] And of all the stages in the complex sequence of operations that culminates in a successful act of vision ('visione verace'), it is the moment of 'seeking', 'searching' or simply 'looking' that Dante describes most often and with the greatest vigour and originality of expression.[30]

First, the whole body must be 'disposed' to see by halting, moving forward, standing up, turning round or leaning out, as the circumstances require.[31] The eyes (alias 'gaze', 'sight' or 'brows') may have to be raised, lowered, directed to the right, to the left or to the other side, or simply made to scan all round.[32] The mind must be applied; indeed, both mind and eye must be 'attentive' and 'intent'.[33]

Next, there begins the phase variously called 'seeking', 'examining', 'eyeing', 'staring steadily' or 'fixing the gaze'.[34] The eyes may have to be 'unbarred', 'opened wider' or 'sharpened', and the eye-string or optic nerve pointed in the desired direction.[35] Dante will then 'move with his gaze', 'cross beyond with his eyes, while his feet remain still', 'get there with his eyes before *he* does', 'move off with his eyes', 'thrust his sight forward', 'proceed with the "course" of his gaze' or 'lead his eyes afar'.[36]

In the *Convivio*, Dante had mentioned the theory of vision, attributed to 'Plato and other philosophers', according to which the 'visive power' of the soul goes out towards the visible object, instead of the visible passing into the eye ('Veramente Plato e altri filosofi dissero che 'l nostro vedere non era perché lo visibile venisse a l'occhio, ma perché la virtù visiva andava fuori al visibile'). This Dante rejected on the authority of Aristotle ('questa oppinione è riprovata per falsa dal Filosofo'). But the sheer number and power of these metaphorical locutions show that he fully understood the psychological truth of Plato's theory.[37]

Before the eye can 'tell' or 'give the answer', it may have to 'struggle' in order to 'disentangle' the visible form.[38] But it must persist until it can 'reach' the object, 'clash' with it, make out the 'figure' and 'recognise' the species or the individual.[39] Only then will it have achieved the purpose for which the sense of sight exists, which is to 'discern', that is, to 'know the differences between things, inasmuch as they are coloured on the surface'.[40]

Cognition and recognition in Antepurgatory

We have seen that Dante's habit of dwelling on the mechanism of perception has the effect of keeping *our* minds in suspense ('l'animo sospeso'), and of forcing us to apply our minds intently in order to apprehend and to comprehend the images which he is seeking to arouse in our imagination through the medium of his verse. The time has now come (as promised earlier) to analyse the ways in which Dante involves us in the process of discovery by freely combining the different sources of error and delay, which we have been examining in somewhat artificial isolation. And there could be few better examples of what we might call 'sensational' narrative than the recurrent scenes in which the protagonist has no difficulty at all in identifying a new *obiectum* as a member of the human species, but fails to recognise immediately the soul as an individual. Let us begin with two scenes from Antepurgatory.

Having left the shore of the island of Purgatory, the two poets come to the foot of the mountain, where Virgil seeks directions from a group of souls who are presented very much as a 'collectivity' (the words used are 'gente', 'popolo', 'mandra').[41] One member of this group asks Dante to consider carefully whether or not he can recognise him.

> E un di loro incominciò: 'Chiunque
> tu se', così andando, volgi 'l viso:
> pon mente se di là mi vedesti unque.'
> Io mi volsi ver' lui e guardail fiso.   *(Purg.* III, 103–6)

And one of them began: 'Whoever you are, *turn your face* while you continue walking, and *reflect* whether you ever *saw* me in the world.' I *turned towards* him and *looked* at him *steadily.*

The numerous and very explicit references here to the preliminary stages in the process of perception (italicised for convenience in the translation) prepare us for the more subtle sequence of impressions conveyed in the two following lines, where we are taken into the protagonist's *sensus communis* in order to register – in a plausible sequence – the un-Italian colour of the speaker's hair, his good looks, his air of nobility and the distinctive slash of a scar above one eye. These four observations (a proper visible, a common sensible and two 'assessments') are more than sufficient to produce a negative result, that is, to convince the protagonist that he has not seen his interlocutor before: cognition, yes; *re*cognition, no.[42]

The fact is, however, that we also claim to recognise people whom we have never seen in the flesh, when, for example, we match the person before us with a mental image formed from a portrait or from a verbal description (hence: 'Dr Livingstone, I presume'). This is the kind of recognition that the protagonist still fails to make, even after he is given a further clue. And so the speaker finally has to identify himself as one of the protagonist's political heroes: a king of southern Italy, who had been killed in battle against the invading French when Dante was still a babe in arms; the grandson of an empress; the last man to resist the unholy alliance between the Pope and the usurping house of Anjou – Manfred. Recognition, in this secondary sense, is delayed no further:

> Biondo era e bello e di gentile aspetto,
> ma l'un de' cigli un colpo avea diviso.
>   Quand' io mi fui umilmente disdetto
> d'averlo visto mai, el disse: 'Or vedi';
> e mostrommi una piaga a sommo 'l petto.
>   Poi sorridendo disse: 'Io son Manfredi,
> nepote di Costanza imperadrice.'   (ibid., 107–13)

He was fairhaired, handsome and of noble appearance; but one of his eyebrows had been split by a blow. When I had humbly denied ever having seen him before, he said: '*Look*', and *showed* me a wound high on his chest. Then he said with a smile: 'I am Manfred, grandson of the Empress Constance.'

The protagonist becomes so engrossed by what Manfred has to tell him that he is impervious for a time to visual impressions and incapable of other mental processes. And the narrative resumes at the beginning of the next canto with Dante's longest and most carefully considered statement about the powers of the soul and the possible hampering of one faculty by another:

> Quando per dilettanze o ver per doglie,
> che alcuna virtù nostra comprenda,
> l'anima bene ad essa si raccoglie,
>   par ch'a nulla potenza più intenda;
> e questo è contra quello error che crede
> ch'un'anima sovr' altra in noi s'accenda.   (*Purg.* IV, 1–6)

When one of our faculties is absorbed by pleasures or pains, the soul may give itself over to this one faculty and seem to ignore all the others (this refutes the mistaken belief that there are several distinct vital principles within us, superimposed one above the other).

> E però, quando s'ode cosa o vede
> che tenga forte a sé l'anima volta,
> vassene 'l tempo e l'uom non se n'avvede;
>   ch'altra potenza è quella che l'ascolta,
> e altra è quella c'ha l'anima intera:
> questa è quasi legata e quella è sciolta.
>   Di ciò ebb' io esperïenza vera,
> udendo quello spirto e ammirando;
> ché ben cinquanta gradi salito era

lo sole, e io non m'era accorto.   (*ibid.*, 7–16)

And so, when something is either seen or heard that imperiously demands the attention of the soul, one is unaware of the passing of time. This is because the faculty that perceives time is distinct from the one that is totally occupying the soul, the former being disengaged, the latter tied down. I had authentic experience of this as I listened in wonder to the spirit, because the sun had climbed through a good fifty degrees without my noticing.

The second scene takes place at sunset on the same day. The reciprocal act of recognition required and finally performed is one of the more familiar kind when two acquaintances meet in strange surroundings after a long interval. And in this case it is slow to happen not only because the light is fading, but also because each of the two has to overcome an initial incredulity. Once again, the effort and the delay in recognition on both sides are enacted for the reader through an insistence on the conditions and processes which concern us (and again, it should be sufficient to indicate these by italicising the relevant words or phrases in the translation).

Dante and Virgil have been standing on a mountain path looking down into a very shallow valley, which is set apart for the souls of European rulers who delayed repentance because of their preoccupation with political affairs. Now they are invited by Sordello to go down into the valley and converse with these 'grandi ombre'.

> Solo tre passi credo ch'i' scendesse,
> e fui di sotto, e vidi un che mirava
> pur me, come conoscer mi volesse.
> Temp' era già che l'aere s'annerava,
> ma non sì che tra li occhi suoi e ' miei
> non dichiarisse ciò che pria serrava.
> Ver' me si fece, e io ver' lui mi fei:
> giudice Nin gentil, quanto mi piacque
> quando ti vidi non esser tra ' rei!   *(Purg.* VIII, 46–54)

I think I took only three steps downwards and I was at the bottom. And I *saw* one of the spirits *looking only at* me, as if he were *trying* to *recognise* me. It was already so late that the *air* was growing *dark*, but it was not yet so dark *between his eyes and mine* that it did not *disclose* what it had been keeping *locked away*. He *turned towards me*, and I *turned towards him*: Oh Nino, judge and gentleman, how I rejoiced when I *saw* you were not among the damned!

109

The moment of recognition itself is not portrayed: it is presupposed in the expression of the joy it causes. The feelings of the protagonist at the time merge with those of the narrator in the present, thanks to the apostrophe and exclamation that seem to burst from his lips as he recalls the scene. And the emotion of joy is mingled with that of relief, because the protagonist clearly had every reason to suppose that his friend had incurred damnation.[43]

Cognition and recognition in Hell

The full significance of Dante's relief, or of Manfred's smile, will emerge all the more forcibly if we return to Hell and examine the representation of the sensory processes in the best known of all these scenes, in which Dante's recognition of the character involved became possible only after the character's recognition of *him*.

Two stone dykes carry a canalised section of the infernal river across a desert of sand in the seventh circle of Hell; and Dante and Virgil were using one of the dykes as a raised pathway. Flakes of fire were falling from above, but the two poets were protected from them by exhalations rising from the boiling, red 'waters' of the canal. They had already gone a considerable distance when they 'met a group of souls, approaching along the line of the dyke; and each of them was *looking at* us, as people do in the *evening* when the *moon* is new':

> quando incontrammo d'anime una schiera
> che venian lungo l'argine, e ciascuna
> ci riguardava come suol da sera
> guardare uno altro sotto nuova luna.   (*Inf.* xv, 16–19)

Light is always deficient in Hell, and the exhalations constituted a further external obstacle to vision. The advancing souls were accustomed to these conditions, but even they had to make a conscious effort to overcome the gloom, and 'they were *sharpening their brows* in our direction, just as an old tailor does at the eye of the needle':

> e sì ver' noi aguzzavan le ciglia
> come 'l vecchio sartor fa ne la cruna.   (*ibid.*, 20–1)

Conditions were so poor that Dante was 'recognised by one of the group' only when the soul was close enough to 'seize him by the hem of the coat, as he called out: "What marvel is this"!'

> Così adocchiato da cotal famiglia,
> fui conosciuto da un, che mi prese
> per lo lembo e gridò: 'Qual maraviglia!' (ibid., 22–4)

The protagonist's difficulties were of a different order, because the soul who challenged him had been cruelly disfigured by the rain of fire. And the six-line sentence that follows enacts, clause by clause, all the effort and attendant pain felt by Dante as he slowly pierced the barrier of the burnt and charred features, matched the present disfiguration with 'the beloved and father-like image' conserved in his memory, and reached down with his hand, in an answering gesture, to touch the soul's face – before identifying him to the reader in what must be the simplest and most poignant rhetorical question in the whole of Italian literature:

> E io, quando 'l suo braccio a me distese,
> ficcaï li occhi per lo cotto aspetto,
> sì che 'l viso abbrusciato non difese
>   la conoscenza süa al mio 'ntelletto;
> e chinando la mano a la sua faccia,
> rispuosi: 'Siete voi qui, ser Brunetto?' (*ibid.*, 25–30)

For my part, when he reached up his *arm* towards me, I *fixed my eyes* on his features, so that the scorched face did not deny *recognition* to my *intellect*; and lowering my *hand* to his face, I said: 'Are you ... here ... Master ... Brunetto?'

The narrator as chorus, commentator, accomplice and composer

After analysing so many examples of 'sensational' narrative, it may be as well to repeat that Dante-the-author never restricts himself literally and totally to the viewpoint of the protagonist, or to the sequence of the impressions he received. It is wholly typical of his flexibility and tact, for example, that the final disclosure of the names of Nino and Brunetto should have been prepared by two long phrases which presuppose the standpoint of the narrator. Moreover, there are many passages where it is unproductive to distinguish the implied perspectives, if only because the two Dantes who take an active part in the poem (neither of whom is to be identified with the author) are simply the same person represented during and after a week-long adventure which radically changed his personality. But before allowing the distinction to lapse and the gap to close, it may be helpful to heighten the contrast between the two Dantes – the protagonist and the narrator – by identifying some of the ways in which the second Dante asserts himself.

What, then, are the main reasons for those innumerable shifts from the past tenses of narration and description to the present tense of commentary and reflection, and what are the roles that Dante plays when he steps forward into the limelight, so to speak, to place himself between the audience and the action on the stage?

First, the narrator periodically suspends the flow of his story in passages where he speaks as a theorist of language, a theorist who is acutely aware that no system of half-sensual, half-rational signs will ever be able to convey phenomena which transcend the senses and the reason. And these moments are closely related to the occasions when he intervenes as poet, to declare that he will now have to wrestle harder than ever in order to make his words 'cousins to the deeds', or when he invokes the Muses, Apollo or God with a plea for inspiration to make good his deficiencies.[44]

Second, he will brusquely interrupt the narrative with apparently spontaneous outbursts of emotion (the earliest comes in the fourth line of the poem), which are occasioned by his recollection of the joys of Paradise, or, more often, by his recollection of the terrible penalties that will be visited on human blindness and perversity in Purgatory and Hell. In these cases he assumes the role of a moralist, educator, preacher or even prophet; and the most conspicuous symptom of his presence will be the rhetorical figure of apostrophe – the words, in this case, being addressed directly to his 'lettore', urging him to take note of some life-saving truth.

Third, the narrator declines to present himself as set apart from, or set above, the rest of humanity. He is at pains to establish that he too has lived in our familiar world, that he has seen and felt what we have seen and felt, and that he has read the same books. He will therefore stand back, momentarily, from straightforward reportage and cast about for analogies, parallels and comparisons drawn from this area of shared experience, comparisons that will convey at least a general notion of the unique and transcendental phenomena in the world beyond the grave. And this, very roughly, is the stance he adopts in the five hundred and more similes in the poem, or in the countless references to legend, to history and to other men's poems.

Lastly (and here it is perhaps artificial to distinguish the 'narrator' from the 'author'), he reveals himself as someone very like the composer of a complex musical work. He prides himself on scoring in such a way that the melody always emerges clearly, but he uses his mastery of harmony and counterpoint to introduce counter-subjects, to reiterate leitmotifs, to establish thematic links with other episodes and, in general, to ensure that every part is integrated into the whole. And in this function, his main stylistic resources are allusion, self-quotation, periphrasis and, above all, patterns of metaphor.

It would obviously be possible to analyse the 'foregrounding' of the narrator with greater finesse by introducing further refinements; and, equally obviously, it would be possible to devote whole chapters to his interventions as poet or preacher, and whole books to his use of simile and metaphor. But even the four rough-and-ready categories just suggested will provide enough scaffolding for the analysis of one last sequence from *Purgatorio*, which is offered as a sample of a kind of reading that would yield similar insights into many other stretches of narrative in the poem.

The passage comes at the end of the tenth canto, and has been chosen to complement and counterbalance the episode discussed at the beginning of this chapter. Both are given over to the approach of something mysterious. But whereas in the earlier canto we were concerned to isolate the successive stages in the protagonist's perception, here we shall study them in the context of the narrator's interventions. We shall consider the interplay between the two perspectives, and admire the skill with which Dante combines 'field recordings' and 'studio commentary' in such a way that the element of suspense is heightened and prolonged rather than dissipated.

'I don't know what': the techniques of suspense in Purgatorio X, 97–139

Dante and Virgil have passed through the Gate of Purgatory and climbed to a deserted terrace, about eighteen feet wide, apparently circling the mountain. On the white marble of the rock face they have found three sculptures in low relief, representing actions of great humility in the lives of the Virgin Mary, King David and the Emperor Trajan. The images are the handiwork of God himself (he is the 'fabbro' of line 99), and are carved with such remarkable expressiveness that the figures seem to move, sing and speak. But they are nevertheless motionless, and it is the protagonist who must move from one scene to the next in order to see them better.[45]

When the narrative resumes, the protagonist is still absorbed in delighted contemplation of the divine images. As so often, however, his attention is deflected towards a new source of impressions by the almost inaudible words that Virgil speaks as if to himself (syntactically, the spoken words interrupt the sentence, coming without explanation between the opening temporal clause and the main verb which governs them, thus mimicking the way in which they penetrated Dante's consciousness). In effect, Dante is invited to look in a certain direction and to register a number of shapes (already identified as human beings, 'molte genti'), who are advancing painfully slowly. (As in earlier passages, the terms relating to the mechanics of perception will be italicised in the translation without further comment.)

> Mentr' io mi dilettava di guardare
> l'imagini di tante umilitadi,
> e per lo fabbro loro a veder care,
>   'Ecco di qua, ma fanno i passi radi',
> mormorava il poeta, 'molte genti:
> questi ne 'nvïeranno a li alti gradi.'   (*Purg.* x, 97–102)

While I was taking *delight* in *looking* at the *images* of such perfect humility (precious to *look* at, too, for their sculptor's sake), the poet murmured: '*Look*, on this side, a host of people, but taking slow steps. They'll direct us to the high levels.'

The next terzina first lingers on the delight and longing felt by Dante, enacting his reluctance to tear his attention away from the images. Then it quickens in rhythm to register the urgency of his impulse to look in the desired direction (which is, as we saw, the first banal, but indispensable, phase in vision).

> Li occhi miei, ch'a mirare eran contenti
> per veder novitadi ond' e' son vaghi,
> volgendosi ver' lui non furon lenti.   (*ibid.*, 103–5)

My *eyes*, which in their eagerness to *see* strange sights had been *gazing* in contentment, were not slow in *turning towards* him.

Now comes the first interruption and change of viewpoint, as the narrator steps forward with a quietly spoken admonition to the reader. This serves to recall the purpose of the whole poem –

namely, to induce a 'proposal' for reform — and to develop the central leitmotif of justice, by means of an allusion to the Day of Judgement and of a metaphor ('to pay the debt') which introduces the concept of retribution. Simultaneously, however, the apostrophe advances the story by making it clear that the visual mystery concerns not the identity of the distant and slowly approaching shapes — we already know they are 'genti' — but the nature of the penalty they have to pay. And by referring to the passion which is likely to follow perception when the *reader* hears of the 'forma del martire', Dante also manages to suggest the passion which the *protagonist* felt on seeing it:

> Non vo' però, lettor, che tu ti smaghi
> di buon proponimento per udire
> come Dio vuol che 'l debito si paghi.
> Non attender la forma del martìre:
> pensa la succession; pensa ch'al peggio
> oltre la gran sentenza non può ire.   (*ibid.*, 106–11)

Reader, I do not want you to be deterred from your good resolution by hearing how God wants the debt to be paid. Pay no attention to the form of the suffering; think of the outcome; remember that, at the worst, it cannot last beyond the Day of Judgement.

The next three terzinas transport us back to the there and then through the direct quotation of the words exchanged between Dante and Virgil (in theory, this is the only way to exclude the editorial perspective of the narrator). But the focus remains on the delayed process of perception, since the poets tell each other of the difficulty each is having, or has had, in interpreting whatever it is that is drawing nearer while they are talking. Dante's sight is 'vain'; he can certainly 'see something moving, but they do not look like people, and he does not know what'. Virgil, too, refers to the 'struggle' his eyes have undergone, and insists that Dante will have to 'look fixedly' in order to see 'the differences between things'. But Virgil has solved the visual puzzle of the numerous, moving shapes, and he now gives the answer — if in very generic terms. The 'people' are hard to recognise as such, because they are bent double 'under those stones':

> Io cominciai: 'Maestro, quel ch'io veggio
> muovere a noi, non mi sembian persone,
> e non so che, sì nel veder vaneggio.'

> Ed elli a me: 'La grave condizione
> di lor tormento a terra li rannicchia,
> sì che ' miei occhi pria n'ebber tencione.
>   Ma guarda fiso là, e disviticchia
> col viso quel che vien sotto a quei sassi:
> già scorger puoi come ciascun si picchia.'   (*ibid.*, 112–20)

I said: 'Master, what I can *see moving* towards us doesn't *look like* people: and I don't know what it is, I'm so blank in my *sight*.' And he answered: 'The grievous condition of their torment crushes them to the ground, so that my *eyes* had to *struggle* at first. But *look closely* there, and *unravel* with your *sight* what is advancing beneath those stones. You can already *make out* how each is beating his breast.'

By the end of Virgil's speech, the 'persone' are close enough for the protagonist to distinguish their individual arm movements. But the figures will not be brought into sharp focus, in close-up, until after another, even longer interruption by the narrator. This time he is more impassioned, apostrophising all proud Christians with an exclamation that develops into two elaborate rhetorical questions. The style is that of the university preacher, at once learned and highly metaphorical. The overlapping metaphors allow the narrator not only to enlarge upon the crucial image of the butterfly, but also to weave in two other recurrent motifs – that of a journey that leads *away* from the desired destination, and that of the diseases that can affect *mental* vision. And in this flurry of imagery, we scarcely notice that we have been given the broadest of hints that the approaching penitents are the souls of the proud – 'superbi':

> O superbi cristian, miseri lassi,
> che, de la vista de la mente infermi,
> fidanza avete ne' retrosi passi,
>   non v'accorgete voi che noi siam vermi
> nati a formar l'angelica farfalla,
> che vola a la giustizia sanza schermi?
>   Di che l'animo vostro in alto galla,
> poi siete quasi antomata in difetto,
> sì come vermo in cui formazion falla?   (*ibid.*, 121–9)

Presumptuous Christians, wretched in your misery, distempered in the *eyes* of your mind, striding out so confidently backwards, do you not realise that we are caterpillars, born to form the angelic butterfly, which soars up unprotected to the judgement-seat? What is it that buoys your minds up so high, since you are like insects with something missing, like caterpillars who fail to form the butterfly!

The voice now becomes quieter and the tone as precise and matter-of-fact as that of a guide book. The narrator is still in the foreground, still between us and the 'forme visibili', but he now assumes the helpful role of a man with a talent for seeing comparisons. We are invited to imagine an Atlas figure (as we should now say), that is, a column supporting a ceiling or roof which has been carved to represent a human figure bearing a weight. But the figure he has in mind is utterly unclassical, and very Romanesque, since it is bent double with its knees drawn up under its chest. We are to think of the kind of art – as the narrator remarks in a final delaying parenthesis – which exploits the 'untrue' to create 'true' distress in the viewer. And with that apt characterisation of his own fiction, the narrator at long last establishes the link between his simile and the 'persons' who were 'beating their breasts under the stones':

> Come per sostentar solaio o tetto,
> per mensola talvolta una figura
> si vede giugner le ginocchia al petto,
>   la qual fa del non ver vera rancura
> nascere 'n chi la vede; così fatti
> vid' io color, quando puosi ben cura.   (*ibid.*, 130–5)

Sometimes you see a *figure* acting as a corbel to support a ceiling or roof, with its knees drawn up under its chest, causing real distress in those who see it despite its unreality – that is how I *saw* them, when I *concentrated hard*.

In the last four lines of the canto the narrator takes a step backwards. He does not completely efface himself, however, and this is one of those passages where there is little to be gained by distinguishing too closely between his retrospective view and what the protagonist 'was apprehending' at the time (although it has to be said that perceptual verisimilitude is respected even here: it is only because the souls of the proud come closer and closer that the protagonist is able to differentiate successively the size of their boulders, the consequent degree of 'contraction' and the different intensity of the suffering which he can read in their expressions). Only in the last line do we finally discover 'what it was, that was coming beneath those stones' or why their 'steps were so few and far between'. And this episode is wholly characteristic of the many stages through which the protagonist and the reader have to proceed in partnership, as they pass from the apprehension of 'common sensibles' to the recognition of fellow human beings:

> Vero è che più e meno eran contratti
> secondo ch'avien più e meno a dosso;
> e qual più pazïenza avea ne li atti,
>   piangendo parea dicer: 'Più non posso.'   (*ibid.*, 136–9)

The truth is they were bowed to varying degrees depending on whether they had more or less on their backs; and even the one whose bearing expressed greatest resignation seemed to be saying, weeping: 'I can go no further.'

CHAPTER SEVEN

Imagining and dreaming

'Imaginary sight' and 'sightless view'

All seeing takes place in the brain. But not all seeing is directly caused from without by the action of reflected light, as we should now say; or, as Dante would have said, not all seeing is caused by the action of opaque bodies, colouring the illuminated atmosphere and thus transmitting 'intentional impressions' of themselves through the pupil of the eye, up the optic nerve and into the common sense. And whichever standpoint one adopts, the *Comedy* is in large measure the result of a second kind of seeing in which the brain becomes aware of images arising from within itself.

Modern readers would probably agree that the poem is a product of the creative imagination, recording what Shakespeare called a 'journey in the head'. Earlier readers accepted not only the Renaissance amendment to the title (*The 'Divine' Comedy*), but a tendentious sub-title: 'The *Vision* of Dante Alighieri'. Many of them felt it was the record of a datable vision of the Trinity, divinely inspired and, to some extent, prophetic of future events. And Dante himself, who took such extraordinary pains to suggest that he really did move as a *corpus mobile* through the afterworld and apprehend things with his external organs of sense, reminds us nevertheless at frequent intervals that what he is putting into verse, in a preordained number of pages, are simply those images which have been preserved in his memory.[1]

Dante and his contemporaries were deeply interested in this area of human consciousness; and they distinguished numerous species of secondary vision – including 'second sight' – according to the formal, final and efficient causes of the phenomena. But they also recognised that all these species shared a common nature, and that they all made use of the faculty of the sensitive soul called *imaginativa* or *phantasia* located near the *sensus communis* towards the front of the brain.[2] And this common nature or common modality is familiar to all of us – not just to seers and scholastic philosophers, not just to 'the lunatic, the lover and the poet' – through our nightly experience of sleep. 'To sleep', one might say, 'is *perforce* to dream'. Indeed, the concepts of sleeping and dreaming are so closely associated in Latin, that the word for 'dream', *somnium*, is derived from the word for 'sleep', *somnus*; and the two nouns are still linked by close similarity of sound in Italian ('sogno', 'sonno').[3]

It can therefore be assumed that everyone knows from recurrent personal experience that dream images appear, move and succeed each other with bewildering speed and a total disregard for such factors as the purity of the atmosphère, lighting conditions, the trigonometry of subtended angles or the conditions of corporeal existence. Similarly, everyone will know that dream images are not perceived after an extended process of searching, gazing, conjecturing and matching appearances with reality: the appearance *is* the only reality.[4] And one of the most characteristic and original features of Dante's poetry, throughout his career, is that he was no less concerned with verisimilitude in the representation of secondary vision than he was in that of normal or primary vision.

In the *Comedy*, he draws upon our shared experience of dreaming to lend greater conviction to his accounts of some of the higher or 'ecstatic' visions which the protagonist is granted during his journey. In perhaps the most remarkable sequence, for example, he will report that the vengeful Procne 'appeared as a trace in his *imaginatio*'; that 'a crucified man then plunged into his *phantasia*'; and, most striking of all, that 'when this image burst of its own accord, like a bubble deprived of the water beneath which it was formed, there arose in my vision a girl':[5]

> E come questa imagine rompeo
> sé per sé stessa, a guisa d'una bulla
> cui manca l'acqua sotto qual si feo,
> surse in mia visïone una fanciulla.   (*Purg.* XVII, 31–4)

Finally, we read, 'this imagining collapsed as soon as a light struck my face, far more intense than any we are accustomed to'; but it gave a last flicker 'in just the same way that sleep does when it is suddenly broken by a new light striking on closed eyes, and, being broken, quivers before it expires completely':

> Come si frange il sonno ove di butto
> nova luce percuote il viso chiuso,
> che fratto guizza pria che muoia tutto;
>   così l'imaginar mio cadde giuso
> tosto che lume il volto mi percosse,
> maggior assai che quel ch'è in nostro uso.   (*ibid.*, 40–5)

This is a writer who knew what dreaming is really like from observing what went on inside his own head, as we can confirm by glancing at one further simile from the last canto of *Paradiso*, where the narrator is preparing himself to describe what he can remember of his culminating vision of God. More than the content of the dream, he retains the feeling of intense pleasure – the 'passione impressa':

> Qual è colûi che sognando vede,
> che dopo 'l sogno la passione impressa
> rimane, e l'altro a la mente non riede,
>   cotal son io, ché quasi tutta cessa
> mia visïone, e ancor mi distilla
> nel core il dolce che nacque da essa.   (*Par.* XXXIII, 58–63)

I am like someone who sees while dreaming, and after the dream the state of feeling it aroused persists, whereas the rest does not come back to mind. My vision has faded almost completely; and yet the sweetness it produced still trickles in my heart.

'Nova fantasia' or 'vano imaginare'?

Visions of various kinds had played a dominant part in Dante's poetry from the very beginning. The first sonnet of the *Vita nuova* recounts a disturbing dream – circulated at the time for other poets to interpret – in which the weeping figure of Love carried away his lady, who is still unnamed at this point in the story. The last sonnet is a consolatory vision of the now nameable Beatrice in heaven. It reveals the 'true meaning' of the earlier sonnet, and establishes it retrospectively as prophetic.[6] And the central poem in the design of the 'little book' gives a long account of another, more terrifying dream of Beatrice's death and ascent to heaven – a dream which almost led the sick and delirious poet to betray his secret to the women who were attending him, by calling out Beatrice's name at the climax of his nightmare.

Written when Dante was in his mid-to-late-twenties, this poem, the canzone 'Donna pietosa e di novella etate', is a minor masterpiece of dream literature in its own right; and it demands our attention here, not only because it is the earliest surviving example (or the earliest acknowledged example) of a piece of sustained narrative in verse by the author of the greatest *narratio poetica* in European literature, but also because it shows how early Dante would achieve that distinctive blend of fidelity to his own experience, creative use of contemporary science and profitable 'trading' with the capital bequeathed him by literary tradition.[7]

The first two stanzas constitute a small-scale 'frame-story'. Piecing together the clues, we are soon able to deduce that the scene is set in a sickroom, where the poet (who tells both stories in the first person) was weeping, calling upon Death and talking incoherently. His 'vain words' frightened his attendant – the 'donna pietosa' of the opening line – so that she too burst into tears, thus causing other ladies to come and relieve her; and they gently roused the dreamer from his delirious nightmare at the very moment when he was calling out the name of his beloved:

> Allor lassai la nova fantasia,
> chiamando il nome de la donna mia.
>
> (*Rime* xx, 13–14; *VN* xxiii, 18)

In the second stanza we learn that his voice was so broken by his anguished weeping that the name was unintelligible to his listeners. But shame at his indiscretion made him turn so deadly pale that the ladies competed with each other in their efforts to comfort him and begged him to tell them 'what he had seen that he should be so faint'. The poet agreed; and the remaining four stanzas purport to be the story of what he had seen in his 'nova fantasia', exactly as he told it to the ladies in the room at the time. So much for the 'frame'.

He begins the story-within-the-story by describing his state of mind and his thoughts in the last moments before he lost consciousness. Personifying and dramatising his feelings and faculties in the way he had learnt from Guido Cavalcanti, he tells the ladies that his own fear of dying led him to think of the frailty of human life in general, and then – with a stab of grief in his heart – to recognise that his lady too must die. It was this thought that successively dazed him, caused him to close his eyes, scattered the animal spirits hither and thither and set him 'imagining, lost to all knowledge and truth' ('imaginando / di caunoscenza e di verità fora'). The dream or vision has begun.

From this point the narration is dominated by verbs of 'seeming' and 'appearing', as the images succeed each other with that inconsequential suddenness which we expect in a real dream (and rarely if ever find in earlier literary dreams). The first image to loom up is that of women's angry or indignant faces – no more than faces – who keep calling out 'Death will take her from you':[8]

> 'Visi di donne m'apparver crucciati
> che mi dicean pur: "Morra'ti, morra'ti".'
>
> (*ibid.*, 41–2; *VN* XXIII, 23)

Next – no explanation is given – the narrator 'seemed to be in an unidentifiable place' and to see dishevelled women lamenting in the street. Then the imagery becomes biblical as he 'seemed to see the sun grow dark and the stars come out and both begin to weep, the birds in full flight fall to the ground, and the earth tremble'. And at that moment 'a man appeared, pale and faint', who gave grim confirmation of what had been foreshadowed in the ladies' keening and the cosmic grief. 'What are you doing? Don't you know what has happened? Your lady, who was so beautiful, is dead':

> 'Poi mi parve vedere a poco a poco
> turbar lo sole e apparir la stella,
> e pianger elli ed ella;
> cader li augelli volando per l'are,
> e la terra tremare;
> ed omo apparve scolorito e fioco,
> dicendomi: "Che fai? non sai novella?
> Morta è la donna tua, ch'era sì bella".'
>
> (*ibid.*, 49–56; *VN* XXIII, 24)

Lifting his weeping eyes (we were told in the frame-story that he had cried real tears), he saw angels ascending into heaven, carrying before them a little cloud and singing the one word 'Hosanna'. Next (again, no link is required), the personified figure of Love invited him to come and see 'our mistress' laid out for burial; and the 'false imagining' took him to see his dead beloved, just before her face was

covered with a veil. Her expression of peace and resignation led him
to entreat Death to come and carry him off as well (and again, we
know that he did indeed call on Death aloud). Then, finding himself
alone, and 'all grieving spent', he looked up to heaven once more and
called out his lady's name – this being the moment just before the
ladies called *him*, as we are reminded in the last line of the poem ('voi
mi chiamaste allor, vostra merzede'), which follows immediately and
brings the poem to an abrupt close.

The narrative, then, is convincingly dream-like. And nothing
could be more plausible than that the imagination of a young
Christian should have been nourished by familiar texts from the
Passiontide liturgy, or by mural paintings of the Dormition or the
Assumption of the Virgin.[9] But there are two subtleties in the
handling of the narrative which look forward to the *Comedy* and allow
us an insight into the author's finesse and conscious control.

First, the narrator who tells the dream to the ladies in the
sickroom is sufficiently alert not to reveal the name of his beloved.
Instead, he substitutes an exclamation beginning with the opening
syllables of her name ('*Beato*, anima bella, chi te vede'). Second, the
narrator insists that his imagining was 'false' and 'wide of the truth'.[10]
Of course, he was right in the obvious sense that Beatrice was still
alive at that moment. But any accomplished reader will assume that a
dream recounted in a work of fiction must have some further
significance, either because it portends some future catastrophe in
the plot, or because it is the allegorical or symbolical vehicle of some
universal truth. So, who is right, narrator or reader?

The answer seems to be: both. In the context of the *Vita nuova*, the
poem is clearly one of a whole series of presentiments of Beatrice's
early death; and it exemplifies in its imagery several distinct species
of prophetic dream as recognised in medieval dream-lore. Yet the
sceptical reader is positively encouraged to interpret the dream as
arising from several, overlapping natural causes, again all recognised
in contemporary theory.

Somnium naturale (intrinsecum, corporale)

By Dante's time, the accepted theory of dreams was a compound of
elements drawn from four main sources: (a) traditional Christian
teaching, as found in the works of St Augustine, with its dual concern

to combat superstition and to vindicate the truth of the prophetic visions in the Old Testament and the Revelation of St John; (b) brief appendices to the *De anima* by Aristotle, entitled *On Sleep and Waking, On Dreams* and *On Prophecy in Sleep*; (c) medical writings by Arab physicians and philosophers, chief among them Avicenna; (d) a fifth-century commentary to a very influential fragment by Cicero known as *The Dream of Scipio*.[11]

It will be remembered that the *imaginativa* or *phantasia* (the organ in the brain, to which Dante gave such prominence in our canzone) was first and foremost a storehouse of images deriving from the real world. These images seemed to be 'preserved' – the ambiguous and metaphorical terminology suggests variously 'suspension', 'imprinting' or 'reflection' – in a medium that was either fluid (the blood and the other humours) or vaporous (the animal spirits).[12] It was assumed, further, that the shape and clarity of the preserved images depended on the relative consistency or purity of the material medium, with the result that the medium was treated in effect as a 'coefficient' in the formation of dream images. People of a choleric disposition were thought to have dreams different in kind and even in colour from people of a melancholic disposition; and it was believed that a temporary predominance of choler or black bile could be corrected with the appropriate 'digestives' or 'laxatives', which would restore the images to normal.[13]

During the process of digestion, new blood and spirit were thought to be generated and successively refined in a series of 'coctions', taking place in the stomach, liver and heart. It seemed self-evident that the inevitable impurities in the newly generated materials could be further clouded by intoxicants or by certain kinds of food. Hence, it was a commonplace that dreams which occur in the first hours of sleep, after a heavy meal, were to be attributed to impurities and turbulence in the material medium and had no further significance.[14]

There is, of course, no mention of 'dispositions' or of food in our canzone. But it is made absolutely clear that Dante was running a high fever; and all fevers were thought to affect the purity and proportions of the humours in the body (which is why we still speak of being '*in*disposed', and why medieval doctors resorted so freely to purgatives and blood-letting). At one level, therefore, his vision could have been fairly described as a *somnium naturale* or *somnium corporale*, which is the term used for a dream which had its origin in the flesh rather than in the mind.[15]

Ambient causes in 'Donna pietosa' and Purgatorio IX

In the third and last chapter of his *De somniis*, Aristotle recognises that lights and sounds from the real environment may strike the eyelids and the eardrums of the sleeper, and that these external impressions may mingle with images being re-presented or newly generated within the brain. (He speaks of cocks crowing, where we might think of an alarm clock.) We may therefore suspect that the 'visi di donne' which appeared in the dream – to be followed by the 'donne disciolte' and by the 'donne' who covered Beatrice with a veil – were masked or semiconscious perceptions of the real 'donne' who were physically present at the bedside.[16]

This line of interpretation is made more plausible by the first of Dante's dreams on the mountain of Purgatory, which we must now examine in some detail. After the dream, from which he awoke in a fright, we learn from Virgil that 'while his soul was asleep within him, in the dawn that preceded day', a lady appeared who introduced herself as Lucia – the name is significant – and begged to be allowed to take hold of the sleeping Dante and to 'ease' his climb. She lifted him up, and, as the day became bright, set off with Virgil behind her. Then she set Dante down; and 'she and his sleep departed simultaneously'.[17]

While this was happening, the sleeping Dante 'seemed to see an eagle with golden feathers and wings outspread, hovering in the sky, poised to swoop'. After a complex thought process within the dream, which led the dreamer to recall the highly relevant myth of Ganymede, the eagle 'seemed to circle a little, then to plunge down as terrifyingly as a thunderbolt and to carry me upward to the fiery heaven. There it seemed that both the eagle and I were ablaze. And the imagined fire burnt so fiercely that sleep was broken':[18]

> In sogno mi parea veder sospesa
> un'aguglia nel ciel con penne d'oro,
> con l'ali aperte e a calare intesa;
> (…)
>   Poi mi parea che, poi rotata un poco,
> terribil come folgor discendesse,
> e me rapisse suso infino al foco.
>   Ivi parea che ella e io ardesse;
> e sì lo 'ncendio imaginato cosse,
> che convenne che 'l sonno si rompesse.
>
> (*Purg.* IX, 19–21, 28–33)

Earlier, in the brief introduction, the narrator had thrown us off the scent, preparing us to believe that it was a prophetic dream by insisting that his vision took place at dawn, when, as we have noted, 'the mind travels most freely from the flesh, is less taken up by thoughts, and is almost godlike in its visions'. In recounting the dream, too, he is careful to insist on the verb 'parere' and on the fact that the burning was 'imaginato'.[19]

On the other hand, Aristotle had reported that, in sleep, 'men think it is lightening and thundering when there are only faint echoes in the ears, and that they are walking through fire and are tremendously hot when there is only a slight heating in certain parts; but the true state of affairs becomes obvious when they wake up'.[20] And we are clearly intended to accept that the 'aguglia', 'foco' and 'incendio' of the vision were veiled and magnified perceptions of Lucia and of the light and warmth of the sun; while the sensation of ascent was real, in that the sleeper was being physically carried up from the valley (where he had met Nino Visconti in the gathering gloom) to reach the Gate of Purgatory.

Somnia animalia

The next main class of dream recognised in medieval theory was the *somnium animale*, in which, to quote Aquinas, '*those* things present themselves to a man's imagination while he is asleep, on which his thoughts and affections had dwelt while he was awake'.[21]

Despite the narrator's insistence that, at dawn, 'our mind is least taken up by thoughts', there is more than a hint of a *somnium animale* in Dante's dream of the eagle, because it is unlikely that Ganymede would have occurred to him if he had not been thinking of himself as a mortal who had been singled out by God and who was to be carried to the top of a sacred mountain. And to return to the *Vita nuova*, there can be no doubt that the nightmare in the canzone is to be attributed in part to the invalid's love and fear. We noted earlier that the third stanza of 'Donna pietosa' dwelt on the patient's mental processes before he lost consciousness; and we can now register, in the light of Aquinas' definition, that those processes took the form of a defective syllogism, in which the major premise is dictated by *cogitatio* ('human life is frail') and the minor premise is suggested by *affectio* ('Love wept in my heart'), to reach the dolorous conclusion which forms the substance of the nightmare ('therefore, my lady will die').[22]

For confirmation that Dante did intend us to interpret the canzone in this naturalistic way, we must look forward once again to *Purgatorio* and examine the second of the three nocturnal dreams, which is described at some length in canto XIX.

Stars were beginning to appear as the protagonist left the circle of the Angry (where he had experienced two waking visions); and Dante only just had time to reach the top of the steps leading to the next circle before the sun disappeared completely, making it impossible to proceed. He begged Virgil to make good use of the enforced delay by explaining to him the nature of the vice being purged on the new circle. And, in reply, he received three of the most important doctrinal speeches in the whole poem, in which Virgil describes how perception leads to passion in human beings, and in which he insists, above all, that our reason and our will are not determined by the laws of stimulus and response, so that men are not necessarily bound to pursue, flee or attack the objects they perceive.[23]

As Virgil concludes his third speech (with a promise of further clarifications from Beatrice about the nature of human freedom), we learn that it is almost midnight, and that Dante is beginning to feel 'sonnolento'. His 'sonnolenza' is temporarily banished by the rapid procession of the souls of the penitent slothful.[24] But it overwhelms him again as the last souls disappear; and the narrator gives a wonderfully exact description of the rambling of his thoughts that led into sleep:

> Novo pensiero dentro a me si mise,
>   del qual più altri nacquero e diversi;
> e tanto d'uno in altro vaneggiai,
> che li occhi per vaghezza ricopersi,
>   e 'l pensamento in sogno trasmutai.   (*Purg.* XVIII, 141–5)

A strange thought intruded, from which there arose other and different thoughts; and I slid so unconnectedly from one to the next that I closed my eyes in pleasurable anticipation and changed my thinking into a dream.

At dawn, so we are told in the next canto, a woman 'appeared' who was hideous in every respect – sallow-skinned, squint-eyed, maimed in her hands, bow-legged and unable to speak distinctly. But as the dreamer looked at her, the effect of his gaze was to transform her into a beauty, standing upright, with a pearl-like complexion and possessing a marvellous gift of song that made it difficult for him to turn his attention away. She is a 'sweet Siren', as she herself tells us in a spell-binding song, a seductress whose regular clients rarely abandon her because she gives them such complete satisfaction.[25]

Before the Siren had finished her incantation, however, another woman appeared and reproached Virgil for his inactivity. As a result, the 'dream-Virgil' moved forward, keeping his eyes fixed on the newcomer, who was described as 'swift, saintly and virtuous'. He seized the Siren and tore open her dress to reveal her abdomen – and the stench that escaped caused the dreamer to wake up and hear the real Virgil saying: 'I've already called you at least three times.'[26]

The sun is up. They pass the guardian angel and begin to climb once more. Dante, however, cannot shake off the thought of his 'novella visione'. He walks with his head bowed, pondering on the significance of what he has seen, until Virgil tells him, rather brusquely, to look up, to fix his eyes on God's 'allurements' in the heavens above and to bestir himself.[27] Virgil then reveals that he is aware of the content of Dante's vision, and goes on to give his own interpretation: 'You saw the primeval enchantress who is now left alone to weep over us. And you saw how a man may free himself from her toils':

> 'Vedesti', disse, 'quell'antica strega
> che sola sovr' a noi omai si piagne;
> vedesti come l'uom da lei si slega.'   (*Purg.* XIX, 58–60)

Virgil is perhaps a little peremptory. He might well have tried to interpret the backwardness of his own counterpart in the dream (presumably, it signifies the culpable inertia of reason before it is roused by grace). And he ought to have brought out the lesson – not mentioned in his preceding account of human perception and desire – that it is the *imagination* which confers a false glamour on the goods of this world (which are faithfully represented by the external senses, as the details of the vision made quite clear).[28]

The narrator is perfectly right, however, in giving so much prominence to the verb 'pensare' and the noun 'pensiero' both before and after the dream, because this is a perfect example of a *somnium animale* in which the images arise *ex praecedenti cogitatione*. It reflects very closely the content of Virgil's three speeches; and this is why it is the least dream-like and the most overtly allegorical of all the visions in the poem.[29]

Somnia caelestia: *(a)* oraculum, visio

Medieval laymen and theologians – and most medieval poets – were interested in *somnia naturalia et animalia* only in so far as they had to clear the ground, so to speak, for the study of the visions that really engaged their attention. What they cared about were visions that were presumed to have their efficient cause in some supernatural power (benign or malignant as the case might be) and which were significant in the sense that they foretold future events.

Characteristically, Dante shows interest in the mechanics of the transmission and reception of such dreams. For example, he introduces the second of his waking visions on the circle of the Angry by apostrophising his image-forming faculty to ask, in effect: 'What is the nature of your efficient cause if the senses do not provide the stimulus?'

> O imaginativa che ne rube
> talvolta sì di fuor, ch'om non s'accorge
> perché dintorno suonin mille tube,
>   chi move te, se 'l senso non ti porge?   (*Purg.* XVII, 13–16)

O imagination, who sometimes steals us away so completely from outward things that we notice nothing, even though a thousand trumpets are sounding, who moves you, if the senses do not offer the wherewithal?

And his brief answer shows that he accepts the kind of explanation given by St Albert, who specifies that such visions or dreams are conveyed by a light ray (*lumen radiale*) proceeding from one of the heavenly bodies, either as a component in its normal 'influence', or by the special action of its angelic mover in response to God's will:[30]

> Moveti lume che nel ciel s'informa,
>   per sé o per voler che giù lo scorge.   (*ibid.*, 17–18)

A light moves you that takes its form in the heavens, either of itself or by an act of will that guides it down to earth.

In his commentary to the *Dream of Scipio*, alluded to above, the fifth-century pagan scholar Macrobius divided these *somnia caelestia* into three kinds, all of which are to be found, in some form, in Dante's poetic oeuvre.[31]

Two of them will not detain us long, precisely because they are so straightforward. In the first, which Macrobius calls *oraculum*, a venerable figure, perhaps an ancestor, appears and prophesies the future in a very *un*oracular way; that is, he foretells 'contingent events before they happen in themselves', 'not through tortuous evasions, but in clear words and precise language'.[32] The phrases in quotation marks are taken from the episode in *Paradiso* involving Dante's ancestor Cacciaguida; and the famous prophecy of his descendant's exile would be a perfect example of an *oraculum* if it had been pronounced by him in a dream.

Similarly, Forese Donati's prophecy of his brother Corso's violent end – dragged to his death and horribly disfigured at the heels of his bolting horse – would be a perfect specimen of a *visio* (Macrobius' second subdivision of the *somnium caeleste*), if it had been represented as witnessed in sleep or in a trance, because a *visio* enacts future events exactly as they will occur.[33] And these two rather eccentric examples may illustrate perhaps why there was not usually much scope for the *oraculum* or *visio* in a work of fiction. Both species are, however, vestigially present in the canzone 'Donna pietosa': the *oraculum* is exemplified in the contribution of the 'omo scolorito e fioco', who simply announces 'Your lady is dead'; while the scenes of mourning in the street and in the house constitute a *visio*, because these would certainly have taken place as described when Beatrice did die.[34]

Somnia caelestia: *(b)* somnium

The prophetic dream *par excellence* – and the literary dream *par excellence* – was called, quite simply, *somnium*. In this type the future actors and events are foreshadowed in symbolic forms, very often involving animals or plants. The general import of the dream will usually be clear enough, but the full significance will only appear retrospectively unless there is a qualified interpreter on hand to decode the messages immediately (as Joseph and Daniel did for the visions of Pharoah and Nebuchadnezzar).[35]

This species, too, is present in 'Donna pietosa' thanks to the biblical imagery – the falling birds, the earthquake and the weeping of the sun and stars – through which Dante was able to suggest a daring parallel between the imminent death of his 'gentilissima salute' and the death of the 'Salvatore'.[36] And it is not the least remarkable feature of that astonishing early poem that it exemplifies all three species of the *somnium caeleste*, as well as demanding attention as a *somnium naturale* and a *somnium animale*.

However, the best example in Dante's work of the kind of symbolic forms a medieval reader would have expected to meet in a prophetic dream is to be found in the last fifty lines of *Purgatorio* XXXII.

The triumphant chariot on which Beatrice appeared in the Garden of Eden is drawn by the 'two-natured' Griffin to the foot of the Tree of Forbidden Knowledge and attached to the tree, causing it to burst into blossom. At this highly charged moment, the protagonist is lulled to sleep by a hymn which is intoned by all the members of the sacred procession. Beatrice subsequently invites him to look closely at the chariot and, on his return to earth, to write down what he sees 'for the benefit of the world that lives in sin'.[37]

First, an eagle plummets down, striking the chariot with all its force like a storm buffeting a ship at sea. A scavenging fox briefly occupies the cockpit of the 'triunfal veicolo' until it is driven away by Beatrice. Then the eagle descends again, this time leaving the whole bodywork covered in its feathers. Next, the ground opens beneath the chariot and a serpent attacks it from below, carrying away part of the undercarriage. After this, the feathers spread like rank weeds over the whole vehicle, which sprouts seven horned and monstrous heads. A brazen prostitute takes over the driving seat, accompanied by a giant who is both her pimp and her lover. Finally, the giant savagely beats his mistress when she makes advances to Dante, before dragging her and the chariot away until they are lost to view in the wood.[38]

For the reader well versed in the Book of Revelation and in the medieval prophetic tradition, this extended sequence is the very 'stuff that dreams are made on'.[39] Until recently, however, commentators have interpreted all but the final scenes with reference to the past history of the Church. And even if we accept the powerful arguments in favour of a purely prophetic interpretation, it must be said that Dante's presentation of the phenomena is not in the least dream-like for the very good reason that the protagonist awoke from his induced sleep before the events took place.[40] Whether it is 'retrospective' or 'prophetic', the sequence takes the form of a celestial pageant, not a *somnium*.

'The nightmare that tore the future's veil'

Somewhat surprisingly, perhaps, there are only two prophetic *somnia* in the *Comedy* which might be said to be 'fulfilled' in the action of the poem itself. The first is retold by a sinner near the bottom of Hell, while the second is experienced by the protagonist near the summit of Purgatory; and they are as different in mood and function as the different locations and dreamers would suggest.

The closing lines of *Inferno* XXXII show Dante the protagonist standing over two sinners who are locked together in the frozen lake of Cocytus. One of them is set slightly higher in the ice, such that his head is like a hat to the other, whose skull he is tearing with his teeth, ravenously and bestially, at the place where the brain joins the nape of the neck. Tempted by the protagonist's offer to make the cause of his savagery known in the world above, the aggressor lifts his head, wiping his mouth on his victim's hair, and promises to speak if he can thereby bring 'infamy to the traitor whom he is gnawing'. The dream that concerns us is part of the story that he goes on to tell. And when we are trying to assess its meaning and impact, we must always remember the horror of the scene and the storyteller's declared purpose of revenge, to which every part of his narrative is subordinated.[41]

There is no need for him to explain the context. It will be enough for him to reveal his own name – Count Ugolino – and the name of his victim – Archbishop Ruggieri – for a citizen of Florence to remember the story of their struggle for power during the 1280s in the nearby city-state of Pisa. And it is equally a matter of common knowledge – so Ugolino makes explicit – that he was 'captured and then killed' by Ruggieri, after he had put his trust in him. But that is not the issue. What Dante cannot have heard is the cruel *manner* of his death ('come la morte mia fu cruda'). It is not the treachery, nor the killing, but the inhumanity of the killing that constitutes the 'offence', which is in turn the ground of Ugolino's revenge in Hell and of the revenge he now seeks among the living.[42]

Ugolino was confined in a garret used to cage falcons during the moulting season. His imprisonment had already lasted several months (as he knew from observing the phases of the moon through a narrow window), when he had an 'evil dream' (or an 'evil *sleep*', 'mal sonno') that 'tore aside the veil of the future'.

This is how he describes the apparitions in his prophetic nightmare (he too insists on the verb 'parere'):

> Questi pareva a me maestro e donno,
> cacciando il lupo e ' lupicini al monte
> per che i Pisan veder Lucca non ponno.
> Con cagne magre, studïose e conte
> Gualandi con Sismondi e con Lanfranchi
> s'avea messi dinanzi da la fronte.
> In picciol corso mi parieno stanchi
> lo padre e ' figli, e con l'agute scane
> mi parea lor veder fender li fianchi.   (*Inf.* XXXIII, 28–36)

This man [i.e., Ruggieri, whose mutilated head is only inches away from the speaker's newly wiped mouth] *seemed* to me to be master and lord, hunting the wolf and its cubs over the mountain that prevents the Pisans from seeing Lucca. He was with a pack of bitches – lean, eager and well-trained – and he had placed Gualandi, Sismondi and Lanfranchi in the front. After a brief chase the father and his sons *seemed* exhausted, and I *seemed* to see their flanks torn open by the sharp fangs.

No dream could be more straightforwardly *animale* than one in which a captive nobleman dreams of open spaces, or sees his enemy as leading a hunt in pursuit of a wolf – a not ignoble animal – with whom the dreamer identifies. For that matter, nothing could be more characteristic of a *somnium naturale* than for an underfed prisoner to wake at dawn with pangs of hunger stabbing at his side. The general import of the dream is in any case quite clear: both waking and sleeping, Ugolino was afraid for his life; and any hearer of his tale should weep even to 'think of what his heart foretold'. But why did the dreamer see 'lupicini' as well as the 'lupo'? And why does he anthropomorphise their relationship as 'padre' and 'figli'? What is the precise relationship between the dream and the future whose 'veil' it 'tore aside'? And what can we infer about the possible supernatural causes of the 'mal sonno'?

The answers follow immediately. The count, we now discover, had been incarcerated with his sons. When he awoke from his nightmare, he heard them whimpering in their sleep and asking for bread. It is further made clear that each of the boys had been visited by a similar dream, and that each was seized by a similar dread ('e per suo sogno ciascun dubitava'). And it is in this mood of shared foreboding that they hear not the expected footsteps of the jailer bringing their daily rations, but the door of the tower below being nailed up. In the instant, they know that they are to be left to starve to death.[43]

The sons, as we learn in the harrowing sequel, will die on the fourth, fifth and sixth days. They survive that long in a petrified immobility, broken only by one despairing gesture from the father and by the children falling as they die, and in a total silence, pierced only by three cries from the boys, calling each time on their 'padre' in outbursts of concern for him, of willingness to sacrifice themselves for him and, finally, of reproach ('padre mio, ché non m'aiuti?'). Only then, in the two days of life that remain to him, does the now blind father give vent to his paternal feelings in loud laments and in groping contact with their dead bodies. That was 'how cruel his death was'. That was why he dreamt of 'lupicini', thought of them as 'figli' and saw their lacerated flanks. The 'hard man' was tortured in his only 'soft spot'.[44]

Dante, as narrator, now condemns this barbarous deed in a passionate outburst directed against Pisa (although not before he has reminded us of the disgusting savagery of Ugolino's eternal revenge on Ruggieri's skull). Whatever fate Ugolino himself had deserved, the children were innocent because of their tender years and should not have been 'crucified' in this way.[45]

The choice of expression here at the end of the episode is probably significant. We cannot interpret the dream until we know what happened in the tower room; and the phrase 'posti a tal croce' would seem to suggest that Dante, as author, wants us to judge those agonising days with Jesus' Passion in mind. We are to recall Christ's dying words on the Cross ('My God, my God, why have you forsaken me?'), in order to be reminded, paradoxically, that God does *not* abandon his children in the hour of their death. We are also to recall the moment of human weakness in the Garden of Gethsemane when Jesus prayed, 'My Father, if it be possible, let this cup be taken from me', only to correct himself immediately: 'Nevertheless, not what I will, but what you will.' When the boys offer their father their own flesh to eat, we are to think of Jesus' invitation to his disciples at the Last Supper ('Take, eat, this is my body'). And, in general, we are to meditate on the second and third petitions in the Lord's Prayer ('Our *Father*, which art in heaven, (...) give us this day our daily bread, and forgive us our trespasses, *as we forgive them that trespass against us*' — words which should also call to mind the dying plea of the first martyr, Stephen: 'Lord, do not hold this sin against them').[46]

These apparently remote texts fit the jagged edges of Ugolino's story as closely as the east coast of South America matches the west coast of Africa. They remind us that we all have another Father, in heaven; and that while eight days is a long time to die, it is also a long time to prepare for the inevitable through remorse, forgiveness and mutual comfort. This is the lesson that will be repeated again and again in the first eight cantos of *Purgatorio*, and the message is encapsulated in the words of King Manfred, who received his mortal wounds in battle and who died in contumacy of the Church. His sins, too, were 'horrible'; but he 'yielded himself, weeping, to him who willingly grants his pardon', because God, in his 'infinite goodness, has such broad arms that he welcomes all who turn to him'.[47]

Armed with this kind of authorial insight into the 'future', we can interpret the nature and origin of the 'mal sonno' with more confidence. Considered as part of Ugolino's passionate rhetoric and special pleading, there is no doubt that the dream is the most important element in the first half of his narrative, and there is equally no doubt that it serves to create in the reader a sense of dread and foreboding which makes us hear the nailing up of the door with the same speechless horror with which it was received by Ugolino and his children:

> E per suo sogno ciascun dubitava;
>   e io senti' chiavar l'uscio di sotto
> a l'orribile torre; ond' io guardai
> nel viso a' mie' figliuoi sanza far motto.   (*Inf.* XXXIII, 45–8)

Considered in the light of medieval dream theory, however, the dream would seem to be attributable to a supernatural cause (it does foretell the future; it is sent simultaneously to all five captives; it does 'cover the truth with figures and veil it with *ambages*', exactly as specified in Macrobius' definition). But not all *somnia* are transmitted to the imagination by a 'light that receives its form in the heavens'. Angels would have sent a very different dream which would have touched and influenced their minds in a very different way. And this dream proves to have been 'evil' not just in the sense that it was a nightmare (which is how Ugolino understood it), but because it was inspired by devils to increase the torment of their last days by excluding any kind of hope.[48]

Later in canto XXXIII we are told – in a curiously un-Christian and un-Aristotelian piece of folklore – that a sinner's soul may be carried down to Hell immediately after committing a grave act of treachery, and that a devil will occupy the traitor's body until the time appointed for his natural death.[49] But demons evidently have other, subtler methods of ensuring damnation. They can send dreams which occupy a man's thoughts and feelings to such an extent that he remains spiritually blind to the hope – and the means – of salvation *in extremis*.

'Sleep knows the news before the fact occurs'

Our last example is a *somnium caeleste* which is clearly supposed to have its efficient cause in a '*heavenly* light'. It is described in canto XXVII of *Purgatorio* at a point in the action where Dante is forced to spend the night on the steps above the seventh circle; and it is the last of the protagonist's three nocturnal dreams, complementing and completing the *somnium naturale* of canto IX and the *somnium animale* of canto XIX.

Its content is extremely simple. In the first of four terzinas we are told (with the usual subordination of the action to the verb 'parere') that 'in dream I seemed to see a young and beautiful girl, walking through open country and gathering flowers as she sang':

> Giovane e bella in sogno mi parea
> donna vedere andar per una landa
> cogliendo fiori; e cantando dicea: (...) (*Purg.* XXVII, 97–9)

The rest of the dream is a transcript of the words of the song, in which the singer introduces herself as Leah, and contrasts her own personality with that of her stay-at-home sister Rachel:

> 'Sappia qualunque il mio nome dimanda
> ch'i' mi son Lia, e vo movendo intorno
> le belle mani a farmi una ghirlanda.
>   Per piacermi a lo specchio, qui m'addorno;
> ma mia suora Rachel mai non si smaga
> dal suo miraglio, e siede tutto giorno.
>   Ell' è d'i suoi belli occhi veder vaga
> com' io de l'addornarmi con le mani;
> lei lo vedere, e me l'ovrare appaga.' (*ibid.*, 100–8)

'Should anyone ask my name, know that I am Leah; and I am busying my hands to make myself a garland. I adorn myself so that I may admire myself in the glass, but my sister Rachel never looks away from her

137

mirror and sits there all day long. She is as eagerly content to contemplate her beautiful eyes as I am to adorn myself with my hands. She is satisfied by seeing, just as I am by doing.'

In the prelude to the dream, Dante as narrator had stressed once again that it took place just before dawn, and that 'sleep often knows the news before the fact exists' ('il sonno che sovente, / anzi che 'l fatto sia, sa le novelle').[50] So, once again, we must look ahead in the action of the poem to discover what figures, places and events may be prefigured in the flowery plain and in the activities of the two women, seen and unseen.

At first sight the solution seems obvious enough. In the next canto, the protagonist enters the idyllic, sylvan landscape of the Garden of Eden or Earthly Paradise, situated on the summit of the mountain. There he meets a 'beautiful woman' (later named as Matelda), 'walking alone, singing, selecting flowers from those with which her path was painted', and, in general, putting Dante in mind of Proserpina and the 'flowers that, frighted, she let fall from Dis's waggon'. Two cantos later Beatrice makes her appearance on the chariot drawn by the Griffin.[51] And it has seemed obvious to a majority of commentators that if Matelda is so self-evidently a fulfilment of Leah, then Rachel must be a prefiguration of Beatrice. At this level, then, the dream would simply be an encouraging and hope-inspiring vision of the two imminent encounters in the Earthly Paradise.

There are, however, weighty objections to this interpretation. It is clear from the characterisation of Leah and Rachel in the dream ('belle *mani*' contrasted with 'belli *occhi*', and 'ovrare' contrasted with 'vedere') that the two sisters appear not so much in their original historical reality (the first and second wives of Jacob), as in the allegorical roles consistently assigned to them in medieval exegesis of the Bible. Like the New Testament sisters Martha and Mary, they had long been taken to symbolise the active and the contemplative life. And an Aristotelian would have understood these traditional terms as referring, respectively, to a life exhibiting the '*moral* virtues' and a life devoted to the '*intellectual* virtues'.

Now, we know from texts in the *Convivio* and *Monarchia* that Dante accepted the usual ranking of the active and contemplative lives – the first being 'good', and the other 'better' or 'best'. But these texts also show that he habitually linked them as being jointly conducive to a purely human happiness attainable during our earthly life, and that he habitually contrasted the moral and intellectual virtues with the 'theological' virtues of faith, hope and charity, which are the necessary precondition of a 'transhumanised' happiness in the life eternal. And in the crucial last chapter of *Monarchia*, Dante specifically says that 'the happiness of *this* life', to which we are led 'by acting in accordance with the moral and intellectual virtues' is 'figured in the Earthly Paradise', whereas the second happiness, which 'consists in the enjoyment of the divine countenance to which our own powers cannot attain', is 'figured in the Celestial Paradise'.[52] In the light of these texts, therefore, Matelda and Beatrice would seem to be paired and contrasted as the 'fully human' and the 'transhumanised', and *not*, as Leah and Rachel were, as the active and contemplative lives.

Returning now to our text, we may venture to conclude that every detail in Dante's third dream will be fulfilled in the Earthly Paradise itself. This is the place which, as Matelda herself will say, 'was chosen as the nest for human nature'. The 'landa' of the dream is a prefiguration of the 'divina foresta' so lovingly described in canto XXVIII. And both Leah and Rachel are subsumed in Matelda – herself almost the *genius loci* – who combines in her character the active propensities of the elder sister and the intellectual rigour of the younger (a quality which becomes very evident in her long speech at the end of canto XXVIII).[53] In this last recorded dream, Dante, the *modern* poet, offers a veiled vision of the Earthly Paradise and of the perfect happiness which we forfeited through the Fall at the very beginning of human history. And in so doing – as Matelda hints – he is matching and fulfilling the dreams of the *ancient* poets, who had written about 'the Golden Age and its felicity, of which they had dreamt, perhaps, on Parnassus':[54]

> Quelli ch'anticamente poetaro
> l'età de l'oro e suo stato felice,
> forse in Parnaso esto loco sognaro.   (*Purg.* XXVIII, 139–41)

CHAPTER EIGHT

Body-language and the physiology of passion

Recapitulation and preview

In the final chapter of part one, we established that the senses of smell, hearing and sight are found only in animals which have the power to move themselves from place to place, and that these senses do not exist simply to supply information about the environment for its own sake, but in order to enable the animal to advance towards a distant good or to retreat from a source of harm while it is still imminent, that is, still only 'threatening'. We also saw that the external organs of locomotion – which may be fins or wings as well as legs – are not moved directly by the combined forces of the *vis apprehensiva*. Between seeing and moving lie the two intermediaries of the *aestimativa*, located in the centre of the brain, and the *vis appetitiva*, whose multiple operations are seated in the heart.

The power of 'estimation', it will be remembered, allows the animal to identify the still-remote source of the incoming image as a *bonum* or *malum* and to anticipate the sensations of pleasure or pain which would result from physical contact or 'union' with that source. The appetites are aroused by such anticipations and produce pleasurable or painful feelings of a special kind, commonly called 'passions', of which the most fundamental and familiar are hunger and thirst. A *passio* is simply an *appetitus in actu*. It manifests itself by causing a bodily change (*transmutatio corporalis*) involving expansion or contraction, warming or cooling, drying or moistening. And it serves as the motive force or *vis motiva*, that is, the efficient cause of the muscular movements which activate the limbs by extension, flexion and rotation.

There will be no need for us to inquire closely into Dante's treatment of instinctive judgement in human beings, even though he knew it to be more important than rational deliberation in the case of children and the majority of adults who live their lives 'according to appearances'. Similarly, it will not be necessary to attempt a detailed study of Dante's representation of human locomotion – of the 'steps we take' to pursue a good or to avoid an evil: it is enough to recall that apart from walking, he describes scree-running, sliding, climbs demanding the use of feet and hands, free ascent through interstellar space, and even the experience of night flying and landing by the light of flares.[1]

He did, however, devote a great deal of poetic energy to the representation of the states of pleasure and pain (the *Comedy* is, after all, an account of the eternal torments of Hell, the never-ending delights of Paradise, and the bitter-sweet, temporal penalties of Purgatory). And he was fascinated by the other 'movimenti umani' – those which take place beneath the skin while the body remains stationary. As a young love poet he was already using his knowledge of contemporary psychology and physiology to dramatise the 'pushes and pulls' of the internal powers. Throughout his career, too, he paid close attention to what is now called 'body-language', the involuntary 'corporal transmutations' that reveal our feelings to others, the shifts of expression which 'bear witness to the heart'.[2] And it is with these effects and signs of the passions, considered as 'testimoni del core', that we shall be concerned in this chapter, where we shall focus for the last time on the human being considered as one of the higher animates, a 'self-moving *body*'.

'The new form called shade'

Even when describing the afterlife, Dante is too faithful an Aristotelian and too instinctive a literary artist to confine his attention to the well-being or otherwise of our eternal soul ('la salute dell'anima'). He does not conceive the human being as essentially a disembodied intelligence, or a 'substance separated from matter'. Those are possible definitions of an angel. Man is a *compositum* consisting of a generated body sustained and perfected by a created 'vital principle' – the *anima humana*. And this *principium vitae*, this 'ground of our being', can exist and fulfil itself only if it structures and animates the organs of a material frame.

The protagonist of the *Comedy* sees the spirits of the dead as Orpheus saw them in Virgil's *Georgics* – *umbrae tenues*. So 'tenuous' are they, indeed, that the arms of a living man will seek in vain to hold them in an embrace (again the motif is borrowed from Virgil); and sunlight passes through them without casting a shadow. Both these facts about the spirits are made evident to the reader's senses of touch and sight through consecutive scenes in the second and third cantos of *Purgatorio*.[3] And immediately afterwards Virgil-the-character is made to state explicitly that the dead do have bodies able to suffer torments involving heat and cold, bodies which are like those of the heavenly spheres in that they do not impede the passage of light rays. Virgil also goes on to insist that these transparent but sentient bodies are 'prepared by a Power who does not wish to reveal to us how he brings this about':

> 'i cieli
> che l'uno a l'altro raggio non ingombra.
>   A sofferir tormenti, caldi e geli
> simili corpi la Virtù dispone
> che, come fa, non vuol ch'a noi si sveli.'   (*Purg.* III, 29–33)

Twenty-two cantos later, however, the 'come fa' is revealed by the Christian convert, Statius, and his revelation makes it clear that the mysterious 'virtue' which 'disposes' the shadow-body may in fact be identified with the 'virtute informativa' inherent in the soul itself.

The torment that occasions this later explanation is more subtly devised than those which require no more than ice or fire. The penitent gluttons are as emaciated as they would have been if they had subjected themselves to a starvation diet by way of penance while they were still alive. And the protagonist is puzzled as to how they can become thin ('come si può far magro') where there is no need for nutrition anyway ('là dove l'uopo di nodrir non tocca').[4]

Statius prefaces his reply with a detailed account of the successive processes of generation and creation. The father's blood becomes semen, the semen produces a plant-like embryo in the womb, and the embryo transforms itself into a sponge-like organism capable of sensation and movement. Then, when all the 'powers' have been given their respective instruments or 'organs' – specifically, at the moment when the three chambers of the brain have been articulated – God intervenes directly as Creator to breathe in the breath of human life. This draws all the existing active powers up into itself to become a single vital principle ('un'alma sola') which lives, like a plant, feels, like an animal, and is self-aware, like an angel ('che vive e sente e sé in sé rigira'). At every stage in this account of human embryology, Statius gives special prominence to what is variously called the 'virtute informativa', 'virtute attiva', or simply 'virtù', that is, the 'structuring power' which is inseparable from the notion of 'soul', whether it be generated or created. And the same noun will recur in the main part of his answer.[5]

At the moment of death, the soul dissolves its bond with the flesh. It retains *in virtute* all its generated and created faculties, with this distinction, however: that the *sensitive* powers are temporarily 'muted' (since they have no 'organ' through which to 'express' themselves), whereas the *rational* powers of memory, intelligence and will are more keenly *in actu* than they had been before:

> 'Solvesi da la carne, e in virtute
> ne porta seco e l'umano e 'l divino:
>   l'altre potenze tutte quante mute;
> memoria, intelligenza e volontade
> in atto molto più che prima agute.'   (*Purg.* xxv, 80–4)

When the soul comes to rest in the appropriate circle of Hell or Purgatory, it is 'circumscribed in space' and immediately irradiates its being into the surrounding atmosphere to provide itself with 'members', which are identical in size and shape to those of its earthly body:

> 'Tosto che loco lì la circunscrive,
> la virtù formativa raggia intorno
> così e quanto ne le membra vive.'   (*ibid.*, 88–90)

The concept is arduous, but the imagery of the following lines helps to suspend our disbelief. These combine metaphor and simile to suggest that the soul imprints itself on the air, thanks to its innate 'virtù', and that it thereby produces a 'novella forma', analogous to a rainbow, which follows the spirit to which it owes its being, just as a flame follows the fire from which it springs, or a shadow clings to the solid object by which it is projected. Indeed, the 'new form' is called a 'shade' – 'ombra' – because its appearance is determined by the spirit in the way these images imply.

Having resolved the question of nomenclature, Statius returns to the powers and organs within the 'shade', insisting that it 'provides instruments for each power of sensation up to and including the sense of sight'. Now, at long last, he is ready to answer the protagonist's original question: 'it is from this same source [ultimately, from the innate 'body-forming' power of the soul] that we are able to speak and to laugh and to produce the tears and sighs that you have been able to hear on the mountain. The configuration of the shade varies in accordance with the desires and the other passions that work on it. And this is the cause of the emaciation that puzzles you.'

> 'Però che quindi ha poscia sua paruta,
> è chiamata ombra; e quindi organa poi
> ciascun sentire infino a la veduta.
> Quindi parliamo e quindi ridiam noi;
> quindi facciam le lagrime e ' sospiri
> che per lo monte aver sentiti puoi.
> Secondo che ci affliggono i disiri
> e li altri affetti, l'ombra si figura;
> e quest' è la cagion di che tu miri.'   (*ibid.*, 100–8)

Spirit and blood

Nothing could be more thoroughly 'psychosomatic' than Statius' account of how the soul (*psyche*) irradiates another body (*soma*), equipping it with organs to discharge its functions, and even modifying its outward appearance in conformity with its desires. In our earthly existence, however, the body is 'organised' more slowly – over months or years – and it is not so immediately responsive to the changing demands of its vital principle, if only because it contains the heavier elements of Water and Earth. And throughout the Middle Ages and the Renaissance, almost all educated people believed that there would be no life, no growth, no sensation and no movement in an animal body if it were not for the mediation of a supremely refined, unimaginably volatile, almost immaterial substance called 'spirit'. This, as we saw in a preliminary way in chapter 4, is the vehicle by means of which the soul penetrates and communicates with the gross and palpable body; and we must now examine in more detail the nature of 'spirit' and its origin and functions in the *human* animal.

Spiritus (in Greek, *pneuma*) exists at three levels of purity which were thought to constitute three distinct species. It is produced in the first instance from blood; and in order to follow the thinking which underlies the medieval theory we must first recall the main differences between our modern conception of the *circulation* of the blood (pumped out of the heart via the arteries, and returning via the veins) and earlier ideas about its *ebb* and *flow*.

From the time of Galen (late second century AD) to that of William Harvey (1578–1657), it was held that there are two distinct kinds of blood contained in two distinct systems of 'canals', connected at only one point by a very narrow 'sluice' or 'weir'. The first system is filled with 'raw' or 'imperfect' blood (*sanguis imperfectus*), which was conceived simply as a liquid food serving to nourish the tissues, muscles and bone of which the body is composed. Generated in the liver, it is dark in colour, and moves only sluggishly in the veins (*venae*). Some of this raw blood passes from the liver into the right ventricle of the heart on its way to feed the lungs; and a very small quantity seeps through invisible pores into the left chamber of the heart. Here – in the left chamber – the filtered raw blood is transformed into 'perfect' blood (*sanguis perfectus*), whose function is to communicate life, warmth and form. This is carried to all parts of the body in the broader channels of the thick-walled arteries (*arteriae*). It is bright red in colour, its flow is vigorous and it 'pulses'.[6]

'Natural', 'vital' and 'animal' spirits

The first two species of spirit are closely associated with the two kinds of blood. The least refined, known as *spiritus naturalis*, is generated from imperfect blood in the liver, while the second, called *spiritus vitalis*, is produced in the left chamber of the heart from a mixture of 'perfect' blood and of air received directly from the lungs. The two spirits travel in the same channels as the blood, that is, in the parallel but distinct veins and arteries, which originate in the liver and heart respectively. And it is from the spirits that the two kinds of blood receive their power to nourish and to structure or 'inform'. The 'pulse' of the heart, varying in response to each new stimulus from the *vis appetitiva*, and detectable throughout the arterial system, was also attributed to the 'vital spirit', since it was assumed that the soul could not act directly on such relatively gross materials.

The third and most volatile or 'subtle' species of spirit was thought to be generated from the vital spirit in a network of fine blood vessels called the *rete mirabile* at the base of the brain (in fact, there is no such feature in human anatomy). This 'spirit of the soul', as it was known (*spiritus animalis*), ascended into the chambers of the brain and filled the hollow tubes of the sensory nerves (*nervi*). It flowed up and down the spinal cord and out into the network of motor nerves. And wherever reference is made to *spiritus*, without further qualification, we are to understand the *spiritus animalis*, the vehicle of all kinds of perception, appetition and locomotion.

The three spirits and the 'passions of extreme youth'

The reader of the *Vita nuova* is introduced to all three spirits on the very first page. Dante explains that he was just nine and Beatrice just eight years old when she 'first appeared to his eyes'; and what his memory retains as a vivid *intentio* some eighteen years later is the crimson colour of her dress. After this rapid but revealing annotation concerning the phase of 'apprehension', he passes on to a very detailed representation of his feelings and their psychosomatic consequences in his spirits and blood.

In bald paraphrase, we could say that he felt the emotions of fear, wonder and grief, accompanied by anticipations of future joy and suffering, and that his whole body began to tremble, with localised feelings of giddiness in the head and discomfort in the abdomen. But he conveys all this information by introducing the three spirits, and by personifying them to the extent that they speak whole sentences in half-biblical, half-scholastic Latin. This is how he describes the three contemporaneous reactions (the technical terms are italicised in the translation):

> In quello punto dico veracemente che lo spirito de la vita, lo quale dimora ne la secretissima camera de lo cuore, cominciò a tremare sì fortemente, che apparia ne li menimi polsi orribilmente; e tremando disse queste parole: 'Ecce deus fortior me, qui veniens dominabitur michi.'
> In quello punto lo spirito animale, lo quale dimora ne l'alta camera ne la quale tutti li spiriti sensitivi portano le loro percezioni, si cominciò a maravigliare molto, e parlando spezialmente a li spiriti del viso, sì disse queste parole: 'Apparuit iam beatitudo vestra.'

> In quello punto lo spirito naturale, lo quale dimora in quella parte ove si ministra lo nutrimento nostro, cominciò a piangere, e piangendo disse queste parole: 'Heu miser, quia frequenter impeditus ero deinceps!'
>
> (*VN* II, 4–6)

At that moment, I can truly say that the *vital spirit*, who dwells in the innermost *chamber* of the *heart*, began to tremble so violently that it became alarmingly apparent even in the weakest of my *pulses*; and trembling he said these words: 'Behold a god more powerful than I am, who comes to rule over me.'

At that moment, the *animal spirit*, who has his seat in the high *chamber* where all the *spirits of sensation* bring their *perceptions*, began to feel great astonishment; and speaking in particular to the *spirits of sight*, he said these words: 'Your joy has appeared.'

At that moment, the *natural spirit*, who resides in the part which provides for our *nourishment*, began to weep; and weeping, he said these words; 'Alas, wretch that I am, for henceforth I shall often be *obstructed*!'

The prophecy made by the vital spirit is fulfilled in the very next sentence, where the 'god who comes to rule' is revealed as a personification of Love, who, we read, 'governed my soul there-after, assuming such confidence and authority, thanks to the power given by my imagination, that I had to carry out his every wish to the full. Often he commanded me to seek out this youngest of the angels.'

> D'allora innanzi dico che Amore segnoreggiò la mia *anima*, (…) e cominciò a prendere sopra me tanta sicurtade e tanta signoria per la *vertù* che li dava la mia *imaginazione*, che me convenia fare tutti li suoi *piaceri* compiutamente. Elli mi *comandava* molte volte che io cercasse per vedere questa angiola giovanissima. (*ibid.*, II, 7–8)

And it will be obvious that although Dante shifts the emphasis from the somatic effects to the psychic causes (specifying 'anima', 'vertù' and 'imaginazione'), he is still reconstructing his childish experience in terms of the scholastic paradigm. The image stored in his imagination awakened and sustained the passion of desire, which fulfilled its proper function by impelling him to move towards the source of that image and to seek out the object of his desire. Hence, Dante is perfectly justified in using the technical phrase *passiones et actus* in his summary at the end of the chapter. Despite all the literary conventions, he has been describing 'le passioni e atti di tanta gioventudine'.

Natural and animal spirits in the prose of the Vita nuova

The prophecy made by the *natural* spirit ('impeditus ero') was not to be fulfilled until nine years after this traumatic first encounter, when Beatrice made a second, definitive appearance in Dante's life, dressed this time not in red, but in pure white. Turning her eyes to the fearful young man, she gave him her greeting; and immediately he felt he could see the uttermost bounds of bliss ('tutti li termini de la beatitudine'). That very night, however, he fell into a 'sweet sleep' and saw a 'marvellous vision', which contained the first intimations of his future bereavement and grief.[7] We may therefore assume that it was a combination of adoration and anxiety that brought about the predicted 'impediment' in the activity of his natural spirit – a condition which is described so lucidly that the sentence would not be out of place in a clinical case history:

> From the time of that vision, my natural spirit began to be obstructed in its functioning ['impedito ne la sua operazione'], because my soul was wholly given over to thinking about this most gracious lady. And so my condition became so frail and weak that many of my friends were worried about my appearance. *(ibid., IV, 1)*

The *animal* spirits, meanwhile, have to wait even longer for their return to the story. Beatrice punished the poet for his indiscreet conduct by denying him her greeting, 'in which all his happiness lay'. The narrator digresses to give some indication of the extent of his loss by describing the 'powerful effects that her greeting used to bring about'. The very hope of that 'mirabile salute', he tells us, would put him into a state of humility and charity towards everyone. But as the moment itself approached, his love-longing would make him oblivious to everything except her. It would enable him, as it were, to experience the greeting even before it was given, pre-empting the sense of sight, with the result that his love could be said to become visible in his eyes.

That is the prose sense of the second paragraph in chapter XI. But what Dante chose to do was to analyse and represent each of the three stages in his feelings by dwelling on their presumed effects on the animal spirits. In this analysis, his desire (which would have been carried to and from the heart by the animal spirits) is actually designated as 'uno spirito d'amore'. His obliviousness is explained by supposing that this spirit of love 'destroyed all the other spirits of sensation'. And his anticipation of the moment of seeing came about because the same spirit of love 'drove out the enfeebled spirits of sight' from the optic nerve, and 'took their place' in his eyes, where the invisible spirit became manifest through the trembling it caused.

The physiological analysis here is almost as respectable as that of the love-sickness and loss of appetite attributed to the 'impediment of the natural spirit', but the fervour of the expression would certainly be out of place in a medical text. Dante throws caution to the winds in his personification of the spirit and in his imagery of invasion, conquest and paying homage. And the rhythms of this remarkable prose-poem transform what might have been mere charm and wit into a moving evocation of the feelings that can overwhelm any adolescent lover.[8]

> E quando ella fosse alquanto propinqua al salutare, uno spirito d'amore, distruggendo tutti li altri spiriti sensitivi, pingea fuori li deboletti spiriti del viso, e dicea loro: 'Andate a onorare la donna vostra'; ed elli si rimanea nel luogo loro. E chi avesse voluto conoscere Amore, fare lo potea mirando lo tremare de li occhi miei.   (*ibid.*, XI, 2)

> And when she was on the point of giving her greeting, a spirit of love, routing all the other spirits of sensation, drove out the weakened spirits of sight, and said to them: 'Go and do honour to your liege lady'; and he remained in their place. And if anyone had wanted to know Love, he might have done so by looking at the trembling of my eyes.

The dramatisation of the passions in the poems of the Vita nuova

During the following period of his disgrace, the 'spiriti del viso' are again defeated and banished by 'Amore' when Dante unexpectedly sees Beatrice among the guests at a wedding banquet. In this episode, however, the prose narrative covers the same ground as the poem allegedly written immediately after the event; and a brief examination of the sonnet in question will enable us to study the evolution of this representational technique during an even earlier phase in Dante's career, a phase when we can still recognise a clear debt to the poetry of the man he called his 'first friend'. For it was Guido Cavalcanti who had greatly extended and refined the analysis of the courtly poet's torments and delights, and who had first given prominence to the spirits as messengers and go-betweens in the theatrical representation of the psyche.

In the opening lines of the sonnet, Dante addresses Beatrice directly after she has teased him about his woebegone appearance. He reproaches her for not reflecting on the internal causes which make his aspect seem so strange to her ('non pensate, donna, onde si mova / ch'io vi rassembri sì figura nova'). Then he dramatises those causes, using already the conceit of Love as an 'invader', but showing him as more vigorous than he would do in the prose of some ten years later, and paying due attention to the laments of the exiled 'spiriti del viso':

> ché Amor, quando sì presso a voi mi trova,
> prende baldanza e tanta securtate
>   che fere tra' miei spiriti paurosi,
> e quale ancide, e qual pinge di fore,
> sì che solo remane a veder vui:
> ond'io mi cangio in figura d'altrui,
> ma non sì ch'io non senta bene allore
> li guai de li scacciati tormentosi.   (*Rime* XI, 7–14; *VN* XIV, 12)

When Love finds me near you he grows exultant and so assured that he strikes into my terrified spirits, killing this one and driving out that, until he alone remains to gaze at you. Hence I am changed into another's aspect – yet not so that I do not then perfectly hear the wails of the outcast tormented spirits.

Two other excerpts from sonnets in the following chapters of the *Vita nuova* will illustrate something of the expressive power that is compatible with a high degree of physiological accuracy. The first boldly attributes all the outward effects of the lover's distress to the seat of his emotions; for it is the heart that is said to grow pale, lose consciousness, seek support as best it may and undergo a violent hallucination:

> Lo viso mostra lo color del core,
> che, tramortendo, ovunque pò s'appoia;
> e per la ebrietà del gran tremore
> le pietre par che gridin: 'Moia, moia.'   (*Rime* XII, 5–8; *VN* XV, 5)

My face shows the colour of my heart which, swooning, seeks support wherever it can; and in the whirl of my violent trembling the stones seem to cry out: 'Die! Die!'

In the prose narrative, Dante portrays this scene as a 'battle' between desire, arising in the imagination, and fear, stemming from the memory. And in the following section, he describes how his 'memoria' used to move his 'fantasia' to 'imaginare' the condition just described, in the hope that 'le passate passioni' would deter him from seeking Beatrice again.[9] But the deterrent fails to work, and the next sonnet ends with a three-line sequence showing renewed perception as followed by an even more tumultuous response in the appetites, resulting this time in a loss of consciousness akin to dying:

> E se io levo li occhi per guardare,
> nel cor mi si comincia uno tremoto,
> che fa de' polsi l'anima partire. (*Rime* XII, 12–14; *VN* XVI, 10)

And if I lift my eyes to look at you, a trembling begins in my heart which drives the soul away from my blood.

The soul's 'departure' from the body was thought to be preceded by the withdrawal of the vital spirits from the arteries ('polsi') to the heart; and this is the medical background to the charmingly operatic scene in Dante's longest and most Cavalcantian essay in this mode – the canzone 'E' m'incresce di me', which was excluded from the *Vita nuova* for a variety of compelling reasons.

The two opening stanzas of the canzone locate it in the period after Beatrice had denied Dante her greeting. At the time of his falling in love, we are told, her eyes had promised 'peace to the heart and delight to the eyes'. But as soon as her forces had captured the citadel of his mind, they withdrew their 'victorious banners' from his sight, with the result that 'the soul, who had been expecting consolation, is left sorrowful; and now she sees the heart, to whom she was joined in wedlock, almost at death's door, while she must take her departure, still full of love'.[10] 'Weeping and disconsolate', the soul retreats to the heart, where she takes a long and sad farewell from the spirits:

> Ristretta s'è entro il mezzo del core
> con quella vita che rimane spenta
> solo in quel punto ch'ella si va via;
> e ivi si lamenta
> d'Amor, che fuor d'esto mondo la caccia;
> e spessamente abbraccia
> li spiriti che piangon tuttavia,
> però che perdon la lor compagnia. (*Rime* LXVII, 35–42)

She has shrunk back into the innermost heart with such life as is extinguished only at the instant of her departure; and there she complains against Love who is driving her out of this world; and embraces again and again the vital spirits who mourn continually the loss of their companion.

Later in the same poem Dante dramatises a nearly fatal seizure caused by shock and sacred fear. He claims it occurred on the day that Beatrice was born (when the poet himself would still have been a baby!); but the physiology of the splendidly vigorous writing is as accurate as ever, and the fear in question is linked to the holy terror that threw St Paul to the ground on the road to Damascus, as well as to the romantic experience of love at first sight:

> Lo giorno che costei nel mondo venne
> secondo che si trova
> nel libro de la mente che vien meno,
>   la mia persona pargola sostenne
> una passïon nova,
> tal ch'io rimasi di paura pieno;
>   ch'a tutte mie virtù fu posto un freno
> subitamente, sì ch'io caddi in terra,
> per una luce che nel cuor percosse:
> e se 'l libro non erra,
> lo spirito maggior tremò sì forte,
> che parve ben che morte
> per lui in questo mondo giunta fosse.   (*ibid.*, 57–69)

The day that this lady came into the world – as I find it written in the book of the mind that is passing away – my childish body felt a strange emotion, so that I was filled with fear; and suddenly a check was placed on all my faculties, so that I fell to the ground; and if that book does not err, the greater spirit then trembled so violently, it seemed just as if death had entered this world to take it.

It is comparatively rare for the passion of love to be represented as the source of 'pace' and 'diletto' in the poems of the *Vita nuova*, but we must not ignore the effects analysed and represented in the very well-known sonnets 'Tanto gentile' and 'Vede perfettamente', which are among the loveliest things that Dante wrote in what he called the 'praise style'.[11] Here Beatrice is portrayed almost as a synthesis of the Virgin and the archangel Gabriel. She causes 'all tongues to fall tremblingly silent', and robs the eyes of courage to look at her. She is so beautiful that she sends an indescribable sweetness through the eyes to the heart, calling forth the muted response of a sigh. And the same reaction will repeat itself every time that the gentleness of her bearing returns to memory:

> Tanto gentile e tanto onesta pare
> la donna mia quand'ella altrui saluta,

ch'ogne lingua deven tremando muta,
e li occhi no l'ardiscon di guardare.

Mostrasi sì piacente a chi la mira,
che dà per li occhi una dolcezza al core,
che 'ntender no la può chi no la prova.

(Rime XXII, 1–4, 9–11; VN XXVI, 5, 7)

Ed è ne li atti suoi tanto gentile,
che nessun la si può recare a mente,
che non sospiri in dolcezza d'amore.

(Rime XXIII, 12–14; VN XXVI, 13)

Nevertheless, the most precise and the most lyrically beautiful analyses of the activity of the passions in the human body come in the poems that express conflict or lament. And our last example from the poems of the *Vita nuova* must be the superb *planctus* which Dante wrote after Beatrice's death: 'Li occhi dolenti per pietà del core'.

The emblematic opening words focus our attention on the eyes – not, however, as the organs of vision, but as tear ducts and 'windows for grief'. (Medieval doctors held that the pressure caused by the expansion of the animal spirits must be vented – 'sfogato' – through one or more of the appropriate outlets.) In their compassion for the heart's distress, the eyes have wept tears and suffered such pain that they can weep no longer. Hence, if the grief is to be eased, the poet must open his mouth and pour out words of lamentation:

Li occhi dolenti per pietà del core
hanno di lagrimar sofferta pena,
sì che per vinti son remasi omai.
  Ora, s'i' voglio sfogar lo dolore,
che a poco a poco a la morte mi mena,
convenemi parlar traendo guai.   (*Rime* XXV, 1–6; *VN* XXXI, 8)

Having insisted that Beatrice's soul is now in heaven, and having dwelt on the inconsolable sadness and 'the longing to sigh and to die of weeping' that afflict all those whose minds are capable of forming an image of the departed, Dante traces the succession of changing emotions that affect him personally. Thinking, imagining and remembering, he first experiences 'anguish', which is a constriction around the heart; then, a longing to die himself (a longing of such sweetness that it steals the colour from his face); then, a new onset of grief from all sides, which causes him to start up in pain; and then, a feeling of shame, which makes him seek to be alone. Finally, as he resumes his weeping and lamentation, he calls on Beatrice – and finds comfort in uttering her name:

> Dannomi angoscia li sospiri forte,
> quando 'l pensero ne la mente grave
> mi reca quella che m'ha 'l cor diviso:
>   e spesse fiate pensando a la morte,
> venemene un disio tanto soave,
> che mi tramuta lo color nel viso.
>   E quando 'l maginar mi ven ben fiso,
> giugnemi tanta pena d'ogne parte,
> ch'io mi riscuoto per dolor ch'i' sento;
>   e sì fatto divento,
> che da le genti vergogna mi parte.
> Poscia piangendo, sol nel mio lamento
> chiamo Beatrice, e dico: 'Or se' tu morta?';
> e mentre ch'io la chiamo, me conforta.
>
> *(Rime* xxv, 43–56; *VN* xxxi, 13–14)

My sighs oppress me grievously when thought brings back to my heavy mind the lady who has cleft my heart; and often, thinking of death, a desire for it comes on me, so sweet that it makes my face change colour. And when my thought is intensely fixed, from every side such anguish comes upon me that I start up with the pain I feel; and I am brought to such a state that shame keeps me apart from everybody: and then weeping, alone, in my lament I call on Beatrice, saying: 'Are you now dead?' And while I call on her, she comforts me.

The power and the signs of former love

When Dante sees Beatrice again – on the chariot in the Garden of Eden – he describes the renewal of 'the power of his former love' by representing once again 'the signs of that earlier flame'. He is seized by wonder to the extent that his vital and animal spirits are 'crushed' and 'trembling'. His 'fear' and 'affliction' make him turn towards Virgil 'like a child to his mother' in order to confess that 'there is not so much as a drop of blood in him that is not throbbing'. And the only significant physiological difference, with respect to the original encounters described in chapters II and III of the *Vita nuova*, is that he cannot continue to look at Beatrice, and cannot therefore receive further information through his eyes. As a result, he has to attribute the resurgence of his emotions to a '*hidden* power' emanating from Beatrice, although this is clearly the same 'exalted power' which 'struck' him and 'pierced' him 'before he was out of his boyhood':

> E lo spirito mio, che già cotanto
> tempo era stato ch'a la sua presenza
> non era di stupor, tremando, affranto,
>   sanza de li occhi aver più conoscenza,
> per occulta virtù che da lei mosse,
> d'antico amor sentì la gran potenza.
>   Tosto che ne la vista mi percosse
> l'alta virtù che già m'avea trafitto
> prima ch'io fuor di püerizia fosse,
>   volsimi a la sinistra col respitto
> col quale il fantolin corre a la mamma
> quando ha paura o quando elli è afflitto,
>   per dicere a Virgilio: 'Men che dramma
> di sangue m'è rimaso che non tremi:
> conosco i segni de l'antica fiamma.'   (*Purg.* XXX, 34–48)

Tears and sighs of repentance

The protagonist is no longer a boy, of course, but a grown man who knows he has been false to his love. And the greatest psychological difference between the original 'innamoramento' and the resurgence of his 'antico amore' lies in the fact that he is overwhelmed simultaneously by the passions of guilt, shame and remorse. Far from welcoming him with open arms, Beatrice attacks her lover with the cutting edge and sharp point of her verbal 'sword', intensifying these emotions in his heart until they are discharged in tears, sighs of repentance and words of confession leading to a loss of consciousness. And if we require further evidence that the protagonist of the *Comedy* is there in flesh and blood, or that the poet of the *Comedy* has not outgrown his interest in the physiology of passion, we cannot do better than examine Dante's psychosomatic responses to Beatrice's reprimand, as portrayed in the second half of canto XXX and in canto XXXI.[12]

Dante's state of stupefaction gives way almost immediately to a grief that 'stains his cheeks with weeping' when he realises that Virgil has disappeared from his side. But the natural course of that emotion is brusquely interrupted when Beatrice addresses him by name from the other side of the stream that separates them and assures him he will have to shed tears for a very different cause. For a moment their eyes meet across the water, but Dante is immediately overpowered by the passion of shame, which produces an almost comic double reaction: first, he looks down at the stream to escape from her accusing gaze; then he lowers his eyes still further to the grassy bank in order to avoid seeing his own reflection in the water:

> Li occhi mi cadder giù nel chiaro fonte;
> ma veggendomi in esso, i trassi a l'erba,
> tanta vergogna mi gravò la fronte. (*Purg.* xxx, 76–8)

My eyes dropped to the clear water, but seeing myself in it, I turned them away to the grass, so heavy was the shame that pressed down on my brow.

The protagonist feels almost an acrid tang in his mouth as he 'savours the bitter taste of sharp-tongued solicitude'; and when Beatrice remains silent, he experiences a sudden numbing drop in his body temperature – a typical symptom of fear or despair – remaining 'frozen' within, like snow on the trees in the Apennines when the winds blow from the North. At this point, however, the angels hovering in the sky above the triumphal chariot strike up the opening verses of David's psalm of hope and trust in the Lord – *In te, Domine, speravi*. Their compassion or participation is no less evident in the sweetness of their song than if they had put it into words. And this has the effect of melting the 'ice' around Dante's heart, just as the Apennine snow liquefies and dissolves into itself when the winds swing round to the South.[13] As it thaws, this 'ice' becomes both 'vapour' and 'water', and these find their separate outlets, through the mouth and the eyes respectively, in the form of sighs and tears:

> Così fui sanza lagrime e sospiri
> anzi 'l cantar di quei che notan sempre
> dietro a le note de li etterni giri;
> ma poi che 'ntesi ne le dolci tempre
> lor compartire a me, par che se detto
> avesser: 'Donna, perché sì lo stempre?',
> lo gel che m'era intorno al cor ristretto,
> spirito e acqua fessi, e con angoscia
> de la bocca e de li occhi uscì del petto. (*Purg.* xxx, 91–9)

[Just as snow is first compacted and then melted] so I remained without tears or sighs until the angels, who model their melodies on those of the eternal spheres, began their song. But when I understood how they took my part in their sweet notes, as clearly as if they had said: 'Lady, why do you mortify him like this?', the ice that had tightened its grip around my heart became breath and water, and issued painfully from my breast through my mouth and eyes.

If the penitent Dante had some initial difficulty in producing the sighs and tears which formed the first 'penalty' he had to pay to divine justice, the same tears and sighs prevented him from using his organs of speech – throat, vocal chords, tongue and lips – when he was called upon to make a public admission of the sins of which Beatrice then accused him. When she demanded that he should 'add his confession to so grave an accusation', he tells us that 'my faculties were so confused that my voice flickered and was extinguished before it could be released from its organs':[14]

> Era la mia virtù tanto confusa,
> che la voce si mosse, e pria si spense
> che da li organi suoi fosse dischiusa.   (*Purg.* XXXI, 7–9)

Pressed for an answer a second time, he became alarmed as well as disorientated, and his 'Yes' was completely inaudible – or, to put it in his own precise words: 'Confusion mixed with fear squeezed the kind of "Yes" from my mouth that you would need eyes to understand':

> Confusione e paura insieme miste
> mi pinsero un tal 'sì' fuor de la bocca,
> al quale intender fuor mestier le viste.   (*ibid.*, 13–15)

Once again the pent-up emotions erupted in a storm of sighs and tears so that he could not articulate the words; and, in a brilliantly realistic simile, Dante now compares his impotence to a crossbow that snaps when the string is wound back too far: 'As a crossbow breaks both string and bow when it is discharged from excessive tension, and the bolt hits its target with diminished force, so I broke down under that heavy pressure, pouring out tears and sighs; and my voice clammed in its passage.'

> Come balestro frange, quando scocca
> da troppa tesa, la sua corda e l'arco,
> e con men foga l'asta il segno tocca,
>   sì scoppia' io sottesso grave carco,
> fuori sgorgando lagrime e sospiri,
> e la voce allentò per lo suo varco.   (*ibid.*, 16–21)

Hence, it was only when he was urged to confess for the third time that the organs of his 'sensitive powers' allowed him to show the specifically human passion of guilt through the specifically human signs of language:

> Dopo la tratta d'un sospiro amaro,
> a pena ebbi la voce che rispuose,
> e le labbra a fatica la formaro.
>   Piangendo dissi: 'Le presenti cose
> col falso lor piacer volser miei passi,
> tosto che 'l vostro viso si nascose.' *(ibid.,* 31–6)

After I had heaved a bitter sigh, it cost me pain to find the voice to reply, and my lips could give it form only with difficulty. Weeping, I said: 'Present things, with their false pleasures, turned my steps aside as soon as your face was hidden.'

Next, Beatrice switched her attack from accusation to reproach, with the declared aim of intensifying the feeling of shame which had overwhelmed her lover at the beginning of their interview. She achieved her purpose so effectively that once again Dante stood 'ashamed, dumb, his eyes on the ground, as children stand when they listen, recognise their faults, and feel sorry for what they have done':

> Quali fanciulli, vergognando, muti
> con li occhi a terra stannosi, ascoltando
> e sé riconoscendo e ripentuti. *(ibid.,* 64–6)

The onslaught on his passions was still not complete. Beatrice insisted that he should endure more pain by 'lifting his beard' and looking at her directly. Reluctantly, he obeyed the command; and, even though she was veiled and did not return his gaze, he found her incomparably more beautiful than she had ever been on earth.[15] But, as Beatrice had foreseen and intended, beauty does not always cause unalloyed delight. Dante was 'stung by the nettle of repentance'; his heart was 'bitten' by self-reproof; and he fell senseless to the ground:

> Di penter sì mi punse ivi l'ortica,
> (...)
> Tanta riconoscenza il cor mi morse,
> ch'io caddi vinto. *(ibid.,* 85, 88–9)

'Witnesses and windows of the heart'

The phrase 'caddi vinto' looks back to two moments at the very beginning of Dante's journey through Hell when he lost consciousness through fear and compassion.[16] It reminds us perhaps that a responsible adult, as opposed to a naughty child, should not be quite so much at the mercy of the 'thousand natural shocks that flesh is heir to'. But if this is one part of the lesson to be learnt, we must not infer that Dante wants us to eradicate the passions altogether. On the contrary, he makes it abundantly clear that he welcomes the spontaneous way in which our feelings find expression in what is now called 'body-language'.

He does not reproach the boisterous devils who signal their spiteful intentions by 'grinding their teeth and threatening with their brows'. What he detests are the smooth-tongued human beings who are able to dissimulate their malicious designs and whose sins of fraud – catalogued in fully sixteen cantos of *Inferno* – are symbolised in the monster, Geryon, the 'sozza imagine di froda', whose swishing tail was charged with poison, like a scorpion's, but whose 'face was the face of a just man'. And what Dante evidently responds to most warmly of all is the outshining of innocent love in the blushing cheeks and laughing eyes of the young and beautiful. Piccarda answers his question 'with such joy that she seemed to burn in the first fire of love'; and Matelda, he surmises, must be 'warming herself in the rays of the planet of love' if he is 'to believe the looks which used to bear witness to the heart':[17]

> 'Deh, bella donna, che a' raggi d'amore
> ti scaldi, s'i' vo' credere a' sembianti
> che soglion esser testimon del core.'   (*Purg.* XXVIII, 43–5)

In writing the *Comedy*, Dante remained loyal to the ideas and ideals he had expounded in a memorable chapter in the *Convivio* (III, viii) which forms the best possible introduction to another important episode in *Purgatorio*.

The major thesis of the *Convivio* chapter is decidedly Platonic, since Dante is primarily concerned to demonstrate that Beauty is Goodness, and Goodness Beauty. He begins by praising Divine Wisdom – first, for the miraculous way in which the human soul unites three natures in itself (the nutritive, sensitive and rational powers); next, for the concord that exists between the soul and the body; and then, for the harmonious proportions obtaining between the various organs of the body. As the chapter develops, however, he shifts the emphasis away from the permanent aspects of this harmony of body and soul towards the transient – that is, away from beauty considered as perfection of form towards beauty considered as the expression of good emotions. And despite the poetic fervour of the language – much influenced by the Wisdom books of the Bible – the fundamental principles and the terminology are Aristotelian. The *anima* is conceived as the *forma* of the body, the ground of its existence, the actualiser of its *potentiae*, the efficient cause of its diverse organs, and the self-moving agent which uses those organs as 'instruments' to carry out its 'operations'.

> The soul dedicates its greatest care and solicitude to those parts of the body where it carries out its proper task most fully. That is why it lavishes such care on the human face, where the highest potentiality of its matter is actualised, such that no two faces are alike. Within the face there are two areas – the eyes and the mouth – to which the soul devotes its greatest efforts, since it could be said that all three powers of the soul have jurisdiction there.
>
> To adopt a beautiful simile, these two places might be called balconies belonging to the mistress of the body's mansion, because it is there that she often makes her appearance, even though she is, so to speak, under a veil. She shows herself so openly in the eyes that any attentive observer can know her current state of feeling. And since there are six specifically human passions – to which Aristotle alludes in his *Rhetoric* – none of them can affect the soul without its likeness appearing in the window of the eyes, unless it is concealed by a great effort.
>
> She stands revealed in the mouth like a colour seen through glass. For what is laughter but the coruscation of the soul's delight – that is, a light whose brightness corresponds to its inner state?
>
> (*Con.* III, viii, 6–10, abbreviated)

'The flicker of a smile'

The material of these paragraphs is transposed from a 'bella similitudine' to poetic drama on the fifth terrace of Purgatory, in a scene that begins shortly after the protagonist has experienced the bodily symptoms of four other passions.

An earth tremor has shaken the whole mountain and left Dante 'frozen' with fear, like a condemned man being led to execution.

Reassured by a fortissimo rendering of *Gloria in excelsis Deo*, he is then 'travailed' and 'warred upon' by the passion of wonder with its concomitant longing to know the causes of the 'tremare' and the 'grido'. But this longing is in conflict with the urgent desire to make haste, which 'pierces' him as he hurries along behind Virgil, picking his way past the recumbent shadow-bodies of the avaricious, whose torments cause him to 'suffer with them in their just retribution'.[18]

While Dante is still in this complex emotional state, he and Virgil are overtaken by a shade who explains that the earthquake and the *Gloria* both marked the moment of his release from a centuries-long period of satisfaction and purification on this very terrace. Without discovering the names of his interlocutors, the shade then introduces himself as the Roman epic poet Statius, and insists that he had been a devoted disciple of Virgil. Indeed, he concludes, his two epics were 'kindled, borne and nourished' by the *Aeneid* – so much so, that he would gladly have remained a further year in Purgatory, in exile from Paradise, if only he could have lived at the same time as his hero.[19]

The declaration is, of course, made to Virgil himself; but it will fall to the protagonist to resolve the dramatic irony of this delightful situation through his inability to disguise his amusement. No further introduction or commentary is required, since even a prose translation can demonstrate that this is dramatic writing of a very high order (although it would require the intimate medium of the television screen to do justice to the facial nuances so lovingly specified in the 'stage directions').

> These words made Virgil turn towards me with a look that, while saying nothing, said 'Say nothing.' But the power of the will is not absolute, for laughter and tears follow the passions from which they spring so closely that they are least subject to the will in those who are most sincere.
>
> I could not help smiling – like someone giving a hint – with the result that the shade remained silent and looked into my eyes, where expressions are delineated most strongly. 'As you hope to gain the summit by your efforts', he said, 'why did your face show the flash of a smile just now?'
>
> I am under attack from both sides at once, one imposing silence, the other begging me to speak. So I heave a sigh – and my master understands. 'Don't be afraid to speak', he says, 'but speak out and tell him what he is asking so earnestly.'
>
> And so I said: 'Spirit from a bygone age, perhaps you were amazed by the smile that escaped me; but now you're going to be seized by even

greater amazement. For the man who is guiding my eyes up to the heights is that very Virgil from whom you derived the power to sing of men and gods.'

(Purg. XXI, 103–26)

'Locus flentium sive lachrimarum' (Judges 2:5)

The moving climax to this scene leads us away from the spontaneous 'coruscation of the soul's delight' back to the problem of the *shadow*-bodies of the dead, with which we began this investigation into the psychosomatic consequences of perception and appetition. For when Statius attempts to embrace Virgil's ankles – in a ritualised expression of reverence and awe – he is restrained with the simple but sublime words: 'Frate, / non far, ché tu se' ombra e ombra vedi.' And he has to excuse himself for the warmth of the affection that had made him 'put our emptiness out of mind, treating shades as though they were a solid thing':

> 'quand' io dismento nostra vanitate,
> trattando l'ombre come cosa salda.'   (*Purg.* XXI, 135–6)

As we saw, however, Dante-the-author does frequently disregard the 'emptiness' of the dead and does represent their phantasmagorical bodies on the assumption that they are 'equipped with organs' for all the faculties of the sensitive part of the soul. Their 'shadows' are certainly sufficiently corporeal for them to experience the primary passions of pleasure and pain, and to express them through the rudimentary natural language of the body.[20]

The 'valle dolorosa' or 'doloroso regno' is filled with the screams and cries that we share with animals in pain. And it is wholly appropriate that, as the protagonist passes through the Gate of Hell, he should hear the wordless 'sospiri, pianti e alti guai', which were resounding through the starless air, before he distinguished the '*parole* di dolore' within the 'whirling tumult'. Similarly, the 'shouts and lamentations' uttered by the carnal sinners in the second circle are registered before their distinctively human blasphemies, directed against the power of God.[21]

As in every system of signs, however, there are differentiations and semantically charged oppositions even within the 'heavy thunder of infinite wailings' that awoke Dante from the first of his swoons on the further bank of the Acheron. The inhabitants of

Limbo, unbaptised but blameless, are 'neither happy nor sad in their aspect'. They suffer no torments, but live in a state of desire for God without any hope of union with him. And this is why 'there were no lamentations there, other than the sighs that caused the eternal air to tremble':[22]

> Quivi, secondo che per ascoltare,
> non avea pianto mai che di sospiri
> che l'aura etterna facevan tremare.   (*Inf.* IV, 25–7)

Turning now from the extrusion of 'vapour' or 'vocal spirit' to 'the waters that grief causes to drip down the cheeks', we shall find Dante at his most inventive in his representation of the tears that flow in the *vallis lacrimarum*.[23]

In an allegory that combines infernal space and human time, the Underworld is irrigated by the tears shed by suffering humanity in the ever-worsening course of our history; and three of the ten circles of Dante's Hell are filled with those tears. Such, at least, is the import of Virgil's description in *Inferno* XIV of the symbolic Old Man, buried deep inside the mountain on the island of Crete, whose chest, midriff, legs and right foot, formed respectively of silver, brass, iron and clay, are 'cleft by a single fissure which drips with tears' – these tears being the source of the single infernal river in its four successive manifestations as Acheron, Styx, Phlegethon and Cocytus.[24]

The tears wept by the 'futile', who are not even allowed to cross the Acheron into Limbo, are provoked by insects stinging their faces. These tears mingle with the blood flowing from the stings, and run down to their feet where the mixture is drunk by revolting worms. But this nauseous spectacle is as nothing compared to the tears shed by the soothsayers in the fourth bolgia of the eighth circle. Their heads are twisted right round so that they can only look backwards. And the macabre detail that makes the protagonist himself stop and weep is the sight of the 'tears from their eyes bathing the buttocks at the cleft'.[25]

Although 'our human image is so distorted' in the punishment of the soothsayers, they do have all their bodily parts (Dante specifies chin, chest and loins as well as buttocks). The suicides, by contrast, have become 'legni animati' in the Infernal Wood and are lacking in all the organs articulated by the sensitive soul. Their torment consists in lacerations, caused either by the Harpies perched on their branches, or by the hounds who hunt the spendthrifts at the base of their trunks. These lacerations produce not only pain, but a 'window for the pain' ('fanno dolore, e al dolor fenestra'). This one 'window', however, has to do the duty of both 'balconies' in the face. For the same wound discharges blood, a hissing of breath in screams and words, and, probably, tears.[26]

As we noted earlier, however, weeping may be more than the effect and sign of a 'desperate grief that oppresses the heart'. It may be, in some sense, an alleviation of that pain; and, as such, it would be inappropriate for the sinners in Hell. It is this grisly insight that underlies Dante's most extensive, savage and original treatment of the tears shed by the damned.

At the very bottom of the pit, the souls of the traitors are frozen in the ice of the lake formed by Cocytus. Near the outer bank of the lake, the sinners' heads project above the surface, with their faces inclined downwards (the detail proves to be important).[27] Their teeth chatter and their eyes are moist with tears, thus providing evidence of the intensity of the cold and of the pain in their hearts:

> Ognuna in giù tenea volta la faccia;
> da bocca il freddo, e da li occhi il cor tristo
> tra lor testimonianza si procaccia.   (*Inf.* XXXII, 37–9)

The protagonist's attention was caught by two heads in such close proximity that their hair was intertwined. When he addressed them, they looked up, and, as they did so, 'the moisture which until then had remained within their eyes dripped down their cheeks.' Immediately, 'the cold froze the tears between them and locked them together. Never did a bar hold wooden door to wooden frame with such a powerful grip':

> Li occhi lor, ch'eran pria pur dentro molli,
> gocciar su per le labbra, e 'l gelo strinse
> le lagrime tra essi e riserrolli.
> Con legno legno spranga mai non cinse
> forte così.   (*ibid.*, 46–50)

After some brutal exchanges of verbal and even physical violence with these 'locked' souls and their near neighbours (all of whom had betrayed their native country or city), and after hearing the harrowing tale of Count Ugolino, Dante and Virgil move across the ice to a second zone where the 'ice roughly swaddles' another group of traitors, whose heads project in the same way, except that their faces are turned upwards.[28] Their crime was more heinous (they had betrayed their own kith and kin), and they are therefore denied the possibility of *any* relief, any 'sfogo', for their pain. As the author explains: 'Crying itself makes crying impossible there, and the pain that finds a blockage in the eyes turns back inwards to increase the torment; because the first tears form a barrier that fills the whole socket under the brow like a crystal visor.'

> Lo pianto stesso lì pianger non lascia,
> e 'l duol che truova in su li occhi rintoppo,
> si volge in entro a far crescer l'ambascia;
>   ché le lagrime prime fanno groppo,
> e sì come visiere di cristallo,
> rïempion sotto 'l ciglio tutto il coppo.   (*Inf.* XXXIII, 94–9)

This ingenious refinement to the tortures of Hell provides the context and the occasion for Dante's last conversation with the damned. One of the sinners – Frate Alberigo – agrees to reveal his name only in the hope that Dante will 'pluck the hard veils from his eyes' so that he may 'give vent for a while to the grief that distends his heart, before the tears freeze again'. But the damned have been warned to 'abandon *all* hope'; and the protagonist becomes both torturer and betrayer by refusing to keep his part of the bargain.[29]

'Tempus ridendi' (Ecclesiastes 3:4; cf. Job 8:21)

In one sense all the damned are bound to experience a temporary increase in their torments as a result of their meeting with the protagonist, since he will inevitably remind them of the 'dolce mondo' and the 'dolce lume'. Francesca is not unrepresentative when she 'weeps as she speaks', because 'there is no greater grief than to remember the time of happiness in the time of misery'. By contrast, the blessed have suffered their 'time of weeping' while they were on earth, and they are now enjoying the 'time of laughing', their *tempus ridendi*.[30]

Their bliss in the requited love of God lacks nothing. But it is nevertheless heightened when they are privileged to welcome Dante in one of the planetary heavens and to answer his questions. He has come 'to increase their loves'; and there is no need to strike dubious bargains to persuade them to talk (although Dante does note with

satisfaction the effect of his blandishments on his ancestor Cacciaguida). They too, however, have shadow-bodies. The happiness they
feel is manifested in those bodies; and any increase in that happiness
– as, for example, in meeting Dante – results in a 'corporeal trans-
mutation'. Specifically, they fulfil the prophecy made by Christ:
'Blessed are you that weep now, for you shall laugh.'[31]

With one major and one minor exception, however, any changes
in their eyes and mouths (those 'balconies' of the soul) are lost on the
protagonist. Their bodies have become sources of light – *corpora
lucentia*. Their *umbrae* are *lucentes*. The brightness of their radiance is
proportional to their joy in the love of God; and any increase in that
joy is signalled by a greater brightness. With the exception of those
in the lowest degree of beatitude – Piccarda and her companions –
the light they irradiate overpowers Dante's mortal eyes, and he
cannot see their human lineaments at all. From the moment (in the
Heaven of Mercury) when Justinian signifies his pleasure at being
able to answer Dante's question, they become simply 'lights', 'suns',
'stars', 'fires', 'lanterns' and 'lamps'.[32]

As bodies, the blessed are located in space and capable of
changing their position. Hence they can use the power of locomotion to express their feelings – for example, in gyration and
dance; in the formation of patterns such as the three circles and the
cross in the Heavens of the Sun and Mars; and, above all, in the
balletic 'semaphore' of the Heaven of Jupiter. As *corpora lucentia*,
however, they can also manifest their feelings through changes of
colour, and, especially, through the intensification of their light or
in the phenomena of 'flaming' or 'sparkling' as opposed to mere
brightness.[33]

The principal exception to these general rules is Beatrice. Once
she has removed her veil, she remains fully visible to her lover
throughout their ascent. And her increased joy as she draws nearer
and nearer to the Empyrean is expressed through the heightening of
her beauty and the power of her smile. Already in the fifth heaven, 'a
smile blazes in her eyes' such that *his* eyes seem to 'touch the
uttermost depth of grace and Paradise'. On their arrival in the
seventh heaven, she refuses to smile lest she reduce him to ashes; and
she will not smile again until the eighth heaven, after Dante has
experienced an ecstasy on seeing the light concealing Jesus, which,
she says, 'has made you strong enough to endure my smile'.[34] And
when the poet now remembers what her smile became as she entered

the *tenth* heaven – the Empyrean – the very memory causes another dysfunction of his mental and sensitive powers:

> ché, come sole in viso che più trema,
> così lo rimembrar del dolce riso
> la mente mia da me medesmo scema.   (*Par.* xxx, 25–7)

Shining like the sun on the weakest of eyes, the very recollection of her sweet smile deprives me of my mind.

Beatrice's smile is often described, as in this passage, through the imagery of light; and, conversely, the effulgence of the blessed is frequently conveyed by means of references to smiling and laughter. But the distinction between 'smiling' and 'light' is important if only because it permits the metaphorical interchange of the two terms, as will be seen in the following example where Beatrice smiles with the power of a light, and Cacciaguida 'blazes' with the same effect as emotion showed in the face:

> Vincendo me col lume d'un sorriso,
> ella mi disse: 'Volgiti e ascolta;
> ché non pur ne' miei occhi è paradiso.'
>   Come si vede qui alcuna volta
> l'affetto ne la vista, s'elli è tanto,
> che da lui sia tutta l'anima tolta,
>   così nel fiammeggiar del folgór santo,
> a ch'io mi volsi, conobbi la voglia
> in lui di ragionarmi ancora alquanto.   (*Par.* xviii, 19–27)

Overpowering me with the light of a smile, Beatrice said: 'Turn and listen; for paradise is not confined to my eyes.' And just as on earth we sometimes see an emotion in the face, if it is so powerful that it occupies the whole soul, so I recognised [Cacciaguida's] desire to talk further with me in the flaming of his holy radiance.

'The human person all entire'

It might seem that any further exploration of the joys of the blessed in *Paradiso* would lead us back to the 'proper visibles' of colour and light and away from the parts and organs of the human body. In fact, however, the two themes flow together and merge in a sublime passage of poetic theology or theological poetry, which is also a

167

vigorous reaffirmation of Dante's belief that the body is not a prison, but the natural dwelling-house for the soul.

This confluence of the themes occurs at the point where the protagonist begins to ask himself how the blessed will experience and express their joy in the not too distant future when 'the sound of the angelic trumpet' will herald the end of the world, and the Son of Man will come again in glory to deliver his definitive verdict on the whole of mankind. On that day – the Day of Judgement – the souls will 'return to their graves' and 'each will put on again its flesh and figure'. And what Dante inquires of the souls in the Heaven of the Sun (the question is formulated on his behalf by Beatrice) is 'whether the flower of radiance that envelops your substances will remain with you eternally as it now is, and, if it does remain, whether seeing will not become painful, once you have become visible again':

> 'Diteli se la luce onde s'infiora
> vostra sustanza, rimarrà con voi
> etternalmente sì com' ell' è ora;
>   e se rimane, dite come, poi
> che sarete visibili rifatti,
> esser porà ch'al veder non vi nòi.'   (*Par.* XIV, 13–18)

The basis of the answer had already been stated in general terms in the sixth canto of *Inferno*. But there the spokesman was Virgil; the argumentation was terse and strictly Aristotelian; and the question centred on the torments of the damned. The protagonist had asked whether 'these torments will increase after the Last Judgement, or whether they will be less, or equally roasting?' And he was invited 'to think back to your science, which requires that the more perfect a thing is, the more it feels both good and suffering. So, although this cursed race will never achieve true perfection, they must expect to be closer to that state, rather than further from it' (and hence their suffering will increase when their former bodies are restored).

The same solution is restated in *Paradiso* XIV. This time, however, it refers to the joys of the blessed. When each individual puts on the garment of flesh again, each will be 'in vera perfezione' and will experience greater bliss. And Dante is given positive assurance that the organs of the resurrected body 'will be strong to everything that can give delight'.

That is the core of the argument. But Aristotelian science gives way to Christian theology; and the promised effects are related to a veritable chain of causality, in which God is the efficient cause of the souls' power to see him and the final cause of their love.

Each soul, we are told, experiences joy in proportion to its love for God. This love, in turn, is in proportion to the measure of its vision (that is, of its power to know God). The measure of its vision, however, is proportional not to its intrinsic deserts, but to the uncovenanted gift of the grace of glory (the 'light' by which man will be enabled to 'see God face to face').[35] Hence, the promised increase in joy will be the result of a further gift from God, which will increase vision or knowledge and thus increase love. And – coming at last to the heart of the matter – this further gift, or this more abundant gift, will be made because each recipient will be more 'pleasing' to God now that he or she has become 'complete' – a soul and a body in one person.

Significantly, this speech is put into the mouth of King Solomon – the presumed author of the Book of Wisdom and also of the Song of Songs. And although he is said to speak with a 'modest voice, perhaps like that of the angel to Mary', he combines the building blocks of metre, logic and rhetoric – the terzina, the syllogism and the figure of repetition called 'climax' – into a radiant unity that is worthy of the theme. Here, if anywhere in Dante, 'three natures are conjoined in one form':

> 'Quanto fia lunga la festa
> di paradiso, tanto il nostro amore
> si raggerà dintorno cotal vesta.
> La sua chiarezza séguita l'ardore;
> l'ardor la visïone, e quella è tanta,
> quant' ha di grazia sovra suo valore.'   (*Par.* xiv, 37–42)

'Our love will irradiate this garment around us for as long as the Feast of Paradise endures. Its brightness matches our warmth, our warmth matches our vision, and our vision is in proportion to the grace it receives beyond its merit.'

> 'Come la carne glorïosa e santa
> fia rivestita, la nostra persona
> più grata fia per esser tutta quanta;
> per che s'accrescerà ciò che ne dona
> di gratüito lume il sommo bene,
> lume ch'a lui veder ne condiziona;
> onde la visïon crescer convene,
> crescer l'ardor che di quella s'accende,
> crescer lo raggio che da esso vene.'   (*ibid.*, 43–51)

'When we are clothed again in the flesh, now sanctified and glorious, our person will be more pleasing to God because it will be complete. In consequence, the light of grace will be intensified, this being the light which we receive as a gift from God, and which enables us to see Him. And there will be corresponding increases in the power of vision, in the ardour kindled by that vision, and in the radiance that issues from that ardour.'

PART THREE

The operations of the rational soul

CHAPTER NINE

Self-direction: the powers of
the mind

Corpora seipsa moventia et seipsa dirigentia

We saw in part one that there is a fundamental difference between
the movement of a stone, as flung by a boy at a passing seagull, and
the movement made by a gull in order to avoid such a missile. The
first body receives its impetus from without, 'by violence'. The
second finds its motive force within itself, 'by nature': and the gull
constitutes a representative example of a 'self-moving body', a *corpus
seipsum movens.*

We also recognised that, at another level of analysis, the self-
caused movements of any animal were assumed to be governed by
factors beyond its control. It owes its existence to a specific form or
vital principle (*anima*) which confers certain limited powers and
certain instinctive needs and appetites. However complex the
mechanism of perception, estimation, passion and locomotion may
prove to be, an animal cannot *not* react in a predetermined way to the
external bodies it chances to encounter. It cannot ordinarily make a
'false move'; but it is 'more acted upon than acting'.[1]

Now, it will be obvious from everything that has been said that, for
Dante, the crucial divide lay not between animate and inanimate
bodies, but between all other animate bodies and man. As a Christian, as a citizen of a self-governing commune, and as an Aristotelian,

he accepted that human beings are genuinely 'masters of their own actions'. The *Comedy* is founded on the premise that normal human adults in normal circumstances are individually responsible for what they do or for what they leave undone; and that they therefore deserve not only praise or blame, but reward or punishment in an eternal afterlife. And we have just seen that when Dante looked into his innermost self, or back into his own past, he was shamed into the awareness that he had been able to *choose*, that he had often chosen *badly*, and that he could still learn to choose *well*. Self-knowledge convinced him that he was not simply 'self-moving', but 'self-directing'. He presents himself in the poem as a *corpus seipsum dirigens*.[2]

On the other hand, it will have been equally obvious from all the material presented in part two, that the opposition between 'animate' and 'human' was by no means absolute. Each one of us, so Dante believed, exists as a living body by virtue of a specific form with certain inalienable faculties. We differ from the 'brute beasts' because our psyche is endowed with a supplementary power, just as all beasts differ from all plants because they possess the powers of sensation and locomotion in addition to those of nutrition, growth and self-reproduction. If we want to understand what is 'human' in our nature, we must simply concentrate on this *differentia*. We must look at the *operationes* that no animal can perform, on the assumption that these consist in the actualisation of a power that is unique to our species and that they constitute the goal or 'final cause' of our existence.

In short, the concepts and axioms with which we 'came to terms' in part one remain relevant to the analysis of 'le *nostre* operazioni'; and the following passage from the *Convivio* (in which Dante is comparing and contrasting the hierarchically conceived powers of 'living', 'feeling' and 'reasoning') offers a characteristically clear illustration of the continuity in the natural order and in the Aristotelian mode of analysis.

> In the second book of the *De anima*, where Aristotle analyses the capacities of the psyche, he asserts that its principal powers are three – life, sensation and thought.
>
> And, as Aristotle says, it is perfectly obvious that the powers are arranged in such a way that each one acts as the foundation for the next. The first can exist independently, but the second must rest on the first. Thus, the vegetative power, which is the principle of life, is the foun-

dation for sight, hearing, taste, smell and touch; but it can also exist as a psyche in its own right, as we see in all the plants.

The sensitive power cannot exist without the vegetative, and it is not found in any lifeless body. This sensitive power is the foundation for the intellectual power, that is to say, reason. In mortal, animate beings, the ratiocinative power is never found disjoined from the sensitive power; but the power of sensation does exist without reason, as we see in beasts, birds, fish and indeed in all brute animals. And the psyche which includes all these powers, being the most perfect of them all, is the human soul.

(*Con.* III, ii, 11–14, abbreviated)

Some metaphors for the operations of the mind

When Dante wants to indicate the distinctively human power in its totality, he calls it 'mind' ('mente', from *mens/mentis*). Mind, he goes on to say in the following chapter of the *Convivio*, is only one 'part' of our psyche, but with respect to the other powers it is the 'most excellent', the 'most precious', the 'most perfect', the 'noblest', the 'ultimate' and 'supreme'. We are linked by the possession of mind to the higher, incorporeal beings in the universe. 'Mind participates in the divine nature like the sempiternal intelligences.' It is 'divinity'; it is 'so ennobled and denuded of matter that the divine light shines into it as it does into an angel'. This is why philosophers call man a 'godlike animal'.[3]

We must not forget the poetic and Platonic fervour of his language in *Convivio* III as we go on now to explore some of the details and technicalities in the Aristotelian model of the mind. But before we try to 'come to terms' with Aristotle again, it will be worth our while to examine the etymology of the principal verbs used to describe the mental operations, and to see what we can learn about the underlying picture language. Words like 'to abstract', 'to analyse' and 'to comprehend' are still current in the modern European languages; but they have lost their medieval connotations and shifted in meaning as they have grown progressively further away from their etymological roots.

Let us begin with the highest level of mental achievement – 'understanding'. English speakers are probably not aware of any relationship between the meaning of the verb 'to understand' and what seem to be its two components ('under' + 'stand'). But the nearest equivalent in medieval Latin – *intellegere/intellectum* – was

175

regularly etymologised and interpreted as a product of *intus* and *legere*, 'to read within' or 'to read beneath the surface'; and it was of course the two participles of this verb which gave the adjectives *intelligens* and *intellectivus* and the nouns *intelligentia* and *intellectus*.

To express the same idea in the vernacular, Dante would probably have chosen the verb 'intendere', which retained something of its root meaning of 'straining' or 'stretching out'. And there are similar analogies embedded in the verbs *comprehendere/comprehensum* and *abstrahere/abstractum*. Today, we may still accept that 'comprehension' requires a measure of 'abstraction'; but we no longer visualise the mind as 'drawing out' (*abs* + *trahere*) a latent meaning and then 'seizing' or 'grasping' it in a 'prehensile' way.

The human mind does not achieve its objectives in an instant, nor retain them for all time. On the contrary, the metaphors of 'reading', 'stretching', 'drawing out' and 'seizing' all suggest a continuing process. Its natural mode is that of a 'discourse' (*discursus*, from *discurrere/discursum*) in the original meaning of that word, charmingly defined by the Oxford Latin Dictionary as 'running this way and that', or 'bustling activity'.[4]

Another metaphor which is applicable to virtually all our mental activities is that of 'taking things to pieces' and 'putting them together again'. The Latin verbs *resolvere/resolutum* and *componere/compositum* yielded the nouns *resolutio* and *compositio*, and these were the normal translations of the original Greek terms 'analysis' and 'synthesis'.

In the task of analysis, the mind could also be said to 'split' things or to 'mark them off' one from another. The relevant verbs here were *dividere/divisum* and *distinguere/distinctum*; and the school of philosophy to which Dante owed his allegiance is of course famous or infamous for its cult of the 'division' and the 'distinction'.

In the task of synthesis, by contrast, reason uncovers likenesses concealed in diversity, or finds a 'oneness' in the midst of an apparent multiplicity. It begins, as we shall see, with individuals and arrives first at the species. It then sets out again from the species to arrive at the 'kind' (in Latin, *genus/generis*). And it is the hallmark of any kind of 'understanding' that it should aspire to the 'general', or that it should comprehend 'universal' categories which do not vary in place or in time (the adjective *universus* comes from *unus*, and its original meanings are defined by the Oxford Latin Dictionary as 'complete', 'regarded as a group', 'occurring all at once', 'forming a homogeneous whole').

Granted the insistence on 'bustling activity', moreover, it is hardly surprising that the mind was also imaged as a womb which must 'conceive' (*concipere/conceptum*) and give birth to its own progeny. A 'concept' was originally a *mente conceptum*, something 'conceived in the mind'.

However, the single most important group of metaphors for the acts of knowing and understanding are all related to 'vision'. The mind 'peers into' things (*inspicere/inspectum*) and 'sees inside' them (*intueri/intuitum*). Its supreme activities were called 'consideration', 'contemplation' and 'speculation'; and these nouns were derived from verbs meaning 'to gaze at the stars', 'to look for omens' and 'to keep a close watch'.

At the very humblest level, we often say 'I see' when we mean 'I understand'. And as we pass on now to a more detailed description of the faculties which make us human, we shall find that the mental powers were usually divided into three, in order to bring out important parallels between them and the main powers of the *anima sensitiva*. The instinctive 'desires' of animals are aroused by 'estimation' which follows upon 'perception' (or, as the scholastics would tend to say, upon 'apprehension'). Fully human 'desires' are consequent upon 'choice', and this presupposes a measure of '*comprehension*'. Seeing and understanding, apprehension and comprehension, do not simply resemble each other. They constitute the opening phases in the two sequences of events which lead to 'self-moved' and 'self-directed' operations respectively.

The speculative intellect and its tasks

In the third book of the *Convivio*, Dante notes that there are several faculties ('più vertudi') in the noblest part of the human soul, and he refers to the first of them as a 'vertù *scientifica*'. Later (in the fourth book and in *Monarchia*), he will prefer the established name, calling it the 'speculative intellect'.[5]

We shall not need to inquire closely into the highest activities of this 'scientific virtue' – that is, into what would have been called *speculatio* without qualification. 'Speculation' had nothing to do with 'guessing'. Dante could define 'l'atto di speculazione' or 'l'uso de lo speculativo' as 'consideration of the works of God and nature'. For him, this constituted the goal of human existence and the fullest happiness possible to our species.[6] And as such it must lie outside the scope of a book concerned primarily with perception and passion. But we must reconstruct, at least in outline, the *early* stages of the process by which the speculative intellect of each and every individual begins to elaborate and then to extend its understanding.

At the very beginning the intellect finds its raw material in the *species sensibiles*, familiarly called 'images' or 'visible forms'. (These, it will be remembered, are received in the common sense and, in optimum conditions, they correspond faithfully to the outward appearance of natural bodies.)

The intellect directs its attention to a number of these *species sensibiles*, stored in the 'treasure-house' of the memory; and it compares and contrasts images deriving from different bodies, or images deriving from one body over a period of time. It attains its first and lowest level of actuality when it grasps a *species intelligibilis* – familiarly, an 'intelligible form' or a 'structure' – which is to say, when it begins to grasp the 'inner nature' or the 'unchanging essence' of a given body. To put it still more simply: the intellect comes into action and reveals its existence when it intuits a set of features or properties which a given natural body possesses throughout its existence, and which it shares with other individual bodies in the same class or species, from which it differs only in 'accidental' or *in*essential ways.

This first stage of 'abstraction from matter' will provide the intellect with a set of notions, which would be expressed, in languages like Greek, Latin, medieval Italian and modern English, by the arbitrary signs which grammarians call 'common' nouns (e.g., 'cow', 'horse'; 'buttercup', 'daisy'). We must also posit similar processes of 'drawing out' information from the images stored in the memory which result in the identification of the kinds of *change* that bodies are perceived to undergo, and also in the identification of the accidental *qualities* that are seen to vary in one body over a period of time (or to vary between different bodies belonging to the same class or species). These parallel processes will furnish the notions conveyed by the basic verbs (e.g., 'to rise', 'to fall'; 'to laugh', 'to cry'), and by the basic adjectives (e.g., 'red', 'green'; 'hot', 'cold'; 'hairy', 'smooth').[7]

In the next phase, the starting point will be the pool of *species intelligibiles* (grouped now into the mental equivalents of common nouns, verbs and adjectives). And the results of the continuing process of 'drawing out' will be so far removed from the original sense impressions that we think of them as 'engendered', call them 'concepts', and refer to the corresponding linguistic signs as 'abstract' nouns.

It would not be appropriate here – even assuming it were possible – to trace all the steps by which the intellect ascends from species, such as 'cow' and 'horse' or 'buttercup' and 'daisy', to kinds, such as 'animals' and 'plants'. Nor do we need to divide and distinguish the stages by which it rises from individual colours or textures to the concepts of 'colour' and 'texture', and from these to the ideas of 'quality' or 'property'. Nor, again, can we follow the processes that lead from a first rudimentary classification of concepts like 'rising and falling' or 'laughing and crying' to the Aristotelian insight that there can be only four kinds of change in natural bodies.

For our present purposes it will be enough to make three main points. First, the parallel and successive processes of abstraction culminate in precisely those concepts with which we came to terms in part one: 'being', 'potency and act', 'form and matter', 'form and accident', 'powers and operations', 'first and second perfections', 'goodness', 'attraction and desire', 'efficient and final causes'.

Second, concepts like 'being', 'goodness' and 'final cause' are the simplest and most universal of categories. No further abstraction is possible. They are the *principia* or 'first principles' from which all subsequent operations of the intellect will start.

Third, the process which leads to the formation of a 'vocabulary' of concepts is clearly inseparable from the development of a conceptual 'syntax'. The conceptual vocabulary is already organised 'vertically', so to speak (in the kind of sequence that rises from 'cow' to 'animal', to 'living body', to 'life' and thence to 'being'). The conceptual syntax is that which enables the intellect to express the 'horizontal' links between concepts, so that we are able to understand that all 'change' must be from 'potency' to 'act', and hence that 'nothing comes of nothing'.[8] It will be seen, further, that this kind of proposition lays claims to 'universality' and 'necessity': the subject of each affirmation states or implies the word 'all'; and the predicate states or implies the words 'must' and 'always'.[9]

Of all the notions to be abstracted and linked by the speculative intellect, perhaps the most important are the concepts of 'form' and 'purpose' and the necessary connection between them in all existing bodies. Once this connection has been grasped, it becomes possible to say that these bodies 'could not be other than they are'; and this is precisely one of the conditions which Aristotle laid down for 'understanding' or *scientia* of the natural world. At this point the intellect has gone far beyond the mere 'cognition' that things are (*quia sunt*) to the 'comprehension' of their nature (*quod sunt*).[10]

A simple way of re-expressing and summarising the principal operations and achievements of the speculative intellect is to say that it ascertains the relationships between the 'intelligible species' which it has abstracted from the phenomena provided by the senses. As we have just seen, these relationships may be either 'vertical' or 'horizontal' in character; and the medieval Latin term which conveys both dimensions is *ordo/ordinis* – 'order'. Hence, the ultimate task of the intellect is to 'discover order' or to 'reduce concepts to order' – *ordinare*. The person who has become capable of performing this distinctively human activity is, literally, a *homo sapiens*. And this is the full meaning of the dense phrase: *sapientis est ordinare* (which Dante translates as 'conoscere l'ordine d'una cosa ad altra è proprio atto di ragione').[11]

Trying another approach, one might also say that the goal of the speculative intellect is *scientia*, and that this consists of a coherent set of acquired concepts and propositions which are 'true' (*verum*). In this context, however, 'truth' (*veritas*) entails a condition which is not necessarily required in ordinary usage: the concepts and propositions must be all-embracing, because 'knowledge bears on universals' (*scientia est universalium*).

In the case of the 'science of *nature*', which is our particular concern, the concepts must correspond to the inner 'structure' or 'essence' of the bodies which make up the cosmos, and the propositions must faithfully represent the recurrent processes of change to which all material bodies are necessarily subject. 'Truth' is the text 'written within' the natural world. 'Truth' is what the mind 'reads' in the act of intellection (*intus legere*) and what it subsequently 'gazes on' in the act of speculation (*speculari*).

Truth and the Beatific Vision

The foregoing sketch is open to objection not only for its many omissions and for its insistence on the paradigm of knowledge concerning *nature* ('la scienza naturale'), but also for its almost exclusively Aristotelian emphases. Dante, it cannot be said too often, was a Christian, a fellow-travelling Platonist, a poet and a man who felt that his own belated quest for *veritas*, *scientia* and *sapientia* had changed the course of his life. We must therefore flesh out the model in at least one important respect by taking account of Dante's conviction – shared with his whole culture – that truth could be read not only in the Book of Nature, but also in the Mind of its Author; or, to put it in other words, that the intellect's desire for truth was nothing other than a desire to contemplate the original order of all concepts in God.

Aristotle himself had shown (as the climax of his work on natural science) that there must be one supreme being, eternally unchanging and unmoved, who is the first or ultimate cause of all movement and change in the universe, in the sense that he is the *'final* cause' of the revolutions of the heavenly spheres. He is the supreme object of their desire towards whom they tend in the mode proper to their being. In Dante's words, he is 'uno Dio / solo ed etterno, che tutto 'l ciel move, / non moto, con amore e con desio'.[14]

Christianity taught that the supreme being – the one God – is also the first *'efficient* cause' of the universe. He is Alpha as well as Omega, 'the maker of heaven and earth, and of all things visible and invisible'. The pagan Greeks, meanwhile, had intuited the existence of a 'First Mind'. And it had become normal to fuse these distinct insights and to speak of the Mind of God or the Divine Mind ('la mente divina').[15]

These intuitions, beliefs and philosophical proofs had long been combined in such a way that the 'intelligible species' – whether considered as abstractions in the human mind or as Platonic entities in their own right – were thought to have pre-existed as exemplars or ideas in the First Mind. From this it seemed to follow that the 'order' which we discern in the parts of the universe and in their regular workings is simply the manifestation of the original order as it existed in the mind of the Creator. To seek the truth is to want to see the 'relationship between all substances and all their accidents' as they are 'bound together by love in one volume'. And this, as Dante makes clear in the climax of his *Comedy*, will be possible only in the Beatific Vision.[16]

Such an utterly un-Aristotelian way of conceiving the thrust of the speculative intellect has the additional merit of reasserting our affinity with the supreme being. We are created in his 'image and likeness', as we are told in the Book of Genesis. There is a resemblance between us from the moment that he breathes the breath of human life into the embryo. We become increasingly 'godlike' as we progressively actualise the potential of our mind, in which the image of God consists.[15]

The 'practical' intellect and its tasks

Understanding of this kind – a complete possession of the Truth in the union of mind with Mind – will indeed make us only a 'little lower than the angels' ('poco minore che li angeli').[16]

The angels were created as pure 'intelligences'. Those who did not join Satan in his rebellion are fully and permanently actualised, always knowing everything that it is possible for a created mind to know. They have never had to learn and never had to recollect. They never cease their contemplation of the Almighty, because they never become tired, never grow old, and are never distracted or turned aside by the pressing needs of daily life on earth, which entails continuous interaction with other bodies – inanimate, animate and human.[17]

Human beings, then, are somewhat less fortunate than the angels. But we are not to be conceived as intelligences *imprisoned* in matter. We are created in order to live out a life on the 'frontier' between the ideal universe of forms and the real world of bodies.[18] And, since 'Nature never fails to provide the necessaries', we are endowed with a second distinctively human power which mediates between the angel and the animal in us, that is, between the competing needs of the eternal 'good' of the speculative intellect and the varying 'goods' of our bodily frame.

This second power is akin to the instinctive faculty of 'estimation'. It enables us to *make* things which are analogous to the nests built by birds, or to *do* actions which resemble the flight of the lamb or the wolf's pursuit, but which are in fact impossible for animals to make or to do. (The distinction between the verbs *facere/ factum*, 'to make', and *agere/actum*, 'to do', has been lost in colloquial modern Italian, but was punctiliously observed by scholastic philosophers.)[19]

The most common name for this power was probably the '*practical* intellect' or the '*practical* reason'. For once, we need not be unduly suspicious of the meaning of this adjective in the modern European languages (although the distinction between 'theoretical' and 'practical' in medieval Latin is perhaps better conveyed by the contrast we make today when we distinguish between different branches of science as 'pure' and 'applied').[20] But it will be worth dwelling for a moment on the etymologies of some of the key words dealing with the activity of the practical reason, in order to become familiar once again with the underlying picture language.

Dante himself begins his description of the practical intellect by using four adjectives. These are 'ragionativo' (which tells us everything and nothing), 'inventivo', 'consigliativo' and 'giudicativo'.[21] 'Inventivo' comes from *invenire/inventum*, 'to find', and it reminds us that this second power of the mind must begin by 'discovering' possible solutions to particular problems, or possible answers to particular questions.[22]

Next, it must examine the advantages and disadvantages of the possible solutions it has 'found'. It must 'weigh them in the balance' (Dante uses the technical verb *deliberare*, which derives from *libra*, 'a scale'). And the noun 'consiglio' (*consilium*) and its derivatives which are used to describe this stage suggest that it is like a 'debate' in some political forum, where numerous participants express their opinions or give advice.

Finally, the practical intellect must give its 'judgement' and 'adjudicate' in favour of the best of the possible ways of doing or making whatever is required; and *iudicium* and its derivatives allude to the 'verdict' given in a court of law by the 'judge' (*iudex/iudicis*), after the two parties to a dispute have argued their respective cases. Another helpful metaphor is the one used by Dante in a very important passage relating to the 'virtue that takes counsel', as he calls it, where he compares its activity to the 'winnowing' which separates grain from the chaff.[23]

Even more than its elder brother, the practical intellect is 'discursive'. But instead of moving ever-further away from the scattered phenomena of the material world towards an ordered set of abstractions and archetypes, it takes these 'universal forms' as its *principia* – its 'points of departure' – and it returns step by step towards the concrete world with the intention of working on particular bodies in a particular place and time, either by 'making' or by 'doing' (*faciendo vel agendo*).[24]

To be a little more precise, the practical intellect (or practical reason) sets out from timeless 'principles', derived from the analysis of past experience, to find particular ways of modifying the present condition of particular bodies in such a way that their immediate future will be other than it would have been without the intervention of mind.[25] Or again – to shift the emphasis from *passatum, praesens* and *futurum* to *principium, medium* and *finis* – the practical reason applies general 'principles' to discover the particular 'means' to bring about a particular 'end'.

The main features of this essentially Aristotelian model will by now be tolerably clear, but there are a number of points concerning the concepts of *finis* and *scientia* in relation to the practical intellect which require clarification.

The practical reason does not 'debate' about the particular goal. All its discursive, inquisitive and deductive activity bears on the 'means' to that 'end': *ea quae sunt ad finem*. And the given end is always so important that it becomes the chief criterion or governing 'principle' regulating all assessment of the means. These will be 'good' if they are conducive to that end; and they will be 'better' if they lead there more economically, more swiftly or more humanely. This is the import of Aristotle's paradoxical dictum that, in ethics, 'the end is the beginning', *principium in operativis est ultimus finis*; or, to put it in modern English, 'the intended goal is the guiding principle'.[26]

It is important to recognise, too, that there is a hierarchy of ends, just as there is a hierarchy of concepts and a hierarchy of being.[27] Something which ranks as a 'mean' at one level of analysis would rank as an 'end' at another. For example, it might be taken for granted that young human beings need a thorough education. At the highest level, a *consilium* concerning the means to give them that education might reach the *iudicium* that the goal would best be achieved by a system of compulsory schooling with a core curriculum taught by professional teachers. At a lower, local level, the desirability of such a system would be taken as given. 'Debate' would focus on the building of the necessary school; and it would concentrate in particular on the site, design, materials and cost with regard to the resources of the particular community.

Reverting now to the crucial difference between human actions and those of animals and inanimate bodies, it will be remembered that all self-moving bodies change their position or state 'for the sake of a goal' (*propter finem*), and that this is tantamount to saying that all self-moving bodies change their position or state for the sake of an appropriate 'good' (*propter bonum*) which they require for their 'exist-ence' or for their 'perfection', and which they therefore desire.

The 'gravity' of a stone may be described, more figuratively than literally, as its permanent desire for the centre of the universe. The appetites of an animal or a human infant, by contrast, are inter-mittent and have to be periodically aroused by its 'apprehension' of some particular good. They move *propter bonum apprehensum*. Adult humans, by contrast, perform their distinctively human actions for the sake of a good or a goal which they have 'comprehended' or understood – *propter bonum intellectum*.

Sound reasoning and true principles

We turn next to consider two areas of doubt ('dubbi', 'dubitazioni') concerning the kind of understanding which is required or achieved by the practical intellect.

It should be clear from what has just been said that the closer one approaches the decisions which lead directly to concrete action in the world of particularity, change and contingency, the further one is removed from the conditions of universality, immutability and necessity which characterise true *scientia*. Aristotle therefore stresses that *scientia moralis* – the discipline which attempts to lay down some general principles for the conduct of our affairs – has to be content with that limited 'degree of certainty which the nature of the subject permits'.[28] Ethics is not like geometry; and practical reasoning is in some ways inferior to elementary arithmetic. People sometimes get their sums wrong, but the errors are easy to detect and there is a 'right' answer. Deliberation, on the other hand, very often results in actions that do not achieve the desired objective. And in such a case, there is rarely any retrospective agreement about which other means might have been effective, or whether the goal had in fact been attainable or even truly desirable.

To these 'dubbi' (which imply that the practical intellect is not much different from, and scarcely superior to, the power of estimation in a fox), Dante and his mentors would have answered that the admitted defects follow from two kinds of ignorance, and that both of these can be remedied. Errors in reasoning as such can be corrected by a proper training in the science of logic. And the errors which result from unimpeachable reasoning based on a false principle can be prevented by a prolonged study of the concepts of 'first philosophy' (such as those presented in part one of this book) and by the application of those concepts to the study of human nature itself.

On the assumption that 'Nature does nothing without a purpose', there must be a supreme goal for the existence of mankind, just as there is for all the other species. And the concept of *operatio propria* entails that this *ultimus finis* must consist in the perfect exercise of our highest, distinctive powers – the powers of the mind.[29]

To understand the 'operations' of these 'specific' powers (as we are beginning to do in this chapter) is simultaneously to know the *optimus finis in rebus humanis* to which all our limited objectives are subordinated as means to an end. To know that 'ultimo fine' is to possess the unshakeable 'principio' on which to found all the logical steps in all the deductive processes which lead to action.

Or, to put it another way, the fundamental knowledge required by the practical intellect is understanding of ourselves. This self-knowledge must take cognisance of our genus as a *corpus mobile animatum* and of the *differentiae* which set us apart as a species. But it must also take account of the aptitudes and talents that we possess as individuals. In Dante's view, the great diversity of human individuals is willed by Nature; and we must respect the 'foundations which Nature has laid'.[30]

The superior appetite: motive and will-power

Most of the actions that result from deliberation and judgement require the flexion and extension of our limbs. And the analogy which obtains between the mental and the sensitive powers suggested that there must be a third component in the mind, something that could act as the 'motive force' or 'efficient cause' of our 'loco-motion'. The Aristotelian natural philosopher would describe this human *vis motiva* as a 'higher appetite' (*appetitus superior*). But in ordinary language it is called the 'will'. Its name in Latin was *voluntas/voluntatis*, which is derived from the verb *volere/volitum*, 'to want', 'to wish'. And it is from the Latin noun that we get the adjective 'voluntary' (*voluntarius*).

In a sequence of events that originate in the mind, the will comes into action at the moment when *deliberatio* has resulted in a *iudicium* to the effect that the best way of achieving a particular goal would be such and such a course of action. It is at this point, on the borderline between 'judgement' and 'volition', that we can legitimately speak of the making of a 'choice' (*electio*).[31]

Once the will has been roused – in principle, it should follow rational choice in the same way that a passion follows instinctive estimation – its function is to provide the energy that will translate the mental resolve into bodily action. It must put the 'judgement' into 'execution' (*executio*, from *exsequi/exsecutum*, 'to follow through', 'to perform'); and it must sustain the motive force until the goal has been attained. Actions which proceed from this 'power of the will' (together with instinctively motivated actions that could have been *prevented* by 'will-power') are called 'voluntary'. And, as we shall see, it is they alone that can properly lay claim to the title of 'operazioni umane'.[32]

'Three and two and one': the unity of the mind

Each of the three components in the mind has its own characteristic excellence or virtue. And each may function more or less well in different individuals. (The natural philosophers Thales and Anaxagoras were proverbial for their unworldliness, even in Aristotle's day; and St Paul was not the first man to realise that he knew what was better and pursued what was worse.)[33]

But although there seemed to be good empirical grounds for a division of the mind into three, the tripartite model was to some extent threatened or undermined by an earlier and even simpler tradition. According to this rival tradition, there are in effect only two kinds of human existence, known as the 'contemplative life' and the 'active life'. This would suggest that all human operations are, in essence, of just two kinds: those which lead to the acquisition of pure knowledge for its own sake; and those – the vast majority – which relate to the rational ordering of our daily existence. And this in turn would imply that one need distinguish only two powers in the mind.

At first sight, there would seem to be no difficulty in reconciling the two approaches, since it would readily be conceded that the practical reason and the will work together as a single unit (the goal of 'deliberation' is action, and there can be no action without 'execution'). But closer analysis reveals that the bipartite model exerted a good deal of insidious pressure on the other. Specifically, it tended to support the assumption that human beings are divided into the great majority who 'do' or 'make', and the happy few who 'think'. It polarised the 'distinction' between the practical and the speculative intellects to the point where it was perceived as an 'opposition'. It made it tempting to argue that each of the two distinct 'kinds' of intellect existed in order to achieve a distinct goal, conferring a distinct kind of happiness. And, lastly, it seemed to demand a different evaluation of the two goals, the two happinesses and the two 'lives'.

Like all members of his culture, Dante knew and accepted this pre-Aristotelian and extraordinarily persistent opposition between the *vita contemplativa* and the *vita activa*. And like all intellectuals in his culture, he believed that the contemplative life was the higher or better of the two.

In the *Convivio*, as we have seen, he expresses his fervent conviction that human beings may fulfil themselves and attain perfect happiness here on earth in the contemplation of the truth (and he repeatedly tries to silence his own persistent doubts as to whether we can ever be fully happy when we are aware that certain truths will always remain beyond our comprehension).[34] Later, in the last chapter of *Monarchia*, he will argue more forcefully than ever before that man does, uniquely, have two distinct goals (*duo fines, duo ultima*). And although he now sees them as successive (the first to be attained in this bodily existence, the second in the afterlife), he still sees the second as higher and as consisting in the eternal contemplation of the Whole Truth. In *Paradiso*, too, he ranks the contemplatives above the rulers, the warriors and the teachers; and in the final cantos of the poem, the blessed are represented as seated in eternal contemplation, while the protagonist reaches the 'term of his desire' when his mind begins to 'circle' around God.[35]

In another context, we should have to discuss these texts and qualify these observations in considerable detail. But for our present purposes it is more important to shift the emphasis firmly in the other direction. Dante did polarise the two 'lives', giving pride of place to the contemplative. Nevertheless, he regarded the active life as good. He knew that it required the use of reason. And he recognised that he had dedicated his own energies to the lower of the two ends.

The 'use' of our practical intellect in the active life, he tells us, is 'full of delight'. It leads along a 'good path' to a 'good happiness'. The moral virtues (consisting essentially in the proper activity of the will) are 'fruits' of a good human 'seed'. Indeed, they are the 'most intimately human of our fruits, since they lie entirely within our power' ('propiissimi nostri frutti sono le morali vertudi, però che da ogni canto sono in nostra podestade'). The moral virtues are also said to be 'more universal, better known and more sought after' than the virtues of the intellect. If we were to compare ourselves to bees, the moral virtues would be the 'honey' rather than the 'wax'.[36]

Morality, Dante claims, is 'the beauty of philosophy'. In his ingenious ordering of the arts and sciences, he places ethics higher than metaphysics, because the understanding of human activity and happiness, which ethics provides, is precisely what impels us to study and to keep alive the other sciences. And by the same token, Solomon is held up for our admiration in *Paradiso* XIII because he asked God for the practical wisdom needed by a ruler ('regale prudenza') rather than the pure knowledge sought by the mathematician or philosopher.[37]

Dante clearly regarded himself as primarily a 'doer'. He tried to influence political events directly through his writings after his exile from Florence. In the *Convivio* and the *Comedy*, he was concerned to impart knowledge that would lead to virtuous action, to 'direct the will' of his readers, and to lead them from a 'state of wretchedness to a state of happiness'. He recognised that as a poet, he was a 'maker' – a maker of verses and a constructor of fictions.[38] He was also the author of a highly detailed treatise on the craft of making songs.

In all these ways, Dante was implicitly stressing that the mind is neither three, nor two, but one. And it is in this spirit that we must read some further passages from the *Convivio*, where he insists that a 'human' life is *any* life that is lived *secundum rationem* – 'in conformity with reason'. (It will be seen that, in these passages, he tends to adopt 'ragione' as the comprehensive name for our 'most noble part'.)

He specifies that the 'rational part' consists of the will and the intellect ('la parte razionale, cioè la volontade e lo intelletto'). He also makes it clear that when he refers to the 'operations which are proper to the rational soul', he is thinking of something as basic as ordinary communication through language and ordinary social intercourse (the verb 'ragionare' was frequently used as a more lofty synonym for 'parlare'):

> The operations proper to the rational soul [are those] in which the divine light shines most clearly, that is, in speech and in the actions which are

usually described as manners or conduct. For it must be made clear that, among animate beings, man alone is able to speak and man alone is characterised by actions or conduct called rational, because he alone has reason. (*Con.* III, vii, 8)

For Dante, the phrase 'living together in accordance with our *humanity*' meant simply 'living according to reason'.[39] To depart from reason, or to fail to use reason (that is, to do no more than vegetate, feel and move about, and never to look to the journey's end or consider how to get there) is to live like a beast, or to be dead!

Things should be defined and named in accordance with the highest perfection of their form, as man is defined by his reason and not by his senses or any less perfect power. Hence, when we say that a man 'lives', we ought to understand that he is using reason, which is the life proper to his species and the actualisation of his most noble part ['sua speziale vita e atto de la sua più nobile parte']. And so the man who abandons reason and uses only the sensitive part of his soul does not live as a man but as a beast. As Boethius puts it so well, 'he lives the life of a donkey'.

(*ibid.*, II, vii, 3)

As Aristotle says in the second book of the *De anima*, living is the mode of being proper to living things. And granted that there are many different forms of life, and granted also that things must be defined according to their most noble part, it is clear that, for animals, living consists in sensation, whereas, for man, living is using reason. Using reason, therefore, is the human mode of being; and so to renounce that use is to renounce being, and therefore to be dead. And is it not renouncing the use of reason if one fails to take thought ['ragionare'] about the end of our life? And is it not renouncing the use of reason if one does not take thought about the route? (*ibid.*, IV, vii, 11–12, abbreviated)

The incorporeality of mind as the condition of self-direction

This chapter began by introducing the concept of 'self-direction'. This was shown to require the existence of a faculty called 'mind' (which proved to be the very faculty that enables us to form concepts, to divide and regroup them, and thereby to 'order' them in their proper vertical and horizontal relationships). A process of analysis and synthesis revealed the presence of a 'trinity' of powers within the mind, which was nevertheless seen to be uncompromised in its essential unity. And we must now close the circle by returning to the original concept of self-direction to discover how this depends on a crucial feature in the relationship between the human psyche and the human body.

Not only is the mind 'one' (rather than three or two separable components), it is a component of the unique 'vital principle' which structures our body and confers vegetative and sensitive as well as self-conscious, rational life on each one of us. As Dante reminds us, we do not have three different souls, one for each level of activity, but 'one soul only', which 'lives and feels and reflects inwardly upon its own nature' ('che vive e sente e sé in sé rigira').[40]

Nevertheless, although this single *anima* is the form of a *corpus*, the mind, which constitutes its 'most noble part', is radically different from the sensitive powers, in that it does not make use of a specific bodily organ. The power of vision requires an eye; the power of locomotion requires limbs; and neither can function if the relevant organs are diseased or cut away. Not so the intellect.

It is admittedly a precondition of rational life that the brain should be 'complete' in its 'articulation'. But the cerebral chambers are the organs of the internal senses of imagination, estimation and memory. The intellect takes the images received and stored in the brain as its point of departure, but – in Dante's view – it does not 'use' the brain in its activity of abstraction, deduction or contemplation. The intellect has no organ.[41]

The distinction between sensing and knowing is of the utmost importance, because the brain – like all the corporeal organs – can be acted upon and subjected to 'enforced' change by other bodies. Of course, these external bodies do not usually make their impact directly, for example, by striking a blow on the skull. But they are continually imparting qualitative changes to the atmosphere which are transmitted via the spirits or the blood to the brain itself. And it was by this kind of corporeal transmission – so it was almost universally believed – that the brain, no less than the heart, liver and loins, could be directly affected by the 'celestial influences' beloved of medieval astrology.[42]

The mind, therefore, is quite different from the faculties of apprehension and feeling. In the opinion of Dante and his teachers, a power which abstracts concepts from matter cannot itself be made of matter or use a material tool. The same seemed to be true of the power to discover 'order' and to reach conclusions of 'universal' import. Rational 'discourse' cannot be caused or altered by any series of events in the material universe. Similarly, the will cannot be material, if it is able to implement conclusions and projects which are 'denuded of matter'. In short, no part of the mind can be 'imprinted', 'impressed', 'stamped', 'sealed', 'influenced' or 'impeded' by images from any earthly body or by the moving light-rays of a heavenly body.[43]

Despite all the difficulties inseparable from this position, Dante held that the mind is capable of initiating action in and through the body (of which it constitutes the highest 'part' of the substantial form), but that it cannot be acted upon by external bodies. This is what is meant by saying that the mind is 'free'. And it is because of this freedom (as will become clearer in the next chapter) that we are not simply 'self-moving' animals, but 'self-directing'.

We owe the 'freedom of our will', or the 'freedom consisting in the possession of will', to the fact that the human soul is created directly (that is, without any bodily intermediary) by God.[44] It is only one of many gifts that we receive from the 'generosity' of our creator (they include our personal immortality, for example, or our ability to understand). But, as Dante makes Beatrice say, it is the greatest and most godlike of them all.

> 'Lo maggior don che Dio per sua larghezza
> fesse creando, e a la sua bontate
> più conformato, e quel ch'e' più apprezza,
>   fu de la volontà la libertate;
> di che le creature intelligenti,
> e tutte e sole, fuoro e son dotate.'   (*Par.* v, 19–24)

'The greatest of all the gifts made by God in the act of creation, the one which most resembles his nature, and the one he prizes most highly, is freedom of the will – a freedom with which all intelligent beings without exception were and are endowed.'

CHAPTER TEN

Aspects of human freedom

On the threshhold

Dante's celebration of the freedom of the will comes at the beginning of the fifth canto of *Paradiso*, where it serves as the preface to a discussion of the most paradoxical use of our freedom, and as the climactic summary of what the protagonist has learnt during his first encounter in the heavens. It is to that encounter we must now return in order to clarify the nature and limits of human freedom.

As we saw in chapter 6, the episode takes place inside the moon itself and it begins when the protagonist catches sight of a group of welcoming faces. These appear so faintly within the luminous and cloud-like body of the moon that he jumps to the conclusion that they must be reflections of people who are standing behind him. His false deduction is corrected first by his sense of sight – he turns round and sees nothing – and then by the words of Beatrice.

His 'sweet guide' smilingly teases him for his 'childish thought', which still lacks the confidence to 'rest its feet upon the truth'. She assures him that the apparitions are 'true beings'; and she urges him to believe what they will say, because their desires are fully satisfied by the 'True Light' who will 'not allow their feet to stray'.[1] Suitably emboldened, her pupil addresses the soul who seems most eager to speak, drawing on the 'sweet' style of his youthful love poetry to express the consummate sweetness of the soul's heavenly bliss and the sweetness of his own desire for enlightenment, which is almost overpowering in its intensity:

'O ben creato spirito, che a' rai
di vita etterna la dolcezza senti
che, non gustata, non s'intende mai,
grazïoso mi fia se mi contenti
del nome tuo e de la vostra sorte.'   (*Par.* III, 37–41)

'O well-created spirit who, in the rays of eternal life, experience the sweetness that can never be understood until it is tasted, it will be a kindness if you satisfy my longing to know your name and the condition of yourself and your companions.'

With 'laughing eyes' and a delightful playfulness in her speech, the soul hastens to comply with this irresistible request. She describes herself as having been a 'virgin sister in the world', and holds back her name until the last possible moment by saying, 'if your mind will look carefully into itself, my being more beautiful will conceal me no longer, but you will recognise that I am – Piccarda':

'I' fui nel mondo vergine sorella;
e se la mente tua ben sé riguarda,
non mi ti celerà l'esser più bella,
ma riconoscerai ch'i' son Piccarda.'   (*ibid.*, 46–9)

The unusual name, the insistence on her beauty, and the delayed recognition should all alert us to the fact that this is one of the encounters for which we have been specially prepared. Twelve cantos earlier, the protagonist had already made an inquiry concerning her whereabouts: 'dimmi ... dov' è Piccarda?'[2] This question was put to her brother, Forese Donati, whom Dante met on the circle of the gluttonous in Purgatory (it may be remembered that Dante was slow to recognise Forese too – in *that* case because of his extreme emaciation). And the protagonist had already been assured that 'she is triumphing joyfully in her crown on high Olympus' – a fact which does not surprise her brother, since he had been unable to decide in his own mind 'whether she had been more beautiful or more virtuous'. So, Dante's first encounter in the heavenly spheres is with a Florentine woman whom he had known personally, a member of the powerful Guelph family into which he had married, the sister of a close friend and companion in revelry – and the sister of a bitter enemy! (Corso Donati, who was still alive in 1300, was to be the prime mover in the *coup d'état* of November 1301, which led to the triumph of the Black faction within the Guelph party and to Dante's exile from his native city.)[3]

However, Piccarda was not chosen as spokeswoman of the first welcoming party simply because of her beauty and virtue, or because of the complex bonds of family and friendship. For Dante, her brief life had evidently come to illustrate two important lessons about the nature of human freedom and therefore about the operations of the will. These are the lessons that the reader and the protagonist will be invited to 'abstract from the particular' and to elevate to the status of 'universal knowledge', as they listen to the details of Piccarda's story, find themselves puzzled and perplexed, and turn for guidance to an authoritative teacher.

Piccarda's story

Pressed to say more about herself, Piccarda devotes the first six lines of her reply to a poetic periphrasis describing St Clare and the 'rule and habit' instituted by the saint in emulation of her contemporary and friend, St Francis of Assisi – a rule established, Piccarda specifies, in order that 'waking and sleeping, women might remain until death with that Bridegroom who accepts every vow that true love aligns with his desire'.[4] Then, in six modestly reticent but delicately revealing lines, she tells of her own entry into the order of Poor Clares, her abduction from the 'sweet cloister' by members of her own family, and her subsequent wretchedness (we are left to deduce that she was forced into a marriage and only released from her misery by an early death).

> 'Dal mondo, per seguirla, giovinetta
> fuggi'mi, e nel suo abito mi chiusi
> e promisi la via de la sua setta.
> Uomini poi, a mal più ch'a bene usi,
> fuor mi rapiron de la dolce chiostra:
> Iddio si sa qual poi mia vita fusi.'   (*ibid.*, 103–8)

'As a young girl I fled the world to follow her, enfolding myself in her habit and promising the way of her order. Then men, more accustomed to evil than good, snatched me out of the sweet cloister. Only God knows what my life then became.'

It now appears that what Piccarda has revealed about herself ('ciò ch'io dico di me') must be valid, in general terms, for the whole group of souls. The pronouns shift from singular to plural again ('la spera *nostra*'), and from the first to the third person, as Piccarda alludes to the similar fate which befell her more illustrious companion, Constance, a daughter of the king of Sicily, who, a hundred years earlier, had been forcibly removed from a convent to marry Emperor Henry of Swabia, and thus to become the mother of Frederick II:

> 'E quest' altro splendor che ti si mostra
> da la mia destra parte e che s'accende
> di tutto il lume de la spera nostra,
>   ciò ch'io dico di me, di sé intende;
> sorella fu, e così le fu tolta
> di capo l'ombra de le sacre bende.
>   Ma poi che pur al mondo fu rivolta
> contra suo grado e contra buona usanza,
> non fu dal vel del cor già mai disciolta.
>   Quest' è la luce de la gran Costanza
> che del secondo vento di Soave
> generò 'l terzo e l'ultima possanza.'   (*ibid.*, 109–20)

'And this other radiance who appears on my right and blazes with all the light of our sphere, refers to her own person what I have said about myself. She was a nun, and the shade of the holy head-dress was plucked from her head in the same way. But when she was thrust back into the world – against her desire and against good custom – she was never stripped of the veil in her heart. This is the light of Constance the Great, who from the second wind of Swabia conceived the third and final force.'

As so often in the Middle Ages, names are assumed to be 'cousins to the deeds' (which is how Chaucer translated the dictum quoted by Dante: *nomina sunt consequentia rerum*).[5] And by defending the 'constancy' of the Empress Constance, Piccarda is of course asserting her own fidelity to the Bridegroom whom she had apparently betrayed when she went through a ceremony of marriage with an earthly groom. She too, had never put aside the 'veil of the heart'.

The 'darker signs'

By concentrating on the moment of meeting at the beginning of the canto, and by giving prominence to the 'splendore' of the 'luce de la gran Costanza', we have done justice to the most important truth which Dante set out to convey in this first encounter with the blessed. Imagery, verbal music and psychological insight all combine to express the souls' joy, their playfulness, their eagerness to please, their love, their ardour – in a word, their 'beatitude'. In the central section of the canto, it is indeed conceded that there are degrees of blessedness in heaven, but Piccarda's first speech is perfectly summarised by the protagonist when he exclaims:

> Chiaro mi fu allor come ogne dove
> in cielo è paradiso, *etsi* la grazia
> del sommo ben d'un modo non vi piove.　　　(*ibid.*, 88–90)

It was clear to me then that every 'where' in heaven is Paradise, even though the grace of the Supreme Good does not rain down equally there.

There is nevertheless an undercurrent of sadness and regret in this episode, a hint of gloom analogous to the dark patches ('segni bui') on the luminous surface of the moon, which had become the major topic in the preceding canto. Beatrice referred to the souls as being 'relegated' here because of some 'shortcoming' in their vows. And although Piccarda has insisted that she is 'blessedly happy among these other blessedly happy spirits' ('con questi altri beati, / beata sono'), she concedes in the same breath that they are in the 'slowest of the heavenly spheres' and admits that their condition ('sorte') does indeed seem very lowly ('giù cotanto'), explaining that it was assigned to them because their 'vows had been neglected and rendered void in some respect'.[6]

Aristotle's discussion of voluntary, involuntary and 'mixed' actions

It is this last phrase which remains in the pilgrim's mind as he listens to the stories of Piccarda and Constance; and it is this which occasions the perplexity ('dubitazione') which makes him turn to Beatrice for enlightenment after the souls have receded into the body of the moon and disappeared from view.

To his mortal eye, heavenly justice seems unjust. He has been told that the souls are given their lowly position because they neglected their vows. But he cannot understand 'how an act of violence done by someone else can reduce the amount of my reward, if my intention to do good persists?':[7]

> 'Se 'l buon voler dura,
> la vïolenza altrui per qual ragione
> di meritar mi scema la misura?'   (IV, 19–21)

Incredibly enough, the challenge posed to Christian justice by the misfortunes of an obscure Florentine nun will be met and turned aside with the aid of concepts, arguments, distinctions and examples which all derive from the analysis of voluntary and involuntary actions given by Aristotle. And since Dante nowhere draws more consistently on a single passage of the Philosopher than he does in *Paradiso* IV, it will be worth looking at the main points in Aristotle's discussion before examining Beatrice's reply.

In the first chapter of the third book of the *Ethics*, Aristotle begins by noting that 'praise and blame are accorded only to voluntary actions'. It therefore 'seems necessary for the student of ethics to define the difference between the voluntary and the involuntary'; and 'this will be of service also to legislators in assigning rewards and punishments'. Next, he notes that 'it is generally held that actions are involuntary when they are done under compulsion [*per violentiam*] or through ignorance'; and that 'an action is compulsory [*violentum*] when its origin is from without, being of such a nature that the agent contributes nothing to it'. His first example, moreover, could hardly be more pertinent, since he invites us to think of 'someone being carried somewhere by people who have him in their power'.[8]

This definition of compulsory actions will be familiar from the distinction between violent and natural motion explained in chapter 4 of this book; but Aristotle does not rest content with such extreme and therefore unenlightening examples as the pebble on the beach and the boy with his sling. He immediately concedes that there is an element of doubt about the voluntary status of 'actions done through fear of a worse alternative [*propter timorem maiorum malorum*], for example, when a man does something shameful on the orders of a tyrant who is holding his parents and children as hostages, or if a merchant jettisons his cargo during a storm'. 'In ordinary circumstances', he continues, 'no one would throw his property away voluntarily, but anyone would do so in order to save his life and the life of his shipmates.' And so Aristotle's preliminary conclusion is that we ought to recognise an intermediate category of actions which could be called composite or 'mixed' (*operationes mixtae*).

No sooner has he made this concession, however, than he insists that 'these mixed actions approximate rather to the voluntary class' (*magis accedunt ad voluntarias operationes*), the reason being that they were 'chosen or willed at the moment when they were actually performed' (*sunt voluntariae tunc quando sunt operatae*). Always mindful of the fact that a human being is a *corpus organicum seipsum movens*, he notes that in such an action 'the origin of the movement of the parts of the body lies in the agent' (*principium movendi organicas partes est in ipso homine*). And he also implicitly reasserts the interdependence of the will and the 'practical intellect' (which is concerned not with the discovery of universal truths, but with decisions as to the best available course of action in a given case), by stressing that all voluntary actions are done 'in particular circumstances at a particular time'. It follows, therefore, that when they are *evaluated* – praised or blamed, rewarded or punished – the evaluation must take account of the particular circumstances (*particulares circumstantiae*).

At the same time, Aristotle is not a dualist or a rigid 'hardliner'. He duly acknowledges the 'absolute and universal' conclusions of the 'speculative intellect' when he adds the rider that 'although these actions are more voluntary than not, they are perhaps involuntary apart from the circumstances [*absolute et in universali considerando eas, sunt involuntariae*], for no one would do such an action in and for itself'. In this frame of mind he can recognise that sometimes men are actually praised – the acid test – 'for deeds of this mixed class, namely, when they submit to some disgrace or pain as the price of some lofty and noble object'.[9] And in other cases, submission may be at least condoned 'when a man does something wrong through fear of penalties that impose too great a strain on human nature, and that no one could endure'.

Aristotle does feel the need to proclaim some moral absolutes. 'There seem to be certain acts', he says, 'which a man cannot be compelled to do, and rather than do them he ought to submit to the most terrible death. For instance, we think it ridiculous that Alcmaeon in Euripides' play is compelled by certain threats to murder his mother!' But having established the philosophical point, Aristotle's experience, tolerance and insight into the complexity of human affairs lead him to conclude his summary with these words of caution: 'It is not easy to lay down rules for deciding which of two alternatives is to be chosen, for particular cases differ widely.'

Beatrice's reply: 'Volontà non s'ammorza'

In her solution to Dante's dilemma about the justice of Piccarda's 'relegation' to the lowest and slowest of the spheres, Beatrice brings the Aristotelian concepts into sharper focus and clarifies the issues by dividing the material into two brief *quaestiones*. Her exposition is so lucid that a slightly expanded translation will be enough to bring out most of the points of interest, without the need for further comment or paraphrase.

In the first *quaestio*, Beatrice asserts the voluntary status of actions performed under duress:

> If we speak of 'violence' or 'compulsion' whenever the patient body does not collaborate in any way with the external body that induces the change, then these souls cannot be excused on the grounds that they acted under compulsion.
>
> The will is not extinguished unless it so wills. It behaves like the nature of Fire [which will always maintain its upward thrust] even though an outside force pushes it aside a thousand times. Hence, if the will 'bends' – no matter how slightly – it is 'following' the external force. And 'follow the external force' is precisely what these souls did when they were physically able to seek refuge again in the holy place.
>
> If their will had been totally unflinching – like the will-power which kept St Lawrence on his gridiron and made Mucius Scaevola punish his hand so severely – it would have driven them back along the road down which they had been dragged, as soon as they were freed from physical restraint. But a will of such integrity is all too rare.[10]　　(*Par.* IV, 73–87)

The intellectual and moral pressure is briefly relaxed in a transitional passage, as we approach the apparent contradiction between the true words spoken by Piccarda, who claimed that Constance had never broken the vows in her heart, and the equally true words of Beatrice, who has just insisted that Constance did 'bend with the remover to remove' at the stage when she could have returned to the convent but failed to do so for fear of the consequences. Then it is back to Aristotle for the second *quaestio*:

> It has often happened, brother, that people have unwillingly done what they ought not to have done in order to avoid danger, as Alcmaeon did when he killed his own mother at his father's instigation, becoming pitiless in pursuit of filial piety.
>
> I want you to grasp that it is at this point that the external force merges with the will, and that their joint action is such that the offences cannot

simply be condoned. The absolute will does not consent to the wrong-doing. But the will does consent to the extent that it fears [and seeks to avoid] the graver sufferings into which it would fall if it continues to resist. When Piccarda expresses her point of view, she is referring to the absolute will; whereas I am referring to the other; and so we are both speaking the truth.[11]   (*ibid.*, 100–14)

Dantean emphases

It seems undeniable, then, that the *Ethics* is the main source of Beatrice's reply at almost every point – from the recognition of actions taken 'unwillingly' in order to 'escape danger' or out of 'fear of greater suffering', to the establishment of a category of 'mixed' actions and the distinction between 'absolute' and 'relative' consider-ations; or, more important, from the example of Alcmaeon, to the literal translation of Aristotle's definition of *violentia* and to the treatment of the will as an internal 'motive force', able to 'follow' or to 'hold itself back' ('seguire' or 'ritrarsi') and capable of 'pushing' the body back along a road, in much the same way that a band of men might have 'pulled' it the other way ('ripingere', 'trarre').

At the same time, there is a profound difference of emphasis. Aristotle does not introduce the distinction between 'instinctive love', which is found in animals, plants, minerals and the four elements, and 'elective love', which is found only in angels and man. For Dante, the likenesses and unlikenesses between the two loves are always of crucial importance.

In the central cantos of *Purgatorio* (where the distinction is intro-duced for the first time in the poem), Virgil leaves the implication that elective love is in a sense inferior to instinctive love, since it alone is 'capable of going astray, either by aiming at the wrong object or by pursuing the right object with too much or too little vigour'.[12] And the story of Piccarda and Constance seems to suggest that human love is weaker than that of the elements, because it can be dimmed or even extinguished by the mere prospect of an obstacle or by the threat of external force.

The first implication is corrected in *Paradiso* I.[13] The second is dealt with in the *quaestio* we have just read. Dante-the-poet recalls the instinctive, inalienable, unerring thrust of the element Fire towards its 'proper place' in the cosmos, only in order to assert that the conscious drive of the will is, or can be, equally inextinguishable. It is for the same reason that he introduces the two positive examples of the Christian martyr, St Lawrence, and the Roman hero, Mucius Scaevola, both of whom continued to defy 'the ruler who had them in his power' even when the flames were consuming their flesh. Not all men are heroes; but human nature is capable of heroism. This is also why Dante transfers the distinction between 'absolute' and 'relative' from the operations of the intellect (which is where it appears in the Aristotelian source) to the operations of the will.

For Dante, the will can be absolute in its own realm. Nothing except an act of the will itself can cause it to abandon its inclination to the object or objectives which the intellect has indicated as good, or to overcome its aversion to those which the intellect has indicated as bad. 'Volontà, se non vuol, non s'ammorza.' This is the most important lesson to be learnt from the encounter with Piccarda. And it is the one which Dante will single out in his summary, as we have already seen, when he praises the *freedom* of the will ('de la volontà la libertate') as the most precious of all God's gifts to human kind.

Other problems concerning freedom in Paradiso III–V

Before we leave the Heaven of the Moon, there are several other lessons to be gleaned concerning the operations of the will and the nature of our freedom.

The opening lines of the fourth canto invite us to reflect on the relationship between the will and the practical intellect in a hypothetical set of circumstances where the intellect is perfectly able to recognise good and bad, but is unable to decide *which* of two objects to pursue or to avoid, because the competing *bona* are equally attractive, or because the alternative *mala* are equally repellent. Dante here subscribes to the view that the will would in effect be paralysed, and the human agent unable to act, if the practical intellect were incapable of preferring one course of action to another.[14] (It will be noticed that Dante, typically, compares the instinctive desire or fear of a dog and a lamb with the elective love of a 'free man'.)

> Intra due cibi, distanti e moventi
> d'un modo, prima si morria di fame,
> che liber' omo l'un recasse ai denti;

> sì si starebbe un agno intra due brame
> di fieri lupi, igualmente temendo;
> sì si starebbe un cane intra due dame.   (*Par.* IV, 1–6)

Placed between two equidistant and equally desirable foods, a free man would die of hunger before he could sink his teeth into one of them, just as a lamb would remain motionless if it were caught between the appetites of two fierce wolves, fearing them equally, or as a dog would remain motionless between two hinds.

More importantly, the central section of canto III requires us to meditate on the relationship between the will of each individual human being and the will of God.

God has created us in his image and given us an unquenchable desire for union with him. Expressed in the spatial imagery of the poem, God's intention is that we should seek him and move towards a particular place in the hierarchy of heaven. Expressed more analytically, his intention is that we should actualise the powers with which he has endowed us. We must actualise, primarily, our intellect and will, which we all possess as members of the human species; but we must also develop to the full our individual talents and aptitudes, which vary in kind and in degree from one person to another (human beings are not created equal).[15]

Once we have used our mental powers to know ourselves – to understand ourselves, both as human beings and as distinct individuals – the best possible use of our practical reason is to choose those objects or objectives which will lead to the fulfilment of our potential; and the best possible use of our will is to pursue those *bona* unwaveringly. We have to '*become* what we are' in the knowledge that 'we *are* what we are' because this was God's intention and will.

Translated back into spatial imagery, the best use of the will is to stay on the 'main road' and to strive towards the successive 'staging-posts' along the route which leads to the destination that God has 'decreed' for us (our 'sito decreto'). We cannot use the 'freedom of the will' better than to will what he willed on our behalf. Only when we freely submit our will to his greater will shall we find peace: 'e 'n la sua volontade è nostra pace'.[16]

The nearest one might come to such an ideal submission in this life might be to enter a religious order. When novices like Piccarda 'fled the world', they dedicated themselves totally to the service of God. They made an irrevocable vow of obedience in the belief that their superiors would henceforth be the best judges of what they should do in order to achieve God's purpose. And this was the concrete situation – extremely common in Dante's society – which gave rise to the last problem concerning the nature of our freedom to be dealt with in the Heaven of the Moon.

As the stories of Piccarda and Constance clearly illustrate, religious vows were often neglected or not fully maintained ('negletti', 'manchi'). Hence, the protagonist wants to know if there is any way of making satisfaction for the broken promise by means of other good deeds or other kinds of service ('altri beni', 'altro servigio') in such a way that the offence would be cancelled and the 'soul made safe from attainder' ('che l'anima sicuri di letigio').[17]

In her reply, Beatrice insists that when a vow is made to God, it is quite impossible to rescind it or to change its terms unilaterally without incurring a divine penalty. (It is, however, also made clear that the Church is empowered to declare the vow invalid or to substitute other, more arduous forms of service.) As far as Dante's immediate audience was concerned, the chief message of this long speech was that Christians should be much less precipitate in making vows.[18] But for our present purposes, we may confine our attention to the lines near the beginning of Beatrice's speech, which immediately follow her fervent praise of the 'freedom of the will':

> 'Or ti parrà, se tu quinci argomenti,
> l'alto valor del voto, s'è sì fatto
> che Dio consenta quando tu consenti;
>   ché, nel fermar tra Dio e l'omo il patto,
> vittima fassi di questo tesoro,
> tal quale io dico; e fassi col suo atto.'   (v, 25–30)

'If you base your argument on the premise [that the freedom of the will is God's greatest gift to man], you will see the paramount value of the vow, if it is made in such a way that God consents when you consent. Because when the pact is sealed between God and man, the treasure I have just described becomes a sacrificial offering; and it does this by its own act.'

There are three points to notice here. First, a religious vow has the same inestimable worth in the eyes of God as the 'treasure' of human freedom for which it was exchanged. Second, there is no 'admixture' of compulsion. Making a vow is not an *operatio mixta*. Renunciation of freedom is a free act of the will. Third, the 'contract' will not be binding unless both partners freely agree to the conditions.[19] And on closer analysis, the most revealing detail proves to be the choice and repetition of the verb 'consentire' in the conditional clause, because it is highly characteristic of Dante's stance with regard to the will that he should denote its supreme activity as 'consent'.

Freedom located in the ability to give and withhold consent

To understand why the notion of 'consent' should be so fundamental, we must bear in mind that Dante would not have given such prominence to the issues of freedom and individual responsibility if he had not known that they were widely misunderstood or denied. He was on the defensive, too, because he was fully aware from personal experience of the weight of the evidence marshalled against his views, and he knew the reasons underlying the popular confusion.

Then, as now, people commonly clung to various forms of fatalism or determinism. Then, as now, they were ready to blame their faults and shortcomings on heredity and environment, or, as they sometimes said, on 'nature and nurture'. They believed that the 'first nature' (the individual temperament produced by the father's seed, the complexion of the elements and the influences of the stars) came together with the 'second nature' (the habits instilled by parents and educators) to 'dispose' and 'incline' each individual to behave fairly consistently and predictably, whatever the circumstances might be, whatever the objectives and whatever the rights and wrongs of the particular case.

Then, as now, it was evident that many people do not devise their own personal plans of action any more than they discover for themselves the truths of mathematics, logic or the natural sciences. With their *speculative* intellect, they learn what others already know and can teach. With their *practical* intellect, they grasp the guidelines provided by the law (Dante called it 'Reason written down') and acquiesce in the decisions taken on their behalf by parents, leaders or rulers. Hence the moment of 'choice' – the moment when *iudicium* becomes *electio* – is usually no more than a willingness to obey the commands of those in authority, or to disobey those commands and risk the anticipated unpleasant consequences.[20]

More important still – and here we link up again with the first part of this book – it was obvious that the will was not the only 'motive force', and that the practical intellect was not the only 'arbiter' able to decide the appropriate course of action in a particular set of circumstances. The muscles of the body are activated by the passions. These are called into play by 'estimation'. This follows spontaneously on apprehension. Apprehension is the result of changes caused to the atmosphere, the organs of sense, the spirits and the brain by external objects – objects which are close, here, and now. In short, the human body, no less than that of brute beasts, is frequently moved by instinctive responses to forces in the outside world before a truly independent, internal principle can come into play.

Dante used a traditional simile when he compared the relationship of the mental and the sensitive powers in man to that between a rider and his unruly horse.[21] Twentieth-century technology allows us to express the same insight by imagining the human body as something like a 'dual-control' car of the kind occasionally used by driving schools.

In this updated version of the image, the sensitive powers are represented by the 'pupil', who sits behind the steering-wheel with the rational 'instructor' at his side. There is one engine, one set of wheels and one system of transmission. But there are two independent brakes and two accelerators; and the 'instructor' can easily grasp the single steering-wheel. What happens in life is that the rash 'pupil' will set this vehicle careering along the road before the 'instructor' has had time to make up his mind about the destination or the route, and before he has had time to think about the obstacles along the way and how best to negotiate them. Most of us would not find it easy to think straight or to override the pupil's controls in such circumstances.

One of Dante's greatest strengths as a poet and a moralist is that he is so vividly and lucidly aware of all the factors that limit our freedom or even inhibit the making of any choice whatsoever. He knows that we are put under pressure by other human beings and by the things which attract and repel us. He also knows that we can often do no better than obey an experienced and prudent leader, or follow the promptings of our instincts which are there, after all, to ensure the survival of the individual or the survival of the species.

It is for reasons such as these that Dante does not devote much attention to the hypothetical model, presented in the previous chapter, in which a totally unconstrained 'human operation' has its origin in the mind of the agent. Instead, he concentrates on cases where a sequence of physiological events has been set in motion by external agents, and where the intellect and the will are sent to 'take over command' from the passions, which are already committed to pursuit, retreat or entrenchment. The newly posted 'commanding officers' may well decide that the 'tactics' adopted by their subordinates are perfectly correct. But their consent is required and must not simply be taken for granted.

These highly relevant analogies from the field of military operations can help us to grasp the two points that Dante most wants to establish. First, the intellect and the will have the power to *withhold* consent and to choose different tactics. Second, whatever they decide to do, the intellect and the will are jointly responsible for all the forces under their command. It is they who are praised for a victory or blamed for a defeat, even though the immediate response came from the passions and it was they who did all the fighting.

Freedom located in the ability to form dispassionate judgements

We have repeatedly seen that the practical intellect and the will work so closely together as a team that it is difficult to determine which of the two powers is directly responsible for the act of 'choice'.

To the Aristotelian, however, their two activities are analytically distinct. And by giving pride of place to the notion of consent, Dante, at least, is implicitly treating the will not only as a separate partner in the team, but as the *senior* partner. We are free, he is saying, to the extent that the passions are governed by the will.

There is, however, an important passage in his *Monarchia* where he once again identifies the unruly passions as enemies of our freedom, but he conceives them as a threat to the phase of *deliberatio* leading up to *iudicium* and *electio*. On this view, we are free only to the extent that the 'power which takes counsel' is able to form its judgements dispassionately. Our freedom is here located not in the will, but in the intellect.

> The first ground or principle of our freedom is the freedom to form unbiased judgements [*principium primum nostrae libertatis est libertas arbitrii*], a phrase to which many people pay lip-service, but which few understand.
>
> Judgement is that which links perception and appetition. First, a thing is perceived; then, it is judged good or bad; and, finally, the person making the judgement pursues the thing or tries to avoid it.

The judgement is free if it is solely responsible for setting the appetites in motion [*si moveat omnino appetitum*] and if it is in no way forestalled by the appetites. If, by contrast, the appetites forestall and move the judgement, it is not free because it is not self-moved, but led captive by another. Hence, brute beasts cannot have free judgement because their judgements are always forestalled by their appetites.

(*Mon.* I, xii, 2–5, abbreviated)

Having noted that the concept of freedom does not exclude the concept of immutability (quite the reverse, in fact), Dante concludes with a by-now familiar quotation from his own poem:[22]

It will be clear that this freedom, or this principle of all our freedom [*haec libertas sive principium hoc totius nostrae libertatis*], is the 'greatest gift bestowed by God on human nature', as I have already said in *Paradiso* in the *Comedy*. It is by virtue of this freedom that we achieve happiness here as men, and happiness in another place as gods.

(*ibid.*, 6)

Other, Christian dimensions

The very last phrase in this passage from *Monarchia* is a timely reminder that Dante is far from being an Aristotelian *tout court*, even when he is composing a work of political philosophy. Writing as a Christian about rewards, punishments and 'corrective training' in a specifically Christian afterlife, Dante is committed, on the one hand, to belief in the Fall and in original sin, and, on the other, to belief in redemption and divine grace.

The first canto of the *Comedy* presents the protagonist as unable to withstand the leopard, the lion and the wolf – the three 'brute beasts' who symbolise the tyranny exercised by the lower appetites in fallen man. The protagonist is not free (on this view of human nature, no unforgiven sinner can be free). He is *seeking* freedom ('libertà va cercando'). And he will not possess it until he has passed through Purgatory into the Garden of Eden. Conversely, the second canto of the poem already shows us a special case of the operation of divine grace, the power which is indispensable – and now freely available – to assist us in regaining our lost freedom.[23]

But there is a sense in which the additional negative and positive factors in the Christian analysis of bondage and freedom 'cancel each other out', leaving the answer to the equation much as it was in the purely philosophical, Aristotelian account. For the plain fact is that human beings – pagan and Christian alike – are punished in Dante's Underworld in much the same way and for much the same reasons as they were in the classical Underworld, as represented in *Aeneid* VI. And whether these punishments are pagan or Christian, they would not be 'just' unless the suffering souls could be held responsible for the deeds they had done on earth, that is, unless they had possessed 'freedom of the will'.[24] This is why it was perfectly appropriate for Dante-the-poet to make *his* Virgil act as spokesman when the issues of freedom and morality are raised in two long speeches at the very heart of the poem in *Purgatorio* XVII and XVIII.

In the first of these speeches, Virgil explains the moral organisation of Purgatory in the light of the axiom that *all* human actions, good and bad, spring from some kind of love. In the second, he describes exactly how and when the instinctive desires, already stimulated by perception and estimation, are subjected to the mental checks of deliberation and consent or dissent. He speaks 'in character' as a representative of what is enduringly valid in classical civilisation. His analysis of the sin of Pride is significantly inadequate; and he explicitly refuses to take the discussion beyond the limits of what reason can see, inviting his pupil to wait and hear what Beatrice will reveal. But there is absolutely no need for him to speak '*out* of character', because there is nothing controversial for the Christian believer in what he has to say at this fundamental level.[25]

Virgil's second discourse is a distillation and recapitulation of virtually all the main ideas which have been presented in the first three parts of this book; and it forms the perfect bridge to part four, where we shall study how three of the principal passions of the sensitive soul – fear, anger and desire – either struggle or collaborate with reason and the will. It is a splendid piece of exposition in its own right; and since all the technical terms have been introduced and set in their threefold context of physics, psychology and ethics, it should be possible to present the speech through the medium of a translation into modern English prose with only a bare minimum of paraphrase and commentary. All that will be required by way of preface are the three lines from canto XVII which give rise to the protagonist's first question.

Perception, passion, deliberation, consent and dissent: Virgil's summary

In canto XVII, Virgil had said that no existing being – neither the Creator nor any part of his creation – is ever 'without love'. Having distinguished, as we noted, between the infallible 'natural love' of the subhuman world and the fallible 'elective love' found in man, he laid it down that 'love must be the seed in man of every virtue and of every operation that deserves punishment':

> esser convene
> amor sementa in voi d'ogne virtute
> e d'ogne operazion che merta pene.   (XVII, 103–5)

This proposition lingers in the mind of the protagonist as he follows Virgil's 'ragionamento' concerning the ways in which human love can lead us astray and 'incur penalties'. And he begs his 'dear father' for a reasoned exposition of the nature of love, 'to which you attribute all good operations and their contraries':

> 'Però ti prego, dolce padre caro,
> che mi dimostri amore, a cui reduci
> ogne buono operare e 'l suo contraro.'   (XVIII, 13–15)

Virgil accedes to the request, beginning with a superbly accurate and economical account of the processes leading from perception to the arousal of the passion of desire. (Typically, the first terzina serves as a 'preview' of what will be elaborated in the lines immediately following.)

> 'L'animo, ch'è creato ad amar presto,
> ad ogne cosa è mobile che piace.
> tosto che dal piacere in atto è desto.'   (*ibid.*, 19–21)

'The mind which is created to be swift in loving is capable of movement towards everything that gives pleasure, as soon as it has been awoken by pleasure.'

> 'Vostra apprensiva da esser verace
> tragge intenzione, e dentro a voi la spiega,
> sì ch l'animo ad essa volger face;
>   e se, rivolto, inver' di lei si piega,
> quel piegare è amor, quell' è natura
> che per piacer di novo in voi si lega.'   (*ibid.*, 22–7)

'Your power of perception derives a mental image from some truly existing object and displays it within you in such a way that the mental power
is made to turn towards that image. If the mental power, having turned to
the image, inclines towards it, that inclination is love: it is Nature, reasserting its bond in you once again through the pleasure-principle.'

> 'Poi, come 'l foco movesi in altura
> per la sua forma ch'è nata a salire
> là dove più in sua matera dura,
>   così l'animo preso entra in disire,
> ch'è moto spiritale, e mai non posa
> fin che la cosa amata il fa gioire.'   (*ibid.*, 28–33)

'Just as the element Fire moves upwards, thanks to its form which has an
innate tendency to climb towards the place where it will retain its matter
longest, so the captured mind enters into a state of desire, which is a
movement of the spirit; and it never rests until the object of desire has
given it joy.'[26]

Virgil now juggles with the distinction between form and matter in
a somewhat elliptical and metaphorical approach to his first conclusion. Considered in itself, wax is always good (it exists; it possesses
the properties distinctive of its form). But this does not mean that
every object made of wax is good: for example, the impression in a
wax seal may be indistinct or otherwise defective. Analogously, an
object of desire is always good, considered in itself. But it is only good
for the *subject* if it is compatible with the nature of that subject, necessary for its survival or fulfilment, and present in the right quantity
and at the right time.

> 'Or ti puote apparer quant' è nascosa
> la veritate a la gente ch'avvera
> ciascun amore in sé laudabil cosa;
>   però che forse appar la sua matera
> sempre esser buona, ma non ciascun segno
> è buono, ancor che buona sia la cera.'   (*ibid.*, 34–9)

'Now it will be apparent to you how far the truth is hidden from those
people who assert that all love is laudable, perhaps because its matter
always seems good. But not every impression is good, even though the
wax is good in itself.'

The master's words have indeed 'demonstrated' the nature of love.
But in so doing they have given rise to a new perplexity, to which his
pupil gives expression by means of an extended metaphor cast in syl-
logistic form.

> Ché, s'amore è di fuori a noi offerto
> e l'anima non va con altro piede,
> se dritta o torta va, non è suo merto.'   (*ibid.*, 43–5)

'If love is offered from outside, and if the soul has no other feet to walk with, then there is no merit attached to its going straight or its going off the road.'

Virgil meets this objection with a superb example of the inductive method proper to the natural scientist, who must study the observable world of phenomena and effects in order to understand the hidden essences and hidden causes. He begins by reminding Dante of the limitations of this method; but he implies that the findings he is about to present are compatible with the truths that the Bible reveals concerning the unseen essences and causes. And the reader of the *Comedy* will recognise that when Virgil asserts that man, too, has an infallible and morally neutral 'natural love', an underlying 'primal desire' for the supreme good and the whole truth, he is referring to what Christians believe to be the soul's 'likeness' to the Creator, and to what they conceive as being the soul's desire to know and be united with its Creator.

> Ed elli a me: 'Quanto ragion qui vede,
> dir ti poss' io; da indi in là t'aspetta
> pur a Beatrice, ch'è opra di fede.'   (*ibid.*, 46–8)

And he said to me: 'I am able to tell you as much as reason can see. As to what lies beyond, you must wait for Beatrice, because it is a matter of faith.'

> 'Ogne forma sustanzïal, che setta
> è da matera ed è con lei unita,
> specifica vertute ha in sé colletta,
>   la qual sanza operar non è sentita,
> né si dimostra mai che per effetto,
> come per verdi fronde in pianta vita.'   (*ibid.*, 49–54)

'Every substantial form that is separate from matter, and yet conjoined with matter, has a power gathered within it which is specific to its nature. This power is not perceived except through its operations and is not revealed except through its effects; as, for example, the power of life is revealed in a plant through its green branches.'

> 'Però, là onde vegna lo 'ntelletto
> de le prime notizie, omo non sape,
> e de' primi appetibili l'affetto,

> che sono in voi sì come studio in ape
> di far lo mele; e questa prima voglia
> merto di lode o di biasmo non cape.'   (*ibid.*, 55–60)

'Hence one cannot know the source of your understanding of primary concepts or the source of your love for primary objects of desire. These powers are simply in you, as the instinct to make honey is in the bee. And this primary desire attracts neither praise nor blame.'

What then is the relationship between the morally 'neutral' primal love for goodness and truth, and the morally 'charged' elective love for the 'esseri veraci' in the universe?

Quite simply, the first inclines us permanently and unconsciously towards our final goal, while the second inclines us consciously and successively to the means necessary to achieve that goal. And this formulation also clarifies the operations of the practical reason and the will. Their tasks are to consider the 'goods' and the 'loves' presented to their attention by the senses and the appetites, to assess their compatibility with the primal good and the primal love, and to give or withhold their assent. They are 'free' because they can refuse. They 'earn' or 'deserve' reward and punishment because they are free. It is this freedom which makes human beings the object of 'moral science', as opposed to 'natural science'.

> 'Or perché a questa ogn' altra si raccoglia,
> innata v'è la virtù che consiglia,
> e de l'assenso de' tener la soglia.
>   Quest' è 'l principio là onde si piglia
> ragion di meritare in voi, secondo
> che buoni e rei amori accoglie e viglia.
>   Color che ragionando andaro al fondo,
> s'accorser d'esta innata libertate;
> però moralità lasciaro al mondo.'   (*ibid.*, 61–9)

'Now in order that every other form of desire should be brought into harmony with the primal desire, you have an innate faculty which deliberates and which should control the threshhold of assent. It is this faculty which makes it possible for you to acquire merit, depending on whether it gathers in or winnows out good loves or bad. Those men who got to the bottom of things by rational inquiry became aware of this innate freedom, and this is why they bequeathed ethics to the world.'

Virgil's discourse has reached its climax in this vigorous linking of the concepts of freedom and morality, and in the reminder that they were discovered by philosophers from his own Graeco-Roman tradition. But he adds two important codicils. In the first, he links his conclusion to his point of departure, by re-emphasising that freedom consists in a capacity to endorse or to reject an initial, instinctive response by the *sensitive* part of the soul. In the second, he gives a single name to the joint faculty of the practical reason and the will, calling it metonymically by the technical term for the effect which it produces – *liberum arbitrium* (often translated as 'free choice', but more accurately rendered by some such locution as 'an unprejudiced and unbiased judgement between competing claims'). There could be no better 'term' with which to 'terminate' this chapter and part three.

> 'Onde, poniam che di necessitate
> surga ogne amor che dentro a voi s'accende,
> di ritenerlo è in voi la podestate.
>   La nobile virtù Beatrice intende
> per lo libero arbitrio, e però guarda
> che l'abbi a mente, s'a parlar ten prende.'   (*ibid.*, 70–5)

'Hence, even if we concede that every love that is kindled within you arises by necessity, the power to retain that love resides in you. It is this noble faculty to which Beatrice will refer as free judgement; so be careful to keep it in mind, if she should have occasion to speak to you about it.'

Combined operations

CHAPTER ELEVEN

Fear

The organisation of part four

In the second and third parts of this book, we have made ourselves familiar with the nature and activity of the sensitive and the mental powers of the human psyche – as these were known to Dante – treating the two sets of powers as far as possible in isolation from each other. In this fourth and final part, we shall be studying some of the most significant representations of human behaviour in the *Comedy*; and we shall therefore be concerned with the *interaction* of all the powers.

In the *Comedy*, as in life, no single affection of the soul is dominant for long at a time, because the passions 'are enwrapped one within another', as Francis Bacon so charmingly put it, and 'do fight and encounter with another'.[1] Characters in the poem rarely give vent to a passion without some element of rational calculation as to its likely effect on the interlocutor or reader. Conversely, the process of deliberation is sometimes shown to be perverted by a prior commitment on the part of the sense-appetites. It is made clear, further, that the passions may be stimulated not only by the present perception of other bodies in the immediate vicinity, but also by the faculties of memory and imagination, or by processes of thought. We are shown that the words of another intelligent being – human, angelic or demonic – may excite feelings such as pity, love, hope, desire and fear. Indeed, it is essential to Dante's concept of rhetoric and poetry that words may convey not only information, but also an 'affective charge' which is capable of arousing the passions and thereby leading to action.[2]

Dante does not represent our instinctive 'estimations' as being necessarily incompatible with our rational judgements. Hence he does not portray the passions as being necessarily at odds with the will. He is far from embracing the Stoic view that the best human life is one totally devoid of passion. For all his readiness to pass judgement on human operations, he is constantly aware of Aristotle's warning that they are to be assessed in the light of the particular circumstances obtaining at the time – *secundum particulares circumstantias*. And we might fairly summarise all these points by saying that he tends to represent virtually all *operationes humanae* as *mixtae*, in the sense that they are the product of the 'collusion' or 'collision' of several motive-forces.[3]

This willingness to recognise the complexity and variety of individual cases is one of Dante's greatest strengths as an observer of human operations. It might well be argued, therefore, that the best way of doing justice to the supreme delicacy of his insights would be to go through a number of revealing episodes from the poem in some deliberately random order. But it remains the central thesis of this book – to quote Francis Bacon again – that Dante's 'active and ample descriptions of the affections' owe a very great deal to the 'subtility of definitions' that he found in scholastic thought. His 'philomythical' powers of synthesis and of representing the particular depend on the analyses and generalisations to which he had been introduced during his apprenticeship as a 'philosopher'. The situations he sets before us are as complex as those we might find in a crucial phase of a game of chess between grandmasters; but the 'board' he plays on is the same as that used by the beginner; and the 'pieces' are the same in number and have the same 'powers of movement'.

It is this train of thought that determines the extremely simple ground-plan of this final part. We have just seen that when Dante thinks of a genuinely self-caused action, his preferred model is that in which the sequence of physiological and mental events is initiated by the perception of some external body, and in which the sense-appetites are called into play in advance of the practical intellect and the will. It seems logical, then, to group the episodes to be discussed in accordance with the passion which predominates.

We also saw earlier that, in the last analysis, there are only three kinds of self-movement: pursuit, flight and attack. This suggests that the internal motive forces may also be limited to three, and that there should be just three chapters devoted to the passions of desire, fear and anger.[4]

It so happens that most of the representations of fear concern Dante as protagonist, and are best examined in the sequence in which they are found in the opening stages of his journey through the terrors and torments of Hell. And this is why this survey of 'combined operations' in the *Comedy* begins with those involving the passion of fear.

The representation of fear in the opening canto

A surprising number of the fundamental causes and effects of fear are powerfully and yet analytically represented in the first sixty lines of the poem. The narrator begins by calling attention to his present fear, 'renewed in his thought', as he recalls the dark wood. And he specifies that the original fear had affected the 'lake of the heart' (considered as the seat of the emotions and the source of the pulsing spirits in the arteries).[5]

This fear had been of a general kind – brought on by the absence of light and the harsh impenetrability of the forest in which he had lost his way. It was 'allayed a little' by the rising of the sun, which began to illuminate the shoulders of a hill. At this point, the protagonist's 'mind was still in flight'; but his bodily panting subsided – so we learn from a simile – as he rested before attempting to climb the hill.[6]

He was immediately deterred from that ascent, however, by some 'textbook' causes of fear in the shape of three advancing predators (*corpora mobilia animata corruptiva*) – successively, a leopard, a lion and a she-wolf. Each time, the moment of perception is strongly stressed, while the effects of fear on Dante's appetites and bodily movements are well differentiated. In the representation of the leopard, there is no mention of the emotions: we are simply shown the consequences for the protagonist's 'locomotion' (his advance was 'impeded' and 'several times he turned to retreat'). In the case of the lion, perception and passion are compressed into one phrase (we read of the 'fear given by his appearance'); and the physiological effects of fear on Dante's body are strikingly transferred to the atmospheric medium ('it seemed that the air was trembling').[7] A first climax is reached in the presentation of the she-wolf. Fear is said to 'issue from her very aspect'; and its effects are indicated both on the body and on the mind ('heaviness' is accompanied by 'lamentation and affliction' in 'all his thoughts').[8] It was strong enough to cast out the rival emotion of hope, which had been generated by the protagonist's recognition that the sun was rising in the Sign of the Ram. And so the advancing beast was able 'to drive him back little by little' to the lower darkness without the direct application of any physical force.[9]

The interaction of rational fear and persuasion in canto II

The fear represented in the opening sequence is not dissimilar in its causes and effects from that which would be experienced by any diurnal, plain-dwelling animal on perceiving three large and aggressive predators. And the same is true of most of the feelings-cum-motives described during the meeting with Virgil, which occupies the rest of the first canto.

The protagonist's underlying *vis motiva* is his desire for the happiness he would find if he could reach the summit of the hill (which is significantly described as 'delightful' and 'the cause of all joy'). The wolf, however, 'impedes' his progress, making his 'veins and arteries tremble' with fear and reducing him to tears of frustration and incipient despair. He therefore agrees to Virgil's proposal that in order 'to escape from this wild place' and 'to flee this evil and worse', he should continue his journey by another route (or, to translate more literally, that he should 'set out on another journey').[10] Nothing could be more generic or more universal than the pursuit of the same 'end' by new and different 'means', as dictated by the 'circumstances'. And the fact that the alternative journey is to take Dante through the three realms of the afterlife does not invalidate the point that the basic model underlying the psychology represented in canto I is almost paradigmatic for any *corpus sentiens et seipsum movens*.

It must also be said, of course, that some of the internal processes portrayed during Dante's first encounter with a fellow human being are distinctively human; and these will be strikingly developed in the second canto, when night begins to enfold the two travellers and Dante 'prepares himself for the war of the journey and the suffering'.[11]

The wolf made Dante turn back by acting on his instinctive

passions as a hostile force. Virgil, by contrast, addressed himself as a friend to his mind. He too effected a change in direction. But the change was in fact due to a free act of will on Dante's part, an act consisting, as always, in *consent* to arguments that have been sifted and weighed by the 'virtù che consiglia'. When Dante explicitly declared: 'Poet, I entreat you to lead me where you just said', he was registering a choice consciously based on the well-founded trust he had placed in Virgil's competence, and on the reasons he had been given for following the alternative plan.[12] It will, however, prove significant that his free decision was based on somebody else's reasoning, because his mind will now generate a series of new thoughts ('novi pensieri') which tend to make him want to 'change his proposal' ('cangiar proposta'). The protagonist is shown as having what would normally be called '*second* thoughts', whereas they are in fact his first recorded rational processes.[13]

It is at this point that Dante-the-narrator intervenes in order to relate the unique situation of the protagonist to the recurrent experience of every 'omo d'intelletto'. In thinking the enterprise through, he had, as it were, already 'terminated' what he began so swiftly. His new thoughts led to a change of plan. He completely abandoned what he had begun. Or, to put it even more simply, he 'unwilled' what he had 'willed'.

> E qual è quei che disvuol ciò che volle
> e per novi pensier cangia proposta,
> sì che dal cominciar tutto si tolle,
> tal mi fec' ïo 'n quella oscura costa,
> perché, pensando, consumai la 'mpresa
> che fu nel cominciar cotanto tosta.   (*Inf.* II, 37–42)

The protagonist's demurral and the author's summary together occupy thirty-three lines; and they are studded with terms relating to the human mind and its distinctive powers of ratiocination and volition. But Virgil is unimpressed. If he has understood Dante's words correctly, the show of reasoning proceeds from a fearful disposition. This is not the kind of salutary fear which an animal experiences and which makes it run away from danger. It is more like the nervous shying of a horse caused by something it did not really see ('falso vedere'). It is 'baseness' – 'viltate' – which 'may affect a man's soul and weigh him down to such an extent that it turns him aside from some honourable enterprise'.[14]

The two words that Virgil uses to denote Dante's fear – 'viltate' and 'tema' – are used only of human fear. And human fear may be dispelled by appeals to the mind – specifically, by an explanation leading to a better understanding of the *propter quid*, the 'wherefore', of a strange and alarming event. So Virgil will help his charge to 'free himself of his fear' by explaining why he has come ('da questa tema a ciò che tu ti solve, / dirotti perch' io venni').[15]

This explanation is dramatised in the form of a flashback to the meeting of Virgil and Beatrice in Limbo, a meeting which contains a further flashback to the scene in Heaven when the Virgin Mary alerted St Lucy, who in turn begged Beatrice to come to Dante's aid. In the course of the linked and encapsulated passages of direct speech, there are numerous references to the protagonist, his fear and his *motus impeditus*, all of which confirm how faithfully Dante is following scholastic theories about perception, passion and movement, and how consciously he is adopting 'locomotion' as the paradigm of every human operation.[16] But we must now focus our attention on two passages in the canto which throw direct light on the coming and going of human fear.

The last twenty-two lines of canto II return us to the present and brilliantly dramatise the moment in which Dante is 'set free' of his fear. Virgil reaches the peroration of his long speech. He galvanises his charge with a series of staccato questions which repeat the accusation of ignoble fear. Then he appeals to Dante's intellect by summarising the reasons for his coming (the three crucial words – 'heaven', 'blessed' and 'promises' – are placed in the rhyme position):

> 'Dunque: che è? perché, perché restai,
> perché tanta viltà nel core allette,
> perché ardire e franchezza non hai,
>   poscia che tai tre donne benedette
> curan di te ne la corte del cielo,
> e 'l mio parlar tanto ben ti promette?'   (*ibid.*, 121–6)

'What is the matter then? Why, why have you come to a halt? Why do you cherish such baseness in your heart? Why don't you have boldness and confidence, since three such ladies in their blessedness are caring for you in the court of heaven and my words promise you so much good?'

These words produce a further 'chain reaction' of responses. But this time they all take place 'inside' the protagonist; and the first four of the five distinct stages are represented out of sequence, in the order 4, 1, 3, 2. A deservedly famous simile describes how his body drew itself up with renewed vigour (stage 4). Then the protagonist himself, speaking like a 'person set free from restraint' ('persona franca'), describes how his understanding of the 'true words' spoken by his guide (stage 1) made his heart ready with desire to return to its first resolve (stage 3), and how his will was thereby brought back into harmony with that of his 'leader' (stage 2). And the canto ends with the resumption of the *motus localis* to which all these *vires motivae* had contributed in turn as Dante 'entered upon the high and savage journey':[17]

> Quali fioretti dal notturno gelo
> chinati e chiusi, poi che 'l sol li 'mbianca,
> si drizzan tutti aperti in loro stelo,
>   tal mi fec' io di mia virtude stanca,
> e tanto buono ardire al cor mi corse,
> ch'i' cominciai come persona franca.   (*ibid.*, 127–32)

Just as flowers which have been weighed down and closed by the chill of night straighten themselves up on their stems and open as soon as the sun whitens them, so did I draw my wearied powers together; and such a surge of courage swept into my heart that I spoke like a man set free.

> 'Oh pietosa colei che mi soccorse!
> e te cortese ch'ubidisti tosto
> a le vere parole che ti porse!
>   Tu m'hai con disiderio il cor disposto
> sì al venir con le parole tue,
> ch'i' son tornato nel primo proposto.
>   Or va, ch'un sol volere è d'ambedue:
> tu duca, tu segnore e tu maestro.'
> Così li dissi; e poi che mosso fue,
>   intrai per lo cammino alto e silvestro.   (*ibid.*, 133–42)

'How kind-hearted was she who came to my aid, and how courteous you were in obeying the true words she spoke. You have made my heart so eager for the journey that I have returned to my first resolve. Lead the way, for there is just one will in both of us. You are my leader, you my lord and you my master.' Such were my words; and once he had moved off, I set out on the great and savage journey.

Such, then, is the way in which a human being can argue himself into a state of fear without any element of sense-perception; and such is the way in which another human being can argue him out of that state.[18]

'In valle mortis non timere malum'[19]

The 'buono ardire' which displaces Dante's 'tema' will soon be challenged by the sights and sounds of the 'valley of death'. But before we examine any of the later episodes involving his fear, we must leave Dante-the-protagonist for a moment and consider the emotions attributed to Beatrice in the course of her visit to Limbo.

We are told – still in the second canto – that she burns with desire to return to her place in the vastness of the Empyrean; that she is 'pietosa' (meaning kind-hearted, or full of pity, or both); and that she had been moved by love to descend to the centre of the universe. There is no doubt, then, that she is capable of experiencing emotions and of acting as a result of those emotions. And the question therefore arises – it is expressed by Virgil – of why *her* descent to Hell was not the occasion of any fear.[20]

To understand the reply, we have to remind ourselves of the relationship between fear, pain and *malum* (as defined in chapter 3).[21] Pain signals the presence of a *malum*. Fear signals the imminence of pain (it results from the present imagining of pain in the future). The reason why animals are 'structured' to experience fear is to enable them to avoid pain, and thus to avoid the *malum* threatening their existence or the fullness of their being.

In this particular case, Beatrice explains that she has been transformed by God (as have all the blessed) in such a way that Hell cannot cause any harm to her mind or her person. Where there is no *malum*, there can be no pain; where there is no expectation of pain, there can be no fear. And that would seem to be the *quod erat demonstrandum*.

But the reason Dante-the-poet chooses to represent his own fearfulness and to dwell on Beatrice's fearlessness is to throw light on the nature of fear in general. As we read the brief exchange between Dante's two guides, we must remember that in this little *quaestio*, as in virtually all scholastic *quaestiones*, the particular solution of the particular doubt or perplexity (lines 91–3) is less important than the universal truth (lines 88–90) which serves as the *principium* on which the formal reply is based.

> 'Ma dimmi la cagion che non ti guardi
> de lo scender qua giuso in questo centro
> de l'ampio loco ove tornar tu ardi.'

> 'Da che tu vuo' saver cotanto a dentro,
> dirotti brievemente', mi rispuose,
> 'perch' i' non temo di venir qua entro.'   (*ibid.*, 82–7)

[Virgil continued:] 'But tell me the cause why you do not shrink from descending to this centre from the vast realm where you long to return.' 'Since you wish to penetrate to the heart of the matter', she replied, 'I will tell you briefly why I am not afraid of entering here.'

> 'Temer si dee di sole quelle cose
> c'hanno potenza di fare altrui male;
> de l'altre no, ché non son paurose.
>   I' son fatta da Dio, sua mercé, tale,
> che la vostra miseria non mi tange,
> né fiamma d'esto 'ncendio non m'assale.'   (*ibid.*, 88–93)

'We should be afraid only of those things which have it in their power to do us harm – not of other things, because they are not fear-inspiring. I have been transformed by God, in his grace, in such a way that your wretchedness does not touch me; nor can any flame from this fire molest me.'

'There are things we ought to fear'

If the impersonal and technical style of lines 88–90 strikes us as incongruously Aristotelian, it is because Beatrice is quoting fairly closely from a passage in the third book of the *Ethics*, and it will be highly relevant to follow Aristotle's train of thought for a moment as he moves forward to the notion that fear is sometimes necessary or even good (the following sentences are translated from the para-phrase and commentary by Aquinas):[22]

We fear things that are terrifying, these being the objects of fear. Gen-erally speaking, terrifying things include all sources of harm [*quaecumque mala*]. Hence philosophers define fear as the 'anticipation of harm' [*expectatio mali*], using 'anticipation' in the broad sense where it refers to any and every movement of the appetite towards something which still lies in the future. (...) It is obvious that we all fear certain kinds of *malum*, for example, disgrace, poverty, illness, friendlessness or death.

A brave man is praised because he has no fear. But there are some things that we ought to fear if we are to lead a good life. It is good to fear such things, because fear of this kind is not only necessary for the

225

preservation of virtue, but is itself something virtuous [*ipse timor est quoddam honestum*].[23]

This is the not entirely predictable conclusion that we must bear in mind as we move from the prologue to the main action of the poem, and as we begin to explore how the insights into the nature and function of fear, adumbrated in the introductory cantos, are developed and refined in the representation of Dante's fictional self during his journey through Hell.

The classical 'guardians' of the Underworld

The three beasts of the opening canto might seem to find their successors in the various 'guardians' whom Dante-the-author took over from classical legend. But although they are certainly portrayed as 'cose paurose', surprisingly little is made of the fear they might have been expected to arouse in the protagonist.

It is not the burning eyes or wild threats of Charon, but the swirling tumult of the lamentations of the futile which 'encircle his head with horror' in canto III. And the successive experiences which 'overpower all his feelings' (rendering him incapable of either perception or passion) are, on the one hand, the sight of a vermilion flash of lightning which accompanied an infernal earthquake, and, on the other, the feeling of 'pietà' which overwhelmed him on learning about the 'mal perverso' of Paolo and Francesca.[24]

Virgil does feel the need to 'comfort' his charge when they are challenged by the incomprehensible 'clucking' of Pluto, but there is no reference to fear during the confrontations with the Minotaur or the Centaurs. And while it is true that in canto XVII Geryon causes Dante to shake all over, as though he were about to undergo a malarial fit, it is not the appearance of the monster which provokes these symptoms, but the prospect of having to fly on his back. Only in cantos XXI–XXIII does Dante-the-author play out the trumps we knew him to hold in his hand; and there, as we shall see in due course, the protagonist's fears are both comically overstated and comprehensively vindicated, while the 'cose paurose' will be the devils of medieval Christian tradition.[25]

Before we study the 'animal fear', however, caused by the boisterous and malevolent behaviour of the devils, we must follow another trail and examine some of the less obvious species and manifestations of fear – emotions such as embarrassment, reverence, suspicion and doubt – which have their origin in the human mind. In the *Comedy*, these are all grounded in the relationship between Dante and Virgil; and they often demand close attention to the ways in which the rapidly developing pupil articulates his questions (or fails to articulate them), and to the ways in which these questions are answered or evaded by the increasingly hesitant master.

Reverence and mistrust in Dante-the-protagonist

Our trail begins in the third canto when Dante is about to enter the gate of Hell, over which he has just read the terrifying inscription warning those who enter to 'abandon all hope'. It is a daunting text and Virgil has to intervene quickly to allay the resultant fear. What Dante must 'abandon' is not 'hope', he says, but his own 'misgivings' ('sospetto'). Similarly, the state of mind he must allow to 'die out' is his 'viltate'. But Virgil's practical knowledge of the human heart ('accortezza') is such that he also knows that there are occasions when body-language is more efficacious than the language of words. In this case it is not so much the balanced rhythms of his speech which 'comfort' his frightened ward, as the squeeze of his hand and his smile of encouragement:

> Ed elli a me, come persona accorta:
> 'Qui si convien lasciare ogne sospetto;
> ogne viltà convien che qui sia morta.'
> (…)
> E poi che la sua mano a la mia puose
> con lieto volto, ond' io mi confortai,
> mi mise dentro a le segrete cose.   (III, 13–15, 19–21)

And showing his insight, he said: 'Here all mistrust must be left behind; and all baseness of soul must be extinguished here.' And after he had laid his hand on mine with a cheerful face, from which I drew comfort, he led me into the hidden world.

Despite this reassurance, however, another form of fear begins to take shape immediately as a result of the three questions which Dante puts to his guide while they are making their way from the gate of Hell towards the bank of the river Acheron. The first question, relating to the sound of lamentation, is answered patiently and in full; so too is the supplementary question concerning the cause of the violence of these laments.[26] But this second answer is pointedly brief and ends with a hint of asperity in the famous dismissive line: 'Don't let us talk about them; but take a look and pass on.' And we have to assume that the protagonist heard a similar note of impatience or reproof when Virgil declined to answer his third question (telling him to wait and see for himself), because Dante-the-author reports: 'Then I refrained from speaking until I reached the river, with my eyes lowered in shame, fearing lest my words had been importunate':

> Allor con li occhi vergognosi e bassi,
> temendo no 'l mio dir li fosse grave,
> infino al fiume del parlar mi trassi.   (*ibid.*, 79–81)

His self-restraint is rewarded after they have reached the Acheron, because Virgil gives him the information he had asked for without any further request.[27] But for the rest of the journey Dante will be mildly inhibited in his desire for understanding by his awe or 'reverence' (the root of *reverentia* is *vereri*, 'to fear').

The protagonist's reverence for Virgil as an 'elder and better' is soon to be complicated by an equally persistent and growing awareness of his master's limitations and fallibility, an awareness which will tend to make him afraid of hurting Virgil's feelings and also to feel alarmed about his own safety.

No sooner does Dante regain consciousness on the further shore of the Acheron than he hears – against a distant rumbling thunder of lamentations – the voice of Virgil urging him 'to begin the descent into the blind world'. But although the air is too dark for Dante to discern who is wailing in 'the dolorous valley of the abyss', it is not dark enough to conceal the fact that Virgil has become 'deadly pale' ('tutto smorto'); and this perception leads to the natural deduction that Virgil himself is afraid of what lies ahead.

> E io, che del color mi fui accorto,
> dissi: 'Come verrò, se tu paventi
> che suoli al mio dubbiare esser conforto?'   (IV, 16–18)

Noting his colour I said: 'How do you expect me to come, if you yourself are afraid, you who have been the comfort of my waverings?'

His inference proves to be mistaken, however. Virgil explains that the emotion which 'paints his face' is not fear, but pity for the 'anguish of those who are suffering below':

> Ed elli a me: 'L'angoscia de le genti
> che son qua giù, nel viso mi dipigne
> quella pietà che tu per tema senti.'   (*ibid.*, 19–21)

Nevertheless, this pallor is an indication of his vulnerability. Beatrice, we remember, had not been 'touched' in any way by the 'misery' of the souls in Limbo. Virgil, by contrast, is not only moved by vain compassion for the eternal deprivation suffered by a 'great throng of men, women and children', he is himself condemned to that same state of 'desire without hope', which constitutes the only (the only!) pain of those who had 'lived without sin', but who had not 'adored God as they should have done'.[28] And there is infinite pathos in his switch from the pronouns and verbal forms of the *third* person plural ('ei non peccaro') to those of the *first*:

> 'Per tai difetti, non per altro rio,
> semo perduti, e sol di tanto offesi
> che sanza speme vivemo in disio.'   (*ibid.*, 40-2)

'We are condemned for these shortcomings, not for any other fault; and our only affliction is that we live without hope in desire.'

The protagonist is deeply grieved by this answer to a question which he had not ventured to express.[29] Simultaneously, he is troubled by a serious doubt. Whom shall he believe, Virgil or the Creed? Can it be true that none of the souls 'suspended in Limbo' have ever satisfied their 'hope and desire' to escape? What about Jesus himself? Or the patriarchs whom he is said to have delivered?

Moved as he is by grief and doubt, Dante cannot restrain his question, which bursts from him with unprecedented urgency ('Dimmi, maestro mio, dimmi, segnore'). And yet he is still sufficiently inhibited by his reverence, and by his fear of hurting Virgil's feelings, to formulate the question rather deviously (the author calls it a 'parlare coperto'), so that it will not seem like a challenge to the authority of his master or a reminder of his 'eternal exile'.[30]

The contested entry into the city of Dis

We must jump forward now to resume our study of fear four cantos later, picking up the narrative at the point where the two poets are being ferried across the river Styx.[31] They approach the high, iron walls of a city, containing mosque-like towers which are glowing red in the reflection of the fires of Lower Hell; and they follow the circuit of the walls until their boatman abruptly orders them to disembark, because 'the entry is here'. Immediately, more than a thousand 'fallen angels' appear over the gate – an occasion for horror, if ever there was one.

Nothing, however, is ever quite predictable in the *Comedy*. If these devils are more terrifying than any of the earlier guardians, it is not because they are trying to prevent the poets from entering, nor because their verbal challenges are full of 'anger' and 'disdain', but because they attempt to drive a wedge between Virgil and Dante. They demand that Virgil shall come forward on his own for a secret parley, and that the living man, who has shown such 'foolhardiness' in entering the kingdom of the dead, shall return alone and find his own way back.[32] The speech in which the protagonist gives expression to his terror at the thought of being abandoned needs no further introduction. But it ought to be noted how we, as readers, are explicitly invited to imagine what we would have felt in similar circumstances. And as we respond to the impassioned rhetoric of Dante's plea to Virgil, we must not fail to register the analytical precision of the opposed nouns 'sicurtà' and 'periglio':

> Pensa, lettor, se io mi sconfortai
> nel suon de le parole maladette,
> ché non credetti ritornarci mai.
>   'O caro duca mio, che più di sette
> volte m'hai sicurtà renduta e tratto
> d'alto periglio che 'ncontra mi stette,
>   non mi lasciar', diss' io, 'così disfatto;
> e se 'l passar più oltre ci è negato,
> ritroviam l'orme nostre insieme ratto.'   (VIII, 94–102)

Just think, reader, how I was cast down by the sound of the accursed words; for I did not believe I should ever return here. 'Dearest leader', I said, 'you who, not less than seven times, have given me back my confidence and rescued me from great danger that confronted me, don't leave me in this plight. If we're not allowed to go forward, let's quickly retrace our steps together.'

Virgil is under pressure, but outwardly he is as steady as a rock. He tells Dante not to be afraid, promises not to leave him and urges him – with biblical solemnity and biblical metaphors – 'to nourish and strengthen his wearied spirits with good hope'. Nevertheless, he orders Dante to wait by himself; and as narrative takes over from dialogue, the verbs remain in the present tense for the duration of one wonderfully vivid terzina, where we see the departing Virgil, see the abandoned Dante, and finally enter into his mind to witness the conflict between the passions of fear and hope:

> Così sen va, e quivi m'abbandona
> lo dolce padre, e io rimagno in forse,
> che sì e no nel capo mi tenciona.   (*ibid.*, 109–11)

Off he goes. And there my sweet father abandons me. And I remain in uncertainty, as Yes and No do battle in my head.

The verbs then revert to the past. Virgil, we read, went forward, and there was a brief, unheard conversation. The devils rushed back inside and slammed the gate in his face. 'He remained outside. He returned with slow steps. His eyes were cast down and his brow shorn of all confidence. He was saying through his sighs, "Who has denied me the mansions of pain?"' Needless to say, the protagonist was dazed and dismayed; and fear 'drove its colour into his face' as he saw his leader 'turned in retreat'.[33]

Virgil tries to to be reassuring. He passes his emotion off as anger. He refers to his earlier experience of the devils' intransigence when they tried – and failed – to prevent Christ from breaking down the Upper Gate. He assures Dante that 'someone' is already approaching who will open the city. But no sooner has he made this attempt to reassure his companion, than he involuntarily begins to frighten him again, because he is simply unable to control his own anxiety. He comes to a halt, straining his ears to hear what his eyes cannot see in the gloom. A phrase that is clearly directed to Dante ('And yet we've got to win the contest') trails away with an uncompleted 'unless ...'. He makes another attempt to pull himself together with the self-reminder that help has been offered by a powerful ally. But his cover-up is, if anything, the cause of greater alarm:

> I' vidi ben sì com' ei ricoperse
> lo cominciar con l'altro che poi venne,
> che fur parole a le prime diverse;
>   ma nondimen paura il suo dir dienne,
>   perch' io traeva la parola tronca
>   forse a peggior sentenzia che non tenne.   (IX, 10–15)

I clearly saw how he covered the beginning of his speech with what came after – the later words being different from the earlier. But nevertheless his words made me afraid, because I attributed a more sinister meaning to the cut-off phrase than it bore.

Fear of being abandoned is replaced by fear that his guide is unqualified through lack of experience; and he will not be reassured until he can discover whether Virgil has ever done this journey before. But fear of giving offence means that he cannot put such a question directly. So, with an apparently innocent change of subject, he inquires:

> 'In questo fondo de la trista conca
> discende mai alcun del primo grado,
> che sol per pena ha la speranza cionca?'
> Questa question fec' io.   (*ibid.*, 16–19)

'Do any of the souls in the first circle, where punishment lies only in the truncation of hope, ever descend to the bottom of this dismal abyss?' This was the question I put.

Virgil's reply is no less tactful. Keeping a straight face, he reveals that, while it is admittedly rare for a soul in Limbo to undertake the journey, he himself has been once before to the very last circle. Only then does he show that he has understood the true import of Dante's question: 'Yes, I do know the way; so put your mind at rest' ('Ben so 'l cammin; però ti fa sicuro').[34]

From 'psychosomatic' to 'somatopsychic'

No sooner has Dante's 'sicurtà' been restored than his eyes are drawn to the most terrifying beings he has yet encountered. On the fiery summit of a watch-tower on the walls, he sees the three Furies, wailing and tearing at their flesh like professional mourners at a funeral. Dante presses close to his leader out of fear, even before he hears them send for their shield with the Gorgon's head in order to turn him to stone for his presumption. Virgil reacts immediately to this 'alto periglio', ordering his charge to look the other way and to cover his eyes with his hands. But he does not stop there. He himself (the words 'elli stessi' are highlighted by the rhyme) physically turns Dante round and then puts his own hands over Dante's hands to make doubly sure:

> Ed elli stessi
> mi volse, e non si tenne a le mie mani,
> che con le sue ancor non mi chiudessi.   (*ibid.*, 58–60)

At this very moment, Dante-the-author intervenes with one of his most famous 'asides', inviting those of his readers who have 'healthy intellects' to 'look at the teaching concealed beneath the veil of the strange lines'.[35] His commentators have not been slow to accept this invitation to look for a 'philosophical' doctrine in the unseen Gorgon's head. But what matters for our purposes are the 'philomythical' insights into the relationship between body and soul. Just as the emotion of fear can produce physiological changes in the body, so contact with another human body can dispel the symptoms of fear. It can even drive the emotion away from the 'psyche'. The 'somatopsychic' reaction (to coin a phrase) is no less important than the 'psychosomatic' one.

The lesson is repeated and amplified in the episode (discussed in chapter 6) in which Dante is ferried down to the ninth circle by the monster Geryon.[36] Other medieval authors might have conceived the composite beast. But few if any could have conceived and represented the emotions of the protagonist at the beginning of the descent.

Already fearful lest he should anger Virgil by staying too long with the usurers, he returns to the edge of the precipice where he had earlier seen the monster waiting with its head on the 'shore'. There he receives the always-frightening injunction to 'be brave' ('sie forte e ardito') and to join Virgil who is already seated on the creature's back. In a simile of medical precision, Dante compares his feelings to those of a victim of malaria at the onset of a periodic cold fit. But he also notes how he tried to conceal his emotions because of the competing 'threats made by shame', the emotion which proverbially makes a servant behave courageously while he is under his master's eyes.[37]

This time the physical contact will involve not hands covering hands, but arms wrapped round the body. And the essence of the 'somatopsychic' moment is that it comes as the fulfilment of an unspoken wish:

I settled myself on those hideous shoulders. I wanted to say 'hold me in your arms', but my voice would not come as I thought it would. But as soon as I mounted, he who had come to my aid on other occasions and in other dangers, folded me in his arms and supported me.

Even this prose translation can suggest something of the emotion generated and resolved. But prose cannot reproduce the way in which rhyme intensifies the affective suffix in 'spallacce' or enhances the emotive verb 'abbracce' in the first terzina. And without the combination of metre, rhythm and the word-order permissible in verse, one cannot convey the delaying effect of the balanced phrases ('altra volta', 'altro forse') or the climactic effect of the paired main verbs at the end of the second terzina:

> I' m'assettai in su quelle spallacce;
> sì volli dir, ma la voce non venne
> com' io credetti: 'Fa che tu m'abbracce.'
> Ma esso, ch'altra volta mi sovvenne
> ad altro forse, tosto ch'i' montai
> con le braccia m'avvinse e mi sostenne. (XVII, 91–6)

'Odi malizia'

We are now in possession of all the information we need to enjoy the most brilliant and the most sustained episode involving the passion of fear. In this case, our interest will be more evenly divided between the two poets and between the external and the internal causes. It will also become clear that instinctive fear may offer better protection against malicious deceit than misplaced confidence.

Dante and his guide have reached the fifth bolgia, that is, the fifth of the ten ditches which make up the ninth circle of Hell. They come to a natural 'bridge' formed by one of the long spurs of rock which span every ditch in the entire circle, converging on the centre like the spokes of a wheel; and they pause on the middle of the bridge to look into the bolgia below, which is filled with seething, bubbling pitch.[38]

The leisurely pace of the opening of canto XXI, in which the scene is set before our eyes, is disturbed by the voice of Virgil urging Dante to 'look, look'. But it is then briefly re-established for the duration of a 'pseudo-simile', in which the author patiently and wittily describes the particular manifestation of his fear *before* he allows us to see the external cause of the emotion:[39]

> Allor mi volsi come l'uom cui tarda
> di veder quel che li convien fuggire
> e cui paura sùbita sgagliarda,

234

che, per veder, non indugia 'l partire.   (XXI, 25–8)

Then I swung round like someone who is anxious to have a better look at
something he ought to run away from, but who is unnerved by sudden
fear, so that his looking does not delay his departure.

The object of this fear-mingled-with-curiosity is a winged devil
who comes racing up from behind, carrying a newly damned sinner
on his back. Paying no attention to the poets, he yells instructions to
some unseen companions and then hurls his victim into the pitch
below. The sinner disappears for an instant, re-emerging with his
face contorted in pain. But he is immediately taken in hand by a
group of devils, who are waiting out of sight under the arch of the
bridge. It is their task to catch any sinner who attempts to alleviate
his torment in this way, to lacerate him with their huge hooks, and to
plunge him back under the surface, like cooks pushing lumps of meat
down into a stew. These are the new adversaries or 'fiends'; and it is
their 'fiendish' behaviour which is going to terrorise the protagonist
himself.[40]

Once again, Virgil prepares to go ahead on his own in order to
parley. But there are significant differences from the last occasion.
He goes unbidden. He reassures Dante in advance, by reminding
him that he has been here before. He warns him not to be alarmed by
any show of violence. And he finds it advisable that Dante should
remain unseen, ordering him to 'squat down' (the verb 'acquattarsi' is
not in the least flattering) behind the rocks that form a sort of parapet
on the bridge. Off goes Virgil, to be met by a violent reception in a
splendidly dramatised scene. When he has quelled the riot, so to
speak, he calls back to the cowering Dante, mockingly drawing
attention to his undignified position, and telling him to come
forward 'sicuramente'.

It would be hard to imagine anyone moving less confidently than
the protagonist now does. He makes a dash for it; he flattens himself
against his leader; he never takes his eyes off the devils. And the black
humour of the scene is enhanced by the 'authenticating' simile describing soldiers, whom Dante had once seen issuing from a besieged
fortress after they had agreed terms of capitulation, and who had
every reason to fear that the enemy would not respect those terms.

E 'l duca mio a me: 'O tu che siedi
tra li scheggion del ponte quatto quatto,
sicuramente omai a me ti riedi.'

> Per ch'io mi mossi e a lui venni ratto;
> e i diavoli si fecer tutti avanti,
> sì ch'io temetti ch'ei tenesser patto.   (*ibid.*, 88–93)

And my leader called to me: 'You there! sitting huddled down among the rocks on the bridge. You can rejoin me in safety now.' So I made a move and rushed to him. And all the devils pushed forward, so that I was afraid they would not keep their pact.

> Così vid' ïo già temere li fanti
> ch'uscivan patteggiati di Caprona,
> veggendo sé tra nemici cotanti.
> I' m'accostai con tutta la persona
> lungo 'l mio duca, e non torceva li occhi
> da la sembianza lor ch'era non buona.   (*ibid.*, 94–9)

It was the same fear I had seen in the soldiers, coming out from Caprona on agreed terms, when they saw themselves among so many enemies. I pressed my whole body right up against my leader; and I never lifted my eyes from their looks, which were not friendly.

Malacoda, the leader of the group, makes an offer of assistance. The spur of rock which brought them over the fifth bolgia, he explains, no longer forms a natural bridge over the sixth. Indeed, with one exception, all the 'bridges' over this bolgia collapsed in an earthquake hundreds of years ago. However, he will nominate a platoon of ten devils (each is individually and grotesquely named) who will escort the poets as far as 'the other spur which crosses all the ditches unbroken' ('l'altro scheggio / che tutto intero va sovra le tane').[41]

Dante listens aghast. He can see no 'sicurtà' in this offer of a safe-conduct. And the fear that first found outlet in his movements is now expressed in his mode of speech, with the words tumbling out in a series of exclamations, impetuous questions, reproaches and requests:

> 'Omè, maestro, che è quel ch'i' veggio?',
> diss' io, 'deh, sanza scorta andianci soli,
> se tu sa' ir; ch'i' per me non la cheggio.
> Se tu se' sì accorto come suoli,
> non vedi tu ch'e' digrignan li denti
> e con le ciglia ne minaccian duoli?'   (*ibid.*, 127–32)

'Oh no, master! What's this I see?', I said. 'If you know the way, please let's go on without any escort. I don't want one for myself! If you are your normal cautious self, can't you see how they're grinding their teeth and threatening no good with their scowls?'

All his protests, however, are to no avail. Virgil insists that he must not be afraid ('non vo' che tu paventi'). The devils salute Malacoda by sticking out their tongues; their officer returns the salute with an anal trumpet-call; and with that 'unusual signal' the 'savage company' set out on their mission.[42]

For some considerable time Virgil seems to be justified. As he had predicted, the devils are indeed taken up with the sinners in the pitch. They catch one. They are tricked into allowing him to make his escape. And two of them become involved in an aerial 'dogfight' which results in their both falling into the pitch themselves. Rescue operations begin; and at this point the two poets leave the devils to their task and set off in single file to find the surviving bridge 'without their escorts'.

If our hero had been an animal — and this area of the *Comedy* abounds with similes comparing human beings to animals — his fear would have subsided once his external organs had ceased to 'apprehend' the *malum* which had caused that fear. But he is a man, endowed with all the powers of the mind; and he is about to be tormented — and saved — by fears arising from his practical intellect and from his distinctively human imagination and memory.[43]

The first of the mental faculties to come into operation is memory — his *literary* memory of a fable attributed to Aesop about 'trickery out-trumped'. The fable tells how a defenceless land animal was deceived by an aquatic animal (a frog offered to ferry a mouse over a river and then attempted to drag it to the bottom in midstream), and how both were seized by an aerial animal in the shape of a passing kite. Dante-the-author goes to unusual lengths to insist that the beginning and end of the fable offer a perfect match to the beginning and end of the quarrel he had just witnessed. But unprompted memories of a literary text are rarely as precise as he suggests; and it may be that the points of contact were less univocal, more numerous and more directly relevant.[44]

Be that as it may, Dante does not often display and exploit his knowledge of the powers of the soul — both sensitive and rational — with quite the same verve as he does over the next thirty lines, which we must read in their entirety. The inductive thought-processes, illustrated in his recollection of the fable, recur in a simile concerning a hare and a dog. He calls attention in general terms to the possibility of instantaneous intellectual events, as when one thought simply 'bursts' or 'pops' out of another. He presents — with comically pedantic precision – all the steps in his deductive process of deliberation, which led first to the conclusion that the devils must by now be in pursuit, and thence to the declared decision that he and his guide must conceal themselves. He recognises that the intellect can influence the imagination, and can lead to the formation of images which are just as vivid and just as compelling as those deriving from the external senses. He introduces yet another physiological consequence of emotion by referring to his hair standing on end. And the words he speaks under the pressure of fear are suitably confused in their syntax:

> E come l'un pensier de l'altro scoppia,
> così nacque di quello un altro poi,
> che la prima paura mi fé doppia.
>   Io pensava così: 'Questi per noi
> sono scherniti con danno e con beffa
> sì fatta, ch'assai credo che lor nòi.
>   Se l'ira sovra 'l mal voler s'aggueffa,
> ei ne verranno dietro più crudeli
> che 'l cane a quella lievre ch'elli acceffa.'   (xxiii, 10–18)

And as one thought springs from another, so a second was born of the first which redoubled my original fear. I reasoned like this: 'The devils have been humiliated, hurt and exposed to ridicule because of us, in a way that I believe must be extremely painful to them. If anger is now added to their malice, they will come after us more cruelly than a hound in the moment that it seizes the hare.'

> Già mi sentia tutti arricciar li peli
> de la paura e stava in dietro intento,
> quand' io dissi: 'Maestro, se non celi
>   te e me tostamente, i' ho pavento
> d'i Malebranche. Noi li avem già dietro;
> io li 'magino sì, che già li sento.'   (*ibid.*, 19–24)

Already I could feel all my hair bristling through fear, and my attention was turned behind us, when I said: 'Master, if you don't quickly hide yourself and me, I'm scared of what the devils will do. We've got them behind us already. I can imagine them so keenly that I can already hear them.'

Virgil answers with the kind of involuntary pomposity which can affect an intellectual in moments of uncertainty. All he is saying in effect is this: 'I knew your thoughts and feelings even before you spoke, because they were identical to my own. There is nowhere to hide, as you suggest, so we must run away. But the devils can run faster than us. *Ergo*, we must find some way of getting down into the next ditch.' And as we read his charmingly and incongruously technical analogy for their shared thought-processes, we must remember that any two rabbits would have reacted in the same way.[45]

> E quei: 'S'i' fossi di piombato vetro,
> l'imagine di fuor tua non trarrei
> più tosto a me, che quella dentro 'mpetro.
>   Pur mo venieno i tuo' pensier tra ' miei,
> con simile atto e con simile faccia,
> sì che d'intrambi un sol consiglio fei.
>   S'elli è che sì la destra costa giaccia,
> che noi possiam ne l'altra bolgia scendere,
> noi fuggirem l'imaginata caccia.'   (*ibid.*, 25–33)

And he said: 'If I were a piece of leaded glass, I wouldn't be able to receive your outer likeness any quicker than I grasped the image of your mind. Your thoughts came among my own just a moment ago, with exactly the same "face" and "bearing", so that I've devised a single plan based on both of them. If the rock-face on the right should slope in such a way that we can get down into the next bolgia, we'll get away from the hunt we've imagined.'

Fear does now give rise to flight, and the fact that the *fuga* is *secundum rationem* ('in accordance with reason') does not make it any the less precipitate. Suddenly the devils are there in reality, with their wings outspread, ready to seize their victims. Virgil takes no thought for his dignity (he is compared to a mother rescuing her child from a fire at night and dashing from the house in her shift). He grasps Dante in his arms and slithers down the hard rock-face of the next ditch faster than water in a mill-race – in the nick of time, because scarcely have his feet touched the bottom than the devils reach the top of the wall above them. Yet, for all the excitement of this dazzlingly kinetic piece of writing, Dante-the-author does not forget to underline the strengthening of the ties between the protagonist and his guide which results from the danger they are sharing. Once again he registers the emotional development through a more intimate physical contact – 'the master', he says, was 'carrying me on his breast like his child, not like a companion':

portandosene me sovra 'l suo petto,
come suo figlio, non come compagno.   (*ibid.*, 50–1)

Antidotes to fear: spurs or apples?

Although Dante will never take such 'evasive action' again, this will
not be the last time he will experience one or other of the many
varieties of fear. On almost every subsequent occasion, too, there will
be some deepening of his bond with Virgil and some growth in his
own fortitude (which is to say, in the ability of his will to conquer
irrational fear). But he will never achieve perfect fortitude, nor will
he ever place a perfect trust in his 'guide-become-father'. And these
are the failings which are dramatised with great pathos in the very
last of their shared experiences.

The scene in question occurs on the evening of their final full
day together. The two poets – accompanied now by Statius – come
to the foot of the flight of steps which leads up to the Garden of
Eden from the highest of the seven circles running round the
Mountain of Purgatory. They have been making their way along
the outermost edge of the relatively narrow terrace, because the
inner part is occupied by a corridor of fire, a 'burning fiery furnace'
where the souls of those who were unable to control their sexual
desire are purified of their carnal lust. And the conversations
between Dante and his fellow love poets have taken place with
them inside the fire and with *him* on the outside (they being as
anxious not to emerge from the flames, as he is reluctant to get too
close).[46]

As the sun sets, the poets see the guardian angel of the circle
'standing outside the flame on the edge' and chanting the Beatitude
which begins 'Blessed are the pure in heart'. He interrupts his chant
to tell them they can go no further without the fire 'biting' them. In
short, they must now pass through the furnace, guided by the singing
they will hear from the inner side.

For the first time on the journey, the protagonist explicitly feels
the fear of imminent death. The author compares his earlier self to a
condemned criminal about to be buried alive. He shows us the recoil
of his body and his instinctive gesture of self-defence. And he allows
us to glimpse the images in his mind – images of human bodies
which he had seen consumed by fire:

Per ch'io divenni tal, quando lo 'ntesi,
qual è colui che ne la fossa è messo.
    In su le man commesse mi protesi,
guardando il foco e imaginando forte
umani corpi già veduti accesi.   (*Purg.* XXVII, 14–18)

When I heard him, I felt like a man who is thrust into the pit. Raising and
joining my hands, I pulled away, looking at the fire and strongly imagining human bodies I had seen burnt.

Virgil now deploys every weapon in his rhetorical armoury in an
attempt to persuade Dante to overcome his fear. Calling him 'my
son', he concedes that there may be 'pain', but assures him there can
be no question of 'death'. He begs him (the repeated 'ricorditi'
conveys the urgency of the plea) to remember the dangers they have
shared, and how he had kept him safe even on the back of Geryon.
He reminds him indirectly of the divine origin of his mission. With
more conventional hyperbole and antithesis, he implores him to
believe with absolute certainty that not a single hair on his head
would be harmed, even if he remained in the fire for a thousand
years:

E Virgilio mi disse: 'Figliuol mio,
qui può esser tormento, ma non morte.
    Ricorditi, ricorditi! E se io
sovresso Gerïon ti guidai salvo,
che farò ora presso più a Dio?
    Credi per certo che se dentro a l'alvo
di questa fiamma stessi ben mille anni,
non ti potrebbe far d'un capel calvo.'   (*ibid.*, 20–7)

And Virgil said to me: 'My son, there may be torment here, but not death.
Think back, think back! If I guided you safe and sound on Geryon
himself, what shall I be able to do nearer to God? Take it as certain that if
you were to remain in the heart of the fire for a thousand years, it would
not make you lose one hair from your head.'

Dante will not, cannot, budge. Not only does he fail to believe on
the basis of their shared experiences, he may even be entertaining
the belief that Virgil is tricking him! And so Virgil treats him like the
apostle Thomas – doubting Thomas – and urges him to base his
belief on the most elementary of all his senses, the one he shares even
with the lowest forms of animal life, the sense of touch:

> 'E se tu forse credi ch'io t'inganni,
> fatti ver' lei, e fatti far credenza
> con le tue mani al lembo d'i tuoi panni.'   (*ibid.*, 28–30)

'And if perhaps you think I'm deceiving you, go close to the flame. Let your hands convince you with the hem of your robe.'

His repetition of the first of the four commands which make up his final appeal indicates how urgently, almost desperately, the words are spoken. But although he succeeds in stirring Dante's moral conscience, he cannot succeed in generating the necessary 'motive force'. Dante remains stock-still:

> 'Pon giù omai, pon giù ogne temenza;
> volgiti in qua e vieni: entra sicuro!'
> E io pur fermo e contra cosci̇enza.   (*ibid.*, 31–3)

'Lay down, lay down all fear. Turn round and come this way. Go in confidently.' And despite all this, I was immovable – against my conscience.

Up to this point, Virgil has been treating Dante like a grown man. Now he will treat him like a child – a child to be bribed with the promise of a sweet, to be teased a little for yielding to the bribe, to be coaxed with constant reference to the promised reward, and to be placed safely between two adults, rather than left to walk on his own:

> Quando mi vide star pur fermo e duro,
> turbato un poco disse: 'Or vedi, figlio:
> tra Bëatrice e te è questo muro.'   (*ibid.*, 34–6)

When he saw that I was still immobile and inflexible despite everything, his face darkened a little and he said: 'My son, look, this wall lies between you and Beatrice.'

The one name is more persuasive than all his rhetoric. Dante's 'hardness' is immediately 'softened', as he indicates by turning to his 'savio duca':

> Ond' ei crollò la fronte e disse: 'Come!
> volenci star di qua?'; indi sorrise
> come al fanciul si fa ch'è vinto al pome.
>   Poi dentro al foco innanzi mi si mise,
> pregando Stazio che venisse retro,
> che pria per lunga strada ci divise.   (*ibid.*, 43–8)

At this, Virgil bowed his head and said: 'What? Are we going to stay on this side?' Then he smiled a little as we do at a child who has been won over by an apple. After that, he led the way into the fire, begging Statius, who had earlier come between us for a long way, to bring up the rear.

> Sì com' fui dentro, in un bogliente vetro
> gittato mi sarei per rinfrescarmi,
> tant' era ivi lo 'ncendio sanza metro.
>   Lo dolce padre mio, per confortarmi,
> pur di Beatrice ragionando andava,
> dicendo: 'Li occhi suoi già veder parmi.'   (*ibid.*, 49–54)

Once I was inside, the blaze was so beyond all measure that I would have thrown myself into molten glass to cool down. My sweet father, to strengthen my resolve, kept talking about Beatrice as he went along, saying: 'I seem to see her eyes already.'

At one level, the episode can and should be read as a 'fable', a fable teaching the best method to overcome fear in oneself or in others. It is better to hold out an apple than to apply the spurs.[47] Virgil fails when he appeals to conscience, reason and experience. He proves his knowledge of the human heart ('accortezza') and he succeeds, when he appeals to love.

It is a grave mistake, however, to try to squeeze a simple, allegorical 'moral' from the richness and complexity of Dante's 'fables'. One cannot interpret this study of the 'antidote' to fear without setting it in the context of the relationship between Dante and Virgil – the context in which we have been taught everything we have learnt about fear itself. In this case, we are probably more involved with the emotions felt by the 'father' than with those of the 'son'. Virgil succeeds by invoking the name of another person, almost a 'rival'. He is 'troubled' by his failure to carry the day by himself, and even more troubled by the success of his alternative strategy. It is true that any good teacher rejoices when his favourite pupil leaves him to study with the greatest authority in the world, or that a father is glad when his son is about to better himself through a good marriage. But there will be a hint of sadness in the recognition of one's own lesser claims, a hint of jealousy, perhaps, when the new name comes to dominate the conversation, and more than a little grief at the thought that one will never see the pupil or son again after he has gone to join the new 'master' or the new 'bride'. And these emotions would be natural enough even if one were not about to return to eternal exile in Limbo! This is the kind of insight Francis Bacon had in mind when he spoke of passions 'enwrapped within another'.

CHAPTER TWELVE

Anger

Ira in universali et in typo

When the protagonist was silently following Virgil along the dyke of the fifth bolgia, his reasoning and imagining sprang not only from fear, but also from a close familiarity with the scholastic analysis of the passion of anger (in Latin, *ira* or *iracundia*). The devils have been put to 'scorn' and they have been 'hurt'. They will therefore feel 'anger', which will move them to give 'chase' not just swiftly, but 'cruelly'.[1] Even the choice of animals in a simile ('più crudeli / che 'l cane a quella lievre') is significant, because the hare was the standard example of a propensity to fear, while the animal proverbial for its anger was the dog.[2]

We can in fact gain a very good preliminary idea of Dante's presentation of anger in the poem by glancing at his references to dogs. They are not symbols of fidelity, watchfulness or protection. They are savage; they snarl, bark and howl; they rush out to attack beggars; they crunch their teeth on bones. In Dante's experience, dogs are 'rabid'. It is no coincidence that the expressive vernacular word 'rabbia' (like the English word 'rage') derives from the Latin *rabies*. And similarly, it is no accident that when Queen Hecuba went out of her mind she 'howled like a dog', or that the protagonist should repel an angry assailant with the words: 'Get back there with the other dogs.'[3]

Unrestrained, furious and violent anger of the kind which will occupy us for most of this chapter is, precisely, an 'ira *bestiale*'. In Dante, the noun 'bestialità' or 'bestialitade' attracts the adjective 'matta'.[4] And anger is a transient 'madness' (*insania, amentia, furor, mania*). It suspends the use of reason, which, as we saw in chapter 10, is the 'activity of our noblest part' and the 'life proper to our species'. 'The person', Dante said, who 'departs from reason and uses only the sensitive part, lives not as a man, but as a beast.'[5]

The treatment of anger in the *Comedy* differs from that of fear in at least three important respects. First, anger had been recognised for centuries as one of the seven Capital Vices.[6] Consequently, separate circles are provided for the souls of the *iracundi* in both Hell and Purgatory. Second, the passion is far from being confined to the protagonist: the guardians and sinners in Dante's Underworld are always likely to 'furiously rage together'. And, third, Dante and his teachers unequivocally admired some manifestations of anger as conducive to a virtuous moral life, in that they help us to 'fight the good fight' or to 'resist the adversary'. 'Righteous wrath' of this kind is shown *by* the protagonist to certain sinners in Hell, and *to* the protagonist by his guides. It is frequently aroused in the souls of the blessed by the wrongs of our world, just as it is one of the most frequent causes of direct intervention by Dante, the author of the poem.

'Trasmutare sembianza'

We saw in chapter 8 that, by definition, every passion of the soul will produce some physiological change in the body – a *transmutatio corporalis*. Aristotle illustrated this point – almost at the beginning of his *De anima* – by noting that a natural scientist would define anger as a 'blazing of the blood around the heart' (*accensio sanguinis circa cor*); and this is the ultimate source of Dante's ecstatic vision of the people who were gathering to stone St Stephen to death, and who were 'blazing with the fire of anger' ('genti *accese* in foco d'ira').[7]

Aquinas reports a commonly held view that the principal signs and effects of anger are five: palpitation of the heart, trembling of the body, puffing of the face, popping of the eyes (*exasperatio oculorum*) and irrational clamouring.[8] And we may use this convenient check-list to establish that Dante is as comprehensive as ever in his attention to 'body-language' when representing anger, and that his imagination is nourished by his learning even when he is describing the guardians of Hell.

Charon has eyes which are not just 'exasperated', but surrounded by 'wheels of flame' such that they seem like 'braziers'. Cerberus suffers from *tremor corporis* to such an extent that he cannot keep any part of his body still ('non avea membro che tenesse fermo'). Pluto has a face so swollen – 'infiata labbia' is a close translation of Aquinas's *inflatio faciei* – that it is compared to sails billowing in a gale. His 'clucking' challenge ('Pape Satàn, pape Satàn aleppe!') is a good example of a *clamor irrationalis*. The same is true of the incomprehensible words of the giant Nimrod, whom Virgil advises to use his hunting-horn if he wants to give vent to his 'anger or other passion'.[9]

Dante, however, does not confine himself to the commonplace. When anger shades into madness, for example, the signs and effects are intensified. If the human Queen Hecuba howled like a dog, the half-human Minotaur is compared by contrast to a man 'biting himself, when overpowered by anger'. The three Furies are appropriately 'furious' as they tear at their breasts with their nails.[10] And the poet is at his most inventive when describing the symptoms of anger exhibited by two popes, whose features are concealed from our view.

The first is Pope Nicholas III, whom we meet in the third bolgia of the ninth circle of Hell. Like his fellow ecclesiastics who had put the gifts of God up for sale, he is buried head-down in the ground as far as his waist, and the soles of his feet are burned by flickering flames. After he has told his story, he is forced to listen to a sermon against simony from the protagonist, to which he reacts by kicking out even more wildly with his feet.[11] And the author records, with deadpan humour, that, in the circumstances, he was unable to tell whether it was conscience or anger that was troubling his audience of one:

> E mentr' io li cantava cotai note,
> o ira o conscïenza che 'l mordesse,
> forte spingava con ambo le piote.　　　　　(*Inf.* XIX, 118–20)

And while I was singing him these notes, whether it was anger or his conscience that was biting him, he thrashed out strongly with the soles of both feet.

The second angry pope is none other than St Peter himself, whom we meet in the Heaven of the Fixed Stars. Together with St James, St John and Adam, he has come forward from the concourse of the blessed to speak with Dante. But throughout the long exchanges described in *Paradiso* XXIV–XXVI, his features have remained concealed (as are the features of all the blessed in the higher heavens) by the very intensity of the light which he irradiates.[12]

As the proceedings draw to a close, the whole 'choir' of the blessed sing a joyous and intoxicating *Gloria* to the Holy Trinity; and the four 'soloists' – so to speak – are described as 'four *torches* blazing brightly before Dante's eyes'. During the singing, however, St Peter's 'torch' undergoes a transformation in its outward appearance ('ne la sembianza sua'): it becomes more radiant ('più vivace'), and changes in colour from white to red. Silence falls. Then Dante hears the voice of the saint telling him not to be amazed at his change in colour:

> Quand' ïo udi': 'Se io mi *trascoloro*,
> non ti maravigliar.'   (*Par.* XXVII, 19–20)

The cause of the 'transcolouration' proves to be the anger felt by the apostle on contemplating the corruption of the papacy; and this anger will erupt into an invective which is even fiercer than the corresponding sermon 'preached' by the protagonist to Pope Nicholas. But on this occasion we are invited to focus, first, on the bodily symptoms of the speaker's own anger, and then on the signs and effects of the corresponding emotion which his words arouse in a sympathetic audience. Peter promises that all the souls of the blessed will 'change colour' as he speaks ('dicend' io, / vedrai *trascolorar* tutti costoro'); and after his opening denunciation of the present 'usurper of his place', we are told that the 'whole of heaven' did indeed 'flush with the colour that paints the clouds at sunrise or sunset':

> Di quel color che per lo sole avverso
> nube dipigne da sera e da mane,
> vid' ïo allora tutto 'l ciel cosperso.   (*ibid.*, 28–30)

At this point our attention is directed towards the figure of Beatrice, whose features have remained visible to the protagonist throughout, and whose aspect is now transformed by a dramatic dimming of her radiance ('così Beatrice *trasmutò sembianza*'). Finally, however, we return to Peter's anger and a new *transmutatio*; for although there is no further change in his appearance, the volume and quality of his voice is said to be totally transformed:[13]

> Poi procedetter le parole sue
> con voce tanto da sé trasmutata,
> che la sembianza non si mutò piùe.   (*ibid.*, 37–9)

Obfuscation and violence

The ensuing diatribe is one of the supreme examples in the *Comedy* of the stylised verbal violence which is the usual consequence of righteous wrath; and it reminds us that all anger, even the most virtuous, results in some kind of attack, rather than in flight or pursuit. But we must retrace our steps a little now and return from justified indignation to the vicious and uncontrollable 'ira bestiale' – punished in Hell and expiated in Purgatory – to consider how Dante represents the unseen effects of anger on the experiencing subject, and how he dramatises the crude physical aggression to which it so often leads.

One of Dante's most common ploys is to take an inert or 'dead' metaphor, of the kind we habitually use to convey the nature of our private feelings to other people, and to give it a new literal life as a punishment or as a feature of the landscape in the other world. For example, we often talk about a 'storm' or 'whirlwind' of sexual passion, as when Dante exclaims in one of his canzoni: 'What rational argument has power to curb when such a tempest whirls within me' ('Quale argomento di ragion raffrena, / ove tanta *tempesta* in me si gira?'). In *Inferno* v, the metaphor is made concrete and visible in the 'bufera infernale' which tosses and buffets eternally the lovers who surrendered to their sensual love.[14]

A similar linguistic process led to the generation of Dante's most successful image for the obfuscation of the rational powers caused by instinctive anger. It will be remembered, from the discussion of vision in chapter 5, that the souls of the penitent *iracundi* on the third terrace of Mount Purgatory are permanently enveloped in a thick cloud of black, acrid smoke. The symbolic point is that good judgement depends on 'discernment', which is made impossible by the 'cloud' of anger, just as good vision depends on the actualised transparency of the atmospheric medium, which is prevented by the presence of particles of dust or vapour. And Dante was conveying the same idea in his description of the corresponding circle in Hell, where he dwelt insistently on the 'suspension of particles of dust' in the infernal river where the *iracundi* are immersed. To be plainer, it is no accident that the Styx is represented as a 'marsh' ('palude', 'pantano'), that its water is 'mud' ('fango', 'belletta', 'loto') or that the sinners are referred to as 'genti fangose'.[15]

In the narrative, we pass immediately from the symbolic description of the condition of anger to a realistic representation of its effects. No sooner has the protagonist followed the 'grey waters' down to the foot of the 'grey malignant cliffs', where the waters spread out into 'the marsh called Styx', than he sees people with an air of grievance brawling with each other. They are not just punching, but head-butting, barging, kicking and biting – for all the world like a Saturday-night fracas outside an inner-city public house, except that the place is a bog in Hell and everyone is naked and covered in mud:

> E io, che di mirare stava inteso,
> vidi genti fangose in quel pantano,
> ignude tutte, con sembiante offeso.
>   Queste si percotean non pur con mano,
> ma con la testa e col petto e coi piedi,
> troncandosi co' denti a brano a brano.
>   Lo buon maestro disse: 'Figlio, or vedi
> l'anime di color cui vinse l'ira.'   (*Inf.* VII, 109–16)

Looking intently, I saw people plastered with mud in that bog, all of them naked and with offended looks. They were striking each other not just with their hands, but with their heads, their chests and their legs, and they were tearing each other to pieces with their teeth. The good master said: 'My son, now you see the souls of those who were overpowered by anger.'

Insults and blasphemy

There are, of course, many other occasions in the poem where Dante represents violent action motivated by irrational anger, with the prize for the most 'bestial signs' going to the sons of Count Alberto or to Count Ugolino in the grip of the ice reserved for the traitors. Their violence is all the more horrific because in each case the paired sinners are frozen in close proximity to each other for all eternity.[16]

Contiguity in misery is also indispensable to the slightly earlier clash between Sinon, who deceived the Trojans into taking the Wooden Horse within their walls, and Master Adam, the forger who counterfeited the golden florins of Dante's Florence. They are seated side by side on the ground, immobilised by appalling afflictions – the Greek steaming and stinking from his fever, the Italian tormented by thirst despite all the accumulated fluids in his dropsical body, which is so swollen that it resembles a lute.[17] Sinon lashes out at his neighbour for revealing his name, punching the taut skin of his belly so that it booms like a drum; and Adam retaliates with a blow from his arm across Sinon's face. The blows are registered with appropriate vigour of rhythm and harshness of sound, but, from the literary point of view, this sudden explosion of reciprocated anger is remarkable chiefly for the slanging-match which follows. Terzina by terzina, the two sinners taunt and curse each other with all the virtuosity shown by the shepherds in Virgil's third eclogue, by epic heroes in a *chanson de geste* or by thirteenth-century 'realistic' poets engaging in a 'tenzone', as we can judge in the final exchange:

> 'E te sia rea la sete onde ti crepa',
> disse 'l Greco, 'la lingua, e l'acqua marcia
> che 'l ventre innanzi a li occhi sì t'assiepa!'
>   Allora il monetier: 'Così si squarcia
> la bocca tua per tuo mal come suole;
> ché, s'i' ho sete e omor mi rinfarcia,
>   tu hai l'arsura e 'l capo che ti duole.'   (*Inf.* XXX, 121–7)

The Greek said: 'And may *you* be tormented by the thirst that is cracking your tongue, and by the putrid water that pushes up your body like a hedge in front of your eyes.' Then the forger replied: 'Your whole mouth is splitting open because of your torment as it always does; because if I'm parched and swollen by fluid, you have the burning fever and the throbbing head.'

The contest has a further link with the subject of this chapter in that it provokes Virgil to a display of justified anger, as he rebukes his pupil for the 'base desire' he showed in listening too intently to these scurrilities. But whether or not the reader is induced to share the protagonist's consequent feeling of shame, there are three main things to learn from Sinon and Master Adam. First, human anger will often take the distinctively human form of linguistic violence (these elaborately studied insults are far from being a *clamor irrationalis*). Second, the obfuscation or degradation of reason leads to a corresponding degradation of language. Third, the tongue can be mightier than the fist, because the wound left by a well-chosen insult may fester and rankle long after the bruise from a blow has been forgotten.

There is, however, one being whom men cannot hurt in any way, no matter how hard they try. He is the three-person God, in whom the Father is identified with Power, and the Son with the Word. But his invulnerability does not prevent men from *attempting* to 'do violence to the deity by blasphemy' ('puossi far forza ne la deïtade, / col cor negando, e bestemmiando quella').[18]

Blasphemy is not necessarily verbal, as we learn from the close of the encounter with Vanni Fucci. Described by the author as 'a man of blood and violent rages', he himself admits that he preferred 'the life of a wild beast to that of a man'. He seeks to hurt the protagonist by prophesying the outcome of a battle in which Dante's fellow exiles will be disastrously defeated, and then shows his defiance of his Maker and Judge by making an obscene gesture with both hands and yelling (in effect) 'Up yours, God.'[19]

Vanni is immediately silenced and punished further for his 'one-off' blasphemous gesture, because although God is not 'hurt', he is certainly 'offended' by the attempt. Indeed, there is a special zone in Dante's Hell which is reserved for habitual blasphemers; and it is there that we meet Capaneus, one of the seven kings who besieged Thebes. Capaneus seems indifferent to the rain of fire under which he lies in the burning sand; and he is allowed the luxury of no less than ten lines of bombastic, mythologising blasphemy, in which he denies the omnipotence of God by claiming that even if 'Jupiter' were to exhaust Vulcan and the giants who supply his thunderbolts, and even if 'he were to hurl those bolts with all his might, he still would not obtain a joyful vengeance' ('non ne potrebbe aver vendetta allegra').[20]

There are several lessons to be learnt from his boasting; and we shall shortly begin to explore the connections in Dante's mind between anger, on the one hand, and joy in revenge, on the other. But for the moment we need only comment that habitual anger (like any other vice) is its own punishment in this life as in Hell. Capaneus is proud that death has not changed him in any way ('qual io fui vivo, tal son morto'). But Virgil, who is made to speak with unprecedented vehemence, is surely right to exclaim: 'Capaneus, it is precisely in that your pride remains undimmed that you are punished most severely. No torment other than your rage could constitute a pain to match your madness.'

> Allora il duca mio parlò di forza
> tanto, ch'i' non l'avea sì forte udito:
> 'O Capaneo, in ciò che non s'ammorza
>   la tua superbia, se' tu più punito;
> nullo martiro, fuor che la tua rabbia,
> sarebbe al tuo furor dolor compito.'   (XIV, 61–6)

Anger and the 'irascible power'

The preceding sections have been structured to suggest that Dante set out to represent, in a bewildering variety of fictional situations, all the effects of anger which St Gregory the Great had metaphorically described as 'daughters of anger' (*filiae irae*): 'brawling, pride, insulting behaviour, uproar, indignation and blasphemy'.[21] But the time has come to tilt the balance more overtly in favour of philosophy once more. Our next task is to establish the formal, final and efficient causes of anger, considered both in its distinctively human manifestations, and as a motive force found among all the higher animals.[22]

The Aristotelian and scholastic analysis of anger embodies a significant revision of the 'binary' paradigm of natural motion in which every self-caused movement is classified either as the pursuit of a future pleasure, stemming from a desired good, or as the avoidance of a future pain, stemming from a feared evil. In this account, anger is caused, not by perception and imagination, but by the passion of present or remembered pain. It normally leads to attack, which is clearly a kind of pursuit; but it seeks to inflict harm and pain on its object, and entails the risk of harm and pain to the subject.

Aquinas treats anger as one of a group of emotions, collectively called the 'irascible power', which were usually distinguished from the remaining passions which together make up the 'concupiscible power'. (The two adjectives are derived from the verbs *irasci* and *concupiscere* meaning 'to grow angry' and 'to desire strongly'.) Aquinas's synthesis is far more complex and far-reaching than anything we find in Aristotle, and there is no evidence to suggest that Dante followed him in detail; but his discussion of the *vis irascibilis* as a whole is well worth attention, because it sets the passion of anger in a context which any intellectual of Dante's time could have accepted.

His reasoning can be paraphrased like this. Some *bona* which are desirable when considered in themselves, without qualification, because they are indispensable to the existence or the fullness of being of the given species, may nevertheless be unattractive to a particular member of that species, in particular circumstances, because they are out of reach or too well defended and cannot be obtained without effort or pain. Seen in this light, such a 'good' may be described as 'laborious' or 'difficult' (*bonum laboriosum, difficile*) or, more expressively, as 'towering' or 'uphill' (*arduum*).[23] Conversely, some *mala* which may cause physical harm or death, and which are certainly to be avoided when considered in the abstract, may, in certain circumstances, have to be sought out or at least resisted, because only by so doing will the animal obtain or preserve a necessary good. (Such a *malum* may also be called *difficile*.)

'Nature is not deficient in necessaries.' The higher animals are therefore endowed with an appropriate power which enables them to resist – to move against or to stand firm, as opposed to moving towards or moving away. This is the *vis irascibilis*.[24]

The first passion contained within the irascible power is called *audacia* (as so often, ordinary modern English has no exact equivalent for the Latin term, and one has to choose, depending on the context and register, between words like 'daring', 'audacity', 'spirit', 'boldness'). It is aroused by the perception of a *bonum difficile* or a *malum difficile*, and it 'stiffens the sinews' and 'summons up the blood' to enable the animal to jump higher or further, for example, or to defend itself with its claws or talons, teeth or beak. The second passion is *ira*. It is aroused by the experience of pain inflicted by a *malum difficile*. And it strongly intensifies the motive force supplied by *audacia*.[25]

These are the ideas which find definitive expression in passages like the following, which culminate in the splendidly affirmative image of the irascible power as a 'champion and defender':

> The sense appetites are divided into two powers, the 'concupiscible', which has as its object any good which is accessible to the senses, considered as good without qualification, and the 'irascible', which has as its object a good considered as inaccessible or arduous; as, for example, victory is regarded as a kind of good, although it is not accompanied by sensual pleasure.
>
> There must be two appetitive powers in the sensitive part of the soul. The first inclines the soul, without qualification, to pursue those objects which the senses indicate as appropriate, or to flee from agents of harm. This is called the 'concupiscible' power. The other enables the animal to resist aggressors or anything that could do it harm. This is called the 'irascible' power; and we say that its object is the 'towering-above' [*arduum*] in that it tries to 'get on top of' its enemies and to 'rise above' them.
>
> The irascible power is, so to speak, the champion and defender of the concupiscible power. It rises against anything that would obstruct or prevent its ward from attaining the proper objects of its desire; and it rises against anything that would bring harm to its ward or cause it to run away.[26]

Aristotelian stresses: (a) anger as bitter-sweet

Keeping in mind this very positive view of the irascible power as a whole, we may now narrow our focus and consider anger as a passion of the sensitive part of the *human* psyche (without reference for the time being to its interaction with the mental powers).

There are perhaps three unexpected emphases in the scholastic account of anger; and they each have their origin in Aristotle's treatment in the second book of his *Rhetoric*, where we read that 'anger may be defined as an impulse, accompanied by pain, to a conspicuous revenge for a conspicuous slight. It must always be attended by a certain pleasure – that which arises from the expectation of revenge.'[27]

Close attention was given, first, to the simultaneous presence of pain and pleasure. The *terminus a quo* of anger is the 'hurt inflicted' by another human being. Its *terminus ad quem* is the hurt to be inflicted on that person in retaliation. It continues to make itself felt as a *motus animae* and a *vis motiva* for as long as the original pain is remembered, and remains unassuaged by revenge. Hence anger involves pain in the past, present and future. But the moment of retaliation will be sweet when it comes. And, more important, there is already a feeling of pleasure in the present, inasmuch as the mind anticipates the satisfaction of revenge.

Aristotle substantiates this last point with an unattributed quotation from the *Iliad*, which appears again and again as a *proverbium*: 'Anger is sweeter by far than the honeycomb dripping with sweetness, and it spreads through the hearts of men.'[28] And just as philosophy was nourished by Homer's poetry in the fifth century BC, so Dante's poetry was to be enriched by philosophy in the early fourteenth century AD, because the 'bitter-sweetness' of anger is portrayed in the damned, in the protagonist and in the persona of the storyteller himself.

The contraries are shown at their most extreme in the character of Ugolino.[29] He 'renews' (and evokes in his hearer and in the reader) the 'disperato dolore' which is the cause of his unappeasable hatred for the archbishop who had been responsible for his 'cruel death'. He can scarcely wait to return to the eternal pleasure of his ghastly revenge. Yet he clearly relishes the unexpected opportunity to avenge himself on his victim in a new way, by blackening his name among the living:

> Poi cominciò: 'Tu vuo' ch'io rinovelli
> disperato dolor che 'l cor mi preme
> già pur pensando, pria ch'io ne favelli.
>   Ma se le mie parole esser dien seme
> che frutti infamia al traditor ch'i' rodo,
> parlare e lagrimar vedrai insieme.'   (*Inf.* XXXIII, 4–9)

He began: 'You want me to renew a desperate grief that crushes my heart even to think of it before I speak. But if my words are to be a seed that will yield a fruit of infamy to the traitor whom I gnaw, you will see me speak and weep at the same time.'

Revenge may also be sweet when the reprisal is carried out 'by proxy'. This is why the protagonist regarded the snakes as 'friends' when they attacked Vanni Fucci for his spiteful prophecy and blasphemous gesture. And this is why he rejoiced when the *iracundi* satisfied his desire to see Filippo Argenti submerged beneath the mud in order to punish his affront.[30]

Dante-the-author comments that he still praises and thanks God for what he saw. And we catch a similar note of joy in the author's voice whenever he imagines and invokes a divine retribution here on earth, as, for example, when he apostrophises the uncrowned Emperor Albrecht and longs for a 'just judgement to fall from the stars' on his descendants – a judgement that will be 'unprecedented and unmistakable, so that your successor may know fear at it'. The most poignant of these angry fantasies, however, comes at the beginning of *Inferno* XXVI. The exile's vengeful pleasure in dreaming of a coming disaster is tempered by the awareness that Florence, despite all the wrongs she has done him, is his native city, and that her misfortune will become harder for him to endure with every year that passes:

> Ma se presso al mattin del ver si sogna,
> tu sentirai, di qua da picciol tempo,
> di quel che Prato, non ch'altri, t'agogna.
>   E se già fosse, non saria per tempo.
> Così foss' ei, da che pur esser dee!
> ché più mi graverà, com' più m'attempo.   (*Inf.* XXVI, 7–12)

But if dreams are true near daybreak, you will shortly experience what Prato, and others, are yearning for. If it had come already, it would not have come too soon. Would that it had happened, since happen it must! For the older I grow, the more it will weigh on me.

Aristotelian stresses: (b) anger in relation to humiliation

The second influential insight in Aristotle's definition of anger is that the 'hurt inflicted' (*tristitia illata*) consists in some form of 'slight' or 'humiliation'. A mild slap in the face may be a serious wound to one's self-esteem. The raising of a hand with two fingers extended in a V or with the thumb inserted between the index and middle fingers may be more provoking than any blow. Dumb insolence can be as enraging as the foulest epithet; and ridicule may well be more effective than either.

There were many synonyms to describe 'slighting' and its effects on the offended party.[31] But the most important for Dante was clearly *despectio* (from *despicere/despectum*, 'to look down on') together with its vernacular derivatives 'dispetto', 'dispitto', 'dispettoso'. The adjective occurs in the examples of pride and anger provided for the meditation of the penitent souls in Purgatory (Michal is 'come donna *dispettosa* e trista', Haman is '*dispettoso* e fero'). Omberto degli Aldobrandeschi, the Tuscan nobleman purging his family pride, held all men in such 'despetto' that it led to his murder. And these are the associations we must keep in mind when reading the opening of the encounter with the Ghibelline leader Farinata degli Uberti.[32]

He towers 'arduously' over Dante, 'as if he utterly despised Hell' ('com' avesse l'inferno a gran dispitto'). It is hardly likely, therefore, that such a figure will treat the protagonist with due courtesy, even though his only reason for accosting him is the desire to speak with a fellow Florentine. No sooner has the trembling Dante been pushed by Virgil to the foot of the fiery tomb which serves as his eternal prison, than Farinata eyes him up and down and asks 'as it were disdainfully, "Who were your forbears?"' (This is a typically aristocratic opening gambit, which will reveal his interlocutor's political allegiances and social status.) And when Dante babbles out the answer (his reverence and over-anxiety are comically underlined), Farinata indicates his contempt by a slight raising of his eyebrows:

> Com' io al piè de la sua tomba fui,
> guardommi un poco, e poi, quasi sdegnoso,
> mi dimandò: 'Chi fuor li maggior tui?'
>   Io ch'era d'ubidir disideroso,
> non gliel celai, ma tutto gliel' apersi;
> ond' ei levò le ciglia un poco in suso.   (*Inf.* x, 40–5)

As I came to the foot of his tomb, he looked at me briefly and asked: 'Who were your ancestors?' And I who was eager to obey, hid nothing from him but revealed everything; at which he raised his brows a little.

To these gestural slights, conveyed by tone of voice, eye and eyebrow, he now adds a totally gratuitous verbal insult, by boasting that he had driven Dante's family into exile – and not just once, but twice! His *sermo durus* produces the inevitable result. The protagonist forgets his reverence and awe (which had earlier led him to inquire as to the whereabouts of Farinata). He does not turn the other cheek or make a 'mild answer to turn aside wrath', as the Book of Proverbs had advised. Instead, he 'gives as good as he got' by retorting that, at least, *his* family had returned from exile on both occasions, whereas the Uberti had not learnt that particular skill ('ma i vostri non appreser ben quell' arte').[33]

This is a shrewd thrust. To understand its full force we should have to examine not only the continuation of the exchange (delayed by the sudden appearance of Cavalcante de' Cavalcanti), but the whole of the sixth canto of *Purgatorio*, which shows how two fellow-citizens ought to behave when they meet in the other world.[34] For the moment, however, we may use the ordinary colloquial English expression 'giving as good as he got' as a link between 'dispetto' and the third main element in Aristotle's definition of anger – the desire for *revenge* (*vindicta*, 'vendetta').

Aristotelian stresses: (c) anger in relation to revenge

Phrases like 'to get even with someone', 'to get one's own back' or 'to pay someone out' are pertinent, because they are easily understood by all members of society, and because they are always used with approval. Despite the reservations of an educated, liberal, tolerant middle class, it is still widely assumed that 'to give as good as you got' is both natural and right. In Dante's day this assumption was even more widespread and even more firmly established. It seemed to be endorsed by the religion in which he believed; it was fundamental to the code of personal and family honour among the aristocratic class to which he belonged (or aspired to belong); and it seemed to embody the underlying principle of natural justice which he so vigorously affirmed – *suum cuique tradere*, 'to give each man his due'.[35]

For Dante's society, then, there was nothing in the least remarkable about propositions such as the following. 'Anyone who is angry
seeks to be revenged for something.' 'The movement of anger does
not arise unless an injury has been done, and unless there is a desire
and hope of vengeance.' 'Anger desires revenge, and the desire for
revenge is good because it pertains to justice.' 'Anger is found only in
the higher animals, because it resembles a rational appetite.'[36]

By the same token, there is nothing remarkable in Dante's own
three-line definition of anger (which takes the form of a characterisation of a typical *iracundus*), or in his slightly earlier presentation of
the vindictive demands made by the wife of Pisistratus, a ruler of
Athens. Both these passages are to be found in the cantos devoted to
the vice of *ira* in *Purgatorio*; and they may be quoted as an admirable
summary of the last three sections, since they demonstrate yet again
that Dante's fictions are rooted in his thought, and that his thought is
representative of his time.

> Ed è chi per ingiuria par ch'aonti,
> sì che si fa de la vendetta ghiotto,
> e tal convien che 'l male altrui impronti.　　(*Purg.* XVII, 121–3)

Then there is the kind of man who seems to grow indignant because of
some hurt, so that he becomes greedy for revenge; and such a man must
inflict harm on another.

> Indi m'apparve un'altra con quell' acque
> giù per le gote che 'l dolor distilla
> quando di gran dispetto in altrui nacque,
> 　e dir: 'Se tu se' sire de la villa,
> 　(...)
> vendica te di quelle braccia ardite
> ch'abbracciar nostra figlia, o Pisistràto.'　　(XV, 94–7, 100–1)

Then another woman appeared [in my trance-like vision]. Her cheeks
were streaming with the waters that are distilled from a pain born of great
disdain against somebody. She seemed to say: 'Pisistratus, if you are lord
of the city, avenge yourself on the arms which dared to embrace our
daughter.'

Quick, slow and cruel anger: the choleric and the melancholic

We have now dealt with the formal, final and efficient causes of anger
considered as a passion of the sensitive part of our psyche. Next, we

must digress a little to consider the possible contribution made by the 'material cause', and to recognise another distinct species of anger.

Why do so many people become quarrelsome when they drink alcohol, and why does nearly everyone in southern Europe become intensely irritable when a hot wind blows from the Sahara? Or again, why are some people chronically quick-tempered, and why are others able to bear a permanent grudge?

In the Middle Ages, questions such as these would probably have been answered in terms deriving from the doctrine of the Four Humours, that is, from the belief that both our temperaments and our transient moods are influenced by the relative proportions in our bodily make-up of the four chief fluids (*humores*) – blood, yellow bile, black bile and phlegm. Each of these was thought to possess a different pair of the four 'contrary qualities' (hot-cold; wet-dry). It was widely believed that there is an excess of yellow bile in the bodily 'complexion' of people who are easily angered. Yellow bile, or *cholera*, is hot and dry; and it this which predisposes such people to be 'hot-tempered' or 'choleric'.

Dante was significantly reluctant to adopt this kind of explanation.[37] But there is no reason to suppose that he would have dissented from the following authoritative paragraph:

> The *iracundi*, that is, those who are quick to anger, grow angry swiftly with the wrong people for the wrong reasons and more violently than they should. But their anger does not last long. They do not retain anger in their heart, but it bursts out immediately, either because they retaliate at once, or because their anger is manifested through various signs in other ways, given that the movement of anger is so swift. Once the anger has been vented, they are calm again. The people who are most disposed to this kind of anger would seem to be the choleric, because of the subtlety and swiftness of choler.[38]

This description comes from Aquinas' paraphrase of the fourth book of Aristotle's *Ethics* (the only significant addition to the original being the reference to 'choler'); and in both spirit and detail it is clearly relevant to most of the manifestations of anger we have examined. More importantly, however, there are good reasons for thinking that Dante knew and was influenced by the continuation of this passage where Aristotle describes a different form of anger, a 'retentive' anger, which Aquinas duly relates to a superabundance of another 'humour', *melancholia* (from the Greek words *melan*, 'black', and *chole*, bile), which was thought to be cold and wet, and therefore thick and sluggish.

> The second kind are the *amari*, whose anger disperses only with difficulty, and who remain angry for a long time because they retain their anger in their heart. Their anger is stilled when they avenge the injury received (punishment allays the impetus of anger as it induces pleasure instead of the preceding pain, inasmuch as a person rejoices in revenge). But if this should not happen – that is, if they do not punish – they are gravely afflicted internally because they do not manifest their anger. No one can alleviate their concealed anger by dint of persuasion; and the 'absorption' of this anger requires a long period of time in which, little by little, it cools and its blaze is extinguished. People who retain their anger for a long time in this way are insufferable [*molestissimi*] to themselves and, above all, to their friends with whom they cannot live together in harmony [*delectabiliter convivere*]; and for this reason they are called 'bitter'. And the people who are most disposed to this kind of excess are the melancholic, in whom sense impressions persist for a long time because of the density of the humour.[39]

Dante-the-protagonist will not actually see any sinners consumed by a hidden and smouldering anger of this kind, because Dante-the-poet has chosen to keep the 'smoke' from their fire purely metaphorical, and to 'hide' them underneath the muddy waters of the Styx. But he does see and learn about some unmistakable *signa* of their condition. What 'his eye tells him, wherever it turns', is that there are bubbles rising to the surface of the marsh. And what Virgil invites him to believe is that these bubbles come from the 'sighs of people who are set fast in the mud under the water', and who are 'gurgling a hymn in their throats' (almost a parody of the psalm *De profundis clamavi*). Virgil then goes on to quote the opening 'stanza' of this sullen 'hymn', and thereby to complete a richly philomythical elaboration of the unusually expressive phrase in Aquinas' Latin: *sunt sibiipsis molestissimi et praecipue amicis cum quibus delectabiliter non possunt convivere.*

> 'Sotto l'acqua è gente che sospira,
> e fanno pullular quest' acqua al summo,
> come l'occhio ti dice, u' che s'aggira.
> Fitti nel limo dicon: "Tristi fummo
> ne l'aere dolce che dal sol s'allegra,
> portando dentro accidïoso fummo:
> or ci attristiam ne la belletta negra."
> Quest' inno si gorgoglian ne la strozza,
> ché dir nol posson con parola integra.'   (*Inf.* VII, 118–26)

'[I want you to believe beyond any doubt that] under the water there are
people sighing and making the water bubble at the surface, as your eye
proclaims wherever it turns. Fixed in the mud, they are saying: "We were
sullen in the sweet air, which is made joyful by the sun, carrying within us
a rancorous smoke. Now we remain sullen in the black mire." This is the
hymn they gurgle in their throats, since they cannot recite it with fully
formed words.'

'Ira mala'

In the passage from the *Ethics* just quoted in paraphrase, Aristotle has
shifted his point of view from that of the 'natural scientist' to that of
the moral philosopher who is 'well versed in human vices and
human worth', and who is prepared to use words like 'should', 'more
than it should' and 'should not'.[40] As we noted earlier, human *ira* is
by no means an infallible 'defender and champion' of our legitimate
needs and desires. And we must now inquire a little more deeply into
the criteria which Aristotle and his successors adopted when they
praised or condemned this or that manifestation of anger.

The criteria are simple enough and contain no surprises for the
modern reader. But it may be helpful to distinguish those which are
more at home in the 'public forum' of law and politics from those
which belong to the 'forum of private conscience', and to present
them under these two separate heads.

We have seen that for Dante, as for Aristotle, human beings are
self-evidently 'companionable animals', fitted by their nature to be
'citizens of a city'.[41] Like other social or gregarious species, we are
'naturally inclined' to love and help each other, because if we are to
'live well' (*vivere bene*) we must 'live together' (*convivere*).[42]

On the other hand, Dante also observed that individual humans
are so different one from another that each constitutes 'almost a
separate species'.[43] Living together is therefore possible only if
individuals are willing to accept that certain people of good judgement and wide experience should dispense justice on behalf of the
whole social unit, in order to resolve disputes and to ensure that
every member does receive his or her due.

From the standpoint of such a *iudex* – who might be the head of a
household, the prior of a guild or the magistrate of a commune – any
operatio humana is *mala* if it weakens or destroys the social bond; and a

vis motiva is *mala* to the extent that it leads to such *operationes*. People who are 'carried away' by anger frequently seek revenge for imaginary or insignificant offences; they attack the innocent; and they try to inflict more pain than they in fact received. Anger, to paraphrase Dante, often goes much further than is right ('assai più là che dritto non volea'). And even if certain acts of revenge are in accordance with natural justice, in that they 'make things even again', angry people frequently act unjustly simply because they take the law into their own hands. They have no authority to punish.[44]

Every human being, however, may be considered not just as a member of a social unit, but as a *corpus seipsum movens*, seeking to actualise its potential and to find fulfilment and happiness in the exercise of the activity proper to its nature. A human life which is given over to the pursuit of its natural goal may be described in a nutshell as a 'life in accordance with reason' (*vita secundum rationem*) as opposed to a life lived in accordance with appearances or with the sense-appetites (*secundum apparentiam* or *secundum appetitum sensitivum*).

Seen in this perspective – the perspective of ethics, rather than politics – the passion of anger is bad to the extent that it obstructs the activity of the mental powers or that it usurps their functions. This is precisely what so often happens. Anger prejudges. It does not allow a *liberum iudicium*.[45] It prevents the *intellectus practicus* from establishing the facts of the case, determining the true responsibility, 'weighing' the offence and 'deliberating' as to the action required in the particular circumstances (action, that is, which would restore the balance without creating a new disequilibrium). It overpowers the *voluntas*, making us turn deaf ears to anyone who gives the proper advice, and driving us precipitately into actions that are cruel and degrading. And by this act of rebellion against the authority of its natural superior, anger brings about a state of metaphorical injustice within the human person. It makes man behave like a brute beast. Indeed, says Aristotle, if anger harnesses the practical intellect to its own perverse ends, it makes us 'ten thousand times' worse than the beasts.[46]

To these purely philosophical considerations, Dante-the-Christian believer would add that irrational anger is bad for three further reasons. First, like any sin, it 'makes the human creature *un*free and *un*like God'. Second, it runs counter to the example of Jesus, whose life, Dante tells us, is 'the archetype and pattern of the

Church on earth', and who said as they crucified him: 'Father, forgive them, for they know not what they do.' Third, it runs counter to the teaching of Jesus, as recorded in the most original and influential 'sermon' ever preached – the Sermon on the Mount. There he tells us that we should not judge; that we should not seek an eye for an eye, or a tooth for a tooth; that we should love our enemies and pray for those who persecute us; that we should forgive our 'debtors', as we hope God will remit our 'debts'.[47]

At the very beginning of the Sermon, Jesus gave his blessing to the 'mild' and the 'merciful' (*mites, misericordes*) and to the 'peacemakers', who 'shall be called the Sons of God' (*beati pacifici, quoniam filii Dei vocabuntur*). And it was this text which Dante chose as the appropriate beatitude for the circle of the wrathful in Purgatory. When a penitent soul leaves the terrace for ever, having been cleansed of the tendency to *iracundia*, the presiding angel says 'Blessed are the peacemakers', adding the phrase, 'who are without bad anger' ('*Beati / pacifici*, che son sanz' ira mala!'[48]

Visions of mansuetude

The technical term to denote a desirable 'mildness of character' was *mansuetudo* (in Dante's Italian, 'mansuetudine'). Etymologically, it was derived – correctly, for once – from *manu assuetum*, 'accustomed or trained by hand', and therefore 'tame'. And it may be wondered whether a poet who could portray people as 'wild beasts' with such vigour and variety would be able to do justice to people as 'domesticated animals'.

To find the answer, we need look no further than the three examples of mansuetude which are contemplated by the *iracundi* in Purgatory as an essential part of their 'reformation', and which represent, in order, the *de facto* head of a household, the magistrate of a city, and the first man to 'follow Christ' uncomplainingly to a violent death in order to be a witness ('martyr') to his faith. All three examples are particularly interesting because they are 'imagined' in the strict sense that they appear as *imagines* in the *imaginativa* of the protagonist when he is caught up in a 'visione estatica' as he walks unseeingly through the cloud of smoke.

We have just looked at the beginning of the scene in Athens where the wife of Pisistratus angrily demanded vengeance on the young man who had publicly embraced their daughter. It continues like this:

> E 'l segnor mi parea, benigno e mite,
>   risponder lei con viso temperato:
> 'che farem noi a chi mal ne disira,
>   se quei che ci ama è per noi condannato?'   (*Purg.* xv, 102–5)

And the lord seemed to answer her, kindly and mildly, with an expression of calm: 'What shall we do to the person who wishes us harm, if we condemn the person who loves us?'

Here, we should notice above all the disarming use of a question as a 'soft answer' and the colloquial simplicity of style (so different from the rhetoric of the wife); but we should also be alert to the fact that the adjectives applied to Pisistratus possess a philosophical dimension as well as a Christian one.[49]

This scene is followed immediately by a vision of the martyrdom of St Stephen; and we can learn a good deal about poetry by comparing the three terzinas with the longer account in Acts 7: 54–9. Dante never forgets that he is describing a 'vision'. First, he draws out implications from his source (without a single direct quotation) to make us see the defenceless youth ('giovin*etto*'), to see and hear the lynching mob as they shout and urge each other on, and to see and almost touch the instruments of death ('ancider con pietre' is much more concrete than the biblical *lapidare*):

> Poi vidi genti accese in foco d'ira
> con pietre un giovinetto ancider, forte
> gridando a sé pur: 'Martira, martira!'   (*ibid.*, 106–8)

Then I saw people, ablaze in the fire of anger, killing a young man with stones and shouting to themselves all the time: 'Kill, kill!'

With the exception of the contextualising metaphor of the 'fire of anger', there is nothing there that could not have been rendered by a contemporary painter (and Dante was doubtless influenced by his memory of some fresco or illumination). In the following lines, however, the resources of language are used to suggest a process. Where the Bible has simply *genibus positis*, 'having knelt down', Dante wants us to visualise Stephen 'sinking to the ground' as 'death was already weighing him down' (the crucial verb, 'aggravava', is in the imperfect tense). Next, he combines two phrases spoken by Stephen at different points in his source, changing the first (line 111) into a metaphorical and antithetical description, and the second into a lyrical passage of reported speech, which is far more moving than the rather unidiomatic and inert Latin of the Bible (*ne statuas illis hoc peccatum*):

> E lui vedea chinarsi, per la morte
> che l'aggravava già, inver' la terra,
> ma de li occhi facea sempre al ciel porte,
>   orando a l'alto Sire, in tanta guerra,
> che perdonasse a' suoi persecutori,
> con quello aspetto che pietà diserra.   (*ibid.*, 109–14)

And I saw him sink towards the ground, since death was already weighing him down. But he continued to make his eyes gateways to heaven, praying to the Lord on high, amid so much violence, that he should pardon his persecutors, with that expression which unlocks compassion.

But even when Dante is using all the resources of language (tense, metaphor, antithesis, allusion, music), he keeps the vision before our eyes. The ferocity of the crowd is recalled in the more abstract phrase 'tanta guerra'; and the last line seems to linger on the saint's expression, which is not just 'temperato', but such as to call forth 'pietà' – the laudable passion which induces us to help our fellows, not to be revenged on them.

The remaining vision is based on the episode in St Luke's Gospel, which is known to art-lovers as 'Christ among the Doctors'. It is the first to be presented in the poem, the shortest and the most memorable.

We are told in the Bible that Mary and Joseph had returned home from Jerusalem after celebrating the Passover, only to discover that their twelve-year-old son was not with the rest of the party. Fully three days elapsed before 'they found him in the temple, sitting among the teachers, listening to them and asking them questions'. And any empathising parent will marvel at Mary's restraint in the circumstances when she said simply: 'Son, why have you treated us so? Behold, your father and I have been looking for you anxiously.'[50]

Dante takes the biblical preamble for granted and sets the scene before our eyes as a painter might – with the refinement that he can control the sequence in which we register the elements that an artist must present simultaneously. We are shown successively the interior of a sacred building and a throng of people. We focus on one woman who is entering, framed by the portal of the door. And we deduce from the mixture of love and concern in her bearing and expression that she is a mother:

> Ivi mi parve in una visïone
> estatica di sùbito esser tratto,
> e vedere in un tempio più persone;
>   e una donna, in su l'entrar, con atto
> dolce di madre.   (*ibid.*, 85–9)

There I seemed to be suddenly caught in an ecstatic vision and to see many people in a temple; and to see a woman, in the entrance, with the gentle bearing of a mother.

Having established the setting, the moment and the principal figure with such economy of means, Dante allows Mary to speak all the words recorded by Luke: *Fili, quid fecisti nobis sic. Ecce, pater tuus et ego dolentes quaerebamus te.* Then he cuts and 'dissolves'. It will be seen that he translates the unadorned words of the Latin very closely indeed, while exploiting the possibilities of the verse-medium to intensify their impact (the word-order gives greater prominence to 'dolenti'; the rhyme dwells on the pronoun 'io'; and the effect of the cut is all the more striking because it occurs in mid-line):

> E una donna, in su l'entrar, con atto
> dolce di madre dicer: 'Figliuol mio,
> perché hai tu così verso noi fatto?
>   Ecco, dolenti, lo tuo padre e io
> ti cercavamo.' E come qui si tacque,
> ciò che pareva prima, dispario.   (*ibid.*, 88–93)

And [I seemed to see] a woman, in the entrance, with the gentle bearing of a mother, saying: 'My son, why have you treated us like this? Your father and I have been looking for you, grieving.' And as she fell silent, that which had been appearing disappeared.

'Good zeal' as a paradigm for 'combined operations'

The New Testament stories of Mary and Stephen cast a powerful retrospective light on the countless examples of choleric, bitter and furious anger represented in *Inferno*, just as the Sermon on the Mount throws down a dramatic challenge to the analysis of anger given by the 'natural scientist'. But Jesus was teaching the way to find reward in the 'kingdom of *heaven*'; whereas Dante continued to believe that it is possible 'to serve two masters'. For him, as we saw earlier, there is a happiness in this life (*beatitudo huius vitae*), as well as in the life eternal. This earthly happiness can be attained 'in the exercise of our own powers' (*in operatione propriae virtutis*). And we reach it 'by different means', namely, 'through the teachings of the philosophers' (*per phylosophica documenta*), 'provided we follow them by acting in accordance with the moral and intellectual virtues' (*secundum virtutes morales et intellectuales operando*).[51]

Earthly mothers are not always as 'gentle, meek and mild' as Mary was in the Temple of Jerusalem. It is quite clear, moreover, that Dante did not think they ought to be. We know from similes in the poem that a mother will face any danger to rescue her child, that she will be indulgent when it speaks deliriously in a fever, and that she will give comfort with the sound of her voice when it is 'pale and trembling' with fear. But we know from the same source that children may also see their mother as 'superba'. Or, rather, they may not be able to meet her angry gaze, but will 'keep their eyes fixed on the ground, silent and ashamed' while she administers a thoroughly deserved scolding.[52]

As we noted at the beginning of this chapter, there are many examples of 'hot speech' in the second and third canticas of the *Comedy*. These fierce reprimands are directed not at children, but at large communities, and indeed at the whole of Christendom. They are attributed not to irate mothers, but to St Peter and other saints, who are of course presented as ideal human beings and as patterns for us to imitate. We must therefore return to theory yet again in order to review some of the ways in which Dante would have argued for the necessity of 'righteous wrath' or 'good zeal'.

All too often we have been forced to describe the interactions of the rational and sensitive powers in the terms suggested by St Paul – 'one law in our members, *fighting* with another law in our minds'.[53] But an examination of the ideal relationship between anger and reason will provide an alternative model which is valid for all the sense-appetites and thus for all the passions. For the first time we shall be in possession of a paradigm for 'combined operations' as they should be, or as they would have been in unfallen man.

The first point to grasp is that Christian 'meekness', of the kind shown in its supreme form by a martyr like St Stephen, is not identical with the mansuetude recognised in 'philosophical documents'. Aristotle's *mansuetudo* is not opposed to *ira* in the same way that *bonum* is opposed to *malum*. Like all his moral virtues (that is, like all desirable dispositions of the will), it is an acquired state of character which inclines its possessor to generate the right amount of a given emotion.

This 'right amount' (*debitus modus*, or, simply, *modus*) will vary depending on the particular individual and the particular circumstances, but it will always lie between the extremes of too little and too much. Courage aims at a 'mean' (*medium*) between cowardice and recklessness, which are both vices. Generosity chooses a 'middle way' (*medietas*) between miserliness and prodigality. A 'moderate' person is one who habitually finds the right *modus*, and is able to 'moderate' his passions. Dante was therefore perfectly accurate when he paraphrased *mansuetudo* – the seventh of Aristotle's moral virtues – as 'that which moderates our anger and our excessive patience with respect to external evils'.[54]

In Aristotle's view, it is possible to be culpably deficient in anger. People are to be regarded as foolish or insensible if they do not feel any pain from an injury done to them. They are to be blamed as 'lazy', 'remiss' or 'servile' if they fail to 'repel injuries' to the proper extent (*repellere iniurias debito modo*), for it is 'vituperable' not to take revenge.[55] When we praise a person as 'good-tempered', therefore, we do not mean that he never 'loses his temper', but that he 'grows angry at the right things, with the right people and, further, as he ought, when he ought, and for as long as he ought' – which is to say, *secundum rationem*.[56]

At this point there arise two related questions bearing on the purpose and the timing of virtuous anger. What is the function of the passion of anger in a being endowed with reason and will? And at which stage in the sequence of events linking perception to action should virtuous anger make itself felt?

The answers are implicit in what has already been said about *ira mala* in human beings and about the *raison d'être* of anger in brute beasts. The practical intellect and the will must be allowed to perform their tasks 'dispassionately'. Good anger should be generated after the acts of judgement and choice – *consequenter*, not *antecedenter*. Specifically, it should come into play between choice and action – *electio* and *executio* – because its function or final cause is to assist the will by providing an additional motive force. It cooperates with the will in order to speed up the result. These ideas are present in the relevant chapter of the *Ethics*, and are duly brought out in the commentary by Aquinas.[57] But they find their classic formulation in the following sentences from the commentator's best-known work, the *Summa Theologiae*.

> Anger may relate to reason either as an antecedent or as a consequence. In the first case, it drags reason from its upright impartiality, and hence it is bad. In the second, the sense appetite moves against vices under the orders of reason. This anger is good. It is called 'anger through zeal'.
>
> The passion of anger is useful, just like all the other movements of the sense appetites, in that it enables one to execute more promptly what reason dictates. Otherwise the sense appetites would exist to no purpose in man; whereas nature does nothing without a purpose.[58]

Earlier in the *Summa*, Aquinas had established that the sense appetites are capable of 'obeying' the higher appetite even in fallen man (if they were not, it would never be possible to use rational arguments to dispel fear, to mitigate anger or to control desire). Indeed, he assumes that the higher appetite will 'overflow' into the lower, or that the lower will 'follow' the movement of the higher, unless there is something that resists. This enables him to champion the followers of Aristotle against the Stoics, who were to teach that all passions are 'perturbations' or 'sicknesses' of the soul. And this in turn enables him to defend the value of a human act to which the passions have made some contribution – always provided that they were *moderatae per rationem*. Far from 'diminishing' the goodness of such an act, they make it 'perfect', as being an expression of the whole human being. This goes well beyond Aristotle, of course, but it is entirely consistent with Dante's thought and poetry.[59]

Anger in the art of rhetoric

Aquinas, in fact, distinguishes two ways in which the will may collaborate with the passions: *per modum redundantiae* and *per modum electionis*. It may simply 'flow over' into the passions; or 'one may choose to be affected by some passion in order to operate more expeditiously with the *co*-operation of the sense appetites [*ut promptius operetur, cooperante appetitu sensitivo*]. In this way, the passion of the soul adds to the goodness of the action.'[60] The second alternative is highly relevant to the way in which anger was treated and justified in the art of rhetoric.

The underlying argument goes something like this. Human animals are unique in that they are both rational and social. Uniquely, therefore, they need and use language to convey their ideas to each other. The primary function and 'goodness' of language, says Dante, is 'to enucleate the concepts of our minds to others'.[61] But a human animal also needs and uses language to induce his or her fellows to work together for the common good. 'Instruction' is not enough. They must be 'moved'.[62]

A tyrant might 'move' his subjects by giving orders and enforcing them. A philosopher might 'move' his equals simply by setting forth irrefutable arguments in favour of a certain course of action. (In theory, the 'cogent' arguments would 'constrain' their intellects to assent, and their wills would choose what 'reason dictated'.) But what happens in a republic like Aristotle's Athens or Dante's Florence is that one citizen (who has no monopoly of power or wisdom) has to induce other citizens (who are disparate in temperament and understanding) to choose one of many possible policies (on the basis of partial information, likelihoods, analogues and opinions), and then to implement that policy of their own free will. In a word, he must 'persuade' them. And experience shows that the most effective way of 'persuading' them is to appeal not only to the will through the reason, but to the passions through the imagination.

With their customary thoroughness, the Greeks studied and codified every conceivable aspect of 'persuasive speech'. They drew up lists of recurrent arguments; they recommended logical 'shortcuts'; they taught memorisation and delivery; they offered detailed precepts about structure and style; and they paid particular attention to the techniques for arousing the desired *emotion* in the audience. The result of these labours was the art of rhetoric (meaning, originally, 'the craft of persuasion'), which was to become the central subject in the schools of the ancient world, and which remained a foundation-subject in the schools and universities of medieval Europe.[63]

Now, a persuasive speech is considered to be 'good' when the audience takes the action which the speaker desires. (A 'good' advocate wins his cases, whether or not his clients have Right on their side.) Hence, it is not surprising that rhetoric was attacked by moral philosophers, both in its infancy and throughout its long life as a school subject, precisely because it seemed to condone demagogy, sophistry, expediency and 'payment by results'. But in the view of the majority – a view endorsed at different times and in different ways by Aristotle, Cicero and St Augustine – rhetoric was regarded as necessary and morally neutral. Like a sword, it was 'good' when it was used by a 'good' man to a 'good' end. And this line of defence extended to the deliberate decision on the speaker's part (*per modum electionis*) to arouse emotions like pity, fear and shame in his hearers; and, above all perhaps, it served to vindicate the arousal of anger because anger gives such an effective impetus to 'prompter action'.

'People smile at those who smile', said Horace in his *Ars poetica*; and, further, 'if you want me to cry, you must first show grief yourself'.[64] By the same token, if you want your hearers to take common action in pursuit of a *bonum arduum*, your best plan will be to arouse their anger against your opponents by taking a 'conscious decision to be affected by that passion' as you speak. The rhetoricians had foreseen your need. From their observation of the spontaneous utterances of genuinely angry people, and from their analysis of the great harangues in the epic poets, dramatists and historians, they had singled out the appropriate figures of speech and thought – short sentences, abrupt transitions, frequent repetitions, exclamations and questions, sarcasm, menaces, hyperbolic metaphor. They had provided their own stereotyped model-speeches for the student to imitate. And thus they made it possible for anyone to *simulate* anger at will, in order to *stimulate* anger at will.

Dante was acutely aware of the harm that can be done when evil or misguided men have mastered the techniques of persuasion. We know from the twenty-sixth canto of *Inferno* that he was fascinated by the figure of Ulysses, who was regarded (in the literary tradition Dante knew) as the crafty speaker *par excellence*. When Ulysses boasts that, after his 'little oration', he could scarcely have restrained his aged crew from setting out on their 'mad flight' beyond the Pillars of Hercules 'in pursuit of the sun', we are meant to admire his extraordinary feat of persuasion, but simultaneously to condemn the 'course' he had advocated in conscious defiance of his ethic and religion.[65]

Nevertheless, Dante became, if anything, increasingly positive in his attitude to rhetoric as he grew older, and increasingly bold in his use of the whole range of devices it offered.[66] When writing the *Comedy* or composing his highly wrought political letters, he clearly believed that 'virtue was guiding him' and that his eloquence was subordinated to a good end.

His first sustained essay in the art of 'directing the will' was the canzone devoted to the virtue of liberality, which he wrote not long after his exile from Florence.[67] The opening lines of this poem are at once a copy-book example of 'angry speech', as this had been codified in the rhetorical tradition, and an almost programmatic description of a desirable 'co-operation' between the emotions and the mental powers. The lines may be paraphrased as follows: 'the passion of grief ["doglia"] has brought the passion of boldness ["ardire"] to the seat of the emotions ["core"] on behalf of a voluntary desire ["volere"], which is an ally of truth':

> Doglia me reca ne lo cor ardire
> a voler ch'è di veritate amico.   (*Rime* CVI, 1–2)

All through the poem, the utterance is that of an angry man, violent, wilful, disdainful of logical arguments and logical progression. The energetic, staccato syntax of the opening is maintained. It leads to climactic repetitions, dense antitheses and teasing word-plays. And it is most conspicuous in the unprecedented abundance of affective figures – exclamations, rhetorical questions, passages in question and answer form, apostrophes and imprecations – which may combine to give a passage like this:[68]

> Morte, che fai? che fai, fera Fortuna,
> che non solvete quel che non si spende?
> se 'l fate, a cui si rende?
> Non so, poscia che tal cerchio ne cinge
> che di là su ne riga.   (*ibid.*, 90–4)

What are you doing, Death? Unfeeling Fortune, what are you doing – that you do not disperse what is left unspent? And if you were to, to whom should it go? I do not know – for there is a circle enclosing us that marks our limits from above.

Needless to say, this 'caldo parlare' is like the surface of the sea 'when it is buffeted by contrary winds'. It does not affect the 'tidal currents' which are governed by the 'moon' of Dante's practical intellect so as to generate a highly complex structure which is as long and as superbly crafted as a canto in the *Comedy*.[69] And we find the same combination of 'storm' and 'tide', passion and 'will', whenever the characters in the *Comedy* are moved by 'good zeal' to arouse 'good zeal' in their hearers. The results are not always happy from the literary point of view (the morally deplorable exchanges of insults in Hell are often more original and more enjoyable!). But at their best, they embody some of the most distinctive features of Dante's poetry.

We have already examined the *visible* symptoms of St Peter's unparalleled wrath against the corruption of his successors, and, in particular against Boniface VIII. (Boniface was the reigning pope in 1300, but here he is immediately denounced as a 'usurper'.) The *stylistic* signs and effects are no less remarkable, as is clearly apparent even in the opening six lines of his invective, which may serve as our last example of anger in motion:

> 'Quelli ch'usurpa in terra il luogo mio,
> il luogo mio, il luogo mio che vaca
> ne la presenza del Figliuol di Dio,
>   fatt' ha del cimitero mio cloaca
> del sangue e de la puzza; onde 'l perverso
> che cadde di qua sù, là giù si placa.'   (*Par.* XXVII, 22–7)

'The man who on earth usurps my place, my place, my place, which is vacant in the presence of the Son of God, has made a sewer of blood and stench of my burial ground; for which the Adversary, who fell from here on high, takes comfort there below.'

The impetus of the pent-up emotion is suggested by the extraordinary triple repetition of 'il luogo mio'. The simple juxtaposition in mid-line of the barest monosyllables ('quà sù, là giù') reinforces the grandiose conceptual and spatial contrast between the judgement-seat of the Son of God (who is resonantly named in full) and the dungeon of Satan (who is indicated in a periphrasis that invites us to visualise his Fall). There is 'height' and 'depth' also in the vocabulary, which ranges from the neutral ('terra', 'luogo') to the legalistic ('usurpa', 'vaca'), and from the coarsely vernacular to the elegantly latinate (from 'puzza' to 'si placa'). But the single most expressive phrase is the hyperbolic metaphor, condensed in three concrete nouns that sprawl across a line-boundary: 'cloaca / del sangue e de la puzza'. The affront to decency and to literary decorum in the very meaning of 'cloaca' is reinforced by its position in rhyme and by its sound: '-aca' is certainly a 'rima aspra', and is meant to offend the sense of hearing. 'Sangue' and 'puzza' are directed at the senses of sight and smell respectively. They are intended to combine with all the other ideas and *impressiones* in order to excite a feeling of angry revulsion in the imagination and the mind. And that – to paraphrase Euclid – is the feeling that was meant to be aroused: *quod erat excitandum.*

CHAPTER THIRTEEN

Desire

A change in polarity and a restriction in field

Let us begin with a simple fable, inspired jointly by Dante and La Fontaine. Two doves, named Constance and Frances, leave their sweet nest to seek sustenance in different fields. Constance is deterred even from landing by a hideous scarecrow. Frances settles where she sees a third dove feeding placidly. Question: which of the two is in the greater danger? Constance, who is repelled by fear of an apparent *malum?* Or Frances, who is called by desire for an apparent *bonum?* Answer and moral of the tale: Frances, because the dove on the ground is a decoy, used to entice her into some hidden nets.[1]

The fable serves to explain the first of the major differences between this chapter and its immediate predecessors. They were structured to culminate with the insights that 'combined operations' can be successful, and that even the painful passions can be good for the experiencing subject in the sense that some fear is 'salutary' and some wrath is 'righteous'. The present chapter inverts the emphasis. It is organised to drive home the point that a pleasurable emotion may be harmful, that not all love for the good is itself good, and that co-operation between the higher and lower powers of the soul is not always possible because there are some situations in which the will should simply say 'no'.

This reversal in 'polarity' is insignificant, however, when compared to the restriction in the 'field'. If we were to examine the representation of attraction in the *Comedy* in the same detail as the representation of anger, this chapter would be as long as the whole of the rest of the book. Dante agreed with Aquinas that 'all things whatsoever perform every action whatsoever out of some kind of love' (*omnia agunt quodcumque agunt ex aliquo amore*). And he is one of the supreme poets of love in all its manifestations.

The only solution to the problems posed by such an embarrassment of riches is to select and exclude. We shall limit the inquiry to one phase of love – the phase of desire – and concentrate on just one species. And this could hardly be other than the desire of man for woman, and of woman for man – above all, the *reciprocated* desire between woman and man, when each partner is simultaneously 'amante' and 'cosa amata'. All other subjects and objects of desire will be banished behind what Dante called a 'wall of disregard', 'una parete di non calere'.

Behind the 'wall of disregard'

We have of course already surveyed a good deal of the ground to be excluded. Part one demonstrated the links between the concepts of *amor* and *bonum*; and it reached its climax with Dante's hymn to the universal *vis motiva* and *virtus unitiva*, which impels all things over the 'great sea of being' to bring them to their preordained 'harbours'. The last chapter of part two reviewed some of the bodily symptoms of human desire and ended with King Solomon's promise that, after the Day of Judgement, the organs of the glorified body 'will be strong to everything that gives delight'. Part three made it clear that Dante chose desire, rather than anger or fear, as the 'paradigmatic' passion of the soul in his analysis of a human operation. It also presented all the concepts and propositions required to understand why it is that our 'amore' may be 'torto' as well as 'diritto', and why it can lead to shipwreck in Hell rather than to a safe haven in Heaven. For the remainder of this section we shall mainly be drawing together ideas that were introduced separately in parts one and three, in order to reassert the conceptual unity of '*natural* science' and '*moral* science'.[2]

It will be remembered that all rectilinear movement must be from a *principium* through a *medium* to a *finis*, and that every such movement begins and ends in 'stillness' (*quies*). It is these three aspects or 'phases' (for want of a better word) that make it necessary to distinguish three possible meanings within the single word *amor*: *inclinatio, desiderium* and *fruitio*. 'Inclination' relates to the *principium*.

It is the innate capacity for loving certain kinds of 'good', which is an inalienable property of every living form. 'Desire' is the phase in which this potential for love is actualised by the perception of a good; and it refers to a particular 'movement of the soul' towards that particular good. Desire is not, or should not be, permanent (the souls in Limbo suffer because they must 'live in desire without hope'). It ceases in the phase called 'fruition', when the movement has come to its 'end'. *Fruitio* is a state of stillness, characterised by a feeling of delight or pleasure, in which the 'amante' is united with and lovingly enjoys the 'cosa amata'. It is the 'final cause' of love. When it is long lasting and only slightly disturbed, it is known as 'happiness' (*felicitas*). When it is eternal and complete in every way, it is called 'blessedness' (*beatitudo*).[3]

Dante excels in the representation of love as both movement and repose; and both have claims on our attention. But in a book devoted to the the study of passion as a *vis motiva*, and in a poem which tells the story of a 'cammino', preference must clearly be given to the stage at which love is still 'un *disio* de la cosa piacente'.[4]

We turn next to the various *species* of love. And perhaps the best way to reopen the discussion will be to read some paragraphs from the third book of the *Convivio*. Having listed the five distinctive kinds of love to be found in the elements, minerals, plants, animals and man, Dante continues like this:

> Human beings may have all these loves and do have them all. By the nature of the simple body [Earth] which is predominant in their material substrate, they naturally love to go downwards, and hence they require greater effort to move upwards. By their second nature, that of minerals, they love the place of their generation, and also the time. Hence they are all naturally more vigorous in the place and the month of their generation.
>
> By their third nature, that of plants, they have a love for certain foods which are perfectly conducive to the operations of this nature, whereas other foods leave them imperfect. By their fourth nature, that of animals – their 'sensitive' nature – men have a further love, through which they love according to the way things appear to their senses, just as animals do. And this love above all has need of a master, because its activity is overwhelming ['per la sua soperchievole operazione'], especially in the pleasure of taste and touch.
>
> And by their fifth and highest nature – the nature that is truly human, or, better, angelic, that is, rational – men love virtue and truth. And from this love is born true and perfect friendship, proceeding from goodness, of which the Philosopher writes in the eighth book of the *Ethics*.
>
> (*Con.* III, iii, 6–11, abbreviated)

Each of these species of love may be resolved into its three constituent phases or aspects (that is, each may be considered as the enabling cause, the efficient cause, and the final cause of a 'human operation'). And each of them may be evaluated and judged within an identical framework of ideas and in accordance with the same rigorous principles. These have been fully discussed in parts one and three; but it may be helpful to summarise them again, rearranging them under the following seven heads, grouped in three paragraphs.[5]

(a) Our nature is composite and has numerous powers. Each power has its own distinct good and its own appetite for that good. (b) These powers are not equal, since some exist for the sake of others. Hence, their goods are not equal in value. And each appetite must be satisfied only in due 'measure', or in the right 'proportion', which is to say, in the proper 'order'.

(c) Our highest and distinctively human powers are the intellect and the will. Their goods are knowledge and virtue, or truth and goodness. These are the objects of our 'speziale amore'. When we are pursuing them or enjoying them, we are 'using reason' and living as human beings rather than as brute beasts. (d) Truth and goodness are not only 'supreme', but 'incommensurable' with respect to the lesser goods. They are incorporeal and infinite. Indeed, in the Christian analysis, the supreme good of both the intellect and the will is none other than God. All his creatures are 'secondi beni'. He alone is the 'primo bene'. He alone can satisfy our every longing.

(e) The intellect and the will confer freedom. Freedom is God's greatest gift to man, but it entails the possibility of error. (f) Error consists in the failure to achieve due measure or proportion. 'Means' are mistaken for 'ends'; lesser goods are desired as if they were greater goods; 'secondi beni' are pursued as if they were the 'primo bene'. Error is disorder. (g) Freedom may be forfeited or destroyed if the actualised appetites of the lower powers – the passions – are allowed to cloud the operations of the intellect or to usurp the authority of the will.

To paraphrase the opening of the passage from the *Convivio*, it was possible for Dante to represent all these loves in the *Comedy*, and represent them all he did! However, not all of them are equally compatible with the declared thrust or 'polarity' of this chapter. And we must now 'pass them through the sieve' to see why sexual desire had to be the residue (what Dante called the *residentia in cribro*).[6]

The protagonist's weariness and the exiled poet's homesickness are portrayed with poignancy; but these 'elemental' and 'mineral' loves are too humble for our purposes. At the other extreme, Dante's 'special' loves for virtue and truth are described radiantly on scores of occasions in *Paradiso*; but they rule themselves out on the grounds that they cannot 'err' either in their objects or in their *debitus modus*. The same is true *a fortiori* of the protagonist's desire for union with God.[7]

To discover human loves that are frequently or universally liable to error, we need look no further than the traditional system which Dante adopted to articulate his vision of Purgatory – the seven Capital Vices, vulgarly known as the seven deadly sins. The first four of these, however, are disqualified for fairly obvious reasons: Anger has been dealt with already; Sloth presupposes a *lack* of desire; and the 'goods' which are 'inordinately' desired by Pride and Envy are not accessible to the senses and cannot be perceived. This leaves us with the three sins of 'incontinence' (as Aristotle called them), all of which do satisfy the criterion that they should involve an excessive desire for a corporeal good.

Greed (*gula*) is a disorder of the love proper to our vegetative nature and would be unduly restricting. By contrast, a study of Covetousness would demand a detailed investigation of Dante's political thought, because this is the vice which is 'most opposed to justice' (*iustitiae maxime contrariatur cupiditas*).[8] And so the 'residue in the sieve' at the end of the process of elimination is Lechery, *luxuria*, which is the uncontrolled and immoderate manifestation of the natural appetite for sex.

Sexual desire, it will now be clear, virtually chose itself as the main subject of this chapter. It is the central phase in a species of love that is neither too high nor too low in the 'hierarchy' of human loves described by Dante in the *Convivio*. It is aroused by the external sense of vision and nourished by the internal sense of imagination. It is the most overpowering ('soperchievole') in its operation. And the pleasure it affords is the most intense (even Aristotle conceded that no one can philosophise while making love).[9]

'Amore e 'l cor gentil sono una cosa'

From the 'philomythical' point of view, erotic love has the additional advantage of having been almost inseparable in Dante's work from the writing of poetry in the mother tongue. Most of his early poems belong to what we now call the 'literature of courtly love'. Every time he represented his feelings as a lover, and every time he theorised about the nature of love, he was taking up a position within, or against, that tradition. In other words, he was qualifying, developing, rejecting or transforming the literary genre which had embodied the most cherished feelings and ideals of high-minded, upper-class young people throughout Western Europe for the previous one hundred and fifty years, and which was not to lose its appeal for at least another two centuries. There was no need for Dante to translate from Latin, to come to terms with the Philosopher, or to seek help from the Commentator. His immediate audience knew and cared as much as he did himself. And rhymed Italian hendecasyllables were the natural vehicle for such discourse.

We cannot possibly turn aside yet again to trace the development of the courtly lyric in Italy between 1265 and 1310, or to describe the revolutionary contributions made by Dante himself in the first two 'ages' of his life.[10] But it may be useful to make three fairly simple observations about the literary context before we begin to study the treatment of love between the sexes in the *Comedy*.

First, then, the emotion celebrated by the courtly poets was not the uncomplicated lust or desire for procreation experienced by the 'base-born' ('villani') or by stallions in the fields. It was complex, exclusive and refined – a '*fino* amore'. Its exquisite torments and delights were the preserve of those who had been born with a 'noble' or a 'gentle' heart. And the goal of such lovers was not a brief shudder of the loins in bodily union, but a permanent state of bliss resulting from an 'unimento *spirituale*', a 'marriage of true *minds*'.[11]

Second, the literature of courtly love offered more than just songs and stories. It put forward what might be called an 'alternative culture' (in the sense in which we speak of '*alternative* medicine'). It projected an ideal of human worth and happiness, and gave precepts and concrete examples to show how these ideals might be attained. Many of its components were borrowed from 'orthodox' philosophy and religion. But its *fines* and *media* were not those indicated by Dante in the passage of the *Monarchia*, quoted in chapter 12, where he described the *beatitudo huius vitae* and the *beatitudo vitae aeternae*.[12]

Third, the 'noble' or 'poetic' lover would frequently assert with pride that his love was an irresistible force. To possess a 'gentle heart' was to become a 'soul in captivity' (this is the implication of the paired phrases 'alma presa' and 'cor gentile' in the first line of the first sonnet in the *Vita nuova*). And in a late sonnet Dante would reiterate and universalise this claim with the words 'Free choice was never free in the circle of Love's arena, so that Counsel looses its arrows in vain there':

> Però nel cerchio de la sua palestra
> liber arbitrio già mai non fu franco,
> sì che consiglio invan vi si balestra.   (*Rime* CXI, 9–11)

The technical phrases 'liber arbitrio' and 'consiglio' in the midst of the daring military metaphors here should be enough to put us on our guard. The *Comedy* is a product of Dante's *third* age. It is a work of fiction, but it passes judgement on the whole of human activity in the world of history. It also puts the author himself on trial, both as a 'doer' and as a 'maker'. *Prima facie*, therefore, we are unlikely to find him rejoicing in any loss of freedom or accepting it as a defence for wrongdoing. It is unlikely, too, that he will prefer the courtly system of values to those of Christianity and Aristotle. On the other hand, it is highly probable that he will have come to question the possibility of a clear separation between 'base' and 'noble' desire, and that he will have asked himself how many of his fellow poets had followed his lead in renouncing all hope of any 'reward' from their ladies – even a smile of recognition – and how many of his less cautious readers might have been led astray by his own rhetoric if they had ever tried to follow his precepts in real life.

The Heaven of Venus: (a) preliminaries

The remainder of this chapter will be given over to a close reading of Dante's encounters with the souls of those who loved 'not wisely, but too well'. These encounters take place in the second circle of Hell, the seventh terrace of Purgatory and the third of the planetary spheres, the Heaven of Venus. But since the chapter is structured to end with the story of how 'sweet thoughts' operated in combination with 'desire' to bring a pair of noble lovers to the 'dolorous pass' of eternal damnation, the three episodes will be presented in reverse order. And we must therefore turn to *Paradiso* VIII.

The first seven cantos of *Paradiso* form an almost seamless narrative sequence. There are very close and ingeniously varied links between the end of one canto and the beginning of the next; and there are full descriptions, placed in mid-canto, of the protagonist's ascents into the moon and Mercury. Canto VIII offers the first major variation.

At line 13, Dante tells us how he suddenly realised he was in the planet Venus, without his having been aware of any leave-taking, departure, climb or arrival. The reader, meanwhile, has just been given a comparable shock, since the new canto began with an apparently gratuitous disquisition on the failings of classical civilisation, a disquisition which constitutes the first significant interruption in the unfolding of the story.

Of course, the 'principio' (as the author calls this introduction to the canto) does have a purely practical narrative function as well. All the 'ancient errors' he mentions are connected with Venus; and we are introduced, obliquely, to some of the more important themes to be dealt with in the Heaven of 'la bella Ciprigna'.

The 'ancient peoples', no less than Dante's contemporaries, we learn, had made a religion of 'il folle amore' – complete with a liturgy, sacrifices and a sort of 'Holy Family'. Their greatest poet, Virgil, had run the risk of deceiving his less sophisticated readers by attributing the onset of Dido's fatal passion to the activity of Cupid. And they had courted the 'danger' of renouncing their human freedom (again, exactly like the courtly lovers of Dante's day) by attributing a blind and irresistible power to the celestial influences which are 'rayed' down from the planet. (Later in the canto, Dante will reassert with great vigour and at great length that the heavenly influences in their totality – 'la circular natura' – are neither irresistible nor without a divine purpose.)[13]

There follows a two-part description of the souls who have gathered in Venus to welcome Dante. This is of the greatest relevance in the way it projects their 'transhumanised' friendship and love; for although there are many aspects of their appearance, movements and speech which are common to all the blessed in *Paradiso*, there are also many implicit contrasts with the appearance, movements and speech of the 'lussuriosi' in *Inferno*.

What the protagonist first sees are lights ('lucerne') moving within the light ('luce') of the planet itself, as one may see sparks within the flames of a fire. Significantly, they are not 'ombre', but *visibilia propria*.[14]

The lights are moving in circles. In other words, they are describing the perfect figure, in the perfect kind of natural self-movement – a movement which, like the revolution of the heavenly spheres, need never come to an end, and which is also emblematic of an eternal contemplation of the Truth or an eternal enjoyment of the Goodness of God. Significantly, they are not tossed up and down or buffeted hither and thither by a violent, external force.[15]

Each of the souls is an individual, differing from and unequal to all the others. They reveal their diversity by moving at different speeds, in proportion – so the author now ventures to infer – to the fervour of the love that provides their motive force, which in turn corresponds to their power to 'see' God. (In Heaven, too, there are necessary links between perception, desire and movement.) Yet there is no lack of order. Their diverse wills are united in freely willing what God has willed for them.[16] And the fact of their diversity makes possible a 'concord' or 'harmony' – the musical metaphor being suggested by a subsidiary simile in which the souls are compared to the voices in a medieval motet, and also by the patterning of syntax and rhythm which is strongly marked here by repetition ('voce', 'voce'), adnomination ('luce', 'lucerne') and alliteration ('fiamma', 'favilla'). Significantly, this is not a 'tumulto', 'turbo' or 'rapina':[17]

> E come in fiamma favilla si vede,
> e come in voce voce si discerne,
> quand' una è ferma e altra va e riede,
>   vid' io in essa luce altre lucerne
> muoversi in giro più e men correnti,
> al modo, credo, di lor viste interne. (*Par.* VIII, 16–21)

And as a spark is seen within a flame, and as voices may be distinguished when one is still and another goes and returns, so I saw several lanterns within the light, moving in circles more or less rapidly, in proportion, I believe, to their inner vision.

The *circular* movement, energised and directed by their eternal love of God, yields to a finite, *rectilinear* movement towards Dante, expressive, in its indescribable velocity, of the intensity of their common love for him. If we fail to imagine the unimaginable (a lightning flash seemed sluggish by comparison!), we can at least experience something of their speed thanks to the very different syntax and rhythm of the new sentence, where tension mounts in the intricately negative clauses of the first terzina, to be discharged in the enjambements of the second. Significantly, the souls do not wait to be summoned; and they are not 'carried by' a wind.[18]

> Di fredda nube non disceser venti,
> o visibili o no, tanto festini,
> che non paressero impediti e lenti
>   a chi avesse quei lumi divini
> veduti a noi venir, lasciando il giro
> pria cominciato in li alti Serafini.   (*ibid.*, 22–7)

Winds, whether visible or not, never descended from a cold cloud so swiftly, but that they would have seemed encumbered and slow to anyone who had seen those god-like lights coming towards us, abandoning the circling they had begun among the Seraphim on high.

The Heaven of Venus: (b) the opening exchanges

A *Hosanna* rings out from those at the front of the group; and one of the 'lights' comes forward to welcome Dante. Significantly, he does not wait to be asked; and although he speaks 'alone' ('solo'), his first word is 'tutti', and he uses the first-person plural consistently to stress that he is the spokesman of them all.[19]

His lyrical speech of greeting dwells above all on the mutuality of pleasure and enjoyment. He and his companions come to do Dante's 'pleasure', so that he may 'enjoy' them. In the fullness of their love, they feel a 'sweetness' that will compensate them for the 'thirst' they will experience on ceasing from their eternal 'gyration' through which they express their love for God. There is exquisite courtesy, too, in the speaker's allusion to the opening line of a canzone by Dante, which took the form of an apostrophe to the angels who move the heavenly sphere in which they now find themselves (Venus is the '*third* heaven'):[20]

> E dentro a quei che più innanzi appariro
> sonava '*Osanna*' sì che unque poi
> di rïudir non fui sanza disiro.
>   Indi si fece l'un più presso a noi
> e solo incominciò: 'Tutti sem presti
> al tuo piacer, perché di noi ti gioi.
>   Noi ci volgiam coi principi celesti
> d'un giro e d'un girare e d'una sete,
> ai quali tu del mondo già dicesti:

> "*Voi che 'ntendendo il terzo ciel movete*";
> e sem sì pien d'amor, che, per piacerti,
> non fia men dolce un poco di quïete.'   (*ibid.*, 28–39)

Within the lights nearest the front, a *Hosanna* rang out – so beautifully, that since that time I have never been without the desire to hear it again. Then one of the lights drew close to us and began on his own: 'All of us are swift to do your pleasure, so that you may take delight in us. We revolve with the heavenly Principalities in one orbiting and one orbit – those whom you addressed from below as: "*You who by intellection alone move the third heaven*". We are so filled with love that, to give you joy, a little stillness will not be less sweet.'

Now it is the protagonist's turn. He can neither 'revolve' nor 'shine'; and he can manage no more than four syllables in reply. But he uses *his* kind of body-language to comparable effect, first turning his eyes to seek and gain permission from Beatrice, and then giving his voice an 'imprint of great love'. This is sufficient to cause a new access of joy to the speaker's existing joys, and therefore to cause an increase in the quality and intensity of his radiance:

> 'Deh, chi siete?' fue
> la voce mia di grande affetto impressa.
> E quanta e quale vid' io lei far piùe
> per allegrezza nova che s'accrebbe,
> quando parlai, a l'allegrezze sue!   (*ibid.*, 44–8)

The speaker now identifies himself rather enigmatically (the reader will not have confirmation of his name until the next canto). He is Charles, the eldest son and heir of the ruler of southern Italy at the end of the thirteenth century; and we deduce from the context that Dante had met him and found him a kindred spirit during Charles's brief sojourn in Florence just a year before his early death at the age of twenty-four in 1295. *Similitudo est causa amoris*. The young poet, we are now told, had 'greatly loved' the even-younger prince, and had been loved in return. (Perhaps we are meant to infer that the rays of Venus may dispose a 'gentle heart' to disinterested friendship, as well as to *luxuria*.)

There is great pathos in the elegiac evocation of 'what might have been' in the speech that Charles now goes on to make. And the general defence of astral influences in his second speech is of the utmost importance for the understanding of Dante's view of human nature. But both discourses must be consigned behind the 'wall of indifference' and we must pass on to Dante's encounter with two further souls in the group, in order to discover more about the links between love and a loving temperament.

The next 'splendore' to introduce herself is Cunizza da Romano. Like Charles, she was nobly born. Like him, she uses high-flown geographical periphrases to introduce herself. Like him, finally, she stresses how different her temperament had been from that of her brother (Ezzelino da Romano had become a byword for cruelty, whereas Robert of Anjou is here reproached for his avarice). The 'foundation laid by nature' had given her a strong predisposition to 'il folle amore'; and she had been notorious for her extra-marital liaisons (most notably with the troubadour Sordello, who appeared in Antepurgatory).

It is made clear that her temperamental *inclinatio* had been some-thing of a handicap.[21] And yet her message is: 'Je ne regrette rien.' She had been 'overpowered by the light of this star'. And yet, she goes on: 'I joyfully forgive myself the cause of my allotted place, which does not offend me, however strange this may appear to the common herd' (the extraordinary sounds of the three Latinisms in rhyme highlight in turn her radiance, her self-confidence and her disdain for the masses):

> 'Cunizza fui chiamata, e qui refulgo
> perché mi vinse il lume d'esta stella;
>   ma lietamente a me medesma indulgo
> la cagion di mia sorte, e non mi noia;
> che parria forse forte al vostro vulgo.'   (IX, 32–6)

Cunizza immediately defers to a third 'splendour'; and in the following encounter the claims she made on her own behalf are shown to be valid for all her companions. Once again the doctrinal point comes as the crystallisation of what has already been conveyed through Dante's imagery, linguistic innovation and power of drama-tic invention.

Here, too, the emphasis falls on joy and radiance. The third light is described as a 'precious and brilliant jewel' and as 'the other glad-ness' ('l'altra letizia'). And when this soul 'rejoices' at the prospect of his conversation, there is a further gain in his 'refulgence', and he becomes like a 'fine diamond struck by the sun'.[22]

Dante devises yet another way of putting the inevitable question by coining three new verbs from the fusion of the preposition 'in' with the pronouns 'me', 'thee' and 'him'. (The coinages are generally appropriate for *Paradiso*, in that they suggest a mutual openness and celestial interpenetration of minds, and particularly appropriate for the Heaven of Venus, in that the same verbs could be used of a more earthly satisfaction of desire.) 'Why do you not satisfy my desires', says the protagonist. 'If I could "in-you" myself, as you can "in-me" yourself, I should not wait for your question. And not one of my wishes can steal itself from you, because God sees everything, and your sight "in-Hims" itself':

> 'Dio vede tutto, e tuo veder s'inluia',
> diss' io, 'beato spirto, sì che nulla
> voglia di sé a te puot' esser fuia.
> 'Dunque la voce tua, (...)
> (...)
> perché non satisface a' miei disii?
> Già non attendere' io tua dimanda,
> s'io m'intuassi, come tu t'inmii.'   (*ibid.*, 73–6, 79–81)

The soul replies with a glorious periphrasis of the Mediterranean Sea, following this with more precise co-ordinates to indicate his place of birth. Then he names himself with great simplicity as Folco – better known to students of Occitan literature as Folquet of Marseilles.

The historical Folquet had ended his days as bishop of Toulouse. But in his youth he had been renowned as a lover and poet of love (one of his poems is quoted with approval in *De vulgari eloquentia*). And it is as an erstwhile 'dicitore d'amore' that he recalls how he had once 'burnt' with love – far more than Dido, Phyllis or Hercules. (The allusion to the classical lovers makes a further contribution to the cumulative definition of 'il folle amore'.) He too had carried the 'imprint' of Venus, just as he now 'stamps' his light on the planet ('questo cielo / di me s'imprenta, com' io fe' di lui').[23]

After this personal testimony, Folco goes on to make a bold and universal statement about the goodness of the sexual appetite in human beings. The 'children of Venus' (as contemporary astrologers would have called the souls we have just met) do not repent in Heaven. They do not recall their guilt. Instead, they rejoice in the understanding of God's order, providence and power as these are manifested in the workings of the physical heavens, to which they owe their temperament. Their mind's eye is directed to God's supreme craftsmanship ('arte'), which gives beauty to so great a handiwork. And they clearly see the good purpose for which the nine angelic hierarchies govern the revolution of the nine ethereal spheres:[24]

> 'Non però qui si pente, ma si ride,
> non de la colpa, ch'a mente non torna,
> ma del valor ch'ordinò e provide.
>   Qui si rimira ne l'arte ch'addorna
> cotanto effetto, e discernesi 'l bene
> per che 'l mondo di sù quel di giù torna.'   (*ibid.*, 103–8)

'Here, there is no repentance but laughter – not for the guilt, which does not return to mind, but for the Worth that imparted order and made provision. Here, we gaze at the craft that adorns so great an effect; and we discern the good, for the sake of which the higher universe causes the lower to revolve'.

The seventh terrace: (a) unrestrained appetite and the 'refining fire'

There is no discrimination between the sexes in the Heaven of Venus.[25] But this impartiality is less remarkable than the even-handedness we find in the representation of the 'lussuriosi' on the seventh terrace of Purgatory.

The penitent souls are there divided into two columns, one containing only heterosexuals, the other only homosexuals. And whereas in Hell there is a sharp distinction between natural and unnatural lust (with one group punished in the second circle, the other in the seventh), here they are treated quite literally 'on the level', as they walk in procession round and round the mountain, singing a hymn and contemplating appropriate examples of virtue and vice in order to expiate their offence and purify their will. They move in opposite directions; and no doubt it is significant that the heterosexuals move to the right (not to the 'sinister' left), in the same direction as Dante and Virgil. But, if anything, the example of the vice to be avoided is less 'opprobrious' – Dante's word – in the second group than in the first, because the homosexuals call out 'Sodom and Gomorrah' in shame and self-reproach, but the hetero-sexuals remind themselves constantly of Pasiphaë, who 'made a beast of herself in a bestial *simulacrum*' by climbing inside a specially made statue of a cow, so that a 'young bull could run to her lust'.[26]

The crucial point is that both groups strayed from the 'diritta via' by 'following their appetites like wild animals' ('seguendo come bestie l'appetito'); and neither group lived 'as virtue and matrimony require'.[27] In Purgatory, moreover, they develop the virtue of self-restraint by the authentically 'peripatetic' method of constantly repeating well-regulated gestures of affection, without letting themselves be carried further than the *debitus modus* allows. Each time the two groups cross, all the members are swift to greet each other in a friendly way ('accoglienza amica'). But they 'kiss each other without pausing, content with a brief celebration':

> Lì veggio d'ogne parte farsi presta
> ciascun' ombra e basciarsi una con una
> sanza restar, contente a brieve festa. (*Purg.* XXVI, 31–3)

There are various passing references and allusions in *Purgatorio* XXV–XXVII which are like little touches of light and shade giving greater relief to the composite picture of sexual desire that Dante is building up, area by area, and layer by layer, in the *Comedy* as a whole.[28] But the dominant image in these cantos is that of the purgatorial 'pena' itself – fire. (We saw in chapter 11 that the two columns circumambulate the mountain within a corridor of fire, which leaves only the narrowest of ledges between the outer wall of flame and the void.)

Like all the 'pene', fire is a 'tortura'. But it also has a complex symbolic meaning. It is one of the most common images for the 'hot' lust which 'burnt' the sinners during their lives. And it is a universal symbol of 'purification' or 'refinement'. Confining ourselves to its use as an 'instrumental cause' in the technology of Dante's time, we may think of it as being like the fire in a brick-kiln that converts the human 'clay' into a new and more noble substance; or as being like the fire in a smelting furnace which separates the 'dross' from the 'pure metal' in the composite human 'ore'. This is a 'fire that refines' ('il foco che li affina').[29]

The seventh terrace: (b) 'versi d'amore' and 'la passada folor'

It cannot be said, however, that these cantos add greatly to our understanding through their narrative action, imagery or explicit philosophical statement. Their chief function is to call attention to the way in which partially sublimated sexual desire had been promoted to the rank of a supreme value in the high culture of Dante's day and in his own early poetry.

In the Heaven of Venus, Dante meets the mistress of a troubadour together with a troubadour who compares himself to victims of passionate love, celebrated by classical poets. Here, on the seventh terrace of Purgatory, only two souls are named and allowed to speak; and they have been singled out precisely because they were the acknowledged masters of love poetry in the vernacular. Arnaut Daniel embodies the literature written in Occitan, the 'lingua d'*oco*'; while the 'lingua di *sì*' is represented by the Bolognese poet Guido Guinizzelli, whose canzone 'Al cor gentil rempaira sempre amore' had been the single most influential and authoritative statement in verse of the relationship between 'gentilezza' and 'fino amore'.[30]

Dante's conversation with the two poets revolves around the acknowledgement of literary debts and corrections to the literary canon.[31] Clearly, the protagonist has lost none of his interest in the craft of poetry or in poems as artefacts (the very ink with which they are written is regarded as precious!). He is still confident that he and his companions – or his 'betters', as he modestly says – had produced 'new rhymes' in a 'new style' which was distinctively 'sweet'.[32] And he seems to remain faithful to the standpoint of the *Vita nuova* in the unspoken assumption that all poetry in the mother tongue should be confined to the subject of love ('sopra materia amorosa'). It is significant, too, that when Guinizzelli describes Arnaut as a 'better craftsman of the mother tongue', he goes on to specify that he 'outdid all metrical compositions about love ["versi d'amore"] and all romances in prose' (literally, 'proses of romances').[33]

The implication is that both the main genres of courtly literature – lyric and narrative, verse and prose – were composed in the vernacular by the same 'dicitori d'amore', who shared the same subject matter, rhetoric and values. And the further implication is that all this literature 'sopra materia amorosa' was tainted with 'lussuria'.

The two poets speak with remorse about their 'love-life'. Guinizzelli says that he has begun the task of purgation so soon, because he had felt genuine grief before his last days. Arnaut is more forceful. He weeps as he sings the hymn of penitence. He 'contemplates his past madness with sorrow' ('consiros vei la passada folor' – where 'folor' stands for a life given over to 'il folle amore'). He looks forward 'rejoicingly' to a true and different 'joy in front of him'. And he concludes by urging the protagonist to 'remember his sufferings in good time':

> 'Ieu sui Arnaut, que plor e vau cantan;
> consiros vei la passada folor,
> e vei jausen lo joi qu'esper, denan.
> (...)
> sovenha vos a temps de ma dolor!' (XXVI, 142–4, 147)

The protagonist, it will be remembered, was terrified of the fire through which he would have to pass. It will now become apparent that the representation of his fear is given such prominence in order to convey in symbolic form some important and closely connected truths about the author – about his personal life, his achievements as a love-poet and the sense of guilt from which the *Comedy* springs.

First, and almost 'trivial' (in both the English and the Italian senses of the word), it implies that Dante knew himself to have a strong and ill-governed sexual drive.[34] Second, it reminds us that the poems for which he was famous in the year 1300 were all 'versi d'*amore*', and, further, that a good many of them were indistinguishable in their attitudes and in their rhetoric from those of the poets who are expiating their lust. And third, it suggests that it had indeed been the attempt to 'reach Beatrice' (it will be her name that gives him the courage to enter the refining fire) which had 'redeemed' the poems he included in the *Vita nuova*. In that work, Dante had narrated – in poetry and in prose – the story of his awakening to a '*new* life'. Beatrice is shown to have inspired 'una dolcezza *onesta* e soave'; and her 'image in his mind had been so powerful that it had never allowed Love to rule without the faithful *counsel of reason*'.[35]

The second circle: (a) the 'subjugation of reason'

With all these insights into Dante's treatment of sexual desire in those who escaped damnation, and with the reminder that Dante is putting himself on trial in the *Comedy*, we are ready to return to *Inferno* V in order to read the first of five particularly significant meetings with the damned (the others come in cantos X, XIII, XXVI and XXXIII).

In each of these famous scenes, we soon recognise that the encounter is so moving because both participants represent different aspects of Dante's inner self. The wavering and fallible protagonist stands for the still-redeemable 'core' of Dante's personality. He is undoubtedly a sinner, but he is still in pursuit of the Supreme Good and aware that he has strayed from the 'diritta via'. He is nagged by remorse, willing to accept correction and help, and therefore still open to a process of 're-formation' and 'transhumanisation'. Each of his interlocutors, by contrast, will embody one or more of the character traits that inclined him to pursue a limited good, or a 'false image of good', with a vigour that was potentially destructive because of its blind obsessiveness.

Dante never met the historical Francesca da Polenta, Farinata degli Uberti, Pier delle Vigne or Ugolino della Gherardesca, any more than he had met Ulysses. He took their names from oral tradition or written sources together with a rudimentary biography, a certain kind of temperament, known or implied, and a calamitous downfall or death.[36] Into that pre-existent shell he 'breathed the breath' of poetic life, drawing the elements into a unique *compositum* which seems 'to live, and to feel and to know itself' because it has been 'created' in the author's 'image and likeness'.[37] Ulysses is endowed with Dante's own thirst for knowledge and experience, his readiness to defy an interdict, his command of persuasive speech. Ugolino acquires his paternal feelings and longing for vengeance on his political opponents. Farinata has the author's love-hate for the city that drove them both into exile. And Francesca is given Dante's tenderness, his literary sensibility and his capacity for sexual love.

Each of the five will seek to win the protagonist's sympathy for the *mis*use they made of the talents they received from their Creator. And the heart of each episode consists in what the souls reveal about themselves in their pleas and special pleading. But no dramatic speech can be properly interpreted in isolation, and before we examine Francesca's *ipsissima verba*, we must gather together a certain number of facts and unequivocal clues which combine to form the appropriate context.

Let us not forget the obvious. The encounter is located in Hell among the 'lost people' who 'lament their second death' and who are 'never comforted by hope of any intermission or reduction of their torment'. (By definition, then, none of the spirits can possess the protagonist's openness to repentance and reform.) But let us not forget, either, that it takes place in the second of the nine circles of the Dantean Underworld, a fact which is significant because we shall be told that those who 'endure punishment above and outside' the fortress of Lower Hell are guilty only of a lack of self-control ('incontinenza'). This 'attracts less blame and gives less offence to God' than mad violence or deliberate malice. And this is why 'divine vengeance "hammers" them less angrily'.[38]

The damned souls in this second circle are described as 'sinners of the flesh', and the nature of their offence is stated analytically in just eleven syllables – 'they subjugate reason to instinctive desire':

> Intesi ch'a così fatto tormento
> enno dannati i peccator carnali,
> che la ragion sommettono al talento.   (*Inf.* v, 37–9)

This brief and abstract definition is amplified and made concrete in their torment. Metaphorically speaking, to renounce reason is to be blind or to live in the dark and hence to lose one's way. To follow instinct is to be driven by a storm of ever-changing force and direction. These are the traditional, inert images which Dante transforms with such extraordinary visual and auditory power. Uniquely in his Underworld, the carnal sinners are suspended in mid-air; and the air is at once their medium and the instrument of their punishment. It is 'malign', 'black', synaesthetically 'dumb of all light'. It is convulsed by a roaring and turbulent typhoon which is said to 'beat', 'toss', 'molest' and 'castigate' them.[39] In short, the situation, appearance and movements of these 'spirits' (the word occurs twice in both *Inferno* v and *Paradiso* IX) could not be more different from those of their 'sisters under the skin' in the Heaven of Venus.

Perhaps inevitably, the air-borne spirits are compared to birds in three extended similes. And if this were a *lectura* of the canto as a whole, there would be a great deal to say about the brilliance of Dante's writing in his contrasting descriptions of the swirling flock of starlings, the honking line of migrating cranes, or the doves about to alight at their nest 'with wings outstretched and still'.[40] Taking these similes simply as part of a context, however, it will be enough to note their ambivalence. On the one hand, these are *birds*, not, for example, flying insects; and Dante gives them endearing human attributes (the cranes 'sing sad lays', the doves come to the 'sweet nest'). On the other hand, birds might be defined as nothing other than brute beasts with wings. Hence, to compare human beings to birds, because they are 'light on the wind' or 'called by desire', is to suggest that they are 'seguendo come bestie l'appetito'. Doves, moreover, were proverbial in Dante's day for their *luxuria*.[41]

The richest and most illuminating contribution to the context, however, does not come from explicit statements or imagery. It is provided by the historical examples and literary allusions in Virgil's annotated list of the souls who are borne along in Francesca's company. Among her peers, he first 'points out and names' two queens from the Orient: Cleopatra is simply labelled as 'lussuriosa', while the incestuous Semiramis is said to have been 'so broken by the vice of *luxuria* that, in order to remove the shame she had incurred, she licensed lust in her law'.[42] To these he adds four names associated with the Trojan War and its aftermath. Paris abducted Helen, with her consent, and thereby 'caused so long a tribulation'. Achilles loved his enemy's daughter and was lured to his death in an ambush. Dido's love for Aeneas was guilty because she had broken her own vow of fidelity ('ruppe fede') to her dead husband Sichaeus, and she 'killed herself for love' on being abandoned.[43]

It will be seen that these 'ladies and knights of yesteryear' ('donne antiche e cavalieri') share two or more of the following characteristics. They loved a partner who was in some way 'forbidden'. Their love brought about their own death. They were rulers, or members of the ruling class, and they therefore had a responsibility towards their subjects – which did *not* include plunging them into a prolonged and bloody war or de-naturing the law of the land. We shall find the same features in the only 'modern' knight to be named – Tristan, who loved the wife of his uncle, King Mark – and in Francesca, wife of the ruler of Ravenna, whose forbidden love was for her brother-in-law.[44] But the most important fact about the last five names in Virgil's list is that their stories were familiar to Dante's first public from the French romances ('prose di romanzi') that had become the favourite reading matter of the courtly classes throughout Western Europe. Indeed, Dante has unwittingly sketched the history of the evolution of the genre by naming the lovers in the order in which the romances had first appeared in the mid-twelfth century (the *Roman d'Eneas*, the *Roman de Troie* and *Tristan*). And if we were to extend the sequence by adding the name of one more legendary modern lover, and one more later romance, it would have to be that of Lancelot, whose adultery with Queen Guinevere (as narrated in *La mort le roi Artu*) was to lead to the destruction of the fellowship of the 'Table Round'.

The phrases used at the beginning and end of the last paragraph are deliberately out of key with the judicial tone of the summary of the charges against Dido's companions. 'Knights of yesteryear' and 'Table Round' have the power to charm 'magic casements, opening on the foam / Of perilous seas in faery lands forlorn'. They remind us that these lovers were the heroes and heroines of the romances – not just in the sense that they were the principal figures, but in the sense that they were admired or 'hero-worshipped' by their readers. Their adventures, their ethos, their feelings and passionate utterances were 'glamorous' and 'romantick' (with a 'k').[45] They were the *raison d'être* of the genre. And as we follow the words and reactions of Francesca and the protagonist, we have to remember that they are fellow 'worshippers'. She will continue to speak like a heroine of a romance, still upholding the values of the courtly world; while he will respond with feelings that are painfully mixed – the immediate and intuitive sympathy of the 'co-religionist' being coupled with the shock of realisation that her 'romantick' actions are being punished and their common 'romantick' values condemned. This is the full meaning of line 72: 'pietà mi giunse, e fui quasi smarrito'.

The second circle: (b) Francesca's first speech

With an 'affettuoso grido' that expresses his 'pietà', the protagonist summons two of the souls in Dido's group who have caught his attention because they seem to be inseparable and 'lighter on the wind' than the others. They approach like doves 'called by desire'.[46] One of them speaks on behalf of both; and we cannot be fair to the intentions of Dante-the-author if we do not allow her words to float towards us 'on the viewless wings of Poesy' *before* our 'dull brain perplexes and retards':

> 'O animal grazïoso e benigno
> che visitando vai per l'aere perso
> noi che tignemmo il mondo di sanguigno,
>   se fosse amico il re de l'universo,
> noi pregheremmo lui de la tua pace,
> poi c'hai pietà del nostro mal perverso.
>   Di quel che udire e che parlar vi piace,
> noi udiremo e parleremo a voi,
> mentre che 'l vento, come fa, ci tace.
>   Siede la terra dove nata fui
> su la marina dove 'l Po discende
> per aver pace co' seguaci sui.'   (*Inf.* v, 88–99)

'O living being, full of grace and kindness, who come through the sable air to visit *us*, who stained the world with crimson, if the king of the universe were our friend, we would pray to him for your peace, since you show pity for our perverse suffering. We shall listen to what you want to say, and speak of what you want to hear, whilst the wind falls silent here, as it does. The city where I was born lies on the shore where the Po descends to find peace with its tributaries.'

The first nine lines constitute what the rhetoricians called the 'seizure of good will' (*captatio benevolentiae*); and they are as beguiling to the ear as the speaker (and the author!) can make them.

The speaker is undoubtedly an 'anima cortese' and possesses a 'cor gentile'. She is gently born, gently bred (as she shows in her concern for Dante's well-being) and, above all, gently spoken: the successive references to Dante's fateful journey (line 89), to the Divine Judge (91) and to their torments (94) are all delicately veiled in euphemism. So too is the discreet allusion to the violent manner of their death (90). It is only with hindsight, if then, that one might reflect that 'delicacy' can be another name for 'evasiveness', or that the first nine lines tell us nothing we do not already know (Virgil has already specified that 'love separated these souls from our life'). If Francesca moves us deeply and unequivocally in these opening lines, it is through her references to peace. The river and 'his followers' will find 'peace' in the Adriatic, near her birthplace at Ravenna; Dante will find 'peace' at the end of his 'fatale andare'; but Francesca will never be 'comforted by any hope of repose or lesser pain' (44–5).

There is a very marked contrast in the next lines, which come like a highly wrought operatic aria after a flowing recitative:

> 'Amor, ch'al cor gentil ratto s'apprende,
> prese costui de la bella persona
> che mi fu tolta; e 'l modo ancor m'offende.
>   Amor, ch'a nullo amato amar perdona,
> mi prese del costui piacer sì forte,
> che, come vedi, ancor non m'abbandona.
>   Amor condusse noi ad una morte.
> Caina attende chi a vita ci spense.'
> Queste parole da lor ci fuor porte.   (*ibid.*, 100–8)

'Love, which is swiftly kindled in a noble heart, seized this spirit for the sake of my fair person, which was snatched from me; and the manner still offends me. Love, which absolves no one who is loved from loving, seized me for the sake of his beauty, such that, as you see, he still does not abandon me. Love brought us to one death. The zone of Cain awaits the man who extinguished our life.' These words were carried to us.

Musically and rhythmically, the three terzinas have an impetus which is all their own, rolling forward, breaking and falling back like successive waves, until the *third* wave (line 106) smashes through our emotional defences with what is more like the glorification of a *Liebestod* than a statement of fact (a fact we already know). In diction and syntax, however, these lines are a re-creation of the love poetry of the 1280s – the decade when the simpler, 'new' style was emerging from the old, the decade when the adulterous pair met their death-through-love, and when Dante was making his mark as a poet 'sopra materia amorosa'.[47]

Francesca has not changed. The key word is 'ancora' (102, 105). She is still a 'captive soul', still under the lordship of Love, still driven by her 'disio de la cosa piacente', still ready to recite unthinkingly the 'Creed' of courtly love, still without remorse.[48] And at this point we must remind ourselves of the only difference between the souls in Hell and those whom Dante will meet on the slopes of Mount Purgatory. All of them had 'erred' in their inclinations, desires and pursuits ('if we deny that we have sinned, we are deceived, and there is no truth in us'). But the souls in Purgatory had felt genuine remorse for the wrong they knew they had done of their own free will. Even in the moment of violent death they had shed a 'little tear' which was enough to rescue them from the devil.[49]

Far from acknowledging a fault (let alone accepting *responsibility* for a fault), Francesca seeks to justify herself by an appeal to the courtly code. And if we consider her speech as a piece of advocacy – rather than as evidence of her temperament or of her literary allegiances – then the two most important lines are those which advance general claims on behalf of 'Amore'. Notwithstanding their lowly grammatical status as relative clauses, lines 100 and 103 are to be considered as *sententiae* – that is, as authoritative statements of a universal truth which are simultaneously rhetorical 'ornaments' because of their memorable form.

Line 100 is a fusion of phrases from Guinizzelli's programmatic canzone. It stops short of asserting the *identity* of love and the gentle heart (which is how the youthful Dante had paraphrased Guinizzelli's message); but line 103 goes well beyond that position by claiming that anyone who is loved is *constrained* to return that love.[50]

The mature Dante certainly believed that we are naturally 'inclined' or 'disposed' to love those who have a similar temperament (*similitudo est causa amoris*). He accepted that the declarations, tokens and 'service' which constitute courtship might 'generate' and 'increase' love.[51] And he would probably not have objected to admitting a kind of 'necessity', if both partners were unattached and if the mutual affection were tending to a 'union of spirits'. But Dante-the-author would never have conceded that we are bound to feel sexual desire for anyone who desires our bodies, or that we are bound to satisfy a mutual lust without regard to what 'human law, virtue and marriage may impose'. Hence, the early commentator Benvenuto da Imola was quite correct in his apparently naive objection that 'this *sententia* is often not true'.

If the proposition were universally true, it would exclude the possibility of human freedom and responsibility. In that case, as we have seen repeatedly, there would be no justice in receiving 'joy for good, and grief for evil' ('per ben letizia, e per male aver lutto'). Hence, the *malum* suffered by Francesca and her companions would really be 'perverso'.[52] But her attempt to shift responsibility onto a literary personification met with no favour from Minos, the judge and 'connoisseur of sin', who consigned her to this second circle of Hell. And it is enough to look again at Virgil's speech concerning love and freedom (analysed as the climax of chapter 10) to see that the 'truth is hidden' from Francesca just as it is from all 'those people who affirm that every love is praiseworthy in itself'.[53]

The second circle: (c) Francesca's second speech

In the narrative, however, Francesca's words pass without challenge. Like most first-time readers of the poem, the protagonist is incapable of distinguishing the truths, half-truths and non sequiturs in Francesca's passionate self-defence. He recognises the fact of damnation, and he is numbed by sadness and pity. But he does not understand the reason.[54]

Everything he now says and does – the bowing of his head, the long silence, the incipient tears, the way he pronounces her name, the use of phrases hallowed in the courtly lyric, even his choice of rhymes – proclaims that he is still a 'faithful member of Love's congregation', a 'fedele d'Amore'.[55]

Quand' io intesi quell' anime offense,
china' il viso, e tanto il tenni basso,
fin che 'l poeta mi disse: 'Che pense?'
    Quando rispuosi, cominciai: 'Oh lasso,
quanti dolci pensier, quanto disio
menò costoro al doloroso passo!'
    Poi mi rivolsi a loro e parla' io,
e cominciai: 'Francesca, i tuoi martìri
a lagrimar mi fanno tristo e pio.
    Ma dimmi: al tempo d'i dolci sospiri,
a che e come concedette Amore
che conosceste i dubbiosi disiri?'   (*ibid.*, 109–20)

When I heard those injured souls, I bowed my head and kept it low until
the poet said: 'What are you thinking?' When at last I replied, I began:
'Alas, how many sweet thoughts and what great desire led them to the
dolorous pass!' Then I turned to them and spoke, beginning: 'Francesca,
your sufferings fill me with sadness and pity, which bring me close to
tears. But tell me: at the time of your sweet sighs, how and by what signs
did Love allow you both to recognise your undeclared desire?'

The most significant feature of the protagonist's complex reactions, however, will prove to be his obsession with the 'sweetness'
of the lovers' 'desire' (113, 118, 120). This almost prurient curiosity is
further evidence of his uncritical involvement with the woman
whom he has now identified. It also enables Dante-the-author to
focus our attention on the crucial moment in the 'combined
operations' of the sensitive and rational powers of the soul – the
moment when 'the mind contemplates the image, inclines towards it
and, having been captured, enters into desire; desire being a movement of the spirit which never ceases until the beloved object gives it
joy'.[56] We are about to witness the crucial moment of consent, which
in this case will be a 'surrender of reason to desire' – and it can rarely
have been expressed with greater truth or immediacy.

Francesca begins her reply with a brief and glorious excursion
into the realm of classical epic poetry. She translates a Virgilian
hexameter (spoken by Aeneas to Dido!) and precedes it with the
saddest lines in the whole poem, which have also become the best
known *sententia* in Italian literature:[57]

E quella a me: 'Nessun maggior dolore
che ricordarsi del tempo felice
ne la miseria; e ciò sa 'l tuo dottore.

> Ma s'a conoscer la prima radice
> del nostro amor tu hai cotanto affetto,
> dirò come colui che piange e dice.'   (*ibid.*, 121–6)

And she said to me: 'There is no greater pain than to remember the time
of happiness in misery; as your teacher knows. But if you have so much
longing to know the first root of our love, I shall speak like someone who
weeps as he speaks.'

At this point she abandons the high style which – in different ways
and with different results – has characterised her utterances until
now. She begins to speak with the utmost simplicity and directness
as she relives the all-too-brief 'tempo felice' which was to lead to the
'doloroso passo'. And it is now, as Francesca seems to 'tell it as it was',
that she wins our empathy and compassion.

It will be immediately apparent that her closing words continue
and intensify Dante-the-author's polemic against the values and
influence of courtly literature by extending it to the 'prose di
romanzi', as well as the 'versi d'amore'. Francesca (the girl 'who
loved things French') was overpowered by her feelings when she and
her brother-in-law identified themselves with Guinevere and Sir
Lancelot while reading a scene in the prose romance in which the
shy knight is brought to the queen by his friend Gallehault and the
'guilty pair' exchange their first kiss. This was the 'means by which
Love allowed them to recognise their "dubbiosi disiri"'. The
romance was the Gallehault (or the 'Pandar', as we now say, with
reference to the story of Troilus and Cressida).

Francesca is still speaking in character as she shifts the blame from
herself to the act of reading, to the courtly 'go-between' in the book
and to the man who wrote it (130–1, 137). Despite the bare simplicity
of her words, the welling up and the release of desire are conveyed
by syntax and rhythm with a climactic effect very similar to that of
her first speech. But she is also as modest and delicately reticent as
ever. She defies literary decorum by using the concrete word 'mouth'
('bocca' is never used in Dante's lyrics; and the passage from
Guinevere's 'riso' to Francesca's 'bocca' marks the passage from
literature to reality). But she allows her interlocutor to complete for
himself the scene she has brought so vividly to life in his
imagination.

Any further comment would be superfluous. This is the moment
when we too must close the book and 'read no further':

'Noi leggiavamo un giorno per diletto
di Lancialotto come amor lo strinse;
soli eravamo e sanza alcun sospetto.

Per più fïate li occhi ci sospinse
quella lettura, e scolorocci il viso;
ma solo un punto fu quel che ci vinse.

Quando leggemmo il disïato riso
esser basciato da cotanto amante,
questi, che mai da me non fia diviso,

la bocca mi basciò tutto tremante.
Galeotto fu 'l libro e chi lo scrisse:
quel giorno più non vi leggemmo avante.'   (*ibid.*, 127–38)

'One day we were reading for pleasure about Lancelot, how love constrained him. We were alone and without any fear. On several occasions,
the reading forced our eyes together, and made our faces change colour.
But it was only one moment that conquered us. When we read how the
desired smile was kissed by so noble a lover, this man, who will never be
divided from me, kissed my mouth, trembling all over. The book was a
Gallehault, and so was the man who wrote it. That day we read no
further.'

Notes

Wherever practicable, straightforward references are grouped in such a way that there is only one note for each paragraph. These references are listed in the order in which the relevant passages are quoted, paraphrased or alluded to in the text (hence a reference to *Purgatorio* may well come before one to *Inferno*).

With two main exceptions, quotations follow the orthography and punctuation of the editions used. The exceptions are: (a) no indication is given when a passage begins or ends in mid-sentence; (b) where the editor has preserved a medieval Latin *e* which corresponds to a classical Latin *ae*, the more familiar classical spelling has been substituted in all cases.

The great majority of the references are to two main sources: the works of Dante himself and the physical, biological and ethical works of Aristotle. The medieval Latin translations of Aristotle's Greek are very literal and often so cryptic as to be unintelligible as they stand. Hence Aristotelian quotations are taken from the Latin paraphrase of the passage concerned in the relevant commentary by Aquinas. Almost all references to Aristotle state the *lectio* and paragraph of this commentary, preceded by a reference to the book, chapter, page and line in the Bekker edition of the Greek original (these page and line references are reproduced in the margin of most modern editions and translations). A complete reference may therefore take the following form: *In De anima* II, iv, 415b 12, *lect.* 7, §319. (In most cases, the chapter of the Aristotelian work and the relevant *lectio* would be the first texts that a reader would wish to consult for a fuller discussion of the topic in question.)

It should be borne in mind that there is nothing specifically Thomist about these paraphrases: they are presented as clear, economical and remarkably faithful expositions of Aristotle's thought. Similarly, references to and quotations from Aquinas' two *Summae* are not to be understood as expressing a distinctively Thomist point of view, unless this is explicitly indicated. And in general – except where there is a specific disclaimer, or where the context suggests otherwise – all references to medieval authors other than Dante are given in the belief that the passages contain representative and uncontroversial formulations of concepts that were current among orthodox, Latin-speaking, Christian Aristotelians in the second half of the thirteenth century.

Dante's Latin works are quoted as they appear in the second volume of the *Opere minori*, published by Ricciardi (Milan and Naples, 1979). Dante's works in the vernacu-

302

lar are quoted from the editions of: Giorgio Petrocchi for the *Comedy*, Domenico De Robertis for the *Vita nuova*; Michele Barbi for the *Rime*; and Cesare Vasoli for the *Convivio*. For Aquinas' *Summa Theologiae* I have used the edition prepared by the Pontifical Institute of Medieval Studies in Ottawa (Ottawa, 1943). All other quotations from Aquinas are taken from the complete edition of his works published by Marietti.

The following abbreviations are used:

I Works by Dante

Con.	*Convivio*
Dve	*De vulgari eloquentia*
Epist.	*Epistolae*
Inf.	*Inferno*
Mon.	*Monarchia*
Par.	*Paradiso*
Purg.	*Purgatorio*
VN	*Vita Nuova*

II Works by Aquinas

(a) Independent works:

S.T.	*Summa Theologiae*
C.G.	*Summa contra Gentiles*

(b) Philosophical commentaries to the works of Aristotle (listed here in the order of Bekker's edition):

In Physic.	*Physics*
In De caelo	*On the heavens*
In De gen.	*On generation and corruption*
In De anima	*On the soul*
In De sensu	*On sense and sensation*
In De memor.	*On memory and reminiscence*
In Meta.	*Metaphysics*
In Ethic.	*Nicomachean Ethics*
In Pol.	*Politics*

1 The prestige and unity of the Aristotelian corpus

1 *Con.* IV, xxiii, 1–7. The signs of 'gentilezza' in the three ages (and in the years we may live *after* our allotted span) are discussed in chapters xxiii–xxviii.

2 Chaucer, *Canterbury Tales*, *General Prologue*, 295–6. The Clerk of Oxenford still shared the same enthusiasm a hundred years later. The story of the re-discovery of Aristotle has been told many times. See, for example, the following works: Copleston, *History of Medieval Philosophy*, pp.153–9, 199–212; Gilson, *La philosophie au moyen âge*, pp. 377–99; Knowles, *Evolution of Medieval Thought*, pp. 185–234; Kretzmann, *Cambridge History of Later Medieval Philosophy*, pp. 43–98, 521–36, 602–28, 657–72, 723–37; Leff, *Medieval Thought*, pp. 171–5, 206–24.

3 References in order: *Inf.* IV, 131; *Con.* III, V, 7; IV, xxiii, 8; vi, 7–8; cf. 16–17.

4 The reasons for the choice of these issues will become clear in chapters 9 and 10.

The crucial words of caution about the degree of certainty are from *Ethics* I, iii, 4, 1094b 24.

5 Among the general studies of Aristotle's thought listed in the Bibliography, Bambrough stresses Aristotle's commonsensical approach to ethics; Lloyd and Randall emphasise the evolution of his thought; while Lear is more inclined to see Aristotle 'whole', as Sir David Ross had done.

6 *Con.* III, vii, 5. The noun 'metaphysics' derives from the adjective referring to the books which used to be gathered together 'after' (*meta*) the works on Nature (*physica*).

7 *Mon.* I, iii, 6, 8.

8 For the distinction between 'generation' and 'creation', see my *Dante Philomythes*, especially chapters 9–11.

2 Movement and change in lifeless bodies

1 The Latin terms are given without the Greek, because throughout this book the medievalised Aristotle will be treated as if he were a Latin author.

2 The shifting usages are nicely illustrated in this short passage from the *Convivio*: '... avvegna che la stella sempre sia d'un modo chiara e lucente, e non riceva *mutazione* alcuna se non di *movimento locale*' (III, ix, 11).

3 It is helpful to pay attention to the different parts of speech and the different interrogatives associated with each of the four kinds of change. The questions to be asked of a body which is assumed to have undergone some sort of 'mutation' will be, in order: Where (*ubi*) is it? How big (*quantus*) is it? How (*qualis*) is it? What (*quid*) is it? The change itself will always be designated by a verb ('to move', 'to increase', 'to alter', 'to generate/corrupt'), but the results of the change will be described respectively by an adverb or adverbial phrase (e.g., 'from Glasgow to Palermo'), an adjective or adjectival phrase ('mature', 'tanned'), and – in the case of substantial change – by a noun or substantive ('John Brown', 'corpse').

These points about the four species of *mutatio* or *motus* may be summarised in tabular form as follows:

(a)	local	*locomotio*	*ubi?*	(adverb)
(b)	quantitative	*augmentum*	*quantus?*	(adjective)
(c)	qualitative	*alteratio*	*qualis?*	(adjective)
(d)	substantial	*generatio/corruptio*	*quid?*	(noun)

4 *Par.* XIV, 114; XXX, 39.

5 *Par.* XIII, 59; XXIX, 50. *S.T.* 1a 75, 2; 3; 7; 118, 1; 2; *Mon.* III, xi, 5.

6 The etymology of *accidens* (originally the present participle of *accidere*, from *ad* + *cadere*, 'to fall') suggests that it 'befalls', or 'happens', or is 'incidental to' a *substantia*.

7 *Mon.* III, xi, 5.

8 *Mon.* I, iii, 4–6; *Dante Philomythes*, pp. 127, 333.

9 Cf. *Con.* I, viii, 9.

10 *In Physic.* III, i, 200b 30, *lect.* 2, §286.

11 It may be helpful to summarise these points in a table:

Kind of change	What undergoes change	What remains unchanged
locomotion	place	body
alteration	accident/quality	substantial form
growth	accident/quantity	substantial form
generation/corruption	substantial form	material substrate

12 Cf. *In Physic.* IV, viii, 215a 15, *lect.* 11, §525.

13 Aristotle devoted a long and characteristically subtle analysis to the relationship between time and movement in the fourth and sixth books of the *Physics*. See, in particular, *In Physic.* IV, xiv, 223a 16ff., *lect.* 23.

14 *Physics* II, i, 192b 21; viii, iii, 253b 8; iv, 255a 8.

15 It would involve a summary of his teaching concerning the elements and their compounds, and of his proof that our earth is at the centre of a single cosmos in the shape of a sphere; see my *Dante Philomythes*, pp. 57–65, 132–3.

16 It is worth remembering that a 'term' is simply a word that has been 'circumscribed' or 'bounded', and thereby 'determined' or 'defined' in a special 'limited' meaning; and the classical Latin word *limes/limitis* denoted a stone or other marker indicating the position of a boundary or frontier.

17 *In Physic.* VII, ii, 243a 15ff., *lect.* 3, §§901–3. In the first phase, the boy drew the pebble closer to him, and his pulling action would be described as 'traction', *tractio* (from *trahere/tractum*, 'to pull', 'drag'). The pebble was then transported horizontally without changing its position in relation to the boy. This is an example of 'carrying', *vectio* (from *vehere/vectum*, 'to carry': the boy was simply the 'vehicle'). In the last stages it was clearly being cast *away* from the boy, and as such was the object of 'propulsion', *propulsio* (from *pellere/pulsum*, 'to push'). As long as it was in contact with the boy's hand, it was being 'impelled' (*impulsio*), but from the moment that he opened his fingers, it was 'expelled', or 'projected' (*expulsio, proiectio*). Whether in lifting, carrying or throwing, the boy was in contact with the stone; and it would have made no difference to the principle involved if he had used a sling, as David did (*In Physic.* VIII, v, 256a 25, *lect.* 9, §§1041, 1044). This was held to be necessary in every case of movement or change; and it leads to the axiom: 'in natural change, agent and patient must always be in contact either directly or through a medium' (243a 4).

18 The full import of this paragraph will emerge in chapter 10 below; see p.198. The classic discussion will be found in *Physics*, VIII, iii–iv.

19 *In De sensu*, 446b 15, *lect.* 6, §236. *Physics*, IV, vii–ix.

20 *Physics*, VIII, x.

21 See *Dante Philomythes*, pp. 64–71.

22 For *principium intrinsecum*, see *In Physic.* II, viii, 199b 15, *lect.* 14, §§267–8. Dante significantly prefers the natural motion of Fire to that of Earth when he is looking for an analogue to the human aspiration towards God (*Purg.* XVIII, 28–33; *Par.* IV, 76–8).

23 *Par.* VIII, 103–5; *In Physic.* II, viii, 199b 15, *lect.* 14, §§261, 267.

24 In human affairs, says Aristotle, in a much-quoted aphorism, the *finis* is the *principium* (*In Ethic.* VI, v, 1140b 17, *lect.* 4, §1170; cf. §139). By this he meant that to know the immediate goal of our activity (or to know the supreme goal of our existence) is to possess the 'principle' that will enable us to choose the 'means' conducive to that 'end'. He himself uses the phrase *primum movens* both of an efficient cause at the *terminus a quo*, and of the goal or source of attraction at the *terminus ad quem*, but it is significant that the Prime Mover *par excellence* in his universe – the Supreme Being or God – causes motion not as an efficient cause, but as the object of desire (*Metaphysics*, XII, vii, 1042bff.). Dante's God is both (both Alpha and Omega).

25 *In Physic.* II, viii, 198b 10ff., *lect.* 13, §§258–60.

26 *Ibid.* 198b 30, *lect.* 13, §253.

27 The example is borrowed from *Dante Philomythes*, p. 52. It has a good biblical pedigree: Genesis 2: 7; Isaiah 4: 9; Jeremiah 18: 1–6; Romans 9: 21.

28 *In Physic.* II, ix, 200a 10, *lect.* 15, §272–4.

29 The example is influenced by two 'philomythical' poems: Leopardi's *Palinodia*, lines 154–81; and Goethe's poem in *West-östlicher Divan*, I, 'Lied und Gebilde'.

30 'Et posita est (…) descriptio "figuraliter", quasi extrinsece et superficialiter et incomplete' (*In De anima*, II, i, 413a 10, *lect.* 2, §244).

31 *In Physic.* III, i, 201b 5, *lect.* 3, §§288–9; cf. §§297, 318, 324–5.

32 *Ibid.*, 201a 5, *lect.* 1, §282; cf. §883.

33 His own expression is 'assommare perfettamente il cammino'; see *Par.* XXXI, 94–5. Like the 'buono camminatore' of his little parable in *Con.* IV, xii, the pilgrim 'giunge a termine e a posa' (19). See also *Con.* IV, xvi, 7–10.

34 Cf. *Con.* IV, xii, 15; *Par.* VIII, 106; XXXI, 94–5.

3   Self-change: growth and reproduction in plant life

1 *In De anima* II, i, 412a 15ff., *lect.* 1, §§220, 224; cf. §§241, 254.

2 *Ibid.*, II, 413a 21, *lect.* 3, §253; cf. §§271, 273.

3 *Con.* IV, vii, 11–12; cf. *In De anima* II, iv, 415b 12, *lect.* 7, §319; cf. §225.

4 'Anima est actus primus (*or* perfectio prima) corporis physici, potentia vitam habentis.' (*De anima* II, i, 412a 30, translated by Moerbeke; the English translation in the text is by J. A. Smith).

5 The content and wording of this paragraph reflect *Purg.* XVIII, 49–54; *Par.* VII, 139–41; XII, 46–8; Rime, C, 40–2; Guinizzelli, *Al cor gentil*, lines 31–2.

6 'Propria autem ratio vitae est ex hoc, quod aliquid est natum movere seipsum, large accipiendo motum (…). Ea enim sine vita esse dicimus, quae ab exteriori tantum principio moveri possunt' (*In De anima* II, i, 412a 15, *lect.* 1, §219). Cf. further *S.T.* 1a, 18, 1.

7 *Quaestio*, 76.

8 *In De anima* II, iv, 416b 22ff., *lect.* 9, esp. §§345–8.

9 *Ibid.*, 415b 5, *lect.* 7, esp. §317.

10 Cf. *Con.* III, iii, 6.

11 A seasoned Aristotelian might make distinctions here to conclude that maturity and generation are mutually subordinate from different perspectives.

12 Cf. chapter 2, note 6.

13 *In De anima* II, i, 412b 1, *lect.* 1, §§230–2.

14 *Ibid.*, 412a 30, 412b 5; §233.

15 Cf. Shakespeare: 'When I consider everything that grows / Holds in perfection but a little moment, (…) When I perceive that men as plants increase, / Cheerèd and checked even by the selfsame sky, / Vaunt in their youthful sap, at height decrease, / And wear their brave state out of memory' (Sonnet 15, 1–2, 5–8).

16 *Dve* I, iii, 1.

4   Self-movement: sensation and locomotion in animal life

1 *In De anima* III, xii, esp. 434a 30ff., *lect.* 17, §§852–3. *In De sensu* i, *lect.* 2, §20. Aristotle recognised that there can be sensation without movement (*De anima* III, ix, 432b 18), although *animalia immobilia* possess only the senses of taste and touch. We shall see that there must be a power of appetition, as well as that of sensation, for local movement to occur (*ibid.*, x, 433b 1–30, *lect.* 15, esp. §§824–5, 827, 833–4).

2 Cf. chapter 1, note 6; chapter 3, note 15.

3 The human powers will be described in detail in chapter 9.

4 Sight involves an *immutatio spiritualis* (which is unlike any species of change studied

in chapter 2), whereas sound and smell involve an *immutatio naturalis* (respectively, a *motus localis* and an *alteratio*): *In De sensu* vi, 446a 20ff., *lect.* 16, esp. §§229–30, 233, 239–40, 243; *In De anima* II, vii, 418a 27ff., *lect.* 14, esp. §§ 403, 417–20; and cf. *lect.* 20, §§491–3; *S.T.* 1a, 78, 3. Sight will be dealt with in detail in chapters 5 and 6. For *sonus*, see also *In De anima* II, viii, *lect.* 16–18. For *odor*, see also *ibid.*, viii–ix, *lect.* 19–20; *In De sensu* ii, 348b 22, *lect.* 5, §§68–9.

5 *In De anima* II, vii, 419a 15, *lect.* 14, §406; *In De sensu* ii, 438a 6ff., *lect.* 4; cf. also §106.

6 See note 4.

7 'Sensibile superpositum sensui non sentitur' (*In De sensu* ii, *lect.* 3, §36). See also *In De anima* III, xii, 434b 27ff., *lect.* 14, §§432–3, 437.

8 *Con.* III, ix, 9. The fullest discussion of such a 'master sense' in Aristotle's work comes in *De somno*, ii, 455a 15ff. See also *In De anima, lect.* 3, §§609–13; *lect.* 12, §768 and esp. §773 ('est quasi *quaedam medietas una* inter omnes sensus, sicut centrum, ad quod terminantur omnes lineae, quasi ad unum medium'). For fuller discussion of the common sense in scholastic thought, see Harvey, *The Inward Wits*, Hirdt, *Wie Dante das Jenseits erfährt*, pp. 56–9, and Carruthers, *The Book of Memory*, pp. 52–3, 58, 78.

9 Cf.: 'li spiriti umani, che quasi sono principalmente vapori del cuore' (*Con.* II, xiii, 24). The function of the 'spirits' is discussed more fully in chapter 8.

10 The distinction was extremely important for Dante, and the 'proper and common sensibles' will be discussed separately and at length in chapters 5 and 6.

11 *Phantasma*, in turn, is related to the noun 'phenomenon', since both are derived from the verb *phainein* meaning 'to appear' or 'to seem'. It is 'almost like a picture', says Aristotle, *quasi quaedam pictura*, or like an impression in wax: 'Motus qui fit a sensibili in sensum, *imprimit* in phantasia quasi quamdam *figuram sensibilem*, quae manet sensibili abeunte, ad modum, quo illi qui sigillant cum annulis imprimunt *figuram quamdam in cera*, quae remanet etiam sigillo vel annulo remoto' (*In De memoria* i, 450b 28, *lect.* 3 §328).

12 See texts cited in note 4.

13 *In De anima* II, vi, *lect.* 13, §§397–8 (there is nothing directly relevant in the original text).

14 *Purg.* XVIII, 23. On the various meanings of the term *intentio* (used as a translation of Arabic terms), see the chapter by Knudsen in Kretzmann (ed.), *The Cambridge History of Later Medieval Philosophy*, pp. 479–95; the entry in the *Enciclopedia dantesca*; Hirdt, *Wie Dante das Jenseits erfährt*, pp. 68–70; and Carruthers, *The Book of Memory*, pp. 53–4, 68 ('each phantasm is a combination not only of the neutral form of the perception but of our response to it (*intentio*) concerning whether it is helpful or hurtful'). Two quotations will help to fix the particular sense in which is is used here. The first is Avicenna's distinction between *forma* (= image) and *intentio* (it was he who did most to give the term currency among the scholastics; and his example deals with a sheep's perception of a wolf): 'Id autem quod de lupo primo apprehendit *sensus exterior* et postea *interior*, vocatur hic proprie nomine *formae*; quod autem apprehendunt *vires occultae absque sensu*, vocatur in hoc loco proprie nomine *intentionis*' (*De anima* I, 5, 96, p. 86). This is summarised by Aquinas in his commentary to *De memoria* as follows: 'convenienter Avicenna dicit quod *memoria* respicit *intentionem, imaginatio* vero *formam* per sensum apprehensam', §343. The second comes from a very important article in Aquinas' *Summa Theologiae*: 'Ad harum autem *formarum* retentionem aut conservationem ordinatur *phantasia*, sive *imaginatio*, quasi thesaurus quidam formarum per sensum acceptarum. Ad apprehendendum autem *intentiones quae per sensum non accipiuntur*, ordinatur *vis aestimativa*. Ad conservandum autem ea, *vis memorativa*, quae est thesaurus quidam huiusmodi *intentionum*. Cuius signum est,

quod principium memorandi fit in animalibus ex aliqua huiusmodi *intentione*, ut puta quod est *nocivum vel conveniens*' (1a, 78, 4; cf. 1a–2ae, 22, 2).

15 For the distinction between memory and imagination, adumbrated in the previous note, see further Hirdt, *Wie Dante das Jenseits erfährt*, pp. 60–8, 70–5; and *In De memor.* §§321–2, 343–4. Dante's concept of the imagination will be illustrated in chapter 7. For every aspect of the faculty of *memoria* in the Middle Ages, see Carruthers, *The Book of Memory*. Memory plays a very important part in Dante's poetry, from the opening of the *Vita nuova* to the last canto of *Paradiso*, but it will not be treated in detail in this book because it does not normally lead directly to an *operatio* in the external world (see, however, Carruthers, *The Book of Memory*, pp. 185–7, for a bold reading of *Inf.* v, 126–38).

16 Petrarch, *Rime* CXLI, 1–4; *Metaphysics* I, i, 980a 28; *In De memor.* i, 449b 5, *lect.* 1, §298 (and cf. §325); *In De sensu* i, 436a 10, *lect.* 1, §§11–12.

17 Cf. Kretzmann (ed.), *The Cambridge History of Philosophy in the Later Middle Ages*, pp. 603–4, for references to the works of St Albert, and *Con.* I, iii, 7–11, for Dante's distinction between 'la cosa imaginata nel vero stato' and 'la imagine per sola fama generata'.

18 'Avicenna vero ponit quintam potentiam mediam inter aestimativam et imaginativam, quae *componit et dividit formas imaginatas*, ut patet cum ex forma imaginata auri et forma imaginata montis *componimus unam formam* montis aurei, *quem nunquam vidimus*. Sed ista operatio non apparet in aliis animalibus ab homine' (*S.T.* 1a, 78, 4).

19 *In De anima* III, ix, 432b 20, *lect.* 14, §808 (and cf. §839). *In Ethic.* III, x, 1118a 20, *lect.* 19, §§610–11.

20 *In De anima* II, iii, 414b 4, *lect.* 5, §§286, 289; *In Ethic.* II, v, 1105b 22ff., *lect.* 5, §§293–6 (and cf. §1571); *In De sensu* i, 436a 10, *lect.* 1, §11. The scholastics did, of course, differentiate between localised pleasure or pain, experienced in the relevant organ, such as the stomach or the genitals, and the general states of 'well-being', 'delight', 'joy' – and their opposites – which affect the organism or *corpus organicum* as a whole. But they were not always consistent in maintaining distinctions between *voluptas* and *delectatio*, or between *dolor* and *tristitia*; and in this introductory sketch, the terms 'pleasure' and 'pain' may be interpreted as broadly or as narrowly as the context requires.

21 *In Ethic.* II, iii, 1104b 15, *lect.* 3, §§265, 268–9; *S.T.* 1a–2ae, 23, 4.

22 'Omnis autem motus appetitivae potentiae reducitur ad prosecutionem vel fugam' (*S.T.* 1a–2ae, 45, 2). *Consecutio*, which is the term preferred by Aquinas in his commentary to the *Ethics*, comes from *sequi/secutum*, 'to follow', while *fuga* comes from *fugere*, 'to run away'. Cf. *In Ethic.* II, v, 1105b 22ff., §§269, 292, 296, 302.

23 *Con.* IV, xxvi, 5.

24 'Ex eadem causa aliquid quiescit in loco, per quam movebatur ad locum' (*S.T.* 1a–2ae, 23, 4). See chapter 2, note 12.

25 E.g.: 'Omnes enim operationes sensitivae partis *passiones* quaedam sunt, secundum quod *sentire pati quoddam* est' (*In De memor.* i, *lect.* 1, §300).

26 '*Actus appetitus sensitivi*, inquantum habent transmutationem corporalem annexam, *passiones dicuntur*' (*S.T.* 1a, 20, 1, ad 1).

27 'Operatio autem virtutis appetitivae perficitur in hoc quod *appetens inclinatur* in rem appetibilem. Et ideo operatio *apprehensivae* virtutis assimilatur *quieti*, operatio autem virtutis *appetitivae magis assimilatur motui*' (*S.T.* 1a, 81, 1; see also *ibid.*, 80, 1; 81, 2).

28 'In motibus autem appetitivae partis bonum habet quasi virtutem *attractivam*, malum autem virtutem *repulsivam*' (*S.T.* 1a–2ae, 23, 4).

29 'Passiones sunt motus appetitus sensitivi qui utitur organo corporali. Unde *passiones*

omnes cum aliqua corporali transmutatione fiunt' (*In Ethic.* IV, ix, 1128b 12, §869; see also §870 for the rest of this paragraph); cf. further *ibid.*, §292; *S.T.* 1a–2ae, 22, 1, 3.

30 'In omni passione animae additur aliquid, vel diminuitur a naturali motu cordis, inquantum *cor intensius vel remissius movetur*, secundum systolen aut diastolen' (*S.T.* 1a–2ae, 24, ad 2). 'Vis enim motiva (...) est principaliter in corde, per quod anima in totum corpus motum et alias huiusmodi operationes diffundit' (*C.G.* II, 72, §1487). Cf. *In De anima*, §§474–5; *In De sensu*, §74. The distinctions made after Aristotle's time concerning the respective roles of the heart and the brain are fairly summed up by Thomas Wright, who came at the end of the tradition, in a chapter in his *The Passions of the Mind in General* (I, 9) entitled 'That the heart is the peculiar place where that Passions allodge'. See also *ibid.*, I, 11, and II, 3.

31 There is a very full summary of the effects of fear in *S.T.* 1a–2ae, 44, 1, 3, 4.

32 *Circumstantiae* is a technical term which will recur in the discussion of ethical issues below (chapters 10 and 13). It referred originally to the objects which 'surround' or 'stand around' (*circum* + *stare*).

33 In each case, the group name is taken from the passion – desire or anger – which is most likely to cause an animal to 'reach out for' an object (*adpetere*) and move towards it.

34 See below, pp. 253–4; *In Ethic.* II, v, 1105b 22, *lect.* 5, §293 (and cf. §544); *S.T.* 1a, 81, 2, 3; 1a–2ae, 23, 1, 2; 25, 1.

35 *C.G.* II, 60, §1374 (and cf. §§1579, 2851).

36 Cf. *In De anima* II, v, 417a 22, *lect.* 11, §§365–7.

37 Cf. *Mon.* I, iii, 8.

5 Perception of light and colour

1 Cf. *Con.* I, xi, 3–4; *In De anima* II, vii, *lect.* 14, §§417–18; Carruthers, *The Book of Memory*, pp. 17–18; Hirdt, *Wie Dante das Jenseits erfährt*, pp. 42–8.

2 *In Meta.* I, i, 980a 28, *lect.* 1, §§6–7. For Dante's awareness of the links between seeing and understanding, see: *Inf.* VII, 40–1; IX, 61–2; XI, 78, 91; *Purg.* VI, 45; VIII, 19; XVIII, 10–12, 46; XXV, 31, 34–6; XXVI, 58, 121; XXVIII, 81; XXXI, 110–12; XXXIII, 102.

3 *Con.* I, xi, 3; *In De anima* II, vii, 418a 27ff., 419a 10–20, *lect.* 14, §§399–403; *lect.* 15, §§428–31.

4 Cf. *Con.* II, iv, 17; *Purg.* IX, 34–42; XVII, 40–2; *Par.* XXVI, 70–5.

5 *In De anima* II, vii, *lect.* 14, §§405, 425.

6 The characteristic words in Dante's Italian are, in the order of the text: 'raggio', 'uscire', 'fonte', 'principio fontale', 'passare', 'scendere', 'fermarsi', 'terminare', 'ripercuotere', 'riflettere', 'rifrangere', 'saltare', 'salire', 'tornare'. The equality of the angles of incidence and reflexion is described in loving detail in *Purg.* XV, 16–24; and cf. *Par.* I, 49–51.

7 *In De anima* II, vii, 418b 10–20, *lect.* 14, §§405–6; *In De sensu* iii, 439a 18, *lect.* 6, §§80–1.

8 'Quod autem dicitur de motu luminis, aut reverberatione ipsius, metaphorice dictum est' (*In De anima* II, vii, *lect.* 14, §413–14).

9 Both light and heat are qualities belonging to the third of the four categories in which a quality can be predicated of a body; cf. *In De anima* II, vii, 418b 14, *lect.* 14, §420.

10 For light as having no contrary, see *In De anima* II, vii, *lect.* 14, §421. For darkness as *absentia lucis*, *privatio lucis*, see *ibid.*, §408; *In De sensu* iii, *lect.* 6, §81, *lect.* 7, §95. For instantaneity, see *In De anima* II, vii, *lect.* 14, §421.

11 *In De sensu* iii, 439a 20, *lect.* 6, §82; *In De anima* II, vii, 418a 27, *lect.* 14, §404.

12 '*Primus* quidem gradus, cum id quod est luminis susceptivum est totaliter lumine repletum, quasi perfecte in actum reductum. (...) Quod quidem inter omnia corpora maxime competit *soli*. (...) Quaedam corpora, quae propter parvitatem sui luminis, non possunt lucere nisi *in nocte*' (*In De sensu* §84; cf. *In De anima* §§429, 436).

13 '*Secundus* gradus est, eorum quae de se non habent lumen in actu, sed sunt susceptiva luminis per totum; huiusmodi corpora proprie dicuntur perspicua sive transparentia, vel diaphana' (*In De sensu*, §85). *Diaphanum* comes from the Greek *dia*, 'through', and *phainon*, 'appearing'; *transparens* is a calque translation of the Greek roots; while *perspicuum* comes from *perspicere*, 'to see through'. For *recipere* and *reddere* ('to give back' or 'to pass on'), see *Epist.* XIII, 56.

14 *In De sensu*, §85.

15 '*Tertius* et infimus gradus est terrae, quae (...) minime nata est recipere de lumine, sed in superficie tantum' (*In De sensu*, §86).

16 *In De sensu* iii, *lect.* 6, §92; *lect.* 8, §115.

17 *In De anima* II, viii, 419b 28, *lect.* 16, §450.

18 The text from St Albert is quoted extensively in Vasoli's commentary.

19 It does not matter whether the colour remains the same, as it would if a gold bar were cut into slices – *aurum depuratum* being Dante's chosen example of a perfectly homogeneous body – or whether it changes, as it would if a goldfish were filleted to expose the flesh beneath the skin, and the bones beneath the flesh. Cf. *Quaestio*, 41; *In De sensu* iii, *lect.* 6, §§89, 93

20 '*Color* est in *colorato* sicut *qualitas completa* in suo esse naturali; in *medio* autem *incompleta* secundum quoddam esse *intentionale*' (*In De sensu*, §62). 'Dupliciter organum animae potest transmutari. Uno modo *transmutatione spirituali*, secundum quod recipit *intentionem* rei. Et hoc per se invenitur in actu apprehensivae virtutis sensitivae; sicut *oculus* immutatur a visibili, non ita quod coloretur, sed ita quod recipiat *intentionem coloris*. Est autem et alia naturalis transmutatio organi, prout organum transmutatur quantum ad suam naturalem dispositionem; puta quod calefit aut infrigidatur, vel alio modo simili transmutatur, (...) puta cum oculus fatigatur ex forti intuitu, vel dissolvitur ex vehementia visibilis' (*S. T.* 1a–2ae, 22, 2 ad 3).

21 It may be helpful to summarise the main points in this section by translating some authoritative formulations, derived from Aquinas' commentaries to *De sensu et sensato* (lower para. numbers) and *De anima* (para. numbers 400 and above):

'Colour as such is intrinsically visible' (400). 'The visible is that which changes a transparent medium' (53). 'Colour is a kind of form, and as such it has the power to induce its likeness in a medium' (425). 'Something becomes visible when a transparent medium is illuminated by a lucent body' (28). 'It is impossible to see without light' (59; cf. 431). 'The active power of colour is imperfect with respect to that of light' (425). 'Colour exists in a coloured body as an actualised quality in its natural mode of existence; in the medium, it exists only incompletely, as an *intentio*' (62). 'The pupil is itself a transparent substance, but a colour must alter an actually transparent body, such as the air; and the organ of sight is altered by this medium, with which it is in surface contact. Bodies only cause change to each other when they are in contact' (432).

22 *In De anima* II, vii, 418b 12; 419a 7, §§405, 425, 430; cf. *In De sensu* iii, 439a 18, *lect.* 6, §81.

23 There is no evidence that Dante knew Aristotle's *Poetics* at first hand, but the concept of *imitatio* or *repraesentatio* would have been well known to him through secondary works; cf. *Con.* III, vii, 9–10.

24 *Con.* II, ix, 4; and cf. IV, xii, 17.

25 *Par.* I, 52–3; cf. *Con.* II, ix, 6–7.
26 *Con.* III, ix, 8, quoted above, p. 71.
27 *Par.* xxx, 122–3. Cf. *Dante Philomythes*, pp. 141, 171.
28 Cf. *Inf.* xxvI, 114–15.
29 Cf. *Purg.* xvII, 40–5.
30 For the colour of Mars, see *Con.* II, xiii, 21; *Purg.* II, 13; *Par.* xiv, 88; xvIII, 67–9.
31 Cf. *Inf.* II, 97–102; *Purg.* IX, 55–7; *Par.* xxxII, 137–8; *Con.* III, v, 11, 16.
32 *Par.* xx, 1–6; xxx, 4–9.
33 References in order: *Con.* II, xiv, 7 (Milky Way); *Purg.* xxIX, 50, 52–4, 73 (candelabrum); *Inf.* xxvI, 25–31 (fireflies); vIII, 3–6 (signalling by flames).
34 For its use as a 'narrative resource', see chapter 6, pp. 110–11.
35 *Inf.* Iv, 10–13, 45, 65–6, 68–9.
36 *Ibid.*, 71–2, 103, 106–11, 116–17.
37 *Con.* II, viii, 14; John 1:5; 8:12; 14:6.
38 *Inf.* xxxIv, 139 (and cf. xvi, 82–4); *Purg.* I, 7, 17–18. In the last line quoted, Dante uses the verb 'contristare', which is the technical term for harming and hurting any sentient body.
39 *Purg.* I, 19–27.
40 *Purg.* vII, 42–60 (no climbing after dark); *Par.* vII, 76–81 (loss of freedom and God's 'light' through sin).
41 See above, p. 77; *Dante Philomythes*, pp. 74–9.
42 *Inf.* vIII, 11–12; xxvI, 133–5; xxxI, 34–7.
43 Dante returns to the theme of the 'soverchio visibile' again and again: *Con.* III, viii, 14; xv, 6; *Purg.* vIII, 34–6; IX, 79–84; xv, 15, 26, 28 (and cf. 139–41); xvII, 52–4, 57; xxxxII, 10–15; *Par.* III, 128–9; Iv, 139–42; v, 1–3; x, 61–3; xiv, 76–84; xxIII, 31–3, 36, 78, 87; xxv, 118–20, 136–9; xxvI, 1–9 (cf. 20); xxx, 25.
44 *Purg.* xxxI, 23–4; *Par.* I, 67–72; cf. *Con.* III, vi, 10; xiv, 7; Iv, xix, 6. For all but St Paul and (in the fiction of the poem) the protagonist, such transhumanisation happens only after death.
45 *Color* is the *obiectum visus* of man as 'generated'; but *lux* – *lux vera, lux aeterna* – is the *obiectum visus* of man as 'created' and elevated by grace.
46 *Par.* xxvI, 117; cf. *Inf.* xxvI, 108–9.
47 *Par.* I, 67–72, 76–8.
48 *Par.* x, 40–2; xxIII, 40–5.
49 *Par.* xxvIII, 13–39, 64–78, 88–96; xxIX, 136–45; xxx, 1–36.
50 *Par.* xxxIII, 22–7, 43, 49–50.
51 *Ibid.*, 115–20, 131–2. Even at this last stage, Dante continues to display his knowledge of optical theory, but the theme of excess gives way to the behaviour of reflected light (119, 128), and to paradoxes drawn from the common sensibles of shape (117, 127–8, 131) and the other proper visible, *color* (117, 130). It is only in the third and final section that he unexpectedly returns to the representation of a 'soperchianza di luce'.
52 The journey of discovery kept to the paradigm of rectilinear movement. Contemplation of the truth is symbolised (not for the first time in European culture) as a circular movement, without beginning or end. The concepts to be explained in chapter 9 below may lend support to the idea that Dante intended to distinguish between the sensitive powers, the intellect and the will. His 'fantasia' was indeed reduced to impotence. But his 'mente' received its desire; and his *velle* responded to the *summum bonum intellectum* by initiating the kind of movement that the angelic movers impart to the heavenly spheres.

6 Perception of shape, size, number and movement

1 *Con.* III, ix, 6, quoted in chapter 5 above, p. 62.

2 *Purg.* I, 117, 127–9 (cf. 95–9); II, 1–9, 14–21, 23–4, 39–40.

3 See chapter 5 above, p. 62.

4 *Purg.* II, 17, 21, 37, 40. The phrase 'venire a riva', which originally meant 'to come to the bank', had already acquired the meaning of 'ar-riv-al', that is, the completion of a *motus*.

5 For 'ali', see II, 26; for 'apparire', see II, 16, 22, 26, 38.

6 II, 28–36.

7 II, 32–3, 41, 43, 100–5.

8 Cf. chapter 9 below, pp. 176, 178–9.

9 This is self evident in the case of *size*. *Shape* demands the simultaneous apprehension of several interrelated dimensions across and around a plane surface. *Number* presupposes the awareness of a space between shapes. *Movement* requires there to be a perceptible distance between a point A, where the *motus* began, and a point B, where it came to an end; while *stillness* can only be registered in a situation where it would have been possible to detect movement. See *In De anima* II, vii, 419a 18, §435; *In De sensu* vii, 449a 25, §§293–6; *S.T.* 1a, 78, 3, ad 2.

10 'Democritus (...) opinatus fuit, quod si medium (...) esset vacuum, quod posset aliquid quantumcumque parvum videri per quantamcumque distantiam, puta *si formica esset in caelo*. Sed hoc est impossibile' (*In De anima* II, vii, 419b 18, *lect.* 15, §433).

11 *Con.* IV, viii, 7; cf. Vasoli's note to this passage; and cf. further, *De somno* i, 458b 28; iii, 460b 18.

12 For cases where movement is concealed, or nearly concealed, by distance, see *Purg.* III, 58–60; XXIX, 58–60.

13 Other brief examples include: *Inf.* XV, 13–15 (cf. *Purg.* XXVII, 22–4); *Purg.* XIII, 55.

14 *Par.* II, 31–2. See chapter 5 above, p. 73, and chapter 10 below, pp. 193–7.

15 *Par.* XXII, 99; cf. 2 Kings 2:11.

16 Cf. *Par.* XXVII, 99–102.

17 For great height or distance surpassing the power of sight, see *Purg.* IV, 40, 86–7; XXIX, 79–80.

18 *Inf.* XXVI, 114–15; cf. *Purg.* XXXII, 108.

19 'Sensus communis, unus numero existens, sola autem ratione differens, cognoscit diversa genera sensibilium, quae tamen referuntur ad ipsum secundum diversas potentias sensuum propriorum' (*In De sensu* vii, *lect.* 19, §293). References in order: *Purg.* XV, 122–3 (wine); IX, 11; XVIII, 145; XXVII, 92 (falling asleep); *Inf.* III, 136; V, 142; VI, 1 (swooning); *Purg.* XV, 134–5 ('corpo disanimato'); *ligamentum sensus* is used in *In De sensu* i, *lect.* 1, §6.

20 *In De sensu* vii, 447a 15ff., *lect.* 17, §§ 253–64. For 'virtù di fuori', see *Purg.* XXXI, 91; for the traditional image of the lady as 'painted' in the lover's heart, see *Rime* L, 22; LIX, 9–10; LXXI, 3; and chapter 4, note 11, above.

21 The most sustained treatment of these themes in the *Comedy* comes in *Purg.* IV, 1–16, translated below. For false imagining as an obstacle, see *Inf.* XXXIV, 106; *Par.* I, 88–90; III, 20; XXVI, 73–5; cf. *Quaestio*, 82. For the mind as seized by the *imaginativa* and then returning to the real world outside, see *Purg.* XVII, 13–24; XV, 115. For greater 'cura' impeding the memory, see *ibid.*, XXXIII, 126. For the eyes taking over from and impeding the other senses, see *Inf.* XXIX, 28–30; *Purg.* VIII, 7–8, XV, 115; XXXII, 92–3; *Par.* III, 7–9; for one object of vision setting up a 'wall of indifference', see *Purg.* XXXIII, 1–5, 17.

22 Cf. also *Purg.* X, 37–45.

23 Cf. also two passages where Dante stresses the activity of several senses in quick succession: *Purg.* XXIV, 145–51; XXVIII,1–3, 6, 8–9, 17–18.

24 *Inf.* XXIII, 4–36 (discussed more fully in chapter 11, below).

25 *Purg.* XII, 91, 98, 118–36.

26 *Purg.* XVI, 1–16, 35–6.

27 The sense of smell may also function as a 'sentry' in the same way: cf. *Inf.* XVIII, 108; *Purg.* XIX, 33. A stench, too, may initially overpower the organ of sense; but one can accustom oneself to the new level (*Inf.* XI, 4–5, 11–12).

28 References in order: *Inf.* IV, 1–2; *Purg.* X, 100–1; V, 4–9; *Inf.* VIII, 65; X, 28; XXVII, 6; IX, 65–6. It is worth noticing the many conscious parallels between sight and hearing. One has to be properly 'disposed' to hear (*Purg.* XXXIII, 21). A noise can 'overpower' the ear (*Inf.* XVI, 1–3 and 92–3). One may have to cover the ears to protect them (*Inf.* XXIX, 45). Sounds get weaker as they recede (*Purg.* XIII, 31–2), and louder as they approach (*Purg.* XXVII, 58–60, cf. XX, 136–7). The mind has to pay attention (cf. *Purg.* XIX, 17–18). A faint sound can be inferred by the sense of sight (*Purg.* XXXI, 13–15). Either sense may awaken compassion (*Purg.* XIII, 65–6).

29 Cf. *Inf.* XXV, 48–9; *Purg.* XI, 76; XIII, 43–57.

30 The principal verbs to be used in their literal meaning are: 'guardare', 'guatare', 'riguardare', 'mirare', 'rimirare', 'sguardare'.

31 The frequency, variety and forcefulness of the expressions noted in this paragraph and the next make it desirable to *quote* one example of each type, rather than simply giving a reference. Examples in order: 'Io era già disposto tutto quanto / a riguardar', *Inf.* XX, 4–5; 'restammo per veder', XXI, 4; 'io stava (...) a veder surto', XXVI, 43; 'novi tormenti (...) / mi veggio intorno, come ch'io mi mova / e ch'io mi volga', VI, 4–6; 'con gli occhi 'n giù la testa sporgo', XVII, 120.

32 Examples in order: 'io levai li occhi', *Inf.* XXXIV, 88; 'li occhi nostri n'andar suso a la cima', VIII, 3; 'ficca gli occhi a valle', XII, 46; 'mi volsi, e vidimi davante / e sotto i piedi', XXXII, 22–3; 'volsimi a' piedi, e vidi', XXXII, 41; 'i' mi volsi a man destra, e puosi mente / (...) e vidi', I, 22–3; 'ciascun di noi si torse / e vedemmo a mancina', *Purg.* IV, 100–1; 'ciascun da l'altra costa li occhi volse', *Inf.* XXII, 119; 'l'occhio intorno invio', IX, 109.

33 Examples in order: 'Allor si volse a noi a puose mente, / movendo 'l viso', *Purg.* IV, 112–13; 'così fatti / vid' io color, quando puosi ben cura', X, 134–5; 'drizzò verso me l'animo e 'l volto', *Inf.* XXIV, 131 (cf. XXII, 16; *Purg.* XXXII, 108); 'la mente mia, tutta sospesa, / mirava fissa, immobile e attenta', *Par.* XXXIII, 97–8; 'attento si fermò com' uom ch'ascolta', *Inf.* IX, 4; 'li occhi miei fissi e attenti', *Purg.* XXXII, 1.

34 Examples in order: 'là giù con l'occhio cerco', *Inf.* XVIII, 115; 'mentre ch'e' tenendo 'l viso basso, / essaminava del cammin la mente, / e io mirava suso,' *Purg.* III, 55–7; 'dintorno mi guardò (...) / e poi che 'l sospecciar fu tutto spento', *Inf.* X, 55, 57; 'se ben ricordo, / già t'ho veduto (...) / però t'adocchio più che li altri tutti', XVIII, 120–3; 'io mi volsi ver' lui e guardail fiso', *Purg.* III, 106; 'con li occhi fitti pur in quella onesta', XIX, 30; 'ma ficca li occhi per l'aere ben fiso', XIII, 43.

35 Examples in order: 'l'occhio intento sbarro', *Inf.* VIII, 66; 'più che prima li occhi apersi', *Purg.* XIII, 46; 'aguzza ver me l'occhio', *Inf.* XXIX, 134; 'li occhi mi sciolse e disse: "Or drizza il nerbo / del viso"', IX, 73–4 (cf. *Con.* II, ix, 5; 'però che 'l nervo per lo quale corre lo spirito visivo, è diritto a quella parte').

36 Examples in order: 'i' mi mossi col viso', *Purg.* X, 49; 'coi piè ristetti e con li occhi passai / di là dal fiumicello', XXVIII, 34–5; 'assai prima / che noi fossimo al piè de l'alta torre, / li occhi nostri n'andar suso a la cima', *Inf.* VIII, 1–3; 'attenti / oltre quanto potean li occhi allungarsi / contro i raggi', *Purg.* XV, 139–41; 'Fa che pinghe / (...) il

viso un poco più avante', *Inf.* XVIII, 128; 'poi, procedendo di mio sguardo il curro', XVII, 61; 'l'occhio nol potea menare a lunga', IX, 5.

37 *Con.* III, ix, 10.

38 Examples in order: 'come l'occhio ti dice, u' che s'aggira', *Inf.* VII, 120; 'ti farà l'occhio la risposta', XXXIII, 107; '[i] miei occhi pria n'ebber tencione. / Ma guarda fiso là, e disviticchia / col viso', *Purg.* X, 117–19.

39 Examples in order: 'sì che la faccia ben con l'occhio attinghe', *Inf.* XVIII, 129; 'li occhi miei in uno / furo scontrati (...) / per ch'ïo a figurarlo i piedi affissi', XVIII, 40–3; 'com' i' odo quinci e non intendo, / così giù veggio e nëente affiguro', XXIV, 74–5; 'avvisava un'altra scheggia', XXIV, 28; 'lo sguardo a poco a poco raffigura', XXXI, 35; 'e ravvisai la faccia di Forese', *Purg.* XXIII, 48; 'e videmi e conobbemi e chiamava', XI, 76.

40 'Però dinanzi mira / (...) se tu 'l discerni', *Inf.* XXXIV, 2–3. See *Con.* I, xi, 3, for the shift from the literal to the metaphorical sense of 'discernere' which yields the noun 'discrezione'.

41 *Purg.* III, 58–9, 67, 86, 100.

42 Cf. *De somno* i, 458b 10.

43 Cf. *Purg.* IV, 130–5.

44 *Dve* I, iii, 2; *Inf.* II, 7–9; XXXII, 1–12; *Purg.* I, 7–12; XXIX, 37–42; *Par.* I, 13–27; XVIII, 82–7; XXIII, 64–9; XXXIII, 56, 67–75; 106–8.

45 *Purg.* X, 46–54, 70–2.

7 Imagining and dreaming

1 See Shakespeare, Sonnet 27, lines 3, 9–10; *Inf.* II, 8–10; *Purg.* XXXIII, 136–41; *Par.* XXIII, 53–4.

2 See chapter 4 above, p. 47; *De somniis* i, esp. 459a 17–22.

3 Ugolino will describe his nightmare as a 'mal sonno' (*Inf.* XXXIII, 26–7).

4 Cf. *Purg.* XV, 93–4.

5 *Purg.* XVII, 21, 19–27. The sequence begins (13–18) with the remarkable theoretical passage considered below, p. 130.

6 *Rime* I, 8–14 (cf. *VN* III, 3–8, 15); XXXV, 10 (cf. *VN* XLI, 13).

7 Both references are to works of disputed attribution: *Epist.* XIII, 29, 32; *Il Fiore*.

8 For the translation of the last half-line, see Foster-Boyde, *Dante's Lyric Poetry*, II, p.117.

9 Cf. lines 49–53, 57–62.

10 Lines 40, 65.

11 *S.T.* 2a–2ae, 95, 6, gives a convenient summary. Steven Kruger's book, *Dreaming in the Middle Ages*, appeared long after this chapter was written. It offers a full description (and bibliography) of all the kinds of dream recognised in the Middle Ages. For his account of the popular tradition and Calcidius (ignored here), see pp. 7–16 and 19–34. For Augustine, see his chapter 3; for 'the new medicine and Aristotelian philosophy', see pp. 70–5 and chapter 5.

12 Cf. *De somniis* iii, 461a 1–8; 461b 12ff.; 462a 9ff.; *De divinatione* ii, 464b 10.

13 Dante avoids this kind of language, even in prose; and the allusions here are to the superbly comic, but learned, debate between Chaucer's hen and cock in *The Nun's Priest's Tale* (ed. Robinson, fragment VII, 2920–83).

14 Cf. *De somniis* iii, 456b 20ff.; 457a 15; 460b 10, 15; 461a 20.

15 Cf. also Foster-Boyde, *Dante's Lyric Poetry*, II, pp. 29–30.

16 *De somniis* iii, 462a 15–30. See *Rime* XX, 1 and 7, for the real women in the room; and lines 41, 46 and 68 for the women in the dream.

17 *Purg.* IX, 52–63.

18 The phenomenon of thought processes occurring within a dream is also mentioned by Aristotle in *De somniis* i, 458b 17–20.

19 *Purg.* IX, 16–19, 28–33.

20 *De divinatione* i, 463a 13ff., translated by W. S. Hett.

21 'Ea occurrunt hominis *phantasiae* in dormiendo circa quae eius *cogitatio* et *affectio* fuit immorata in vigilando' (*S.T.* 2a–2ae, 95, 6). Cf. *De somniis* ii, 460b 3ff.; *De divinatione* i, 463a 25.

22 *Rime* XX, 29–34 (cf. *VN* XXIII, 3, 21).

23 *Purg.* XVII, 70–8. See chapters 10 and 13 below, pp. 210–14 and 278.

24 *Purg.* XVIII, 76–90.

25 *Purg.* XIX, 7–24. The 'pearl-like' complexion is a deduction from line 15 and *Rime* XIV, 47 (cf. *VN* XIX, 11).

26 *Purg.* XIX, 25–36.

27 *Ibid.*, 40–2, 52, 56–7.

28 The ears (7) and the eyes (8–9) registered the Siren as she was, well before the nose added its confirmation (33).

29 For 'pensare' and 'pensiero', cf. *Purg.* XVIII, 141–5; XIX, 41, 57. The doctrinal passages most closely reflected in the Siren sequence are *Purg.* XVII, 97–102, 133–9; XVIII, 19–39, 61–72.

30 Aristotle excluded the idea of dreams sent by God (*De divinatione* i, 462b 22). For Albert, see his commentary to *De somno*, pp. 188b, 190a, 192a, 193b, 195b. Cf. also *S.T.* 2a–2ae, 172, 2; Nardi, *Saggi*, pp. 55–8; Kruger, *Dreaming in the Middle Ages*, pp. 99–115.

31 Macrobius had found elements of all three in the *Somnium Scipionis*, cf. Kruger, *Dreaming in the Middle Ages*, p. 35.

32 'Le cose contingenti / anzi che sieno in se', (...) 'né per ambage (...) ma per chiare parole e con preciso / latin' (*Par.* XVII, 16–17, 31, 34–5). The last words reflect Macrobius; cf. Kruger, *Dreaming in the Middle Ages*, p. 23.

33 *Purg.* XXIV, 82–7.

34 *Rime* XX, 54–6 (*oraculum*), 45–8, 66–70 (*visio*). The literary objection to the *oraculum* and the *visio* is that the author would be forced to repeat himself, using the same words in his representation of the actual event as he had in the dream which had foretold it.

35 Genesis 41, esp. 25ff.; Daniel 2, esp. 1–11, 31–45. Both dreamers are, typically, named in *C.G.* III, 154, §3271.

36 *Rime* XX, 49–53; cf. *VN* XXIII, 5; Matthew 27: 51–3; Luke 23: 44–5; Foster-Boyde, *Dante's Lyric Poetry*, II, p. 118.

37 *Purg.* XXXII, 16–105. The Griffin is called an 'animal binato' (47) and 'biforme fera' (96).

38 *Ibid.*, 109–60.

39 Shakespeare, *The Tempest*, IV, i, 157 (it might be said that some of the details in the pageant are not unrelated to the 'skimble-skamble stuff' parodied by Hotspur in *1 Henry IV*, III, i, 146–52).

40 The protagonist's awakening is described in *Purg.* XXXII, 70–2. On all aspects of the 'pageant', see the major book by Peter Armour, *Dante's Griffin*. In the opinion of earlier commentators, as Armour shows, only the scenes involving the Giant and the Whore allude to events that will take place 'in the future' with respect to the fictional date of Dante's journey in 1300; but even these scenes would not have been considered genuinely prophetic, since they have always been interpreted as allusions to the departure of the Papacy from Rome to Avignon, which occurred after

1300, but before the time Dante wrote this part of the poem, probably some fifteen years later.

41 *Inf.* XXXII, 124–39; XXXIII, 1–9. The warning is necessary because the first Englishman to retell the tale (Chaucer in *The Monk's Tale* (ed. Robinson, fragment VII, 2407–62) omitted the setting and the speaker's exordium, and cast the narrative in the third person.

42 *Inf.* XXXIII, 11, 13, 14, 18–21.

43 *Ibid.,* 37–48.

44 *Ibid.,* 51, 58, 61, 68–9, 71, 73–5. There is a strong implication that Ugolino's 'groping' ('brancolar', 72) refers to an act of cannibalism. But this is not the surface meaning; and it has nothing to do with Ugolino's avowed attempt to revenge himself on Ruggieri through defamation.

45 *Ibid.,* 76–90, esp. 87.

46 Matthew 6:9–14; 26:39, 42; 27:46; Acts 7:60.

47 *Purg.* III, 118–23; cf. XI, 1, 12–18.

48 For dreams inspired by devils, see *C.G.* III, 154, esp. §§3268–9; *S.T.* 1a–2ae, 80, 2; 2a–2ae, 95, 6; Kruger, *Dreaming in the Middle Ages,* pp. 43–9; 110–12.

49 *Inf.* XXXIII, 129- 47.

50 *Purg.* XXVII, 92–3.

51 For Matelda, see *Purg.* XXVIII, 36, 40- 2, 49–51 (cf. Shakespeare, *The Tempest,* IV, iv, 116); for Beatrice, see *Purg.* XXX, 1–39.

52 *Mon.* III, xv, 7–10.

53 *Purg.* XXVIII, 77–8; and cf. 88–144. Needless to say, there are many other, more complex interpretations of the figure of Matelda – for which, see Armour, 'Matelda in Eden' – but these lie beyond the scope of a chapter on dreams.

54 This is Matelda's 'corollary' (XXVIII, 136). Through the medium of the dream, Dante is able to adumbrate some more tentative and yet more challenging insights into the 'operations' that constitute the 'second perfection' of our human nature. There is nothing surprising in his description of Rachel (XXVII, 104–8), for it had been traditional in the visual arts to represent philosophy or the contemplative life as a woman gazing into a mirror. But it was not traditional to represent the *vita activa* as a girl gathering flowers – let alone such a radiantly attractive girl as the one into which Dante has transformed the 'blear-eyed' or 'weak-eyed' Leah of the Bible. Nor would it have been usual to insist that she is *satisfied* by her activity ('appagare' is a strong verb in a strong position, XXVII, 108), or that she too will gaze at herself in her mirror (103). All these features may be interpreted as pointing to a more positive, less grudging valuation of the active life than one would expect to find in a philosopher or theologian.

We may also deduce a final 'corollary' about the relative values of 'doing' (*agere/ actum*) and 'making' (*facere/factum*). Leah insists that she is '*making* herself a garland' ('*farmi* una ghirlanda', XXVII, 102), which suggests that she symbolises not only moral virtue, defined as the 'recta ratio *agibilium*' or the 'norm of actions to be performed', but also the skill of the craftsman or artist, whose 'art' was defined as the 'recta ratio *factibilium*', the 'norm or measure in making things'. And the fact that she is seeking to 'adorn herself' (103) suggests that Dante was thinking specifically of his own craft – the art of poetry (cf. *Con.* I, x, 12). He was, variously, philosopher, politician and poet; and his dream suggests that all those distinctively human 'operations' lead to the perfection of our 'natural human powers' which constitute 'the happiness of this life, which is figured in the Earthly Paradise': 'beatitudo (...) huius vitae, quae in operatione propriae virtutis consistit et per terrestrem paradisum figuratur' (*Mon.* III, xv, 7).

8 Body language and the physiology of passion

1 References in order: *Inf.* XII, 1–10 (the scree); XXIII, 36–51 (sliding); I, 29–30; XXIV, 25–63; XXVI, 13–18; *Purg.* IV, 25–45 (various climbs); *Par.* I, 75, 90–2, 124–6, 136–41; II, 19–24 (space flight); *Inf.* XVII, 82, 97–126 (night flying).

2 *Purg.* XXVIII, 45; cf. XXI, 106–11.

3 *Georgics* IV, 472; *Purg.* II, 76–85; III, 16–28.

4 *Purg.* XXV, 20–1.

5 *Purg.* XXV, 37–75. This part of the speech is analysed in greater detail in my *Dante Philomythes*, pp. 271–9. The noun 'virtù' occurs, in the various spellings, in lines 41, 52, 59, 72, 80, 89; and cf. 96.

6 Cf. *Purg.* XXV, 37, 40–1. For the spirits, see St Albert, *De spiritu et respiratione*; *Dante Philomythes*, p. 372, note 7; Foster-Boyde, *Dante's Lyric Poetry*, II, p. 80.

7 *VN* III, 1, 3.

8 For further revealing paragraphs on the role of the 'spiriti del viso', see *VN* XIV, 5–6, 8, 14.

9 *VN* XV, 2; XVI, 2–4.

10 *Rime* LXVII, 15, 18–28.

11 Strictly speaking, 'the style for praising Beatrice', 'lo stilo de la *sua* loda', *VN* XXVI, 4.

12 Cf. *Purg.* IX, 10; XI, 43–5; XXVI, 56–7.

13 *Purg.* XXX, 80–90.

14 *Ibid.*, 103–8, 130–2, 136, 144–5; XXXI, 5–6.

15 *Purg.* XXXI, 67–84.

16 *Inf.* III, 130–6; V, 141–2 (cf. VI, 1).

17 *Inf.* XVII, 7, 10, 25–7 (Geryon); XXI, 131–2 (the devils); *Par.* III, 67–9 (Piccarda).

18 *Purg.* XX, 127–9; 133–41, 145–51; XXI, 1–6.

19 *Purg.* XXI, 7–12, 40–2, 55–72, 82–102.

20 *Purg.* III, 31–3; XXV, 101–2; cf. *Con.* III, viii, 1.

21 *Inf.* III, 22–30; V, 35–6.

22 Cf. *Inf.* IV, 35–42, 84; *Purg.* VII, 28–36.

23 Cf. *Purg.* XV, 94–5; *Par.* XVII, 137; Psalm 83:7 (Vulgate).

24 *Inf.* XIV, 89–90, 103–20 (cf. 130–8). The Acheron marks the 'frontier' of Hell, the other three are places of punishment for the angry, the violent and the treacherous.

25 *Inf.* XX, 4–25.

26 *Inf.* XIII, 28–45, 91–2, 101–2, 131–2, 137–8. One has to say 'probably', because the verb 'piangere' does not always imply weeping.

27 *Inf.* XXXII, 16–24, 31–7.

28 *Inf.* XXXIII, 91–3.

29 *Inf.* III, 9; XXXIII, 113–18, 148–50.

30 *Inf.* VI, 88; X, 69, 82; XXVII, 26; XXVIII, 74 (for the 'sweetness' of the world and the light); V, 121–3, 126 ('no greater grief'); Eccl. 3:4 (the different 'times').

31 *Par.* V, 105 ('increase'); XVI, 30 ('blandishment'); III, 34, 67; V, 107 (the blessed as 'ombre'); Luke 6:21 ('quia ridebitis'; cf. Matthew 5:4, 12).

32 *Par.* V, 105–8, 118–20, 124–6, 130–8 (Justinian); IX, 70–2 ('joy and radiance').

33 Technically speaking, the blessed are still *corpora mobilia secundum locum*. For their powers of movement to express joy, see *Par.* VIII, 19–21; XIV, 109–11; XXIV, 13–18. For changes of colour, see XXVII, 10–15, 19–21, 28–36. For 'flaming', see V, 1; XVI, 28–9; XVIII, 25. For 'sparkling', see XVIII, 71; XXI, 41.

34 References in order: *Purg.* XXXI, 136–45; *Par.* XV, 34–6; XXI, 4–12; XXIII, 46–8.

35 Line 42 must be interpreted in the light of *Par.* XXVIII, 112–13, and XXIX, 61–6. In

Catholic doctrine, however, no human act can be meritorious of heaven, unless the agent is in a state of grace, having received 'sanctifying' grace as an undeserved gift from God. (It was earned for all mankind by Jesus on the Cross.) The grace which enables the blessed to see God is called 'glorifying'. It is given in differing degrees, in proportion to the soul's deserts, as just explained; but it is still a gift, not a contractual right. And since this 'grazia' is far higher in value than the soul can ever strictly deserve, it is '*sovra* suo valore'.

9 Self-direction: the powers of the mind

1 See above, p. 55; cf. further, *S.T.* 1a–2ae, 1, 2; 26, 1.
2 For 'principium suarum operationum', 'dominium sui actus' and similar phrases, see *In Ethic.* III, iii, 1112b 32, *lect.* 8, §479 (cf. §§526, 1125, 1127); *S.T.* 1a, 23, 1, ob. 1; 82, 1, ob. 3; 1a–2ae, 6, 2, ad 2; *C.G.* III, 155, §3282–3. For responsibility, reward and punishment, see *Epist.* XIII, 25; *C.G.* III, 73, esp. § 2491.
3 The key adjectives in Italian are: 'eccellentissima', 'preziosissima', 'nobilissima', 'perfettissima', 'ultima', 'sovrana' (*Con.* III, ii, 14–19). All the other words and phrases quoted in this paragraph are from this section.
4 Cf. *S.T.* 1a, 59, 1 ad 1; 58, 4; 64, 2; 79, 8.
5 *Scientificus* derives from the present participle of the verb *scire*, 'to know'; *scientia* should often be translated as 'knowledge' or 'understanding'; *intellectus speculativus* was the accepted translation of Aristotle's 'theoretical intellect'.
6 It is that 'in which the intellect and the reason find contentment' (*Con.* III, xiii, 5–7; IV, xxii, 11).
7 The less formal word 'notion' is here preferred to the term 'concept', which is reserved for the next stage of abstraction – that which results in the 'abstract nouns'. It is impossible to separate the analysis of concepts from the analysis of language (as is shown by the original ambiguity of *logos* in Greek and exemplified by the problems of translating posed by 'ragionare'). But the possibility of translating from one language to another – illustrated in the four languages which concern us in this study – would have been taken as the clearest proof that the mind 'seizes' something other than a mere sign.
8 The 'vertical' process leads to the philosophically exact definition, the 'horizontal' to the logically correct syllogism.
9 In the study of nature, one must always be prepared to add the phrase 'or, at least, in most cases' (*ut in pluribus*).
10 Cf. *Purg.* III, 34–45.
11 *Con.* IV, viii, 1 (cf. II, xiv, 14); *In Ethic.* I, i, 1094, *lect.* 1, §1.
12 *Par.* XXIV, 130–2. This is Dante's own very revealing paraphrase of the opening words of the Creed. Cf. further, I, 107, 112–26; XXXIII, 145; Aristotle, *Metaphysics* XII, VI–VIII, esp. 1072b 4ff.
13 In Dante's words: 'la prima Mente, la quale li Greci dicono Protonoè' (*Con.* II, iii, 11). For Alpha and Omega, see Revelation 1:8; for the 'maker of heaven and earth', see the Nicene Creed.
14 *Par.* XXXIII, 82–105; cf. I, 103–5.
15 Cf. my *Dante Philomythes*, pp. 276–9, 283–8.
16 Psalm 8:6, translated by Dante in *Con.* IV, xix, 7.
17 Cf. my *Dante Philomythes*, pp. 191–3.
18 Dante visualises the material and immaterial parts of the cosmos as two 'hemispheres' with a common 'horizon' (*Mon.* III, xv, 3).

19 Cf. *In Ethic.* VI, iv, 1140a 1ff., *lect.* 3, esp. §§1151, 1154; *Con.* IV, ix, 5.

20 *Ibid.*, VI, ii, iv–v, *lect.* 2–4; *Con.* IV, xxii, 5; *Mon.* I, iii, 9; *Purg.* XVIII, 61–3. The medieval Latin forms are: *intellectus practicus* and *ratio practica.* 'Intellect' and 'reason' are often interchangeable, but there is perhaps a greater likelihood that 'ragione', 'ragionare' and 'ragionativo' will be used in contexts where the activity in question clearly belongs to the 'practical' rather than to the 'speculative' intellect.

21 *Con.* III, ii, 15.

22 Cf. *In Ethic.* VI, x, 1143a 5ff., *lect.* 9, §1238 (cf. §484).

23 *Purg.* XVIII, 66.

24 'Intellectus practicus ad conclusionem operativam recipit maiorem propositionem ab intellectu speculativo, et sub illa particularem, quae proprie sua est, assummit et particulariter ad operationem concludit' (*Mon.* I, xiv, 7). The process of reasoning from effects to causes, or from the particular to the universal, is called *inductio*; while reasoning from first principles to conclusions is called *deductio.*

25 The intervention may affect the state, position, or even the existence of the body in question – which is often the body of the person who is 'taking counsel'. The consequent action may well inhibit as well as initiate change.

26 *Ethics* VI, v, 1140b 15. The quotation is from *In Ethic.* I, viii, 1098b 10, *lect.* 12, §139. Cf. further, *ibid.*, III, iii, 1112a 20ff., *lect.* 7–8, esp. §475 (and cf. §23); *Mon.* I, ii, 7–8.

27 See chapter 3 above, p.000.

28 *In Ethic.* I, iii, 1094b 23–7, *lect.* 3, §36; cf. *Con.* IV, xiii, 8; *Mon.* II, ii, 7.

29 *In Ethic.* I, vi, 1098a, *lect.* 10, esp. §§119, 128.

30 Cf. *Mon.* I, iii, 6; *Con.* IV, vi, 6–8, 13–16; *Par.* VIII, 127–48.

31 *In Ethic.* III, iii–iv, *lect.* 5–6, 9; VI, ii, 1139b 7ff., *lect.* 2, §§1133–4, 1138 (cf. §1040); *S.T.* 1a, 83, 4.

32 *Con.* IV, ix, 7.

33 Ovid, *Metamorphoses*, VII, 20–1; Romans 7:15–20 For the 'virtues' of the intellect, see *Ethics* VI; for the 'virtues' of the will, see *ibid.*, III–V.

34 For Dante's 'conviction', see *Con.* I, i, 1; II, xiii, 6; III, xiii, 14; XV, 4; for the 'attempt to silence his doubts', cf. *Con.* IV, xii, 11–12; xiii, 1–9.

35 *Mon.* III, xv, 3–10; *Par.* XXXIII, 143–5.

36 References in order: *Con.* IV, xxii, 10–11; xvii, 9, 11; xvi, 10; xvii, 2 ('fruits'). The moral virtues are listed, after Aristotle, as eleven in IV, xvii, but as (the Stoic) four in xxii, 11. The comparison with the bees comes in IV, xvii, 12.

37 References in order: *Con.* III, xv, 11; II, xiv, 18; *Par.* XIII, 91–108.

38 The political letters are *Epistles* V–VII, XI. For the practical goal of the *Comedy*, see *Epist.* XIII, 40; for 'direction of the will', see *Dve* II, ii, 7 (cf. *Mon.* III, xv, 10); for the definition of poetry, see *Dve* II, iv, 2.

39 *Con.* III, xi, 14.

40 For a reference to *three* 'natures' in the soul, see *Con.* III, vii, 8; for the *two* intellects, cf. IV, xxii, 10; for the *one* human soul, see *Purg.* XXV, 74–5; and cf. IV, 5–6.

41 *Purg.* XXV, 61–6.

42 Cf. *Dante Philomythes*, pp. 252–5.

43 *Purg.* XVI, 67–84; *Par.* VII, 67–72 (cf. 124–44).

44 Cf. *Dante Philomythes*, pp. 278–88.

10 Aspects of human freedom

1 *Par.* III, 25–33. In the narrative, the threefold stress on 'truth' serves to highlight the difficulties that the protagonist will experience when he detects an apparent

contradiction between what he is told by the spokeswoman of the souls and what he will be told by Beatrice herself. But this insistence is also part of a systematic set of contrasts in the canto between the ordinary human way of knowing (based on perception, requiring deductive processes, prone to error) and the perfect under-standing enjoyed by the blessed and the angels.

2 *Purg.* XXIV, 10. For other examples of this kind of preparation, see *Inf.* VI, 79–80, which is 'fulfilled' in *Inf.* X, 32; XVI, 41, 44; XXVIII, 106. For the delaying technique used in the episode itself, see chapter 6 above, pp. 106–11.

3 *Purg.* XXIV, 13–15 (Piccarda), 82–7 (Corso); cf. *Rime* LXXIII–LXXVIII (Dante's 'tenzone' with Forese).

4 *Par.* III, 97–102.

5 *VN* XIII, 4; Chaucer, *Canterbury Tales, General Prologue,* line 742.

6 *Par.* III, 30, 50–7. The participle 'rilegato' had been used of Virgil's eternal exile in Limbo (cf. *Purg.* XXI, 18), while the noun 'manco' (30) contrasts with the insistence on fulfilment in the verbs 'appagare' (32) and 'contentare' (40).

7 *Par.* III, 55–7, 122–6; IV, 19–21, 64, 67–72.

8 *Ethics* III, i, 1109b 30–1110b 17. The passages in quotation marks in this and the following paragraphs follow very closely the translation by H. Rackham in the Loeb edition. The Latin phrases are from the commentary by Aquinas, *In Ethic.* III, *lect.* 1–2.

9 The case of the Sienese nobleman Provenzan Salvani, whom Dante encounters on the terrace of the Proud, is relevant here: see *Purg.* XI, 121–3; 133–8.

10 'Se vïolenza è quando quel che pate / nïente conferisce a quel che sforza, / non fuor quest' alme per essa scusate: / ché volontà, se non vuol, non s'ammorza, / ma fa come natura face in foco, / se mille volte vïolenza il torza. / Per che, s'ella si piega assai o poco, / segue la forza; e così queste fero / possendo rifuggir nel santo loco. / Se fosse stato lor volere intero, / come tenne Lorenzo in su la grada, / e fece Muzio a la sua man severo, / così l'avria ripinte per la strada / ond' eran tratte, come fuoro sciolte; / ma così salda voglia è troppo rada.'

11 'Molte fïate già, frate, addivenne / che, per fuggir periglio, contra grato / si fé di quel che far non si convenne; / come Almeone, che, di ciò pregato / dal padre suo, la propria madre spense, / per non perder pietà si fé spietato. / A questo punto voglio che tu pense / che la forza al voler si mischia, e fanno / sì che scusar non si posson l'offense. / Voglia assoluta non consente al danno; / ma consentevi in tanto in quanto teme, / se si ritrae, cadere in più affanno. / Però, quando Piccarda quello spreme, / de la voglia assoluta intende, e io / de l'altra; sì che ver diciamo insieme.'

12 *Purg.* XVII, 94–6 (cf. 97–102).

13 In *Paradiso* I, the implication that human loving is somehow inferior to that of irrational beings is corrected in two important respects. First, it is made clear that intellectual beings do have their own kind of unerring natural love for a 'place' proper to their species – an inherent, inalienable, if confused, attraction to the Supreme Good, which keeps them at least oriented towards their 'sito decreto' in the Empyrean with God. 'Elective' love – which is simply the actualisation of the will – bears on the means to the end, not on the 'ultimo fine' itself. Second, we are reminded that elective love would not be free if it did not have the 'power to bend in another direction' ('podere / di piegar (...) in altra parte', I, 131–2). If it were impossible for us to 'stray', 'bend', 'turn aside' or 'go backwards' (Dante rings the changes on these journey metaphors), there would be no merit in our continuing along the 'diritta via'.

14 Consistently, Dante says that his inactivity was deserving of neither praise nor blame in this case ('me non riprendo (...) né commendo') because it was 'necessario'

(*Par.* IV, 7–9) Cf. the classic study by Bruno Nardi, 'Il libero arbitrio e la storiella dell'asino di Buridano', in *Nel mondo di Dante*, pp. 287–303.

15 Our intellect and will are 'created' directly by God; our temperaments and talents are 'generated' by natural causes; but all our powers come from God. See *Dante Philomythes*, chapter 11.

16 *Par.* III, 70–87, enriched with allusions to *Con.* IV, xii, 14–19, and *Purg.* XVI, 67–81 (esp. 79–80).

17 *Par.* IV, 136–8, rephrased in V, 13–15 (cf. 46).

18 *Par.* V, 19–84. The plea for caution with regard to the will in this speech (64–84) is matched in canto XIII, 112–42, by a plea for caution in the intellectual sphere. We should beware of 'rushing in', whether it is to make vows or to draw conclusions in philosophy and theology.

19 *Par.* III, 73–8, 101–2.

20 *Con.* IV, ix, 8.

21 *Con.* IV, xvi, 6–9.

22 On the first point, Dante specifies that the will of the angels and the blessed is perfect simply because they never cease to will what God wills (*Mon.* I, xii, 5). The self-quotation ('sicut iam dixi in *Paradiso Comediae*') is so surprising that it was treated as spurious by earlier editors. It was, however, restored to the critical text by Ricci; and Prudence Shaw has indicated, in a private communication, that it has unimpeachable manuscript authority.

23 *Purg.* I, 71; XXVII, 140; XXXIII, 127–9; *Par.* XXXI, 85–7 (cf. X, 88–90).

24 *Purg.* XVI, 70–2.

25 The premisses now required depend on divine revelation and are a matter of faith ('opra di fede', *Purg.* XVIII, 48). The speeches to which Virgil looks forward are those examined at the beginning of this chapter.

26 In line 33, it is possible to translate 'fin che' as 'for as long as', rather than 'until'; and it is true that in Dante's vision of virtuous love between two human beings, or between a human being and God, the phase of 'fruition' is represented with all the urgency of the phase of 'desiring' (see chapter 13 below). But in the context of this speech – valid for all species of desire and dominated by the paradigm of locomotion – 'gioire' seems to refer to the moment of 'quiete' when the 'moto spiritale' has reached its *terminus ad quem*.

11 Fear

1 The passage is quoted in full as the fourth epigraph to the whole book.

2 The three *officia* of classical and medieval rhetoric were 'to teach, to please and to move'; see further, for the notion of 'direction of the will', *Dve* II, ii, 7 (in the light of *Mon.* I, xiv, 5; xv, 9; III, iv, 14).

3 See chapter 10, p. 199. Aristotle, of course, reserved the term *mixtum* for actions which result from joint action by the reluctant will and the passion of fear caused by the threats of an external agent.

4 The passions were divided and subdivided in different ways by each of the thinkers who influenced Dante. Cicero, for example, made do with four main categories, based on the permutations of pleasure and pain, present and future; Aristotle listed six; Aquinas proved that there must be eleven in all. None of these schemes proved compatible with the thrust of this book.

5 *Inf.* I, 6, 19–20.

6 *Inf.* I, 16–18, 22–30.

7 For stress on the moment of perception, see I, 31 ('ecco'), 34 ('volto'), 45, 53 ('vista'); for the leopard, see 35–6; for the lion, 44–8.

8 I, 52–3, 57.

9 I, 37–43, 54, 58–61.

10 I, 76–8, 88–96, 132.

11 II, 1–6.

12 I, 130–1. The trust is based on what we read in I, 73–87; the reasons are given in lines 91–3 and 112–23.

13 II, 10–36, ending with the verb 'ragionare'.

14 *Inf.* II, 43–8. 'Viltate' (cf. 'viltà' in II, 122, and III, 15) is the opposite here of 'magnanimitate' or 'greatness of soul', a term which Dante had used in *Con.* IV, xxvi, 7 as a synonym for courage or fortitude. It is no accident that the narrator here refers to Virgil periphrastically as 'del *magnanimo* quell'ombra' (44).

15 II, 49–50.

16 Dante is 'impeded', II, 62, 95. The 'short route' has been cut off by the wolf, 120. He has 'turned back through fear', 63. His pitiful laments reach heaven, 106. Help is required if he is 'to escape', 68–9, 104. Beatrice is 'moved' by love to descend; but 'desires' to return to her place on high, 71–2. The 'chain reaction' – from the Virgin to Lucy and on to Beatrice and Virgil – illustrates how the human will can and should be activated or changed: *not* by fear or through blind obedience, but either through compassion aroused by the spectacle of another person's distress (Lucy can *hear* Dante's laments and see him locked 'in combat with Death', 106–7), or by means of a courteously expressed and rationally motivated request to perform a good deed.

17 The logical order of events would be (1) understanding, (2) willing, (3) desiring in the heart, (4) straightening up and (5) beginning to move 'locally'.

18 There is a significant contrast to this moment in *Purg.* XXXIII, 130–4.

19 Cf. Psalm 23:4 (= Psalm 22:4, in the Latin version 'iuxta Hebraeos').

20 Cf. *Inf.* II, 61, 71–2, 84, 98, 133. In *Con.* II, x, 6, Dante defines 'pietà' in a broad sense to mean a 'noble disposition of the mind which is ready to receive love, *misericordia* and other charitable passions'. *Misericordia* is there defined as 'dolersi de l'altrui male', which is what 'la volgar gente' understand by pity. In the context of canto II, Beatrice seems to be 'pietosa' in both the broad and the narrow senses because she is currently distressed by the misfortune of her 'friend' and 'faithful servant'.

21 See p. 43 for a discussion of the neutrality of the Latin word *malum* and for its wide range of meanings, which in English have to be rendered variously as 'injury', 'harm', 'hurt', 'hardship' or 'damage', as well as 'evil', 'wrong' or 'tort'.

22 *Ethics* III, vi, 2, 1115a, 8–10. In the translation by Moerbeke it begins: '*timemus* autem *terribilia* (...) haec autem sunt *mala*'. The precise location of the source is not without significance. The passage comes at the very point where Aristotle closes his discussion of the issues presented in chapters 9 and 10 of this book and passes on to consider the relationship between the passions and moral virtue for the first time. He illustrates the concept of moral virtue (defined as a disposition to choose the mean between two extremes) by examining the nature of true courage ('buono ardire', 'fortitudine', 'magnanimitate'), conceived as a disposition lying between foolhardiness (cf. 'folle', ii, 35) and fear ('paura', 'tema', 'viltate').

23 *In Ethic.* III, vi, 1115a 8, *lect.* 14, §§531, 533.

24 *Inf.* III, 22–31; 91–102, 109–11, 130–6; v, 93, 140–2; vI, 1–3.

25 VII, 1–9 (Pluto); XII, 12–27 (Minotaur); 55–87 (Centaurs); XVII, 85–93, 106–14 (Geryon); for the devils, see below, pp. 243–9.

26 This same episode illustrates in copy-book fashion the relationship between sensa-

tion and intellection. We are shown (a) how *auditory* impressions (III, 25–30) stimulate desire to know their cause (32–3); (b) how the explanation (34–42) demands another explanation (43–51); (c) how the second explanation enables Dante to interpret successive *visual* impressions (52–60) and thus to reach 'understanding and certainty' (61–3).

27 III, 121–9. Significantly, Virgil is described as the '*courteous* master'; and significantly, too, he addresses Dante for the first time as 'my *son*'.

28 IV, 28–39.

29 Cf. 'Tu non dimandi . . .', IV, 31. The justice of the treatment of the virtuous pagans is called into question in *Par.* XIX, 70–8.

30 *Inf.* IV, 46–51.

31 In the interim we have learnt much more about *other* passions of the soul, because we have been escorted through the four circles of Upper Hell which punish the uncontrolled satisfaction of the natural human appetites for sex, food, possessions and revenge.

32 'Foolhardiness' translates the adjectives 'folle' and 'ardito' which are used in successive lines. This brutally reductive summary ignores all the subtleties of the representation in VIII, 64–78, which exemplifies many of the procedures illustrated in chapter 6. It also fails to convey the superb cross-cutting between narrative (76–80, 82–3, 86–8) and vivid dramatic speech (81, 84–5, 89–93).

33 VIII, 112–20; IX, 1–2. Dante's confusion is deduced from Virgil's command in VIII, 122 ('non sbigottir').

34 IX, 19–30.

35 IX, 61–3.

36 See pp. 104–5.

37 See in particular, *Inf.* XVII, 76–7, 81, 85–8, 89–90.

38 This paragraph combines information revealed in XVIII, 1–18 and XXI, 1–21. To visualise and understand the events in canto XXIII it is important to remember that the arrangement of the bolgias resembles a series of concentric moats around a castle, except that each successive ditch is lower as well as smaller than the one before it.

39 The resultant inversion of the moments of perception and passion is especially appropriate here, because he is analysing the conflict between the desire to get away and the desire to have a longer look at the *obiectum timoris*.

40 XXI, 22–57. 'Fiend', like 'Satan', means 'enemy' or 'adversary'.

41 XXI, 103–26. The date given in lines 112–14 is in fact exact to the very hour. The earthquake really did take place and is the one which occurred at the time of Christ's death on the Cross. We later learn that it did not leave even the one single bridge intact. Hence, if the poets are to be 'safe until they reach the unbroken bridge', they are either receiving a safe-conduct for the whole circle, or not receiving one at all – which is clearly how the devils understand the order. For the moment, however, we are concerned with fear, not with the art of lying.

42 XXI, 133, 136–9; XXII, 1–15.

43 Animals have memory and imagination, but theirs are 'sensitive' powers and cannot store concepts or words. Hence, they could not have recalled a fable or formed an image in response to words and reasoning.

44 XXIII, 4–9. The immediate stimulus to the protagonist's thought-processes would seem to have been the remembered image of an unseen, hovering predator about to carry off two victims. There would also seem to be links between the unfordable river and the unbridged bolgia; between the water in the river and the pitch; even, perhaps, between Virgil and the mouse. There is certainly a connection between the

kite and the devils: first, Alichino (XXII, 130–2); second, Calcabrina (133–41); and, third, the whole group of devils, when they appear 'con l'ali tese (...) per volerne prendere' (XXIII, 35–6). One might even recall that Virgil and Dante will be almost tied together, like the mouse and the frog, when they slide down into the bottom of the sixth bolgia (37–40, 50–1). But perhaps the most important points are these: (a) Dante learns from the dangers of others ('aliena pericula') and becomes cautious ('cautus') in good time, thus exemplifying the tag, quoted by Benvenuto da Imola, 'Felix quem faciunt aliena pericula cautum'; and (b) this is the way Dante intended his poem to work on his readers – making us wise before the event.

45 Dante insisted that animals do not need language because all members of the same species have the same *actus et passiones* (*Dve* I, ii, 5); while the prime function of fear, throughout the animal kingdom, is to provide the motive force for running away.

46 *Purg.* XXV, 112–17; XXVI, 14–15, 28–30, 102.

47 In the simile where Dante compared reason and the sense-appetites to a rider and his horse, he said that the 'rider' should use the 'spur' of fortitude when the 'horse' inclines to 'run away': cf. *Con.* IV, xxvi, 6–7; *Purg.* VI, 91–9. For the 'apple', see *Purg.* XXVII, 45, 115 (and cf. 119; XXVI, 106–11).

12   Anger

1 Among the abstract terms used in *Inf.* XXIII, 1–33 ('ira', 'schernire', 'noiare', 'caccia', 'crudele'), the only important absentee is 'vendetta'.

2 Cf. *S.T.* 1–2ae, 46, 5 ad 1.

3 References in order: *Inf.* V, 4; VI, 14; XXXII, 105; VI, 19, 28; XXI, 67–9; XXXIII, 78; XXX, 20; VIII, 42.

4 *Inf.* XII, 33; XI, 83–4; *Par.* XVII, 64, 67; cf. further *Con.* II, viii, 8.

5 *Con.* II, vii, 3–4 (cf. IV, vii, 10–15; *Inf.* XXVI, 119–20; and chapter 9 above, p.190). For madness, cf. *In Ethic.* I, x, 1100b, *lect.* 16, §197.

6 *S.T.* 1a–2ae, 46–8; 2a–2ae, 158, 1–8. Aristotle recognised it as a form of *incontinentia* in *Ethics* VII, v–vi, 1149b 2ff.; cf. also, *ibid.* IV, v, 1125b 28ff.; *Rhetoric* II, ii, 1377b 30ff.

7 *De anima* I, i, 403a 32; *Purg.* XV, 106.

8 *S.T.* 1a–2ae, 48, 2; 2a–2ae, 158, 4 (quoting St Gregory, *Magna moralia*, v, 45).

9 References in order: *Inf.* III, 99, 109; VI, 24, and cf. 13–18; VII, 1–2, 7–9, 13–15; XXXI, 67–72.

10 References in order: *Inf.* XXX, 16–21; XII, 14–15; IX, 38, 45, 49–50.

11 *Inf.* XIX, 4, 6, 13–15, 22–33, 64, 79–81. It was the extra vigour of the pope's kicking in response to the greater redness of the tormenting flame which first drew him to the protagonist's attention.

12 He is referred to successively as a '*foco* benedetto', an 'amore *acceso*', a '*luce* profonda' and an 'apostolico *lume*': *Par.* XXIV, 31, 82, 88, 153.

13 Apart from the passages quoted as verse in the text, the references in this section are to the following lines in *Par.* XXVII: 1–3, 10–15, 19–20, 22, 31–6.

14 *Rime* CXVI, 26–7; *Inf.* V, 31–3, 42–3, 49, 75, 79, 82–7, 96.

15 *Inf.* VII, 100–8, 121, 124, 127–9; VIII, 10–12, 21, 32, 39. The image carries, of course, the additional connotations of degradation and defilement: the waters are not just 'grey', but 'filthy'; the animals who love to wallow in mud are 'pigs': VIII, 10, 50.

16 For example, a giant thrashes a whore (*Purg.* XXXII, 152–8); a crowd stones a martyr (XV, 106–14); a devil attacks another in mid-air (*Inf.* XXII, 132–44). For the anger of the traitors in the ice, see *Inf.* XXXII, 43–51, 124–34; XXXIII, 1–3, 76–8.

17 *Inf.* XXX, 49–57, 61–9, 73–5, 88–90, 92–3, 97–9.

18 *Inf.* XI, 31–2, 46–7.
19 *Inf.* XXIV, 124–6, 129, 142–51; XXV, 1–3.
20 *Inf.* XIV, 52–60.
21 'Rixa, tumor mentis, contumelia, clamor, indignatio, blasphemia' (*S.T.* 2a–2ae, 158, 7, quoting St Gregory, *Magna moralia*, XXXI, 45).
22 Cf. *In De sensu* i, *lect.* 1, §12.
23 Other synonymous expressions used by Aquinas which underline the idea of 'inaccessibility through height' include 'cum quadam *elevatione* sive *magnitudine* existens' and 'sub ratione cuiusdam *altitudinis* sive *ardui*'. The hill in *Inferno* I would be a classic example of a *bonum arduum*.
24 *S.T.* 1–2ae, 25, 1, 3. There is a particularly useful and charming account of the irascible power in Thomas Wright's *The Passions of the Mind in General*, I, chapters 5–6, pp. 103–8.
25 *S.T.* 1a–2ae, 25, 3; and 25, 4, ad 3.
26 *In Ethic.* II, v, 1105b 20, *lect.* 6, §293; *In De anima* III, ix, 432b 5, *lect.* 15, esp. §804; *S.T.* 1a, 81, 2; 82, 5; cf. 1a–2ae, 25, 1; 46, 2, ob. 1.
27 *Rhetoric* II, ii, 1378a 32, translated by W. Rhys Roberts. The word he renders as 'conspicuous' is translated in Latin as *apparens* and could mean 'apparent' or 'real'.
28 *Rhetoric* II, ii, 1378b 7, quoting *Iliad* 18, 109.
29 See chapter 7 above, p. 133.
30 References in order: *Inf.* XXV, 1–24; VIII, 52–60.
31 For example, Italian words like 'scorno' and 'schernire', 'disdegno' and 'sdegnoso', or Latin words like *minoratio, parvipensio* and *contemptus*.
32 References in order: *Purg.* X, 69; XVII, 26; XI, 64. A moralist or theologian would have to note that Farinata's truculent attitude is as absurd as that of Capaneus, who was described as '*dispettoso* e torto' (*Inf.* XIV, 47).
33 *Inf.* VI, 77–87; X, 25–7, 29–30, 35–6, 46–51; Matthew 5:38–9; Proverbs 15:1.
34 *Inf.* X, 73–93, 109; *Purg.* VI, 58–96 (especially 70–5), 124–51. This later episode provides a damning indictment of the perpetual feuds which were to destroy the Italian communes (and it is there that the Montagues and Capulets make their first appearance in European literature).
35 For 'la vendetta divina', see *Inf.* XIV, 16–18, and *Par.* VII, 18–21, 49–51; for Dante's not unambiguous attitude to the nobility and the need to avenge insults to the family honour, see *Par.* XVI, 1–6; *Inf.* XXIX, 18–21, 31–6. A just ruler gives each man the reward or the punishment he deserves. A just reward will pay and cancel the debt incurred by society for the services rendered by citizen X, and a just punishment will pay and cancel the debt incurred by citizen Y for the *dis*service he did to society: both citizens are 'quits'. Justice seeks to maintain or to restore the equilibrium; it makes things 'even' again.
36 *S.T.* 1a–2ae, 46, 1 and 2; *In De sensu* i, *lect.* 1, §12.
37 It seems to encourage determinism and to involve a culpable confusion between an 'efficient' cause on the one hand, and 'material', 'instrumental' or 'dispositive' causes on the other: cf. *Dante Philomythes*, pp. 54, 227.
38 *In Ethic.* IV, xi, 1126a 12ff., *lect.* 13, §809; cf. §§1391–2.
39 *Ibid.*, §810.
40 Cf. 'esperto / e de li vizi umani e del valore', *Inf.* XXVI, 98–9. In Latin, the normative phrases are such as: *oportet, magis quam oportet, non oportet*.
41 *Politics* I, ii, 1253a 1; *Ethics* I, v, 1097b 11; *Con.* IV, iv, 1; *Par.* VIII, 114–20; cf. *Purg.* XIII, 94–6.
42 *In Ethic.* VII, vi, 1149b 25ff., *lect.* 7, §1391.

43 *Dve* I, iii, 1.
44 *Purg.* V, 77–8; *Mon.* II, xi, 4; *Par.* V, 33.
45 See chapter 10 above, p. 207.
46 *Ethics* V, xi, 1138b 5ff.; VII, vi, 1150a 7; *Inf.* XXXI, 55–7.
47 *Par.* VII, 73–81; *Mon.* III, xiv, 3–4; Luke 23:34; Matthew 5:5, 7, 9, 38–45; 6:12; 7:1.
48 *Purg.* XVII, 68–9.
49 'Temperato' is the adjective related to *temperantia*, 'self-control', the cardinal virtue which 'reins in' desire and anger; 'mite' is one of the epithets used by Jesus in the Beatitudes.
50 Luke 2:41–8.
51 *Mon.* III, xv, 7–8; cf. pp. 139, 188 above. Jesus had made explicit that he was not concerned with the 'kingdoms of this world': see Matthew 4:8; 5: 3, 10, 12, 19, 45; 6:4, 6, 18, 19 and especially 24.
52 References in order: *Inf.* XXIII, 37–42; *Par.* I, 101–2; XXII, 1–6; *Purg.* XXX, 79–81; XXXI, 64–6.
53 'Video aliam legem in membris meis, repugnantem legem mentis meae', Romans 7:23.
54 *Con.* IV, xvii, 5. *Modus* originally meant 'measurement', or 'unit of measurement', and it early acquired the senses of 'measure', or 'the proper measure'. *Moderatio* comes from the verb derived from *modus* – *moderari/moderatum* – meaning 'to find the right *modus*', 'to regulate', 'to control'.
55 Cf. *In Ethic.* IV, v, 1126a 5, *lect.* 13, §§805–6.
56 *Ibid.* 1125b 32, §801.
57 *Ibid.* §§801, 805.
58 'Dicendum quod ira dupliciter se potest habere ad rationem. Uno quidem modo, antecedenter. Et sic trahit rationem a sua rectitudine, unde habet rationem mali. Alio modo consequenter, prout scilicet appetitus sensitivus movetur contra vitia secundum ordinem rationis. Et haec ira est bona, quae dicitur "ira per zelum".'

'Dicendum quod passio irae utilis est, *sicut et omnes alii motus appetitus sensitivi*, ad hoc quod homo promptius exequatur id quod ratio dictat. Alioquin frustra esset in homine appetitus sensitivus, cum tamen natura nihil faciat frustra' (*S.T.* 2a–2ae, 158, 1, ad 2; 8, ad 2).
59 *Ibid.* 1a–2ae, 24, 3.
60 *Ibid.* ad 1.
61 *Dve* I, i, 2; cf. *Con.* I, ii, 7 ('le parole son fatte per mostrare quello che non si sa'), and X, 12.
62 Horace had said: 'Non satis est *pulchra* esse poemata; dulcia sunto / et *quocumque volent animum auditoris agunto*' (*Ars poetica*, 99–100).
63 For this section, see the introduction to my *Dante's Style in his Lyric Poetry*, and section IV of the Bibliography there.
64 Lines 101–3. Lines 93–106 are particularly relevant to this section.
65 The protagonist had to cling to a rock to prevent himself from falling into the bolgia where Ulysses is damned for his rhetorical triumphs. Dante-the-author protests that he is still so pained by his memory of the subsequent encounter that he 'must rein in his *ingenium* more than usual, in order that it may not run where virtue does not act as guide' ('perché non corra che virtù nol guidi'); cf. *Inf.* XXVI, 19–24, 43–5, 69, 94–6, 108–9, 112–26.
66 Cf. *Dante's Style in his Lyric Poetry*, chapters 6–8.
67 It is cited in *De vulgari eloquentia* as the only Italian example of *directio voluntatis*. It is also an example of a poem devoted to the theme which Dante variously describes as *virtus, honestum, rectitudo* (*Dve* II, ii, 7–8).

68 This paragraph contains several self-quotations from the last chapter in *Dante's Style in his Lyric Poetry.*

69 The allusions are (in order) to: *Purg.* XXX, 72; *Inf.* V, 29–30; *Par.* XVI, 82–3.

13   Desire

1 Cf. *Inf.* V, 82–4; *Par.* III, 118; IV, 101, 110–11; *Fables* IX, 2.

2 See the passage by Thomas Wright quoted as the third epigraph on p. vii.

3 *In Ethic.* II, v, *lect.* 5, §293, in the light of §§21, 1505, 1511, 1519, 1598, 2025–6, 2038, 2052, 2056; *S.T.* 1a–2ae, 23, 4; 25, 2; 26, 2; 27, 1, 3; 28, 1–6. In its transhumanised condition, the underlying disposition, eternally actualised, is better called *caritas.* Lino Pertile, who is writing a book on the 'metaphorics of desire' in the *Comedy*, has pointed out in preliminary articles that *Paradiso* is the cantica of the protagonist's *desire* for God, rather than of his *union* with God, and that the poet represents the blessed as eternally possessing what they desire and eternally desiring what they possess ('"La punta del disio"'; and '*Paradiso*: a drama of desire').

4 *Rime* XVI, 11 (= *VN* XX, 5).

5 The grouping is inspired by Virgil's speech explaining the organisation of Purgatory in which he reduces the *seven* Capital Vices to *three* kinds of error in elective loving; see *Purg.* XVII, 94–139.

6 The following description of the process which led to the elimination of all candidates except *sexual* love is modelled on Dante's survey of the Italian dialects in *De vulgari eloquentia*, during which he uses the metaphor of 'sifting' and looking for a 'residue in the sieve' (cf. *Dve* I, xi, 1, 2, 6; xii, 1; xv, 8).

7 For weariness and the desire for rest or sleep, see *Inf.* I, 11, 28; II, 1–6; *Purg.* IV, 43, 52; IX, 10–11; XI, 43–5. For the exile's love of Florence, see *Inf.* X, 79–84; *Purg.* VIII, 1–6; *Par.* XVII, 55–60; XXV, 1–9; *Rime* CIV, 73–107; CXVI, 76–84; *Con.* I, iii, 3–5. It is worth adding that the desire for truth can err if it takes the form of 'curiosity' or the mere accumulation of sense data; and that the desire for goodness can err if it takes a friend or the beloved as its '*ultimo* fine' (cf. *VN* XVIII, 4).

8 *Mon.* I, xi, 11. The term *avaritia* is sometimes used as a synonym for *cupiditas*, but on other occasions it refers specifically to the phase of 'hoarding' as opposed to that of 'acquisition'. A study of the canzone *Doglia mi reca*, and of *Convivio* IV, xii, would show that Dante has a very subtle view of the error involved in covetousness. It is not simply that the covetous or avaritious man amasses more material goods than are necessary for living happily and well. He is also vainly trying to satisfy his innate longing for an *infinite* good (God) by pursuing an ever-greater number or quantity of finite goods, not realising that no number is so great that it cannot be increased by one.

9 *Ethics* VII, xi, 1152b 18.

10 See above, p. 3. Dante entered his *third* age when he became forty-five in 1310.

11 *Rime* XVI; *Con.* III, ii, 3; Shakespeare, Sonnet 116.

12 See above, p. 268

13 For the 'holy family', see *Par.* VIII, 4–8 (Venus corresponds to Mary, Cupid to the Christ child, and Dione to St Anne). In Virgil's narrative, Cupid assumed the form of Aeneas' son and 'wounded' Dido while being cuddled in her lap (*Aeneid*, I, 685–8, 717–19). We know from *VN* XXV that the young Dante had no objection to personification as such, provided that there was a 'naked body' of truth beneath the 'garment' of the rhetorical figure. But the reader should be able to 'uncover' the veiled truth for himself. For the 'influence' of Venus, see *Par.* VIII, 1–3, 97–111, 127–35; *Con.* II, v, 13–14.

14 See above, p. 166, and *Inf.* v, 49.

15 *Inf.* v, 29–33, 42–3, 49–51, 75, 79, 96. The 'king of the universe' is the 'friend' of the blessed (cf. *ibid.*, 91).

16 See *Par.* III, 52–4, 70–90.

17 *Inf.* III, 28, 30; v, 32.

18 Dante is drawing on orthodox meteorology when he describes lightning as 'visible winds descending from a cold cloud'; see *Dante Philomythes*, pp. 76–9, 89. But it seems likely that he intended the reader to remember an *earlier* 'vento' (alias 'bufera' or 'fiato'); cf. *Inf.* v, 31, 42, 79.

19 Contrast *Inf.* v, 80–1, and 90–5, where Francesca's 'noi' refers to her and Paolo as opposed to the other isolated lovers.

20 There is admirable tact also in the speaker's unobtrusive correction of the error Dante had made in his *commentary* to the canzone (*Con.* II, v, 6, 13, 15), where the angelic hierarchy responsible is named as the 'Thrones' (following the order proposed by St Gregory the Great; cf. *Par.* XXVIII, 130–5). Here (line 34) and in *Par.* XXVIII, 125, they are named as 'Princes' or 'Principalities', following the order given by Dionysius. The 'poco di quiete' recalls the moment in *Inf.* v, 96 when the 'wind falls silent' to allow Francesca to tell her story; but everything turns on the contrast between the cessation of a *vis extrinseca* and a voluntary stillness. As we shall see, Francesca makes frequent allusions to Dante's lyrics, thereby reminding the protagonist that his poems, like those of his peers whom we meet in Purgatory, were written 'in suo periclo' (cf. *Par.* VIII, 1).

21 Like all the souls we meet in the lower heavens, she enjoys a relatively lowly status in Paradise because she had not struggled sufficiently against her inclinations, whereas the souls we meet in the higher heavens had clearly been assisted by their 'natural gifts'. See *Purg.* XVI, 73–84; *Par.* III, 55–7; VI, 112–26 (especially 115–17); IX, 118–19.

22 *Par.* IX, 37, 67–70.

23 *Par.* IX, 97–102; cf. Ovid, *Heroides*, II, VII, IX.

24 Justification for this rather lengthy paraphrase will be found in *Dante Philomythes*, pp. 152–4, 194–8, 232–4, 266–9. In line 107, Petrocchi reads 'affetto', understanding it as the subject of 'addorna', to give the sense that 'God's love makes his handiwork so beautiful'.

25 If we include the silent figure of Rahab (*Par.* IX, 112–26), we are introduced to an equal number of men and women.

26 The result of her bestiality was the Minotaur. *Purg.* XXVI, 40–2, 79–81, 85–7.

27 *Ibid.*, XXV, 133–5; XXVI, 83–4.

28 Lust is a '*poison* of Venus' (XXV, 132). It leaves an open wound ('piaga') which must now be sewn together ('ricucire') with the appropriate treatment and diet ('cura', 'pasti', 138–9). Shame is a help to self-control (XXVI, 81; cf. *Inf.* XVII, 89–90). One should keep a 'close bridle on one's *eyes*' (XXV, 116–20). The example of Julius Caesar is not always to be followed (XXVI, 76–8; contrast *Par.* VI, 55–81); but Mary is a model in everything, particularly in her inviolate virginity (*Purg.* XXV, 128).

29 XXVI, 148. As a 'tortura' (XXV, 109), the 'pena' is closely linked to the fire which destroyed Sodom and Gomorrah, and which eternally punishes the sinners against nature in *Inferno* XIV–XVI. As an image of lust, whether heterosexual or 'hermaphrodite' (cf. *Purg.* XXVI, 82), it is more akin to the 'bufera' in *Inferno* v because, in both cases, the souls *continue* to exist in the same state as they had done on earth. And to the metaphorical meanings drawn from medieval technology we could add the

process called 'sublimation', that is, the converting by heat of a solid substance into a vapour which resolidifies, in purer form, after cooling.

30 *VN* xx, 3 (= *Rime* xvi, 2); xxv, 4.

31 In his *De vulgari eloquentia*, Dante had given equal prominence to Arnaut and Guiraut de Bornelh (they receive four mentions each); while the *historical* Guinizzelli, in the first line of a dedicatory sonnet, had saluted Guittone as 'O caro padre meo'. Here it is the protagonist who hails Guinizzelli as 'padre / mio', whereas the *fictional* Guinizzelli disparages Guittone and Guiraut, and points to Arnaut as the 'better craftsman of the mother tongue' (*Purg.* xxvi, 117, 120, 126).

32 The crucial adjective recurs twice in the phrases 'rime d'amor usar *dolci* e leggiadre' and '*dolci* detti' (*Purg.* xxvi, 97–9, 112). These lines, like the whole passage (109–26), are to be read in the context suggested by xxiv, 49–62.

33 xxvi, 117–18. The earliest French romances, dating from the middle and later twelfth century, were written in octosyllabic couplets, as were both parts of the *Roman de la rose*. By the middle of the *thirteenth* century, however, prose had become the preferred medium for what Dante called the 'enchanting adventures connected with King Arthur' ('Arturi regis ambages pulcherrimae', *Dve* i, x, 2). This passage suggests, further, that line 118 could be paraphrased as 'written in Occitan or French'.

34 His reaction to the 'pena' on the seventh terrace should be compared with his attitude to those on the first and second terraces (xi, 118–20; xii, 1–9; xiii, 133–8) where he, in effect, pleads 'guilty' to Pride, but 'not guilty' to Envy.

35 *VN* ii, 9; iv, 2; xxvi, 1–3 (and contrast xxxviii, 4–7; xxxix, 1). The only poems which were beyond all reproach were those which had been devoted to praise of Beatrice without any hope of reward: see xviii, 6–9; xxi, 1; xxvi, 4; xlii, 2. We may also recall that in *Par.* xxxi, 85, Dante, in taking leave of Beatrice, praises her because she has 'led him from slavery into freedom': 'Tu m'hai di servo tratto a libertate.'

36 With Francesca and Piero it was presumably the manner of their death (murder *in flagrante delicto*; suicide) that captured his imagination; whereas with Ugolino and Ulysses, it must have been the mystery surrounding their deaths. In the case of Farinata, it would have been the death in exile of the defeated patriot and the persecution *post mortem* of his family and his mortal remains. In each of the five cases, though, the death and/or defeat of the historical original must have struck him as, in some sense, a necessary consequence of the temperament and the life. Dante's task as *poet* was to structure the meeting in such a way that their '*second* death' – that is, their damnation, their eternal loss of the true good – should strike the reader as at once the consequence and the symbol of their dominant obsession.

37 Like the reader of this book, Dante would have 'raised his eyebrows a little' at such amateurish psychology; but he would have recognised the analogies between divine and poetic creation: see *Purg.* xxv, 70–5.

38 *Inf.* i, 117; iii, 3, 9; v, 44–5; xi, 78–90.

39 v, 28–33, 42–3, 51, 86. For medieval ideas about 'typhoons' (*typho/typhonis*) see *Dante Philomythes*, p. 320. The four verbs applied to the action of the 'bufera' are 'violent' in the obvious sense of the word, and also in the specific sense that 'violent motion' is that which has its cause 'outside the agent' (see above, p. 200). Even so, they are perhaps less revealing than the apparently colourless verb 'menare', meaning 'to lead' or 'to lead *captive*', which recurs four times in the canto, twice with the infernal storm as its subject (lines 32, 43), and once each with 'amore' (78) and 'disio' (114).

40 v, 40–3, 46–8, 82–4.

41 Later in the poem, however, St Peter and St James will 'express their affection' like

two 'colombi'. Birds, of course, do well to follow their 'natural love which cannot err'; and, in any case, the first simile makes it clear that the starlings are self-moved, whereas the spirits are driven from without. On flattering and unflattering comparisons between animals and humans, see *Dante Philomythes*, pp. 118–23.

42 'Libito fé licito in sua legge.' One must not be too heavy-handed in glossing a line which depends so much on alliteration and adnomination; but it might be worth bearing in mind that Dante believed that law should be 'reason written down' (see above, p. 205), not the caprice of a woman; and that many English churches still display a table of the prohibited degrees of consanguinity ('a man may not marry...') alongside the table bearing the Ten Commandments.

43 Dido's story is also recalled allusively on the seventh terrace of Purgatory and in the Heaven of Venus; and Dante keeps very close to the account of her love in *Aeneid* I and IV. The story of Paris and Helen comes in part from Ovid (*Heroides* V and XVI) and in part from Guido delle Colonne's *Historia destructionis Troiae*, and this last is probably the direct source for the story of Achilles' love for Polyxena.

44 This relationship is not made explicit until line 2 of the following canto.

45 The adjectives are meant to point up the similarities with later popular fiction and later audiences: 'romantick' was a pejorative term in the eighteenth century denoting the sort of 'stuff' one would find in a 'romance' of the period.

46 V, 82–7. Other details in these lines confirm that the protagonist and Francesca are 'on the same wavelength'. His attention is caught by the 'romantick' inseparability and lightness of the pair (lines 74–5). He hails them as 'anime affannate' (80), using an adjective which is perfectly at home in the courtly lyric (it occurs twice in rhyme in Dante's poems) to express not the torments of Hell, but the lover's *chagrin d'amour*. In this choice (and, no doubt, in his tone of voice), he has in effect followed Virgil's double-edged advice to call the two lovers 'per quell'*amor* che i *mena*' (cf. note 39 above). 'Forte' (87) is the quintessential courtly adjective or adverb to express the irresistible power of 'true' love.

47 The elements common to both the old style and the new include the quasi-personification of 'Amore', the choice of refined words like 'persona' and 'piacere' (lines 101, 103) and the semi-technical use of 'prendere' (101, 104) coupled with the adverb 'forte' to describe the all-conquering power of love. The triple anaphora of 'Amor' and the triple word-play on the root 'amare' in line 103, on the other hand, are perhaps more typical of the earlier Tuscan poets; while the close association of 'amore' and 'morte' is particularly characteristic of the 'new' lyrics of Cavalcanti and of the phase in Dante's career when he was most under the influence of his 'first friend' (although *there* the lover had claimed to be at the *point* of death through *unrequited* desire).

48 There is, indeed, more than a hint of vindictiveness in her oblique reference to the fact that she was killed *treacherously* by her husband, who, on his death, will be punished for his crime in the *lowest* circle of Hell, 'Caina' (line 109; XXXII, 58).

49 References in order: 1 John 1:8–10; *Purg.* III, 121–35; V, 97–108.

50 'Amore e 'l cor gentil sono una cosa / sì come 'l saggio in suo dittare pone', *Rime* XVI, 1–2; *VN* XX, 3. See Guinizzelli, 'Al cor gentil', lines 1 and 11. The second claim is tantamount to asserting the identity of the passive and active infinitives, such that: *amari = amare*, or *amare = redamari*.

51 *Con.* I, xii, 3; xiii, 10.

52 *Inf.* V, 93; *Purg.* XVI, 72.

53 Minos' activities are described in *Inf.* V, 4–15. The differing truth-content of Francesca's two *sententiae* may be assessed by measuring them against Virgil's speech.

Line 100 proves to be true and unobjectionable, if it is understood to extend no further than the phase of perception and instinctive attraction which Virgil describes in *Purg.* XVIII, 19–24. But line 103 is patently untrue because it implies that the mind is not free to withhold consent (XVIII, 25–7, as explicated in lines 61–75).

54 To put it in the technical terms alluded to by Virgil in *Purg.* III, 34–45, he knows the *quia*, but he does not understand the *propter quid*. If he had been able to act as judge at this point in the narrative there would have been no need for him to undertake the 'fatale andare'. Showing him 'le perdute genti' was a last extreme remedy for his 'fall', as Beatrice will make clear in *Purg.* XXX, 127–45.

55 This is how Dante himself paraphrased the nouns in the opening line of the first sonnet in the *Vita nuova*, 'A ciascun' alma presa e gentil core'. For the strength of emotion which is implied by the bowing of the head, see chapter 11 above, p. 242. The length of his silence is unequivocally conveyed through the adverb and conjunctions ('tanto', 'fin che', 'quando'). 'Oh lasso' is one of the most common exclamations in the poetic lovers' complaints. 'Martiri' was used of the lover's torments, usually in rhyme with 'sospiri'. The key epithet 'dolce' is used twice (lines 113, 118), so too is the key noun 'disio', 'disiri'. 'Amore' is duly personified (although the critical text does not capitalise the noun, as printed here). And 'Francesca' proves to be a name as full of meaning as 'Dominic' or 'Beatrice'.

56 *Purg.* XVIII, 31–3, quoted above, p. 211.

57 'Sed si tantus amor casus cognoscere nostros', *Aeneid* II, 10.

Select bibliography

Aelred of Rievaulx. *De anima.* C. H. Talbot (ed.). London, 1952.
  Dialogue on the Soul. C. H. Talbot (trans.). Kalamazoo, Michigan, 1981.
Armour, Peter. 'Matelda in Eden: The Teacher and the Apple.' *Italian Studies,* 34 (1979),
  pp. 2–27.
  Dante's Griffin and the History of the World. Oxford, 1989.
Avicenna. *Liber de anima seu sextus de naturalibus.* S. Van Reit (ed.). 2 vols., Leiden,
  1968–72.
Bacon, Francis. *The Advancement of Learning and New Atlantis.* London, 1951.
Bambrough, Renford (ed.). *The philosophy of Aristotle.* New York, 1963.
Bartholomaeus Anglicus. *On the Properties of Soul and Body.* R. James Long (ed.). Toronto,
  1979.
Blund, Johannes. *Tractatus de anima.* D. A. Callus and R. W. Hunt (eds.). London, 1970.
Boyde, Patrick. *Dante's Style in his Lyric Poetry.* Cambridge, 1971.
  Dante Philomythes and Philosopher: Man in the Cosmos. Cambridge, 1981.
Bundy, Murray Wright. *The Theory of Imagination in Classical and Medieval Thought.*
  Illinois, 1927.
Carruthers, Mary. *The Book of Memory: a Study of Memory in Medieval Culture.* Cambridge,
  1990.
Charlton, W. *Aristotle's Physics I, II* (translated with Introduction and Notes). Oxford,
  1970.
Chaucer, Geoffrey. *The Complete Works.* F. N. Robinson (ed.). London (2nd edn.), 1957.
Chiavacci Leonardi, Anna (ed.). *Dante, L'inferno.* Milan, 1991.
Copleston, F. C. *A History of Medieval Philosophy.* London, 1972.
Corti, Maria. *La felicità mentale.* Turin, 1983.
De Robertis, Domenico. *Il libro della Vita nuova.* Florence, 1961.
De Robertis, Domenico (ed.). *Dante, Vita nuova.* Milan and Naples, 1980.
  Guido Cavalcanti, Rime. Turin, 1986.
Di Scipio, Giuseppe and Aldo Scaglione (eds.). *The Divine Comedy and the Encyclopedia of
  Arts and Sciences.* Philadelphia, 1988.
Enciclopedia dantesca. U. Bosco (ed.). 6 vols., Rome, 1970–9.
Foster, Kenelm. *The Two Dantes and Other Studies.* London, 1977.
Foster, Kenelm and Patrick Boyde. *Dante's Lyric Poetry.* 2 vols., Oxford, 1967.

Gilson, Etienne. *La philosophie au moyen âge.* Paris (2nd edn.), 1952.
> *Dante et la Philosophie.* Paris (2nd edn.), 1953.

Gregory, Tullio (ed.). *I sogni nel Medioevo.* Rome, 1985.

Halbertsma, K. *A History of the Theory of Colour.* Amsterdam, 1949.

Hamlyn, D. W. *Aristotle's De anima II, III* (translated with Introduction and Notes). Oxford, 1968.

Harvey, E. Ruth. *The Inward Wits. Psychological Theory in the Middle Ages and the Renaissance.* London, 1975.

Hills, Paul. *The Light of Early Italian Painting.* New Haven and London, 1987.

Hirdt, Willi. *Wie Dante das Jenseits erfährt.* Bonn, 1989.

Kemp, Martin (ed.). *Leon Battista Alberti: On Painting.* London, 1991.

Knowles, David. *The Evolution of Medieval Thought.* London, 1962.

Kretzmann, Norman, Anthony Kenny and Jan Pinborg (eds.). *The Cambridge History of Later Medieval Philosophy. From the Rediscovery of Aristotle to the Disintegration of Scholasticism, 1100–1600.* Cambridge, 1982.

Kruger, Steven F. *Dreaming in the Middle Ages.* Cambridge, 1992.

Lear, Jonathan. *Aristotle: the Desire to Understand.* Cambridge, 1988.

Leff, Gordon. *Medieval Thought from Saint Augustine to Ockham.* London, 1958.

Lindberg, D. C. *Theories of Vision from Al-Kindi to Kepler.* Chicago, 1976.

Lloyd, G. E. R. *Aristotle: the Growth and Structure of his Thought.* Cambridge, 1968.

Nardi, Bruno. *Nel mondo di Dante.* Rome, 1944.
> *Dal 'Convivio' alla 'Commedia' (Sei saggi danteschi).* Rome, 1960.
> *Saggi di filosofia dantesca.* Florence, 1967. (1st edn. 1930).

Pertile, Lino. '"La punta del disio": Storia di una metafora dantesca.' *Lectura Dantis,* 7 (1990), pp. 3–28.
> 'Paradiso: a drama of desire', in *Word and Drama in Dante,* ed. J. C. Barnes and J. Petrie, Dublin, 1993, pp. 143–80.

Randall, John Herman Jr. *Aristotle.* New York, 1960.

Ross, Sir David. *Aristotle.* London, 1964. (1st edn. 1923).

Spearing, A. C. *Medieval Dream Poetry.* Cambridge, 1976.

Van Steenberghen, Fernand. *Aristotle in the West. The Origins of Latin Aristotelianism.* (L. Johnston trans.). Louvain, 1955.

Vasoli, Cesare (ed.). *Il Convivio* (in *Dante, Opere minori,* vol. I, part 2). Milan and Naples, 1988.

Wolfson, Harry A. 'The Internal Senses.' *Harvard Theological Review,* 28 (1935), pp. 69–133.

Wright, Thomas. *The Passions of the Mind in General.* W. W. Newbold (ed.). New York and London, 1986.

Index of Latin terms

Index of longer quotations from Dante's works

General index

flight 51, 52, 54, *see also fuga*
Florence 256, 273
Folco, *see* Folquet of Marseilles
Folquet of Marseilles 287
Forese Donati 131, 194
foretasting, of pleasure or pain 50, *see also*
   expectatio
form (structure) 16, 25, 29, 179, *see also forma*,
   formal cause
   contrasted with matter 211
formal cause 25, 26, 27, 28, 39, 42, 55, 85, 253
Francesca 165, 226, 292, 295, 296, 297, 298,
   299, 301
free will, *see* choice, freedom, *liberum arbitrium*,
   voluntas
freedom of the will 128, 174, 208
   and bondage, in Christian analysis 208
   and individual responsibility 205, 298
   and morality 209, 213
   and obedience to God's will 203, 204
   and persuasion 271
   as ability to withhold consent 213
   entails possibility of error 278
   God's greatest gift 192, 202, 278
   how forfeited 278
   impossible in fallen man 208
   its nature and limits 193, 195
   its renunciation as free act 204
   see also determinism, instinct
fruition 277
fulfilment 39, *see also* actualisation, *perfectio*
Furies 247

Galen 145
Galileo 18, 21
Ganymede, myth of 126, 127
generation 17, 18, 25, 30, 31, 35, 38, 49, 141,
   142
   as opposed to creation 10
gentle heart, in courtly poetry 280, 296
geometry, of vision 97, 100
Geryon 159, 226, 233, 241
God 14, 57, 80, 91, 113, 121, 129, 142, 165, 169,
   188, 192, 202, 203, 229, 241, 251, 252, 256,
   264, 274, 283, 284, 287
   as Alpha and Omega 181
   as 'primo bene' 278
good 44, 48, 49, 51, 56, 211–13, 277
   absolute and relative, contrasted 211
   and love 278
   as 'laborious' or 'arduous' 253–4
   the infinite Good (God) 85
   see also bonum, desire, goodness, scale of
   value, value
goodness 41–3, 179, 277
grace 86, 91, 129, 169, 208, 316–7
gravity 22
Green, Thomas (in example) 30

Gregory, St 253
growth 13, 17, 18, 30, 31, 35, 37, 38, 44, 49, 76,
   174, *see also incrementum*
guilt, as specifically human passion 158
Guinizzelli, Guido 290, 297

happiness 5, 8, 9, 148, 166, 178, 188, 220, 263,
   277, *see also beatitudo*, pleasure
Harvey, William 145
hearing, as complementing sense of sight
   103–4
heart, as seat of emotions 53, 101, 140, 145,
   147, 148, 150, 151, 153, 165, 219, 223
heat, contrasted with light 64
heterogeneous parts (in plants and higher
   organisms) 39, 43
higher appetite 186, *see also appetitus*, will
hope 136, 137, 148, 156, 163, 220, 227, 229,
   231, 296
Horace 272
horror, as species of fear 230
human actions, as product of several motive
   forces 218, *see also* human operation
human being: and 'life on the frontier' 182
   and supreme goal 186
   as 'fallen' 208
   as 'godlike' 175, 182, 203, 212
   as rational and social 271
   'companionable animal' 262
   comparable to animals 45, 174, 237
   diversity of powers in 43
   has two distinct goals 188, 268
   three natures in one soul 191
   see also intellect, mind, reason, will
human nature 8
human operation 9, 43, 206, 276, 278
humanity, and conformity with reason 189,
   190
humours (the four fluids) 260

illumination 64, 66–9, 70, 89, 97
illusion 76, 77, 84, 96, 97, 98
image 48, 53, 71, 72, 92, 101, 102, 107, 111,
   114, 147, 178, 191, 192, 211, 238, 239, 240,
   see also imago, intentio
imagination 50, 72, 73, 87, 92, 119, 147, 150,
   191, 217, 238, 271, 279
   as conferring false glamour 129
   in relation to fear 237
   see also imaginativa
impression, in sensation 46, 48, 53, 55, 101,
   114
imprint, as metaphor of sensation 46
inclination 202, 276, *see also* love, temperament
incontinence (weakness) 293
increase, *see* growth
individual humans, constitute 'almost a
   separate species' 262

3 5282 00621 0317

Printed in the United States
58757LVS00004B/43-69

9 780521 028554